AFRICA AND OTHER CIVILIZATIONS

Africa and other Civilizations
conquest and counter-conquest

Collected Essays of
Ali A. Mazrui
Volume II

Edited by
Ricardo René Laremont
Fouad Kalouche

Toyin Falola
Series Editor
Classic Authors and Texts on Africa

Africa World Press, Inc.

P.O. Box 1892
Trenton, NJ 08607

P.O. Box 48
Asmara, ERITREA

Africa World Press, Inc.

P.O. Box 1892
Trenton, NJ 08607

P.O. Box 48
Asmara, ERITREA

Cover design: Ashraful Haque

Library of Congress Cataloging-in-Publication Data

Mazrui, Ali Al_Amin
    Africa and other civilizations : conquest and counter-conquest / edited by Ricardo René Laremont, Fouad Kalouche.
      p. cm. -- (Collected essays of Ali A. Mazrui ; v. 2) (Classic authors and texts on Africa)
    Includes bibliographical references and index.
     ISBN 1-59221-010-4 -- ISBN 1-59221-011-2 (pbk.)
     1. Africa--Civilization. 2. Africa--Civilization--Western influences. 3. Africa--Foreign relations.   I. Laremont, Ricardo René. II. Kalouche, Fouad. III. Title. IV. Series: Mazrui, Ali Al_Amin. Essays. Selections ; v. 2. V. Series: Classic authors and texts on Africa.
    DT14.M386 2002
    960--dc21

                    2002009190

TABLE OF CONTENTS

EDITORS' NOTE ix

ACKNOWLEDGMENTS xi

INTRODUCTION

From the Semites to the Anglo-Saxons: Culture and
Civilization in Changing Communication (1986) 1

**PART I: AFRICA BETWEEN CULTURE AND
CIVILIZATION**

Chapter ONE: Africa And Cultural Dependency: The
Case of the African University (1975) 57

Chapter TWO: Ideology and African Political Culture
(1992) 95

Chapter THREE: Africa in the Shadow of a Clash of
Civilizations: From the Cold War of Ideology to the
Cold War of Race (2000) 147

PART II: AFRICA AND OTHER CIVILIZATIONS

Chapter FOUR: The Dual Universalism of Western
Civilization: The Ethnocentrism of Progress and of
Western Social Sciences (1988)   169

Chapter FIVE: Africa Between the Meiji Restoration
and the Legacy of Atatürk: Comparative Dilemmas
of Modernization (1981)   203

Chapter SIX: Islam in Africa: An Overview (1991)   225

Chapter SEVEN: Africa and Asia in the Postcolonial
Experience (1997)   255

PART III: AFRICA AND THE INTERNATIONAL ORDER

Chapter EIGHT: Human Obligation and Global
Accountability: From the Impeachment of Warren
Hastings to the Legacy of Nuremberg (1993)   281

Chapter NINE: The Frankenstein State and the
International Order (1988)   303

Chapter TEN: Global Apartheid: Race and Religion
in the New World Order (1991)   329

PART IV: PHILOSOPHICAL AND LITERARY PERSPECTIVES

Chapter ELEVEN: Ancient Greece in African
Political Thought (1966)   345

Chapter TWELVE: Rousseau and Intellectualized
Populism in Africa (1968)   379

Chapter THIRTEEN: Edmund Burke and
Reflections on the Revolution in the Congo (1963) 397

Chapter FOURTEEN: Towards the Decolonization of
Rudyard Kipling (1972)   417

Chapter FIFTEEN: Eurafrican Lessons from
Shakespeare, Shaka, Puccini and Senghor (1982)   431

CONCLUSION

Africa and Other Civilizations: Conquest and
Counter-Conquest (1995)   449

INDEX   473

EDITORS' NOTE

This collection of essays, *Africa and Other Civilizations: Conquest and Counter-Conquest*, is the second volume of three-volume set of books that will provide readers with a broad spectrum of Ali A. Mazrui's scholarly writings during his four decades as both a scholar and a public intellectual. The dates of the original publication of all essays are provided after the title, in order to give the reader a more precise way of assessing the historical relevance of Mazrui's writings. This second volume considers the interaction of Africa with other civilizations from various perspectives. An introductory piece presents the historical development of political power in terms of a transition from the interconnected domains of Semitic religions to Anglo-Saxon technologies—via the sovereign-state, capitalism, expanding communication and diminishing dialogue. The first part starts out with situating Africa in relation to discourses of culture and of civilization, discussing cultural dependency and African higher education systems, ideology and African political culture, as well as the place of Africa in what has been termed a "clash of civilizations." The second part assesses the complex interactions between Africa and other civilizations, and analyzes Western Universalism and theories of progress as well as the comparative effects of modernization on Turkey,

Japan, and Africa, before assessing to the historical role of Islam in Africa and economic and political interactions between Asia and Africa. The third part considers international order from the perspective of its implications on Africa and the rest of the "Third World." Starting from a study of global accountability and international law, part III moves to discuss the changing role of the state in the international order and in liberation struggles worldwide before assessing the "new world order" in terms of a "Global Apartheid." The fourth part reproduces Mazrui's analyzes of Africa's engagement with political philosophy, literature, and art. Starting with an essay written on the relation between Ancient Greece and Africa years before the "Black Athena" debate, the fourth part highlights philosophical and literary perspectives of Africa's particular experiences of, and interaction with, other cultural and civilizational traits. A concluding piece sums up Africa's relation with other civilizations where conquest is inextricably linked to counter-conquest. A discussion of *Pax Africana* and of Africa's self-reliance concludes this rich volume. The third and final volume of the *Collected Essays of Ali A. Mazrui* will focus on Power, Politics, and Africa's global role.

Ricardo René Laremont
Fouad Kalouche

ACKNOWLEDGMENTS

The editors wish to thank Tracia Leacock Seghatolislami and Michael Toler for their contributions to this volume. Also instrumental to the finalization of this volume were Nancy Levis, Barbara A. Tierno, AnnaMaria Palombaro, and Goretti Mugambwa. We appreciate their constant support and their diligence. Last but not least, we acknowledge Connie Ciancio who, on very short notice, was able to go over the text, format it, and develop an index. We thank her for her extraordinary efforts.

Ricardo René Laremont
Fouad Kalouche

FROM THE SEMITES TO THE ANGLO-SAXONS
CULTURE AND CIVILIZATION IN CHANGING COMMUNICATION (1986)

"God, gold, and glory!" Captured in a slogan, these are in fact the three basic imperatives in the history of cultural diffusion. Why do men burst forth from their boundaries in search of new horizons? They are either inspired by a search for religious fulfillment (the God standard), or by a yearning for economic realization (the gold standard), or by a passion for renown (the quest for glory). It was John Milton, author of *Paradise Lost,* who described the quest for glory as "that last infirmity of the noble mind." In reality, all three elements have always been present in the history of cultural expansionism. But there has always been the issue of which is "first among equals." Which particular force—God, gold, or glory—is supreme in the particular case of cultural expansionism? In this essay, we are not dividing world history into feudal, capitalist, and socialist epochs. We are dividing world history into the God standard, the gold standard, and the quest for glory. Simplistically, we might say that the pre-capitalist world was a universe of the supremacy of God, the capitalist phase is the supremacy of gold, and the post-capitalist world is the supremacy of glory The main issue here is whether the glory is sectional or planetary, chauvinist or humane.

In the search for the God standard in world culture, especially important have been the Semitic peoples, particularly the Jews and the Arabs. In the search for the gold standard in our special sense, particularly important have been Europeans and their extensions in the Americas. In the search for glory, there are two ultimate routes: one is through outer space and the other is through grass-roots social movements. The quest for ultimate human glory is at the crossroads. It must either emphasize the flight into outer space or stress putting the local human house in order. The former needs cosmonauts and astronauts; the latter requires grass-roots social movements. It was Julius Nyerere of Tanzania who once said: "while they are trying to reach the moon, we still are trying to reach the village." And yet, the most momentous social movement may well turn out to be the women's movement to which we shall return. Meanwhile, let us take history on its own terms. The first forces to teach the world that the human race was one were religious forces. The most universalist of all religions were Semitic religions, especially Christianity and Islam. Precisely because Christianity and Islam wanted to convert every human being, they were the most militantly globalist of all cultures. Yet their ambitions exceeded their communicative capabilities. It is still worth following this remarkable story of the impact of the Semites on our consciousness of a single world. Part of the story is religious bigotry, part of it is militarism and conquest, and part of it is ethnic exclusivity. But when all is said and done, it was the Semitic belief in the oneness of the human race that led to Christian crusades and Islamic *jihads*. These involved a commitment to global conversion. Let us take a closer look at this religious dimension before we turn to the imperatives of the gold standard and beyond.

Between God and Gold

"What do you think of Western civilization?" asked the interviewer. "That would be a good thing!" replied the Mahatma. This reported interchange between Mahatma Gandhi and a questioner captures one of the most important debates of the twentieth century: what is the moral worth of the West's contribution to the human condition? Has the West left the human race better off or worse off than it found it? Part of the discussion requires a clarification of terms. Gandhi was not disputing that the West had a culture; he was raising the question of whether it had a civilization. We define "culture" as a system of interrelated values, active enough to condition perception, judgment, communication, and behavior in a given society. We define "civilization" as a culture that has endured, expanded, innovated, and been elevated to new moral sensibilities. It was presumably the last criterion of "moral sensibilities" that Mahatma Gandhi was implicitly questioning when he queried whether the West had as yet evolved as a civilization. And yet the two biggest contributors to world culture are the Semites on one side and Europeans on the other. The Semitic peoples (especially Jews and Arabs) helped change the world through religion—a theocratic approach to cultural universalism. Europeans have helped to change the world through technology and science—a technocratic approach to cultural universalism. Let us explore this remarkable impact of the Semites and the Europeans upon the nascent global civilization. In a sense, this is a study in macro-history rather than a general theory of causation. We are not trying to explain why the torch of universalism passed from the Semites to the Anglo-Saxons. We simply show the transition. We are not theorizing about the story of changing human pursuits in a cultural perspective.

"God, gold, and glory!" This triple ambition had been at least as important in the history of cultural expansionism as the aspiration of *"liberté, égalité, fraternité"* has been in the history of modern revolutions. As we have indicated, religious fulfillment (God), economic gain (gold), and political ambition (glory) have been three of the most decisive factors behind cultural diffusion and institutional transfers in world history. These three ambitions have constituted the ends of cultural expansionism What about the means of this conquest? Three primary forms of technology have facilitated the spread of cultures: the technology of production (with economic output), the technology of destruction (with military output), and the technology of communications (with the output of messages). We have here three goals (God, gold, and glory), and three paths towards these goals (economic, military, and communicative). The relative weight of the three goals has, of course, varied in different periods and for different societies. The economic determinists would insist that the pursuit of gold and its equivalents were the most paramount. As a poet once put it when characterizing the Arab *jihads* and conquests of the seventh and eighth centuries:

> No, not for paradise didst thou
> the desert life forsake;
> Rather, I believe, it was thine
> yearning for bread and date.

However, the primacy of economic gain is a much more recent phenomenon than outright economic determinists would argue. Earlier phases of history did sometimes witness the tilting of the balance in favor of God in preference to "pure" economic gain. In other words, there was a God standard before there was a gold standard in the history of culture. Our second argument here is the simple one that the pursuit of gold had reached new global proportions with the rise of Western Capitalism. Economic gain has been put on the world stage, with considerable implications for culture change and cultural diffusion. Western Capitalism holds the reins of both the technology of production and the technology of communication. Our third argument is that the pursuit of glory under European leadership has now taken the form of the sovereign state, which has also been globalized. The sovereign state holds the reins of the technology of destruction. Our fourth concern is with grass-roots movements that, in the second half of the twentieth century, are up against Capitalism, on one side, and the state-system, on the other; and what is at stake is the nature and texture of world civilization itself.

That the God standard in our sense was often the dynamo of large-scale cultural expansion can be discerned from the simple fact that religious movements were for so many centuries among the major carriers of new values and norms across societal boundaries. The banner of religion has had a lot to do with the evolution of something approaching a world culture. The biggest exporters of culture in history have been India, the Middle East, and Western Europe. India's most important cultural export has been religious, but not necessarily a religion that has been triumphant within India itself. But while Buddhism is indeed a major case of cultural export, it is less central to world culture than are the contributions made by the Semites and the Europeans. We define "world culture" as a shared heritage that has spread to at least three continents and, in different degrees, affects the lives of at least half the human race. Humanity in the twentieth century has only just begun to evolve something approaching a world culture. And within that heritage the contributions made by the Semitic and European peoples are immense and disproportionate.

1. The Semitic and European Impact

Let us first look at the history of this Semitic and European impact before we examine its contemporary implications. The Jewish impact on world culture has been through both Judaism and Christianity, through both the Old Testament and the New. Judaism itself is more transterritorial than international. It makes better sense to talk of "the Jewish nation" scattered in different countries than to talk of "international Judaism." The Jewish community worldwide is relatively small and the Jews can therefore be deemed an ethnic group, to some extent a biological group of shared descent. This is a small group but with an enormous impact on world industry. The Jews gave birth not just to Judaism but also, of course, to Christianity. Christianity is the most international of all religions. The internationalization of Christianity had basically five major stages. There was first the conversion of Paul with all its consequences. In time, this was followed by the conversion of the Emperor Constantine I resulting in the Christianization of the Roman Empire. Third, there was the Reformation and the inauguration of competitive proselytization. Fourth, there was the peopling of the Americas under Christian umbrellas. And, fifth, there was, as part of the internationalization of Christianity, the European colonization of the African continent. Let us first look at the two ancient stages more closely (conversions of Paul and Constantine) before we examine more recent history.

The first stage of Christian internationalism was the de-nationalization of the religion—delinking it from the Jews. After all, Christianity began as a Jewish sect. Early Christians accepted Jewish rituals: the early Jerusalem Church regarded circumcision as obligatory and the Mosaic Laws as binding. It was the Jews of the Diaspora who initiated the trend towards Christian universalism. An early convert called Stephen demanded the abrogation of the Mosaic Code and denounced official Judaism as unreceptive to the Holy Spirit. He was dragged before the Jewish Sanhedrin and stoned to death. Stephen was perhaps the first Christian martyr. There followed persecution of liberal Jews, and many fled and sought asylum in Antioch. It seems to have been the Antioch Christians who began to convert gentiles. What is more, they said that gentiles did not have to be circumcised. A new frontier in the de-nationalization of Christianity had been reached. The conversion of Paul helped to start the process of the true internationalization of Christianity. Paul was probably the first to preach a thoroughgoing universalism. As he declared in his letter to the Romans: "There is no distinction between the Jews and the Greek; the same Lord is Lord of all and bestows his riches upon all who call upon him."[1] Between the years 48 A.D. and 58 A.D., Paul covered much of Asia Minor and Greece, traveling and preaching the Gospel to Jews and Gentiles alike. Christianity began to penetrate the eastern provinces of the Roman Empire before even Rome itself had a Christian community. Meanwhile, tension developed between Jewish Christians and universalist Christians. The Jewish Christians were under the Jerusalem Church, the universalists under the Church of Antioch. James, Jesus' brother, was the central figure in the Jerusalem Church; Paul presided over the destiny of Antioch. The Jerusalem Church was Jewish orthodox; the universalists were liberal. Jerusalem insisted on circumcision for Christians. On the other hand, Paul denounced those who insisted on "mutilation of the flesh." Paul was imprisoned for two years and was probably executed by Emperor Nero.

Paul had in any case fulfilled his historical destiny, becoming the second founder of Christianity. The legacy of the Antioch Church continued, while the Jerusalem Church died. Christianity became primarily a Gentile movement and was, fundamentally, a grass-roots movement. The new Christian religion began to spread further. It became at once internationalized within the Roman Empire and isolationist. It was internationalized in the sense of making converts across ethnic, national, and provincial frontiers. But Christianity was also isolationist and separatist because of the tendency for believers to live apart, while rejecting the pagan worship of the god-emperor. Christians regarded emperor-worship as idolatry. The Roman government in turn regarded the Christian rejection of the god-emperor as treason punishable by death. The grisly game of throwing Christians to the lions was inaugurated. The followers of Jesus had to pray in secret. By the fourth century, the Christian community had grown to such an extent that recognition seemed politically prudent. Emperor Constantine proclaimed the Edict of Milan in the year 313 A.D., extending toleration of Christians alongside followers of other religions of the Empire. Constantine apparently procrastinated over his own formal conversion until rather late in his life. Indeed, in the eastern part of his empire, he never quite abandoned the concept of god-emperor. But he did lay the foundations of the Christianization of the Roman Empire, which served as the genesis of the Christianization of Europe as a whole. One more step had been taken in the slow process of evolving a global political culture.

We started by saying that the biggest contributors to world culture have been the Semites and the Europeans. When the Roman Empire was converted to Christianity, the two universalist legacies were for a while fused. The Graeco-Roman heritage and the Judeo-Christian legacy had a rendezvous with destiny and started their joint adventure towards changing the world. The God standard had taken over an empire and shared the glitter that went with it. European Christianity became less of a grass-roots movement and more of an imperial system. On the other hand, the idea that the world was one involved a merger between the Graeco-Roman and the Judeo-Christian legacies.

2. Islam: A New Semitic Impact

While Christianity was slowly consolidating itself in Europe, another branch of the Semitic peoples, the Arabs, burst into the world stage with the banner of Islam. The expansion of Islam in its first century was much faster than the expansion of any previous religious movement. Furthermore, unlike Christianity and Buddhism, Islam has remained successful where it was born, as well as abroad, in its cradle as well as in exile. This has made the Arabs the most successful exporters of their own religion in human history. Europe has exported a religion it borrowed from others (Christianity); India exported a faith it had basically rejected for itself (Buddhism). Only the Arabs among the cultural exporters stand out continuously as leaders in the religion that they themselves produce and continue to profess. When we focus more exclusively on the period of human history since the birth of Islam in the seventh century, the Arabs are in any case ahead of India in cultural expansionism. Within a brief period following the death of the Prophet Muhammad, in 632 A.D., the Arabs had taken on two mighty empires of the ancient world, the Byzantine and Persian empires. Syria fell to the Muslims in 636 A.D., Iraq in 637 A.D., Mesopotamia in 641 A.D., Egypt in 642 A.D., and Persia itself in 651 A.D.

Two processes of slow acculturation were set in motion: Arabization (through language transfer) and Islamization (through religious conversion). Countries like Egypt underwent both processes and eventually became both Arab and Muslim. Persia, on the other hand, underwent mainly Islamization without becoming an Arab country by linguistic definition. In subsequent centuries, other parts of Asia were also Islamized without becoming Arab countries: from Afghanistan to Indonesia, from Asia Minor to large parts of the Indian subcontinent. In time, Islam became the most widespread religion in Asia. The biggest Muslim societies are now outside the Middle East, including Indonesia, Bangladesh, Pakistan and indeed the remaining millions of Muslims in the Republic of India. Islam's future rival in expansionism was, however, Europe. Centuries before Europe colonized the world of Islam, Islam had attempted to take over Europe.

In this ambition Islam was partially and temporarily triumphant. In 711 A.D., the Muslims crossed with an army from North Africa into Spain and defeated the Visigoth king, Roderick. By 715 A.D., Muslims had either captured or indirectly controlled the main cities of Spain. Narbonne in the south of France was also occupied as part of the Visigothic Empire. Spain became a province of the Islamic Empire, controlled for a while from Damascus under the Umayyad dynasty. Islam, inspired by a new universalism, wanted to take over the world in the name of God. Its ambition outstripped both its power and its means of communication, but a globalizing mission was nevertheless attempted.

The Umayyad dynasty of Cordova flourished and reached the height of its power and prosperity under Abdulrahman III (912-961 A.D.), when the Muslims controlled most of the Iberian Peninsula. But fragmentation soon began and, with it, the political decline of Islam in Iberia. In 1030 A.D., there were some 30 independent rulers in Muslim Spain. The spirit of universalism was cracking under the strain of political rivalries. Some of these rulers appealed to the Almoravids, rulers of the Berber empire in North Africa. The Almoravids defeated a Christian challenge in Spain and then ruled Spain themselves form 1090 to 1145 A.D. Fellow Berbers, the Almohads, succeeded them and ruled Muslim Spain until 1223 A.D. The Almohads subsequently withdrew, under pressure, to North Africa as Christian Spain sought to reassert itself. Cordova fell to the Christians in 1236 A.D., Seville in 1248 A.D. In 1492, Granada (with Alhambra) was incorporated into the new United Kingdom of Aragon and Castile. The stage was set for the expulsion of the Moors and for the dark period of the Inquisition. Both Islamic and Christian universalisms were under siege. The desire to convert the world had resulted in a new fragmentation of the world. Universalism wore the frightening mask of sectarianism.

Elsewhere, the first Islamic raid on Sicily was in the year 652 A.D., but the final occupation was not completed until 902 A.D. Parts of mainland Italy were also threatened: the Arabs arrived at Naples in 837 A.D. Indeed, in 846 A.D. and 849 A.D. Rome itself was threatened, but it was neither invaded nor captured. There is reason to believe that Pope John VIII (reigned 872-882 A.D.) had to pay tribute to the Muslims on his borders for about two years. Once again, competitive universalism was a prescription for strife and dominion. Before the end of that century, Byzantine power began to reassert itself in southern Italy. This resulted in ending the Arab occupation of mainland Italy. As for Sicily, it was recovered from the Muslim conquerors in the year 1091 A.D. The crusading movement of the later eleventh century arose further north in Europe, and failed to reconquer the holy land. But at least the bulk of Europe managed to keep Islam at bay. In the year 732 A.D., a Muslim raiding expedition had penetrated to the area between Poitiers and Tours and was defeated by Charles Martel. This has been acclaimed by Europeans historians as one of the most decisive battles of all history. In a sense, it marked the utmost military expansion of Islam into Western Europe. But, in the intellectual field, Islam still continued for a while to outshine Europe. The "Dark Ages" in Europe coincided with the flourishing of Islamic science and scholarship. The Muslim world reintroduced Europe to the intellectual glories of classical Greece. Geography and the nautical sciences received a new stimulus from Islam. The zero entered the world stage, and what we now call the Arabic numerals replaced the numerals of Rome, under the mathematical tutorship of both the Muslim world and India. Today, words of Arabic derivation in English include algebra, amalgam, average, atlas, chemistry, cipher, drug, tariff, zenith, and zero. The scientific foundations of all three forms of modern technology (production, destruction, and communication) were slowly being laid. But all this time, science and scholarship were still primarily theocentric. Islam had expanded the horizons of learning *fi sabil el-lah* (in God's path and in God's name). Cultural expansionism was still animated by a universalist fervour. The God standard continued to outshine the gold standard, at least in the field of culture.

3. Monotheism and the Origins of the State

The most important political contributions to world culture that the Semites have made include ideas of centralized government and the principle of patriarchy. Both of these contributions have been of immense relevance to the evolution of the modern sovereign state. Ideas about God can condition ideas about government. It is not always easy to determine where theology ends and political philosophy begins. In Semitic terms, the first world government was the Government of God on earth. Planet Earth itself was not a state, but God was certainly king. The Semitic concept of God envisaged God in anthropomorphic, royal, masculine, and judgmental terms. God was man writ large, and was king and ultimately male. The Almighty expected loyalty and obedience. Indeed, in Christian terms, the original sin was the sin of disobedience—and God was supreme judge. The hereafter was intended to be a centralized and absolutist dominion, divided between the paradise of the pious and the ghetto of the sinner under the kingdom of God.

What God decreed was good. The history of theology and philosophy is replete with debates as to whether God could be omnipotent if he could not help being good. Does good define God, or is God the ultimate definition of what is good? The early debates were a precursor of the issue as to whether "the king could do no wrong." The origins of state sovereignty do lie in the conception of royal absolutism, and this in turn was greatly influenced by the absolutism of the Semitic kingdom of God. The idea of a supreme subversive incarnated in Satan ran into difficulties when liberalism started glorifying opposition to absolutism. Nobody felt this more keenly than John Milton, author of one of the most eloquent defenses of liberty (*Aeropagitica*) and at the same time defender of the ways of God to man (*Paradise Lost*). This lover of earthly freedom was also a defender of divine absolutism. And yet the love of freedom crept into Milton's treatment of divine absolutism. Satan in the earlier phases of *Paradise Lost* certainly assumes heroic proportions. After all, he is rebelling against a king who demands absolute obedience and seems to enjoy the servility of constant prayer and hymns in his glory. God seems to revel in creating politically conscious creatures that are challenged to declare their unqualified allegiance to the Creator. God becomes absolute vanity. Satan becomes a freedom fighter rebelling against the absolutism of the Almighty and the servility of the politically conscious part of creation.

In reality, the New Testament's conception of God is more complex than that of the Old Testament. Under the New Testament, God is indeed still king in heaven, yet He resides among the wretched of the earth. The crucifixion is a process by which God humbled Himself before men. The humility of God was part of the majesty of God. Jesus declared that his kingdom was not of this world: he advised his followers to give unto Caesar what was Caesar's and unto God what was God's. Jesus' recognition of Caesar as sovereign on earth was part of the background to modern European conceptions of sovereignty. As we have indicated, there are occasions when theology is the mother of political philosophy. Ideas about divine governance are often interlinked with ideas of politics among men. Under the Semitic impact, what is the relationship between heaven and earth as political entities? In Orthodox Judaism and in Islam the pull is towards a kind of divine unitarism linking heaven and earth. In the final analysis, theocracy is triumph in the Judeo-Islamic tradition where heaven and earth are together a unitary kingdom under God. On the other hand, the modern

Christian tradition is more federalist than unitary as between the kingdoms of heaven and earth. The move towards liberal secularism in culture was linked to the move towards the federalization of politics. Separating church from state was like separating the kingdom of heaven from the kingdom of this earth. The Semitic emphasis on patriarchy pushed the trend towards divine masculinity in polities. Polytheistic or pantheistic traditions in world history—including those of ancient Egypt, ancient Greece and Rome, and the "tribal" religions of the world—allowed considerable room for female deities. But Semitic monotheism was the great destroyer of the female factor in the character of the deity. From the Semites onwards the great symbols of fertility became masculine: no more goddesses, only one God, and it is a "He" with a capital H! This is in spite of the matrilineal principle in the lineage system of the Jews. We shall return to patriarchy later in the analysis. Suffice it to say for now that the God standard in politics was in part the cradle of the sovereign state. The Semites were ironically the midwives of the concept of sovereignty. But who were the midwives of the gold standard? Let us now turn to the grand transition from God to gold.

Europe and the Rise of the Gold Standard

As Islam went into decline, the torch of science, technology, and scholarship was being passed to a newly awakened Europe. In the fourteenth century of the Christian era, the classical poet Petrarch was among the first to interpret the preceding thousand years of European history, including his own day, as an age of darkness: culture and virtue had declined. Petrarch called for a renewed study not of the Gospel but of Europe's own Graeco-Roman antiquity, setting the stage for the Renaissance based on the twin myths that Europe's antiquity was the zenith of human creativity and the "Dark Ages" were the nadir. It was up to Europe to revive the spirit of its own classical past, innovative and dynamic. Three interrelated European movements were to play a critical role in the emergence of modern Europe: the Renaissance, the Reformation, and the Enlightenment. The Renaissance helped to free European art from excessive service to God and church and laid the foundations of aesthetic individualism. The Enlightenment helped to secularize European science and scholarship and gave new prominence to the role of reason as against faith. Great figures of the Enlightenment included Francis Bacon and his method of induction, Descartes and his method of deduction, Galileo who pushed the Copernican revolution a stage further with telescopic observation, Isaac Newton who formulated new heavenly laws based on gravitation, such empirical philosophers as David Hume, such romantic thinkers as Rousseau, such epistemological innovators as John Locke, and such incorrigible skeptics as Voltaire. They were part of the constellation of stars that constituted the Enlightenment. Then there was the Protestant Reformation as another constellation. Martin Luther (1483-1546 A.D.), son of a miner who had become an Augustinian friar, was appalled by the abuses of indulgences under Pope Leo X. Luther posted his 95 theses on the church door at Wittenberg, one of the great gestures of protest of all time. He proclaimed that faith was the true salvation and that the truly repentant did not need priestly intercession or the Church's indulgences—thus calling for direct communication between the creature and his maker. What should be borne in mind is that these three European movements—the Renaissance, the Reformation, and the Enlightenment—were part of the origins of the sovereign state, on the one hand, and of European Capitalism, on the other. The Renaissance as period did indeed generate artistic independence and innovative individualism. But the Renaissance was also the period of the new monarchies and the renewed doctrines of royal absolutism. The years of new individual liberation in the arts were also the years of the new political centralization of the state. The glories of the palace of Versailles as an artistic achievement are inseparable from the politics of Louis XIV who proclaimed: "I am the state!"

The Protestant Reformation was linked both to the origins of the modern sovereign state and the origins of Western Capitalism. In the evolution of the state system, the Reformation contributed to the breakup of what remained of the Holy Roman Empire. Quarrels among the different principalities resulted in the Peace of Augsburg of 1555 A.D., which formulated a formula of state sovereignty based on the principle of religious nonintervention. Hence the convention or *modus vivendi* agreed upon among Europeans princes, founded on the idea that the religion of the ruler was to be counted as the religion of the society. The whole exercise was designed to reduce interference and intervention across the territorial boundaries of each prince's domain. The idea of the sovereign kingdom was directly at stake in the Treaty of Augsburg. But this 1555 treaty did not end the religious wars in Europe that the Protestant Reformation had unleashed and Europe was later to plunge into another 30 years of conflict. Out of this particular period of internecine religious warfare emerged at long last the Treaty of Westphalia of 1648 A.D., widely regarded as the true genesis of the modern system of sovereign states on the world scene. The conflicts unleashed in Europe by the Protestant Revolution had set the stage for the whole modern state system, which today governs the diplomacy and destiny of the human race. Similarly, the Reformation was not only part of modern statecraft and of the dynamics of sovereignty. The Protestant Revolution was also part of the genesis of modern Western Capitalism. It is to this part of the global equation that we must now turn. A new tilt was beginning to take place form the God standard to the gold standard in a fundamental but subtle transition.

The story of "the Protestant ethic and the spirit of Capitalism" is familiar enough, thanks largely to the brilliant pioneering work of Max Weber. By eliminating priestly intercession in man's relations with God, Protestantism promoted a new spirit of personal accountability and initiative. Laymen and laywomen could interpret for themselves what was "avarice" and what was "usury" without reference to priests or church officials. Acquisitiveness assumed a new legitimacy. Piety was no longer equated with poverty, regardless of the challenge of squeezing a rich man through the eye of a needle! John Calvin (1509-1564 A.D.) pushed the Protestant ethic even further. It was at the age of 20 that he had his "conversion" and began to preach a return to Christian simplicity. In 1536 A.D., Calvin published his *Institutes of the Christian Religion* that stripped the church of pomp, much of the splendor, and much of the ritual. The impact on the new converted bourgeoisie was to discourage ostentation and to discredit elaborate consumption. And so, the new Protestantism was, on the one hand, giving acquisitiveness greater legitimacy than ever and, on the other, denying legitimacy to pomp and ostentation. The implicit and compelling message was: "Acquire, but don't consume! Make money, but don't spend it!" The stage was set for primitive accumulation; the trumpet had sounded for a crusade of savings and reinvestment. John Calvin also preached predestination and the doctrine of the Elect and the saints. To prosper was regarded as a possible sign of God's favor, a signal that one might be among the Elect. Economic exertion became a form of prayer, and success could be God's pat on the back. The God standard and the gold standard were being merged.

Under Protestantism guilt was removed from the pursuit of wealth. A new economic morality came into being. Protestant Europe and Protestant North America took the lead in the new capitalist revolution. It was therefore not an accident that Protestant England was industrially ahead of Catholic Italy, that Protestant Ulster was industrially ahead of the Irish Republic, that Protestant United States was ahead of Latin America, and Protestant Scandinavia was ahead of Catholic Iberia. Only France retained a uniqueness of its own: it was Catholic by religious allegiance but basically Protestant in its culture. The French Revolution of 1789, with its massive attack on the church and the monasteries, had been France's equivalent of a Protestant Reformation. French individualism and the liberalism of the legacy of 1789 transformed France into a country that was at once denominationally Catholic and culturally Protestant. At the center of it all has been the newly emergent Capitalism and the newly triumphant sovereign state. The foundations of the West's hegemony had been set and a new global history was being born.

THE RISE OF THE WEST

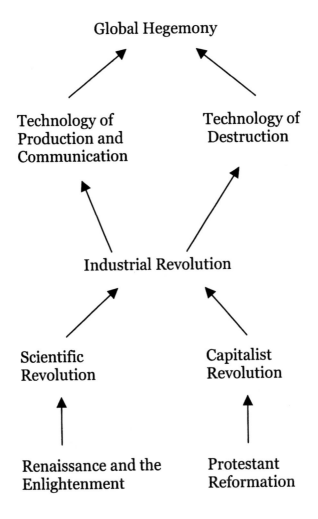

Global Hegemony

Technology of
Production and
Communication

Technology of
Destruction

Industrial Revolution

Scientific
Revolution

Capitalist
Revolution

Renaissance and the
Enlightenment

Protestant
Reformation

On Race, Imperialism, and Communication

It was not merely Europe's technology of production that was stimulated by the Reformation and the scientific revolution; it was also Europe's technology of communication. We have already noted that production helped to consolidate Capitalism. We must now also note that communication helped to expand imperialism. The genius of Western Capitalism is indeed the sheer capacity to keep on producing; the genius of Western imperialism involved effectiveness in communication. At least in a crude way, it can be argued that Capitalism involved the pursuit of gold through production, whereas imperialism has increasingly involved the pursuit of glory through communication. But in Western history the two are wedded together almost indissolubly. Indeed, whether or not Protestantism was the midwife of Capitalism, there is little doubt that Capitalism was the midwife of Western imperialism. Imperialism was linked to the globalization of the gold standard and to the marriage between expanding Capitalism and expanding communications. Imperialism required a strange intimacy between the technologies of production, communication, and destruction. What is more, imperialism fused racist ideology with triumphant technology.

The communication revolution in the modern world did not begin with Sputnik or with the invention of the telephone; it began with European explorations and voyages of discovery, especially from the fifteenth century onwards. That is why the revolution had been linked not only to advances in technology but also to stages in imperialism. The stage was being set for European penetration of the rest of the world, with considerable danger to cultural autonomy and global human diversity. But today, a very curious but still major point to bear in mind is that while the communication revolution is indeed bad news for cultural autonomy in the Third World, it is at long last good news for the struggle against racism. Cultural authenticity among non-Westerners has never been in greater danger. Western culture is penetrating deeper and deeper in much of the Third World. On the other hand, the communications revolution has now become an ally in the struggle against racism. Blatant racial discrimination is on the defensive: the language of racial abuse is looking around for euphemisms. The racists have never been more reluctant to proclaim their prejudices in public. Racism on the world scene is at best declining and is at worst in search of disguise and camouflage. In a sense, the decline of cultural autonomy and the retreat of racism are interconnected. There was a time when racism was itself regarded as an area of cultural autonomy. The southern states of the United States were permitted to invoke the dictum of "Separate but Equal" and thus "enjoy" their own Southern authenticity. There was also a time when South Africa could insist on the principle of "domestic authenticity" and "separate development." The communication revolution is making it harder to use cultural autonomy as a justification for a racist ideology.

What should be remembered is that the link between communication and racism has not always been so positive. Indeed, the story of the relationship between these two has been tumultuous and variable across the centuries. There is, for example, that whole complex story of Europe's interest in finding a sea route to Asia. This involved a major problem in communication. The imperatives of trading with Asia forced Europeans into an age of discovery and exploration. At that time, Africa was just a stumbling bloc on the way to Asia. Western Europeans felt they had to sail around the landmass called Africa in order to get to Asia. Bartolomé Diaz tried to circumnavigate Africa and gave up at the Cape, calling it "The Cape of Storms." Vasco da Gama made a more successful bid, renaming the Cape "Good Hope." The "hope" was not about what Africa might have to offer but about communication with Asia by sea. If Europeans could have abolished or sunk Africa, they would have done it for the sake of trade with Asia! If Africa had not existed, or if it were a much smaller obstacle, the chances are that the "discovery" of the Americas by Europeans would probably have been delayed by another century or longer. The search for an alternate sea route to Asia became financially viable only when alternative routes, like the one round Africa, seemed so expensive and uncertain. Christopher Columbus would have had a much harder time raising money for western-oriented exploration if the sea-route around Africa towards Asia had been less strenuous, less hazardous, and less expensive. Africa was the world's second largest landmass after Asia. Circumnavigating Africa was a demanding assignment. Because Africa existed and was hard to embrace easily, the Americas were "discovered" sooner by Europeans. The American route to Asia was, in the ultimate analysis, an alternative to the African route to Asia. Africa was a difficult option and Christopher Columbus set sail westward instead. And yet, history had its cruel revenge upon Africa. Christopher Columbus did not realize what damage he had done to the African continent by "discovering" the American hemisphere. In a relatively short time the demand for slaves in the "New World" played havoc with population patterns and social institutions in Western Africa. A substantial part of Africa was dragged, kicking and screaming, and was shipped to the new plantations of the Americas. The maritime and nautical achievements of Europe and the "discovery" of new worlds to conquer did irreparable damage to Black Africa. Today, one of every five people of Black African ancestry lives in the Americas. From Africa's point of view, Christopher Columbus and his navigational skill have a good deal to answer for. No people in history have been forcibly exported in such large numbers as Africans, and the Americas were the largest recipients of these reluctant immigrants.

The next link between communication and racism came with the Industrial Revolution proper and its impact on European imperialism in Africa and Asia. On the one hand, the Industrial Revolution helped to make slavery obsolete and generated support for the abolitionist movement. On the other hand, the Industrial Revolution created in Europe new demands for raw materials and other commodities, and resulted in Europe's economic and political expansionism. The subsequent invention of the steam engine and a new wave of interest in building railways strengthened the penetrative capabilities of Europeans in parts of Asia and Africa and created an entirely new and repressive colonial order. The third link between communications and racism was more positive. The colonized peoples in different continents began to know about each other and to learn how to confront racism and imperialism. The anti-colonial movement in India under the leadership of Mahatma Gandhi was particularly influential at a certain period. Africans would not have known much about what was going on in India had Gandhi's movement taken place 50 years earlier. After all, very few Africans knew about the Indian mutiny in the nineteenth century. Communication between Africa and India at the time did not lend itself to such mutual familiarization. But by the 1930s, African nationalists were already able to follow from the radio and from newspapers the whole exciting unfolding of *Satyagraha* against British imperialism. Future African historical figures inspired by the Indian national movement included Kwame Nkrumah (later founding president of Ghana), Kenneth Kaunda (later founding president of Zambia), and Obafemi Awolowo (later one of the giants of independent Nigeria). The communication revolution had made it possible for the oppressed to learn from each other.

It is not often remembered that modern war involves a revolution in communication. World War II, and its aftermath, was beneficial, from a very narrow point of view, for the Third World. The European imperial order was mortally wounded by the war. France emerged from the war humiliated and to some extent humbled. Britain was impoverished and exhausted. The imperial will and World War II seriously shook the will to grandeur. For the British it was not long before they had to give up India. And almost exactly ten years after India's independence came the independence of Ghana, the first Black African country to attain sovereignty after European colonization. These events took place in the full glare of world publicity. Part of the whole process of liberation was the experience of expanding political horizons among the colonized. The war had conscripted large numbers of people from the Third World: Africans were fighting in Burma; Gurkhas were fighting in the Middle East. Village lads were seeing the rest of the world and, later on, some of these ex-servicemen became part of the vanguard of anti-colonialism in their own countries. A world war is indeed a globalizing experience; it is a brutal way of communicating the fact that we belong to one world. But the best phase in the alliance between communication and the struggle against racism is the present one of global exposure. The communication revolution has militated against racism in a variety of ways. There is, first, the instant reporting of racial unrest or racial atrocities thousands of miles away. A *de facto* monitoring system has emerged upon the racial situation in the world as a whole. Major racial convulsions are guaranteed instant publicity from continent to continent. Second, modern communication networks are a constant reminder to humanity how diverse humankind is. Television news cover events in obviously varied racial situations. Familiarity may sometimes breed contempt, but at least as often it can ameliorate a pre-existent disdain. Half of prejudice arises out of ignorance. Modern communication help to remind the world that humankind is, like love, a many-splendored thing. The globalization of communication has also helped to give more meaning to the concept of "world opinion." There is more participation of the weak in the global system than there has ever been.

The Language of Power

A central feature of this phase of world cultural history is that White Anglo-Saxon Protestants (WASPs) have presided over the two most momentous centuries of all time, the nineteenth and twentieth centuries. The Anglo-Saxons have been the most effective in using the language of Capitalism and the technology of production. They have mobilized the symbols of the state-system and the technology of destruction. And they have exploited the medium of their own culture through their technology of communication. The Anglo-Saxons are the new "Semites" of the technocratic era. But who are the Anglo-Saxons? Our sense of "Anglo-Saxon" is almost purely Gaullist, rather than genealogical. Like Charles de Gaulle, we mean by "Anglo-Saxon" in this period those "white" nations whose mother tongue is the "English" language. It is a combination of pigmentational and linguistic criteria. Jamaicans are not Anglo-Saxons, although their mother tongue is English. Cypriots are not Anglo-Saxons in this sense, although their skin is white. But the people of the Falklands are indeed "Anglo-Saxons" because they are both white and native speakers of English. What Charles de Gaulle called "Anglo-Saxons," Winston Churchill called "the English-speaking peoples." Both de Gaulle and Churchill excluded, on the whole, non-white native speakers of the English language, who may already outnumber the population of the United Kingdom.

In this section of the essay, we are concentrating on the political and state manifestations of Anglo-Saxon supremacy in these two centuries. In the next section, we shall focus on Anglo-Saxon hegemony in the language of Capitalism. In the third section, our concern will be with the Anglo-Saxon role in world culture. An underlying motif in all three sections is the dialectic between Anglo-Saxon insularity and Anglo-Saxon expansionism: the political culture of insularity and the political economy of expansionism. In the history of the Anglo-Saxons, insularity has itself taken two forms. England has represented the insularity of an island people. The United States has signified the isolationism of a continent nation. Western expansionism has also taken more than one form. Territorially, the United States expanded as a state but not as an empire. Territorially, Britain expanded as an empire but not as a state. The doctrine of "Manifest Destiny" inspired the United States to swallow neighboring territory, from the purchase of Louisiana to the conquest of California (contiguous expansionism). The doctrine of *Pax Britannica* inspired Britain to annex distant territory, from creating an Indian Empire to establishing the protectorate of Zanzibar. Territorially, the United Kingdom will be smaller at the end of the twentieth century than it was at the beginning of the nineteenth century. On the other hand, the United States will be larger at the end of the twentieth century than it was at the beginning of the nineteenth. In this context, the Anglo-Saxons communicated with the world in three forms of political language: the power of intimidation (mainly military), the power of persuasion (mainly diplomatic), and the power of control (basically imperial). These three forms of power are closely interrelated.

1-The Language of Intimidation

In this period, means of intimidation have ranged from the Maxim gun to nuclear weapons, from British naval pre-eminence in the nineteenth century to Reagan's grand design about militarizing outer space before the end of the twentieth century. The Anglo-Saxons were the first to produce nuclear weapons. They were the first to use nuclear weapons (with Hiroshima and Nagasaki in August 1945 as the first targets). They were the first to take the world to the brink of a nuclear war (in the Cuban missile crisis of 1962). And they are the foremost in refusing to outlaw nuclear first-strike capabilities. On the other hand, the Anglo-Saxons have also led in seeking to control nuclear testing. In July 1963, British negotiators, led by Lord Hailsham, and American negotiators, led by Averell Harriman, arrived in Moscow. After five days of negotiations, a tentative agreement was reached and a copy of the draft treaty was publicized on 24 July, banning all tests in the atmosphere, under water, and in space, but not underground. On 5 August 1963, Soviet Foreign Minister Andrei Gromyko, US Secretary of State Dean Rusk, and British Foreign Secretary Lord Home, put their signatures to the document. The United States Senate ratified it on 24 September after a lengthy debate (the vote was 80 to 19). A large majority of the world's nations followed suit and signed even though France and China were militantly opposed to the treaty.[2]

By this time, the Americans were already the senior Anglo-Saxons. The transition form British global preeminence to American global hegemony was sometimes subtle and sometimes dramatic. The drama of the transition occurred partly through World War II, as American leadership consolidated itself in the course of the war. But it was not until the Suez war of 1956 that the torch seemed to have clearly passed from London to Washington: Anthony Eden was decisively humbled by Dwight Eisenhower and Secretary of State John Foster Dulles. Britain's power of intimidation in world politics was definitely overshadowed by American power when the British were forced to withdraw from Suez. Both the gold and the "glory" of Empire were disappearing. In the era of the balance of power in the preceding three centuries, Britain had been the queen of changing alliances. She could side with Austria against France and Prussia in one decade, and side with Prussia against France and Austria in the next decade. But now, the world of balance of power (with conventional weapons) had given way to a world of balance of terror (with nuclear weapons), and Britain was no longer in the first league of this new Anglo-Saxon roulette.

But Britain preferred to retain a "special relationship" with the senior Anglo-Saxon across the Atlantic.

2-The Language of Persuasion

The global political role of the Anglo-Saxons did not simply rely on instruments of intimidation (military power) but also on means of persuasion. The Anglo-Saxon nations took the lead in the creation of both the League of Nations and the United Nations; but Britain and the Unites States were not consistent in supporting these institutions. Woodrow Wilson inspired the formation of the League of Nations, but his country did not ratify its own membership. Britain was lukewarm in supporting the League's sanctions against Mussolini for his invasion of Ethiopia. The United States played midwife to the birth of the United Nations at the formative conference in San Francisco in 1945. Many Anglo-Saxon ideas influenced the text of the Charter. The Security Council became the equivalent of the House of Lords—"war lords" with veto power. The General Assembly was the House of Commons, based on more democratic ideas of representation. The history of the United Nations has witnessed the greater democratization of the General Assembly. But in the Security Council two out of the five "war lords" are Anglo-Saxon. The Council has two English-speaking vetoes out of five.

In addition to the means of intimidation and persuasion, the Anglo-Saxons have also utilized instruments of control. The British, as we know, created the largest political empire in human history; the Americans created the largest economic empire ever. Their means of intimidation and their techniques of persuasion helped to consolidate their capacity for control. In terms of territorial control, the United Kingdom was virtually the architect of modern imperialism. Curiously enough, the Americans became the pioneers of modern anti-imperialism. The American Declaration of Independence remains one of the landmarks of the history of decolonization in the modern world. The two Anglo-Saxon powers also played fascinating roles in the history of politicized hereditary status in world affairs. The American Revolution (even before the French Revolution) attacked the principle of monarchy and a hereditary aristocracy. Britain, on the other hand, took the lead in attacking the principle of slavery and hereditary servitude. The Americans were pioneers in ending the hereditary humiliation of an underclass (slaves). But by the twentieth century, neither the Americans nor the British were prepared to tackle the new equivalents of heredity, such as ecological privilege and ecological servitude. The people of the northern hemisphere have become the Brahmins of affluence and geo-historical advantage. The people of the southern hemisphere (the Third World) have become the untouchables of servitude and geo-historical poverty.

The Anglo-Saxons have been among the foremost opponents of the New International Economic Order and the New World Information Order. The budgets of the UN and a number of other world organizations are one-third Anglo-Saxon. Alas, the one-third is opposed to fundamental change in favor of the under-privileged. What is more, the Anglo-Saxons can sometimes decide to switch off and not listen. They can use power to break off communication rather than promote it. One example is America's technique of withdrawing from such bodies as the International Labour Organization (ILO) or the United Nations Educational, Scientific, and Cultural Organization (UNESCO). This is a combined power of silence and of the purse. Anglo-Saxon threats of withdrawal have been, in part, a mechanism of censorship, a brutal leverage to change the agenda of international discourse. The sovereign state system is manipulated as a method of silencing certain voices of the South, certain messages from the dispossessed. The state is not only a medium of communication; it is also a guillotine for cutting off further dialogue. But the Anglo-Saxons have not only dominated the state system; they have also presided over the fortunes of Capitalism—and for good reason. The Anglo-Saxons have provided the greatest stability to both liberalism and Capitalism. It is to this area of hegemonic Capitalism that we must now turn.

3-The Language of Capitalist Power

What is the link between liberalism as a political system and Capitalism as a mode of production? Part of the answer lies, again, in the history of the Anglo-Saxon states, especially Britain and the United States. We define "liberalism" in this essay as a pluralistic system of government that puts a special premium on political choice and individual freedom. We define "Capitalism" as an industrial system in which the means of production, distribution, and exchange, are under mainly private control and operate in the context of unequal class relations. Of all the peoples of the world, the Anglo-Saxons have perhaps been the most successful in stabilizing liberal democracy in their own countries. The Anglo-Saxons have also been the leaders in stabilizing Capitalism as a global system. In other words, they have presided over the fate of liberalism domestically and of Capitalism globally. This liberal stability at home and capitalist stability abroad have been interconnected.

All countries with liberal systems are capitalist in their economic organization. Is this a historical accident or a logical causal necessity? England, from the seventeenth century onwards, was a laboratory of modern Capitalism. In the same period, England was evolving into a laboratory of liberal ideas. How causally connected were these trends? Modern liberalism was born out of three revolutions, two of them Anglo-Saxon. These were the 1688 Glorious Revolution in England, the American Revolution from 1776 onwards, and the 1789 Revolution in France. The Anglo-Saxon revolutions were decidedly different from the French; and the difference goes towards explaining Anglo-Saxon stability. The English and American revolutions were revolutions from above that were led by members of the disgruntled establishment. The French Revolution, on the other hand, was an explosion from below, symbolized by the mob onslaught on the Bastille. The Anglo-Saxon revolutions engaged in selective transformation, upholding the Burkean principle that a people should "neither entirely nor at once depart from antiquity." The French Revolution, on the other hand, was an exercise in comprehensive transformation, aspiring to wipe the historical slate clean. The American Revolution, especially, was more liberal than democratic, as it sought to protect the people from the power of the government. The French Revolution was more democratic than liberal, as it sought to increase the power of the underprivileged. In other words, the American Revolution was preoccupied with checking the power of the mighty; the French were obsessed with enhancing the power of the meek.

Checks and balances, separation of powers, and federalism were America's answer to despotism. Mass involvement, referenda, and Bonapartism were France's prescription for popular participation. The ethos of American liberalism was decentralization; the ethos of the French version was centralization. The English and American revolutions were basically elitist; the French Revolution was mass-oriented. It is precisely these contrasting factors that helped to make Anglo-Saxon liberalism so stable and French liberalism so changeable. The French have had many constitutions since 1789. The Americans have had only one since the late 1790s. Particularly relevant for the link with Capitalism was the convergence between stability of government and stability of property. The French Revolution was no respecter of property. The Anglo-Saxon revolutions, on the other hand, were preoccupied with property rights. John Locke was the philosopher-prophet of both Anglo-Saxon revolutions. He stood for "Life, Liberty, and the Pursuit of Happiness"—

Jefferson might still have meant "the pursuit of property." Locke was the forerunner of a long list of Anglo-Saxon communicators who helped to rationalize Capitalism and thereby helped to stabilize it internationally. Adam Smith is regarded as the founder of the classical school of economics. Born in Scotland in June 1723, he lived to become the first systematic economist. His message was brilliantly communicated. His impact demolished feudal economics: the medieval guilds and mercantilism. The Capitalism of the division of labor in production prepared the way for today's Capitalism of mass production. Another British communicator who helped to rationalize and stabilize Capitalism was David Ricardo. Born in London in 1772, he lived to develop influential theories of rent and of labor that had considerable impact on the evolution of modern economics. Karl Marx's theory of surplus value owed a good deal to Ricardo. He wrote on money and trade and helped to develop the iron law of wages based on the doctrine of scarcity of economic goods. The new culture of "gold" was getting truly sophisticated. And when Capitalism faced its worst crisis in the twentieth century, it was once again a British thinker and communicator who rationalized the necessary reforms and helped to rescue the global system. Born in Cambridge, England, in June 1883, John Maynard Keynes lived to become the most influential economist of the first half of the twentieth century. He was the founder of the expansionist school of economics who formulated a strategy for overcoming unemployment and deflation through public works. He helped to rescue that other Anglo-Saxon power across the Atlantic: his ideas influenced President Franklin D. Roosevelt's New Deal strategy against the Great Depression.

From the eighteenth century onwards, the English-speaking peoples have communicated to the world by far the most brilliant theories in defense of Capitalism: from Smith to Friedman, from Malthus to John Kenneth Galbraith. These intellectual foundations have helped to give the global capitalist system both durability and resilience. Not surprisingly, the very paradigmatic quality of Anglo-Saxon Capitalism also provided the setting for the most brilliant critiques of Capitalism. After all, where would Marxism be without Marx's close study of the workings of Capitalism in England? Similarly, the paradigmatic quality of Anglo-Saxon imperialism provided the ammunition for the most brilliant attacks against imperialism. Where would Lenin's theory of imperialism be without Hobson's prior theory? Where would theories of dependency be without a study of American economic imperialism? But the Anglo-Saxon impact on the world economy has not been merely in terms of brilliant rationalizations or critiques of Capitalism; the impact has taken more direct forms as well. There was, first, England's leadership in the Industrial Revolution and her emergence as a "workshop of the world." There was also England's role in stabilizing for many decades the principle of "free trade," which was so important in the evolution of Western Capitalism. England's role in stabilizing the principle of the gold standard as a basis of international exchange was also an important, if temporary, factor in the development of a capitalist world economy. The economic torch was once again passed from the British to the Americans. In time, the United States became the most important national economy in the global system. The collapse of Wall Street in 1929 sentenced the rest of the world to the deprivations of the Great Depression. From then on, the health of the world economy as a whole was indissolubly linked to the health of the American economy. Before long the gold standard was, to all intents and purposes, replaced by the dollar standard. After World War II, Western Europe's reconstruction depended on the enlightened self-interest of the United States and its Marshall Plan. And the Bretton Woods Conference in New Hampshire, in July 1944, laid the foundations of the post-war international monetary and banking system dominated by the United States. Symbolically, the president of the World Bank is always an

American. And the International Monetary Fund and International Development Association needed the good mood of the American Congress to keep them in business.

The Anglo-Saxon factor in the world economy continues to be pronounced and critical. For better or worse, the English-speaking nations continue to be both the most stable liberal democracies in the world and the greatest stabilizers of international Capitalism. They have been more successful in exporting Capitalism to others than exporting democracy. In this leadership of the world of Capitalism, do the Anglo-Saxons now see a potential rival on the horizon? If Japan is emerging as a super-industrial state, will its importance for the health of the world economy ever approximate the importance of the Anglo-Saxons? There was a time when Japan appeared to be another England. Britain led Europe in the industrial revolution; Japan led Asia. Both were island nations that managed to combine attachment to tradition with a spirit of modernization. Both were monarchies with elaborate class structures that combined feudal and bourgeois elements. Both became expansionist imperial powers. In many ways, Japan appeared to be the England of the Far East. But while England helped to demonstrate that liberalism without Capitalism was not possible, Japan demonstrated that Capitalism could exist without liberalism. It is indeed true that all liberal democracies have capitalist economies; but it is not true that all capitalist economies are within liberal democracies. Japan, before World War II, demonstrated, convincingly, that the growth and maturation of Capitalism need not be accompanied by the evolution of a democratic political system. But apart from that major difference, Japan before the war did appear to be another England in its political economy. Since World War II, has Japan been developing into another United States? In industrial might, Japan has certainly left England way behind, and has narrowed the industrial gap between itself and the United States. Japan is now the second industrial giant of the capitalist world, and its share of international trade is now a critical factor in the world economy. But while Japanese industrial expertise is catching up with that of the United States, Japanese natural resources are almost nonexistent when compared with the natural endowment of America. And in population, Japan is, of course, less than half the size of the United States. It therefore seems unlikely that Japan will ever overshadow the Anglo-Saxon factor in world Capitalism, no matter how large Japan's industrial output becomes.

But will the Anglo-Saxons remain capitalist? Marx was wrong in having ever expected a communist revolution in either Britain or the United States. There is probably a phase in capitalistic development below which a socialist revolution is indeed feasible, but above which a proletarian revolution becomes impossible. Almost all the Anglo-Saxon countries in our sense of the term (Britain, the United States, Australia, Canada, New Zealand, etc.) may have reached and passed that stage. Perhaps only Ireland among the white English-speaking countries is still at a stage of capitalist development at which a socialist revolution is conceivable. But elsewhere in the white English-speaking world, internal liberal stability and external capitalist equilibrium have already produced a different result. The Anglo-Saxon nations are the least likely to vindicate Marx's prediction that advanced Capitalism inevitably leads to a proletarian socialist revolution. Liberal Anglo-Saxons have presided over the destiny of Capitalism for two centuries and their nations seem to be even further away from a Marxist revolution today than they were during Marx's own lifetime. The Anglo-Saxons have switched on their amplifiers to convey their capitalist message to the rest of the world. But they have switched off their hearing aid and turned a deaf ear to the global call for social justice.

4-The Language of Culture Power

As indicated earlier, a special dialectic between insularity and expansionism is discernible in the history of the Anglo-Saxon peoples. This dialectic has operated in both the political economy and the political culture of the Anglo-Saxon experience. In this section, we place particular emphasis on political culture. We are examining the interplay between Anglo-Saxon history and global culture transfers, especially trends in religion, race, language, and leisure. In a sense, the interplay in religion goes back to the Tudors. There is, first, the Anglo-Saxon impact on the relationship between church and state—a major aspect of the recurrent contradictions of world culture. The Protestant Reformation had, in retrospect, three major founders: two theologians and one king. The theologians we mentioned before were Germany's Martin Luther and France's Jean Calvin. The king was Henry VIII of England (1509-1547 A.D.). Luther and Calvin challenged the church on matters of theology and doctrine. Henry challenged the Pope on issues of authority. In the ultimate analysis, Henry's protest was political rather than spiritual. While Luther and Calvin were redefining the relationship between individual and priest, Henry was redefining the relationship between church and state. The history of the world would have been very different if Henry VIII had had a marriage counselor or a good psychiatrist. The story is all too familiar. The second Tudor king had had problems with his marriage to Catherine of Aragon, widow of Henry's brother, Arthur. Henry wanted the marriage annulled on the grounds that the law forbade a man to marry his brother's widow (advance shades of Hamlet's self-torment over his mother's marriage to his uncle). Pope Julius II had granted the original dispensation authorizing the marriage, but Henry was now disputing the Pope's authority. Pope Clement VII procrastinated and Henry decided to catch the "Papal Bull" by the horns. In 1531 A.D., Henry forced an assembly of clergy to recognize him as the supreme head of the English Church. He forced parliament to stop payments to Rome and to appoint bishops without the permission of the Pope. Archbishop of Canterbury, Thomas Cranmer, declared Henry's marriage to Catherine null and void, under duress, and declared his marriage to Ann Boleyn valid. In 1534 A.D., Henry forced Parliament to pass the Act of Supremacy declaring the English monarch to be "the only supreme head on earth of the church of England." Theologically, Henry did not depart form the Catholic creed except on this issue of papal authority. He retained the articles of faith of he Catholic Church, keeping distant from both Lutheranism and Calvinism. It was Edward VI (1547-1553 A.D.) who presided over the true transition to Protestantism, when altars and images were brought down and "mass" gave way to "holy communion." The right of the king to marry (which had obsessed Henry) was now followed by the right of the priest to marry. In their own pragmatic way, the Anglo-Saxons were forging their own version of Protestantism.

What did all this mean from the point of view of the dialectic between insularity and expansionism among the Anglo-Saxons? The birth of Anglicanism signified the nationalization of Christianity; for it inaugurated the principle of creating an established church within the state, fusing a national monarch with a universal church. The Church of England was born, and Christianity was nationalized. Henry VIII had struck a blow against religious dependency, for better or worse. Protestantism as a whole came to signify a movement for greater liberation of the individual from the centralized church, but Anglicanism in its origins seemed more concerned with the greater liberation of the nation-state form the universal church. The King of England was standing up against the Roman Pope. For quite a while, Anglo-Saxon Protestantism was more preoccupied with the rights of the state against the church than with the rights of the individual against priestly power. The Anglo-Saxons were engaged in religious insularity in this phase of their history. As Anglo-Saxon culture and thought became more diverse, and as Anglo-Saxons migrated and populated other areas, striking differences developed. The two leading Anglo-Saxon powers signified drastically different relationships between church and state. The United States became a model of the principle of separation of church and state. Even today the issue of prayer in public school is a matter of heated constitutional debate in the United States. England, on the other hand, is a model of integration of church with state. The Queen is both head of state and governor of the Church of England. Major doctrinal changes in the Church of England need the implicit approval of the British Parliament (delegated to the synod), and the Archbishop of Canterbury is technically appointed by the Prime Minister. The two largest Anglo-Saxon nations thus provide contrasting paradigms for the rest of the world on the issue of church and state. And it is the American ethos of separation, rather than the British model of integration, which is gaining ground in contemporary world culture.

As to the actual doctrinal content of Anglo-Saxon religious denominations, their spread has been less dramatic than one might have expected. The Anglo-Saxons have been more effective in spreading their language than their religion. They have beaten the Latin countries linguistically, making the English language a bigger global force than French, Spanish, Portuguese or Italian, but they have failed to make Protestantism a bigger religious force in the world than Roman Catholicism. Perhaps part of the explanation lies in the pluralistic nature of Protestantism as contrasted with the monolithic nature of Roman Catholicism. British imperial policy was more tolerant of competitive evangelization and proselytization than was the imperial policy of even France, let alone Spain and Portugal. There was even an ecumenical principle in British immigration policies into the American colonies: Catholics to Maryland, Congregationalists to New

England, Quakers to Pennsylvania, Anglicans to Virginia, and Dutch Reformed colonists to old New York and New Jersey. Partly because of the basic expansionist pragmatism of the Anglo-Saxons, they have had a role in the destiny of other faiths as well. We have already referred to their innovation in nationalizing Christianity during the days of Henry VIII. Four centuries later, the Anglo-Saxons presided over the nationalization of Judaism as well by playing midwife to the birth of the state of Israel and, later, committing themselves to the survival of Israel. Britain's role in the history of Israel had, of course, been different from that of the United States; but both roles by the Anglo-Saxons have been fundamental for the destiny of Zionism and the Jewish state.

Britain was the power entrusted with the Mandate of Palestine after World War I. The Balfour Declaration of 1917, issued even before the end of the war, is widely interpreted as a landmark in the legitimization of Zionism as a force and in the validation of the principle of a Jewish homeland. With typical British contradiction and ambivalence, the Balfour Declaration affirmed as follows:

> His Majesty's Government view with favour the establishment in Palestine of a national home for the Jewish people, and will use their best endeavors to facilitate the achievement of this object, it being clearly understood that nothing shall be done which may prejudice the civil and religious rights of existing non-Jewish communities in Palestine, or the rights and political status enjoyed by Jews in any other country.[3]

The declaration was very influential and President Woodrow Wilson approved it before publication. The declaration was subsequently endorsed by France, Italy, and other allied governments. Many international instruments incorporated the words of the Balfour Declaration, including the

League of Nations Mandate for Palestine in 1922, and US-British Palestine Mandate convention in 1924. Later on, the United States more than Britain presided over the destiny of Zionism and the dream of the Jewish state. President Truman's role was critical in determining the vote in the United Nations in favor of the partition of Palestine. From then on, the United States has remained the patron of the state of Israel, providing moral, military, and economic means of survival. The Anglo-Saxon factor in the history of the Jews in the twentieth century is second only to the role of the Jews themselves. It is not for nothing that the English language is now second only to Hebrew in the state of Israel.

What about the impact of the Anglo-Saxons on Islam? Has there also been a nationalization of Islam? In a sense, there has been a similar tendency in the Anglo-Saxon impact. The British ruled India and presided over the partition of India, in many ways similar to the partition of Palestine, as Pakistan nationalized Islam. Lawrence of Arabia (T.E. Lawrence) played a role in making the Arabs rebel against Turkish imperialism. In so doing, the Arabs replaced Ottoman overlords with European overlords. They exchanged fellow Muslims for Christians as masters as new Islamic nations were created. The compartmentalization of the Ottoman Empire was a trend towards the nationalization of Islam, and the Anglo-Saxons have been central to the process. To the present day, Mecca and Medina are, in a sense, in the custody of the United States. The *de facto* alliance between Saudi Arabia and the United States leaves the Islamic holy places in the care of the Anglo-Saxons. The British and the Americans continue to play a historic role in the smaller Gulf states, from Kuwait to Oman, that share an Anglo-American fascination. But where does the Iranian revolution fit into this interplay between Islam and the Anglo-Saxons? In a way, the Iranian revolution is an effort to resurrect an Islamic Empire and to revive a kind of "Ottoman Empire" in a more radical incarnation. Once again, the Anglo-Saxons are quite central to Iranian sensibilities, as the crisis of the American hostages during the Iranian Revolution dramatically illustrated. If the heartland of Sunni Islam is Saudi Arabia, the Sunnis are in alliance with the Anglo-Saxon. If the heartland of Shiite Islam is Iran, the Shiites are in a relationship of daggers drawn with the Anglo-Saxons. The Shiites are out to internationalize Islam in its radical form, rather than bow to Anglo-Saxon preference for national "churches."

Finally, there is the issue of Hinduism and the Anglo-Saxons. The heartland of Hinduism was India, and the British ruled India. India borrowed from the Americans the principle of the secular state and the principle of federalism, however modified or even distorted to suit local conditions. India borrowed from Britain more profound levels of political culture. Thanks to the Anglo-Saxon impact, Hinduism has changed internally and found a new relationship with Western Civilization. Even figures like Mahatma Gandhi were themselves products of the interplay between Hindu nationalism, the Yogic tradition, and Anglo-Saxon liberalism. Three of India's prime ministers, Jawaharlal Nehru, his daughter Indira Gandhi, and Nehru's grandson, Rajiv Gandhi, remained amongst the most Anglicized Indians that the British Raj ever produced. In short, the Anglo-Saxons presided over the modernization of yet another great religious civilization, Hinduism.

Anglo-Saxon influence in the colonies included racial issues along with religious ones. A US Ambassador to the United Nations, Andrew Young (himself black), accused the British of having "invented modern racism." While this was definitely an exaggeration, the Anglo-Saxon peoples did take a major lead in the modernization of racism and its application to historical conditions in the last three centuries. A major product of racism before the twentieth century was, of course, the trade in black slaves, especially across the Atlantic. In time, the British became the biggest carriers of slaves from Africa to the Americas, selling slaves not only to their own colonies but also to Spanish and Portuguese America. In time, the southern states of North America evolved what was probably the most race-conscious form of plantation slavery in the Western Hemisphere where "miscegenation" between masters and slaves was not a way of liberating the offspring (as was often the case in Latin and Islamic forms of slavery). In the United States, children of slaves were indeed slaves even if the father was the master himself. Although the Anglo-Saxons played such a major role in commercializing racism and making money out of the humiliation of Africa, history also gave the Anglo-Saxons a leading role in the fight to abolish slavery. British ships rescued many a slave on the high seas, and it was the Anglo-Saxons who helped promote Black Zionism, the call to the return of former black slaves to their ancestral Africa. That is how Liberia, the oldest African republic, was born. The American Colonization Society created a government of repatriated Black Americans (Americo-Liberians) over the indigenous African population in 1816. The Society handed over political control more fully to the immigrant Blacks in 1947. Sierra Leone was, in turn, once a British settlement for emancipated slaves. The Creoles, some of the leading citizens of Sierra Leone, are basically descended from those. Nowhere else in the world is descent from ex-slaves as much a matter of pride as it is in Liberia and Sierra Leone. The Anglo-Saxons had a good deal to do with creating such a sense of privilege for the imported Blacks as opposed to the indigenes. Yet, this itself was part of Anglo-Saxon racism since semi-westernized ex-slaves were constructed as superior to the non-westernized "natives."

As part of the modernization of racism, the Anglo-Saxons also played a leading role in two interrelated processes: the scientification of racism and the poetification of racism. The influence of Charles Darwin on racial theories symbolized the process of scientification. The influence of Rudyard Kipling symbolized the process of poetification. Darwin's biological ideas about natural selection and the survival of the fittest were applied to racial graduation. Social Darwinism became, in part, a theory to justify white supremacy. Kipling turned racism into an imperialist crusade for the white man. Kipling's poem "The White Man's Burden" remains the most imperialist poem in the English language. The poetification of racism is captured in such images of the "native" as "half-devil, half-child." And white patriotism is stirred by such lines as:

> Take up the white man's burden
> —The savage wars of peace
> Fill full the mouth of famine
> And bid the sickness cease.
>
> The ports ye shall not enter.
> The roads ye shall not tread,
> Go make them with your living,
> And mark them with your dead.[4]

This brings us to the linguistic impact of the Anglo-Saxons upon world culture. Some would say this is by far the most important contribution that the Anglo-Saxons have made to world culture. The English language has become the most widely spoken language in human history, in terms of distribution. Sometimes the linguistic impact is linked to such other Anglo-Saxon roles as international trade and imperialism. Until the second half of the twentieth century, the biggest disseminator of the English language was Britain, especially in relation to its territorial empire. Since World War II, the biggest promoter of the English language is the United States and its economic empire. The English language is tied also to racism. Shakespeare was probably more anti-Semitic than anti-Black. Certainly, the *Merchant of Venice* (with its Shylock) is a more racist play than *Othello* but subsequent Anglo-Saxons became more anti-Negro than anti-Jewish.

Other areas of culture with Anglo-Saxon leadership include some fields of leisure. Pop music (from jazz to rock) had been disproportionately influenced by Anglo-Saxons and "Afro-Saxons." The United States' impact on world cinema and television has been enormous. American pop-culture as a whole has been expansionist; a coca-colonization of the world is under way. Popular American culture ranges from jeans to hamburgers. American high culture, on the other hand, tends to be derivative and influenced by Europe. It has been less successful on the world scene. American soft drinks have taken over the world, especially Coke and Pepsi. American magazines have triumphed globally (especially *Time* and *Newsweek*), but American newspapers are far less successful (except in the peculiar case of the *Herald Tribune* which is not read in the United States itself). The dialectic between insular newspapers and expansionist magazines becomes symbolic of a wider Anglo-Saxon predisposition. And cultural autonomy elsewhere has continued to be on the defensive as a result of the conquering power of Anglo-Saxon culture.

The State Triumphant

As we approach the twenty-first century, another curious trend has been unfolding. Two legacies from vastly different Semitic figures have been challenging Western hegemony and its Anglo-Saxon vanguard. One legacy is, once again, Islam and its restlessness whenever threatened by the West. The other legacy is that of Karl Marx, sometimes regarded as the last of the great Semitic prophets. A new battle is joined between the exported cultures of Semitic prophets, on one side, and the exported ways of the Anglo-Saxons, on the other. There is little doubt that Marxism and Islam are the most universalistic of all the challenges to Anglo-Saxon hegemony. Marxism is especially concerned with the triumph of Capitalism and seeks to undermine it. Islam is most concerned with the triumph of Western culture and seeks to arrest it. What neither Marxism nor Islam in the twentieth century is particularly worried about is the triumph of the sovereign state-system.

Two types of revolutions have arisen as a result of these concerns: revivalist and innovative revolutions. Revivalist revolutions are animated by nostalgia for the past; innovative revolutions aspire to an idealized future. Islam has provided a stimulus for revivalist revolutionary movements; Marxism has inspired innovative revolutionary trends. The revivalist movements are culturally defensive; the innovative movements are structurally transformative. The revivalist movements are usually nationalist; the innovative ones are usually socialist. The revivalist movements are born of a crisis of identity; the innovative ones come out of a crisis of inequality. The revivalists tend to be focused on the nation and its sanctity; the innovative ones are concerned with the state and its powers. But in reality neither revivalist Islam nor innovative Marxism challenged the victorious status of the sovereign state. Two Third World revolutions provide some of the most striking contrasts between these two trends. Iran under Shah Pahlavi was one of the richest of Third World countries; Ethiopia under Emperor Haile Selassie was one of the poorest. The Iranian Revolution intended to reverse the modernizing autocracy of the Shah; the Ethiopian revolution intended to accelerate the modernizing autocracy of the Emperor. The revolution in Iran was in search of a new Islamic theocracy; the revolution in Ethiopia was engaged in terminating an ancient Christian theocracy. The Iranian Revolution in 1979 was a spontaneous revolution of unarmed civilians; the Ethiopian revolution in 1974 was a creeping coup by armed soldiers. The Iranian revolution was opposed to Anglo-Saxon cultural imperialism; the Ethiopian revolution was opposed to Anglo-Saxon economic imperialism. What neither Islam in Iran nor Marxism in Ethiopia focused upon or opposed was the state-system. The legitimacy of the sovereign state seems to be the least endangered of all the methods by which the West and the Anglo-Saxons have sought to control the modern world.

The three most universalistic movements founded by Semitic prophets are Christianity, Islam, and Marxism. All of them started as grass-roots movements. Of the three, only Islam captured the state during the Prophet's own lifetime. Christianity had to wait until three centuries after the death of Jesus before capturing the Roman Empire. Marxism had to wait from Marx's death in 1883 until the Russian Revolution of 1917 to capture the Russian state. But what is clear is that whenever grass-roots movements have captured the state, it is not the state that has changed; it has been the grass-roots movements. There is compelling evidence that whoever captures the state is in mortal danger of being captured by it. When liberation movements succeed in capturing the state, the leaders become converted to the state-system itself, sometimes almost fanatically. When workers capture the state in the name of socialism, they too soon develop state consciousness rather than class-consciousness. They seek to protect the interests of the state that they now control, rather than continue to struggle to realize the interests of the workers in whose name they captured the state in the first place. Classical Marxism and orthodox Leninism have always envisaged "the withering away of the state" as a kind of ultimate utopia. Since the state had been seen ideologically as the instrument of the ruling class, it has been theoretically taken for granted that the withering away of classes would inevitably result in the withering away of the state. It is our contention that any capture of the state by the proletariat would be a Sisyphean exercise (an endless labor of pushing a large round stone uphill, only to have it roll down, and then to push it uphill again, an so on repeatedly). Should any section of the working class ever capture the state, its class-consciousness is often rapidly transformed into state consciousness. That is why a preoccupation with class interests is often replaced by a preoccupation with the interests of the state. Whoever controls the state is compulsively tempted to preserve it. It is because of this that we have concluded that whoever captures the state is captured by it. The conqueror's orientation changes: the survival of the state becomes the paramount aim even if it means repressing fellow workers or fellow nationals.

Social movements are held hostage not simply by the system of sovereign states, but also by the machinery of Capitalism worldwide. Indeed, the future of social movements in the world is subject to a dual hegemony: a condominium being exercised by Capitalism, on one side, and the state-system, on the other. The capitalist world economy and the state system are two distinct prison houses in which our era finds itself, and the Anglo-Saxons are still presiding over both. The most ambitious global reform for the future may have to include a search for alternatives not only to Capitalism but also to the state. Partly because of the state-system, the world has developed the most destructive arsenals ever accumulated in history. Partly because of the state-system, the resources of this planet (including the sea bed) are still disproportionately controlled by principles of state sovereignty and national jurisdiction. Partly because of the state-system, governments are prepared to go to war for the sake of inches of barren territory. Impossible as the task may be at the present time, there is a compelling case for exploring both alternative state-systems and alternatives to the state. For the time being, however, we are prisoners behind the bars of Westphalia. If the struggle for cultural and class utopias has not left any dent on the prison walls of these capitalist and state systems, is the situation hopeless? We have sought to demonstrate that the underprivileged races and cultures have attempted to capture the state and have been captured by it. Nationalists of Asia and Africa sounded the knock of entry into the world system and then became the high priests of the state-system itself. The underprivileged classes have also sought to capture the state and, when they did, were captured by it. The socialists and workers sounded the knock of exit from the capitalist system and at the same time sounded the knock of entry into the state system. The question now arises whether the underprivileged sex or gender could hold the secret of global transformation. Can women guide us away from both the excesses of the Semites and extremities of the Anglo-Saxons?

God, Gold, and Gender

Until now, the state has been tied to patriarchy, including its central primordial principle of male dominance. If the state is an institutionalized monopoly of the legitimate use of physical force, and if women are less physically inclined to violence than men, the very concept of legitimate use of physical force may change when the state becomes androgynous. The state's ultimate instruments of coercion have so far been disproportionately men. The same goes for all those who challenge the state's monopoly of the legitimate use of physical force. Ironically, both Anglo-Saxons and Semites have experimented with female leaders of the state, but what happened in those situations where a woman has been at the pinnacle of the state, seemingly in control of its destiny? What has happened when Queen Elizabeth I (Anglo-Saxon), Mrs. Golda Meir (Semite), or Mrs. Margaret Thatcher (another Anglo-Saxon) took charge of the state? In reality, in political systems that are primarily male-dominated, a single female at the top does not change the fundamental masculine dynamic of the structure. The women who succeed in a male-dominated world have themselves to display male-derived perceptions of strength. The question for the future is whether a real feminization of the state would reduce its propensity for violence. On the whole, it is arguable that the feminist movement has been seeking mechanisms for sharing rather than monopolizing power. It is also arguable that feminism, given that men and women need each other more than races or classes do, might result in reducing polarization in the struggle for equity. Feminist styles and aspiration should help to minimize the game of post-liberation violence.

Capitalism at a primitive state is androgynous, involving both men and women in comparable productive capacities. But as Capitalism became more internationalized, it also became more masculine dominated. Similarly, as Capitalism became more mechanized and industrialized, it became more male dominated. The gender of Capitalism is still more androgynous then the gender of the state-system; but this is only a relative measurement. On the whole, both the state-system and the capitalist global economy are major universes of the male of the human species, awaiting fundamental reform through partial feminization. God and gold have never been enough foundations for social justice. The missing "g" is no longer "glory" in Milton's sense of the applause of one's peers. The missing "g" is gender. By moderating the excesses of both the God standard and the gold standard, women may hold the secret map of escape from the dominion of Semitic absolutes and Anglo-Saxon versions of "compromise."

Conclusion

We have sought to demonstrate in this essay that the history of world culture is, at least in part, a transition from Semitic ideas to European technique, from the spread of Semitic religions to the triumphs of Anglo-Saxon technology. From the point of view of world order, this grand cultural transition has given birth to two mighty forces of the past few hundred years: the power of the sovereign state and the force of Capitalism. The modern sovereign state can be traced back to a marriage between Semitic ideas and European experience. The transition was, at one level, from God as king to the king as God's anointed. And then the absolute monarchy became the absolute state. The other Semitic tradition (Islam) was also evolving towards a concept of the absolute state. Indeed, the Prophet Muhammad lived to preside over a nascent Islamic state, and thereby helped to bequeath a tradition of theocracy to future generations of his followers. But, on the whole, Islam produced either city-states or empire states. It was Christianized Europeans who were destined to develop the nation-state. The idea of sovereignty emerged out of the principle of absolutism, which in turn was for a while an earthly translation of the Kingdom of God. Semitic monotheism influenced the history of European monarchies, and must be seen as part of the intellectual and normative origins of the sovereign state. Europe evolved from a culture of the absolute deity to a culture of the absolute monarch, and then onto a culture of the absolute state.

As for Capitalism, this, too, was partly a case of Europeanizing the Semitic heritage, subjecting a Semitic legacy to the changing material realities of European experience. This developed in the economic face of the Protestant Reformation, as has been indicated. In Islamic history, there was, for a while, a strong possibility of a parallel evolution of a capitalist tradition. The Prophet Muhammad had himself been a merchant, and some of the verses of the Qur'an praise trade as a calling. Islam is distrustful of interest, but not of the profit motive. The early Islamic empires, especially under the Abbasids, displayed signs of vigorous entrepreneurship as a way of life. It appeared as if the foundations were being laid for what we were later to label as "Capitalism." Islam did contribute to the early stages of the technological and capitalist revolution in Europe, but Islam fell short of evolving its own industrial revolution. On the whole, it was revised Christianity, rather than revised Islam, that culminated in what Max Weber later described as "the spirit of Capitalism." In the evolution of the gold standard, the Europeans have been the senior partner within the coalition of Semitic ideas and European experience. But in the earlier evolution of the

God standard, the Semites were the senior partner and original inventors of the standard. In the last 200 years, the torch of leadership in the world system has been passed to the Anglo-Saxons. Great Britain presided over the fate of Capitalism and empire in the nineteenth century. The United States has increasingly assumed a dominant role in the twentieth century. The Anglo-Saxons have become the "Semites" of the technocratic era. The Jews and the Arabs had once forged a theocratic approach to universalism through the God standard. The Anglo-Saxons have attempted to chart out a technocratic approach to universalism through the gold standard.

The world has since discovered that it is within the prison walls of two new absolutes: the state-system and Capitalism. Those who have wanted to abolish Capitalism by capturing the state have found themselves captured by the state. When socialists capture the state, it is not the state that withers away; it is in fact socialism. What is the way out of this interconnected maze of the absolutes of Capitalism and the state-system? The most promising solution lies neither in a new God standard nor in a revised gold standard. It lies in the androgynization of both and in the partial feminization of the state. It seems probable that the androgynization of church, state, and economy will substantially moderate the tendency of each to become absolutist. By the very nature of their predicament, women cannot seek to replace men; they aim at political and economic equality and not political and economic monopoly. The retreat from the excesses of the Semitic heritage and the abuses of Anglo-Saxon legacy may require the equal status of women as both guides and commanders.

Let us conclude with the imagery of three ships in history: the Bounty, the Titanic, and the Californian. They are symbols of a world in partial communication. On His Britannic Majesty's ship Bounty, there had in fact been tyranny under the rule of Captain William Bligh. In desperation the men ultimately rebelled in the same year that the French people did: 1789. The mutineers on the ship overcame the captain and his supporters, put them in lifeboats and let them loose in the sea, and took charge of the ship themselves. The Bounty attempted to disengage from the international nautical system, and to keep its distance from Britain's law, after the mutiny. The mutineers then retired to an island, an exercise in primordial delinking and a severance of communication. Today, the world itself is an island; no mutiny on the Bounty can be an escape in its own right. No mutineers from the Bounty could find refuge in such stark terms. The world is now faced with omni-communication—if it only cares to listen. The tragedy is that of expanded communication and diminishing dialogue. Our other image of a ship is that of the Titanic, the supposedly unsinkable vessel that sank on its maiden voyage when it hit an iceberg on 15 April 1912. There was another ship near by, the Leyland Liner, the Californian, less than 20 miles from the stricken Titanic. The radio of the Californian was switched off that momentous night, and they could not hear the distress signals from less than 31 kilometers away. Once again, human beings failed to rescue each other because they had switched off avenues of communication. You may have noticed that all three ships (the Bounty, the Titanic and the Californian) were "Anglo-Saxon." But none of the captains or the radio operators were women. So what? If I were a Semitic prophet in the grand tradition, I would describe all this as "a parable." The fate of humanity may indeed depend upon creative communication and androgynization of the command structure. Those social movements that enhance contact and communication and those that seek to expand the role of women are needed in the struggle to tame the sovereign state, civilize Capitalism, and humanize communication. To the question "what is civilization?" it may one day be possible to answer "human communication in a truly androgynized world." Such a message has yet to find a prophet of

Semitic proportions. It cannot even find Anglo-Saxon "packaging" for the time being. Perhaps "civilization" is a word ahead of its time. Perhaps it has always been.

NOTES

This chapter is a revised version of an essay entitled "From the Semites to the Anglo-Saxons: Culture and Civilisation in Changing Communication," originally published in *Alternatives*, volume XI, No 1, January 1986, pp. 3-43.

1. *The Holy Bible*, Romans X: 12, Revised Standard Version.
2. See John G. Stoessinger, *The Might of Nations* (New York: Random House, 1981), pp. 352-353.
3. J.C. Hurewitz, *Documents of Near East Diplomatic History* (New York: Columbia University Press, 1951), pp. 25-26.
4. Reproduced in Louis L. Snyder (ed.), *The Imperialism Reader: Documents and Readings in Modern Expansionism* (Princeton, NJ: Van Nostrand, 1962), pp. 87-88.

PART I

AFRICA BETWEEN CULTURE AND CIVILIZATION

ONE

AFRICA AND CULTURAL DEPENDENCY
THE CASE OF THE AFRICAN UNIVERSITY (1975)

Introduction

African universities have often been expected to serve as major instruments of development in their societies. But what if those universities also constitute links in a chain of dependency? As instruments of potential development, the universities have been called upon to produce high-level intellectual contributors, "relevant" research and training, "appropriate" skills, and potential innovators. Many universities have failed to live up to those developmental ideals, but development has continued to be regarded as a relevant basis for evaluating the performance of any African institution of higher learning. But let us again ask the basic question: What if the institution is also a link in a chain of dependency? Is it possible that the developmental lapses and deficiencies are connected with the constraints of dependency? How can the dependency be transcended? Some aspects of academic dependency in Africa are clear and unmistakable. In structure, virtually all universities in Africa south of the Sahara are based on one or more Western models. Virtually all these African universities use a Western language as the primary medium of instruction. Many rely overwhelmingly on books and articles published by Westerners or in the West to fill the shelves of their modest libraries. Some continue to have large numbers of Western instructors and professors on their faculty. Qualifications for student admission and staff recruitment continue to put a high premium on prior assimilation into Western culture among the candidates. Among the most prestigious of African universities are precisely those that were at one time, or continue to be, overseas extensions of some university in Europe. Among them are the universities of Ibadan, Ghana at Legon, Dakar and the old Makerere in Uganda. Because our concern in this essay is partly with the search for a new international cultural order, we shall go beyond examining the intrinsic academic dependency of the African university in itself. We shall also explore the wider effect of that dependency on the society as a whole. An institution can itself be dependent without necessarily spreading dependency over the wider society. But the university in Africa itself is not only sick; it is also a source of wider infection and societal contagion. That is why this essay is about cultural dependency and not merely about academic dependency within the university structure on its own. We should thus begin with what we mean by culture and then advance some working definition of our sense of dependency.

The Seven Functions of Culture

For our purposes in this essay, culture serves seven fundamental functions in society. First, it helps to provide lenses of perception and cognition. How people view the world is greatly conditioned by one or more cultural paradigms to which they have been exposed. A graduate from an African university thus views the world around him qualitatively different from how he would have viewed it had he never gone to Western or neo-Western educational institutions. The second function of culture lies in providing motives for human behavior. What makes a person behaviorally respond in a particular manner is partly cultural in origin. Ghanaian undergraduates have been known to laugh at Shakespearean tragedy on the stage. Is this partly because they are caught up in a cultural ambivalence of some kind? What about the students' motive for being at the university at all? Is that also a product of culture change in Ghana? The third function of culture lies in providing criteria of evaluation. What is deemed better or worse, ugly or beautiful, moral or immoral, attractive or repulsive, is partly a child of culture. The evaluative function of culture need not always correspond with the behavioral. Many African university graduates would condemn ethnic nepotism or "tribalism" as immoral. This is an evaluative position derived partly from Western influence. But the same graduates may find themselves practicing ethnic nepotism in spite of their new values. This would be a case of behavioral dissonance. The fourth function of culture provides a basis of identification. Ethnic nepotism is itself a product of culture in this identity sense. Western culture as transmitted in African educational institutions provides rival forms of identification, some of them related to the emergence of new elites and new social classes. Fifth, culture is a mode of communication. The most elaborate system of communication is language itself. In East Africa in the first two decades of colonial rule, there was considerable debate about language policy. Should the ethnic languages be given priority in the new imperial system? Or should Kiswahili be promoted as a *lingua franca*? Or did the cultural logic of European imperialism imply the promotion of European culture and languages first and foremost? At the level of higher education when the time came, there was little debate. The relevant medium of higher education was the imperial language itself. This decision, as we shall indicate later, had fundamental consequences in matters that range from intellectual imitation to elite-formation. The sixth function of culture lies precisely in providing a basis of stratification. Class, rank and status are profoundly conditioned by cultural variables. University education in Africa became a major factor in redefining status and gradation in modern African societies. The seventh function of culture lies in the system of production and consumption. In our scheme of analysis, patterns of consumption sometimes affect production as profoundly as production helps to shape consumption. Universities in Africa have played a part in distorting consumption patterns as well as in influencing productive trends. These seven functions of culture have relevance for the new international cultural order. What lies in the way is the whole problem of dependency.

Types of Dependency

In the context of our present analysis, dependency involves at least one of two forms of relationship. One is a relationship of surplus need: society B is dependent on society A if B needs A more than A needs B. The second type of dependency involves deficit control: B is dependent on A, if B'has less control over their relationship than A has. In a colonial relationship proper, A is the imperial power and B is each colony. After independence A's control may decline in some spheres. But which spheres? For analytical purposes, we may distinguish among the following spheres of dependency: the political, the economic, the military, and the cultural. In terms of surplus need, it was A that "needed" B economically before B became annexed as a colony. Colonies were perceived by A as potential sources of raw materials, or potential markets, or a source of labor or recipients of surplus population from A. Technically, therefore, England was a dependency of its own Empire in this special sense of England's economic needs, real or imagined. In terms of deficit economic control, the colonies were dancing to England's economic commands instead of the other way round. The factors that made the difference in control at that time were political and military. By definition, the colonies were political dependencies of Great Britain and subject to its monopoly of physical force over their territory. But while the British and the French were covetous of Africa's economic resources, they had little interest in Africa's cultural resources. Indeed, the French doctrine of assimilation was even prepared to exchange French culture for African economic riches. This introduces a fundamental difference between economic dependency and cultural dependency. While economic dependency has always included some leverage on the part of the "colony" upon the metropole (since the center needs the periphery economically), cultural dependency has been much more of a case of one-way traffic. The imperial power was prepared to dump its cultural goods on the African market, but it was not interested in purposefully importing African culture back into Europe. Whatever African culture has penetrated Europe has been due far less to organized European policies than to the activities of individual scholars, artists and antiquarians, and to the cultural impact of African slaves imported into the Western world. Europe was prepared to offer its religion, languages, and culture to Africans, but only in exchange for land, mines, labor, energy, and other economic riches of Africa. It was a classic case of offering culture in exchange for material goods, exporting arts and ideas and importing economic riches. By the time African universities were established, Africans themselves were all too eager to scramble for Western culture. On the basis of surplus need, there was no doubt Africans felt a need for Western culture far greater than the West felt it needed African culture. On the basis of deficit control, Western institutions exerted disproportionate control over African institutions. Cultural dependency was becoming much more acute and less reciprocal, than economic dependency.

The Impact of World War II

This brings us to the strange and paradoxical role of World War II in the history of the different forms of dependency in Africa. Politically, the war weakened imperial control and prepared the way for the disintegration of the empires of France and Great Britain. But economically the war helped to integrate the colonies more firmly into the global capitalist system as the economies of the periphery were made to serve more systematically the war needs of the center. As for the cultural impact of the war, it broadened Africa's exposure to alien influences, and later resulted in the new imperialism of building higher educational institutions for the colonies. Militarily, the war initiated more firmly the idea of recruiting African soldiers and setting-up African armies equipped with modern weapons, with all the consequences that process has had for both military dependency and the tensions of civil-military relations in the former colonies.

Our focus in this particular section is on the impact of World War II on cultural dependency. But that requires some understanding of the other effects of the war. Politically, imperial control was being weakened partly because of the weakening of the imperial powers themselves. France had been humiliated and partly occupied by the Germans, which put a strain on the old mystique of imperial invincibility and the grandeur of France that had been propagandized in the colonies. Great Britain was getting exhausted and impoverished as the war dragged on. British India was restive, though loyal, while the Japanese played havoc with Burma and the Malayan peninsula. The British empire in Asia was not going to last long after the war even if Britain won. African nationalists like Awolowo, Nkrumah, Kenyatta, and Azikiwe were watching these developments in the old empires with rising hopes and aspirations for Africa's own liberation. Even for those Africans who had not been abroad the war was helping to broaden their international horizons in the very effort to follow the fortunes of the different battles on the radio and in "vernacular" newspapers. Never before had so many ordinary Africans tried so hard to understand conflicts in such remote places as Dunkirk and Rangoon, Pearl Harbor and even El Alamein. In addition, there were the African servicemen themselves who experienced combat thousands of miles from their villages, who learnt new skills and acquired new aspirations, and who witnessed the white man in a new light, both as an enemy on the other side and sometimes as a frightened comrade in the trenches. But while the war was thus undermining the political control of the old empires, it was also increasing temporarily Europe's need for the products of the colonies. There was rationing throughout the empires and a continuing effort to make the colonies produce what Europe most needed. New food products were cultivated with Europe's hungry mouths in mind; new raw materials were produced in the periphery with Europe's industries as the intended market. There was a war boom in the colonies, followed later by a new depression. The very dialectic between this kind of boom and depression in Africa was a symptom of Africa's new level of economic integration into the international capitalist system. The same war weakening Britain and France's political control over their colonies was, at the same time deepening Africa's economic dependency upon the Western world as a whole. What about the cultural impact of the war on Africa? This was partly related to the other processes we have mentioned. As more and more people in Britain realized that the colonies could not be held in subjection forever, and a new timetable was needed for imperial policy, a new commitment to "colonial development and welfare" emerged. It was no longer enough merely to maintain law and order in the colonies and let social change take its own slow course. A new sense of developmental urgency began to influence policymakers at the colonial office in London. It was partly out of this developmental urgency that the idea of accelerating higher education for the colonies was elaborated further. In 1945, the Asquith Report was submitted to the British government; the report was a blueprint for higher education in the colonies. One of its basic assumptions was that the colonies needed the kind of indigenous leadership that had acquired Western skills and a "modern" outlook. The stage was being set for new forms of cultural penetration into the colonies.

But it should be emphasized at once that the motives were often of the highest. It was true that Africa had been left behind in certain basic skills of the "modern" technological era. Unfortunately, the universities emerging were not primarily designed to help Africa close the technological gap with those who were more advanced. On the contrary, the new colonial universities imported the same contempt for practical subjects that had characterized the academic ethos of the West for centuries. While the West had evolved safeguards against this academic arrogance and produced other ways of fostering technology and engineering, the colonies imported the academic arrogance without its safeguards. The contradiction was not always recognized either by Britain or by the new spokesmen of African aspirations in the colonies. It was an often-stated British imperial policy to offer Africans the education best suited to African conditions and needs. Educators such as Carey Francis in East Africa were most anxious not to de-Africanize African youth through Western education. But as a result of the educators on the ground not being sufficiently innovative, they ended up doing what they probably knew best: duplicating what was offered in Europe. Bishop Masasi's more distinctive experiments in Southern Tanganyika stood out among the rare innovations.

In some cases, the new post-war policy of "universities for the colonies" partially diluted an earlier imperial commitment to vocational and practical training. In its pre-university incarnation, Makerere in Uganda was noted less for its liberal arts than for professional training in "MAVE" (Medicine, Agriculture, Veterinary Science, and Education). While these subjects continued to be a major concern after Makerere attained university status (Veterinary Science was later transferred to University College, Nairobi), the proportion of students enrolling in these courses drastically declined. The appeal of the liberal arts deprived the Faculty of Education of its fair share of the brightest students for many years to come. In Makerere's pre-university days, the Education faculty had a significantly higher proportion of the most gifted students than it did later. The most illustrious of this earlier batch of Makerere's trained teachers turned out to be Mwalimu Julius Nyerere, destined to become the philosopher-president of Tanzania several years later. What all this means is that the new welfare colonialism that ensued upon World War II gave a new impetus to liberal arts and literary education, sometimes at the expense of earlier progress in more practically oriented educational policies.

In this connection, it is worth bearing in mind important differences between the Westernization of Africa and the modernization of Japan after the Meiji Restoration of 1868.[1] Japan's original modernization involved considerable selectivity on the part of the Japanese themselves. The whole purpose of selective Japanese Westernization was to protect Japan against the West, rather than merely to submit to Western cultural attractions. The emphasis in Japan was therefore on the technical and technological techniques of the West, rather than on literary and verbal culture. The Japanese slogan of "Western technique, Japanese spirit" at the time captured this ambition to borrow technology from the West while deliberately protecting a substantial part of Japanese culture. In a sense, Japan's technological Westernization was designed to reduce the danger of other forms of cultural dependency. The nature of Westernization in Africa has been very different. Far from emphasizing Western productive technology and containing Western life-styles and verbal culture, Africa has reversed the Japanese order of emphasis. Among the factors that have facilitated this reversal has been the role of the African university. In order to understand this role more fully, let us examine it in relation to those seven functions of culture that we defined earlier, though not necessarily in the order in which those functions were originally enumerated.

The African University and Dependent Paradigms

As we indicated, one primary function of culture is to provide a universe of perception and cognition, a societal paradigm, a worldview. Kuhn's work on the structure of scientific revolutions has provided new insights into the process through which scientific paradigms shift, and how new alternative systems of explaining phenomena come to dominate scientific thought. But what about shifts in cultural paradigms? How are cultural shifts related to scientific innovations? Religion is often a cultural paradigm in its own right. Copernicus and Galileo, by helping to transform scientific thought on planetary movements, in time also helped to change the Christian paradigm of the universe. Charles Darwin, by helping to initiate a revolution in the biological sciences, also started the process of transforming the Christian concept of "creation." Paradigmatic changes in the sciences have led to paradigmatic changes in religion in these cases. Historically there have also been cases where religious revolutions have resulted in scientific shifts. The rise of Islam gave the Arabs for a while scientific leadership in the northern hemisphere. Puritanism and non-conformity in Britain in the eighteenth century were part of the background to both a scientific and an industrial revolution in that country.

But paradigmatic changes are caused not merely by great minds like those of Copernicus, Newton, Darwin, and Einstein, or only by great social movements like Islam and the Protestant revolution, but also by acculturation and normative diffusion. It is in this sense that colonialism constituted a major shift in the cultural paradigm of one African society after another. Traditional ideas about how rain is caused, how crops grow, how diseases are cured, and how babies are conceived, have had to be re-examined in the face of the new scientific culture of the West. If African universities had borrowed a leaf from the Japanese book, and initially concentrated on what is indisputably the West's real area of leadership and marginal advantage (science and technology), the resultant African dependency might have been a different kind. But the initial problem lay precisely in the model of the university itself, the paradigm of academia, with its distrust of direct problem solving in the wider society:

> There is much in our education system (in Britain), which makes it easier to define problems in terms of narrowly scientific objectives. The existing relationship between universities (with the unidirectional flow of "experts" and advisors, the flow of overseas students to this country, etc.) have tended to transfer the same standards and expectations to the LDCs... Technologies for the satisfaction of basic needs and for rural development have received little attention... curricula, text books and teaching methods are too closely imitative of practice in industrialized countries. This has spilled over from teaching into research expectations. Universities have aimed to achieve international standards in defining the criteria for staff recognition and promotion; in practice this means using the international scientific and engineering literature as the touchstone. However, applied work directed at the solution of local problems... can rarely be associated with publication in "respectable" journals: a far better test is

the local one of success or failure of the particular project in the LDC environment.[2]

The one paradigmatic change that was necessary for the imported universities did not in fact occur. The missing factor was a change in the conception of the university itself and its purposes. But the "lack of change" in the conception of the transplanted university caused a lot of changes in the attitudes, values, and worldview of its products. Since the university was so uncompromisingly foreign in an African context, and was transplanted with few concessions to African cultures, its impact was more culturally alienating than it need have been. A whole generation of African graduates grew up despising their own ancestry, and scrambling to imitate others. It was not the traditional African that resembled the ape; it was more the westernized one, fascinated by the West's cultural mirror. A disproportionate number of these cultural "apes" were, and continue to be, products of universities. Those African graduates who have later become university teachers themselves have remained intellectual imitators and disciples of the West. African historians have begun to innovate methodologically as they have grappled with oral traditions, but most of the other disciplines are still condemned to paradigmatic dependency. This includes those African scholars that have recently discovered Karl Marx. The genius of Marx did indeed initiate a major international paradigmatic shift in social analysis. But Marx's theories were basically Eurocentric, and his legacy constitutes the radical stream of the Western heritage. Those African scholars that have replaced a Western liberal paradigm with a Western radical paradigm may have experienced a palace coup in their own minds or a changing of the guards within the brain. But they have not yet experienced an intellectual revolution in this paradigmatic sense. The ghost of intellectual dependency continues to haunt the whole gamut of Africa's academia for the time being.

The African University and Borrowed Languages

An important source of this intellectual dependency is the language in which African graduates and scholars are taught. For the time being it is impossible for an African to be even moderately familiar with the works of Marx without the help of a European language. *Das Kapital* is not yet available in Hausa or Kiswahili, let alone in Kidigo or Lutoro. Parts of the *Communist Manifesto* have already been translated into Kiswahili and Amharic but it may take some time before even a quarter of the literary output of Marx and Engels is available in one single African language unless there is a genuine educational revolution involving widespread adoption of African languages as media of instruction. As matters now stand, an African who has a good command of a European language has probably assimilated other aspects of Western culture as well. This is because the process of acquiring a European language in Africa has tended to be overwhelmingly through a formal system of Western-style education. It is because of this that the concept of an African Marxist who is not also westernized is for the time-being a socio-linguistic impossibility. This need not apply to a Chinese or Japanese Marxist, where it is possible to undergo an ideological conversation at a sophisticated level without the explicit mediation of a foreign language. Japan especially has tamed its language to cope with a wide range of intellectual discourse. Of course, the Japanese range goes beyond ideological and political literature. But in Black Africa, for the time being, a modern surgeon who does not speak a European language is virtually a socio-linguistic impossibility. So is a modern physicist, a zoologist, or an economist. Nor is this simply a case of the surgeon, the physicist, or the economist acquiring an additional skill called a "European language," which he is capable of discarding when he discusses surgery or physics with fellow professionals in his own society. Professional Japanese scientists or social scientists can organize a conference or convention and discuss professional matters almost entirely in Japanese. But a conference of African scientists, devoted to scientific matters, and conducted primarily in an African language, is for the time being sociologically impossible.

Almost all black African intellectuals conduct their most sophisticated conversations in European languages, as well as their most complicated thinking. This intellectual and scientific dependency in Africa is inseparable from linguistic dependency. Since a major function of culture lies, as we indicated, in providing media of communication, the choice of European languages as media of instruction in African universities has had profound cultural consequences for the societies that are served by those universities. It is possible that outside Arab Africa and parts of Eastern Africa the imperial founders of African universities had no choice. The great majority of African languages did not have enough speakers to justify the massive financial and intellectual investment necessary for making them effective media of higher education. But even those African languages, like Kiswahili, that stood a chance of developing in that direction did not receive adequate imperial support. As for Arabic in the Sudan, there continues to be discordance between the English language as a medium at Khartoum University and the Arabic-orientation of pre-university education, with severe costs in quality for all levels of instruction. What should be remembered is that by the time these African universities were being established, African intellectuals had already become so mentally dependent that they themselves insisted on considerable imitation of Western educational systems—including the importation of Western media of instruction for African use. Dependency is cumulative; cultural dependency is particularly prone to this tendency.

The African University and Derivative Stratification

Concurrently with these other cultural changes came changes in stratification. What is a social class? Some have defined it in terms of "who owns what." But in the new Africa a social class was beginning to be defined in terms of "who knows what." Familiarity with certain aspects of Western culture began to be particularly crucial among the new forces of elite-formation. In most African countries, independence meant the transfer of power from the West to the western-ized. The new politicians were those with a good command of the imperial language and a substantial imitation of the Western life-style. In the earlier days of colonial rule there had been a debate about which African the imperial system should support—the "native in a blanket" or the "native in trousers." Many colonial policy-makers had distrusted West-ern education and strove hard to protect the "native in a blanket." Lord Lugard, perhaps the greatest of British colo-nial administrators in Africa, was particularly concerned about the disruptive consequences of Western civilization in African societies. His philosophy of "Indirect Rule" as a sys-tem of governing African societies through their own institu-tions was partly designed to contain and regulate, and some-times even prevent, the process of Westernization in places like Northern Nigeria. But in much of Africa (though not necessarily in Northern Nigeria), power was finally trans-ferred to "the native in trousers." Once dismissed as "arro-gant upstarts," the westernized and semi-westernized Afri-cans were now being viewed seriously as heirs-apparent to the imperial system. The founding fathers of the new inde-pendent African states were disproportionately of this cate-gory. They included such figures as Nnamdi Azikiwe of Nige-ria, Kwame Nkrumah and Kofi Busia of Ghana, Jomo Ken-yatta and Tom Mboya of Kenya, Felix Houphouët-Boigny of the Ivory Coast, Léopold Senghor of Sénégal, and Julius K. Nyerere of Tanzania.

The initial constitutional arrangements in most African states seemed designed to maintain power among the acculturated. No African could become a member of parliament unless he had a command of the relevant European language. An African who spoke seven of the indigenous languages of, say Nigeria, but could not speak English, was *ipso facto* disqualified from representing his people in the federal parliament. On the other hand, a Nigerian politician might hypothetically speak only English, and be incapable of using any indigenous Nigerian language, yet still be constitutionally eligible to sit in the federal parliament. Most of this was also true in the majority of other countries south of the Sahara. To represent an African constituency required competence in a European language. Because one could not be a member of an African Parliament without a European language, neither could one be a Minister in an African government. Moreover, because one could not be an African Minister without such European credentials, one could not ascend to the very pinnacle of power—the presidency. In other words, Westernization of the candidates for office predicated access to the commanding heights of African political systems.

African universities played a leading role in fostering this new basis of stratification by giving Western culture (as a whole) greater legitimacy in African societies. They produced teachers for lower levels of education and thus helped to continue the Eurocentric tradition of the colonial educational system. The universities also produced opinion-leaders in other public pursuits. The university degree itself was for a while a major passport to influence and opportunity. The class-systems of African societies were in a state of flux and cultural dependency was part of this problem of re-stratification. In fairness to some African governments and educational reformers, we must recognize some of the agonized efforts that have been made to modify the colonial heritage. In Kenyatta's Kenya alone, at least three major educational commissions (Ominde 1964, Ndegwa 1971, and Gachathi 1978) dealt with educational reforms—not to mention numerous workshops and seminars. However, reforms in Daniel Arap Moi's Kenya came faster. Some important concessions have been made to Kiswahili. It enjoys more attention at the University of Nairobi and Kenyatta University than ever before, though the attention is still modest by absolute standards. The status of Kiswahili at lower levels of Kenya's educational system is also modest, in spite of its elevation to the "national language" of Kenya with English as the "official language." English continues to overshadow Kiswahili decisively at least from the third year of schooling onwards.

In terms of political stratification, an important step was taken when Kiswahili was adopted as the language of Kenya's parliament from 1974 to 1979. But significant anomalies remained. Whereas legislation in Kenya's parliament was still presented in English, the debate on that legislation was conducted in Kiswahili. The speech on the budget continued to be made in English with full political and diplomatic ceremony. The minimum qualifications required of a parliamentary candidate continued including competence in the English language—but not necessarily competence in Kiswahili. Nowadays debate can be in either language in parliament. The most important language of national politics is now Kiswahili, but the official language of the Kenya constitution continues to be English. Because of these continuing anomalies, the political establishment of the country continues to consist disproportionately of those who have been initiated into the culture of the former imperial system. The University of Nairobi is central to the structure that is perpetuating the Britannic factor in Kenya's system of political stratification. What is true of Kenya is basically true of most of former colonial Africa south of the Sahara. Indeed, those countries that do not have the equivalent of Swahili as a *lingua franca* are condemned to even more severe cultural dependency than Kenya, with all the consequences of derivative elite-formation.

Identity, Values, Motives, and Economic Culture

We have so far examined the African university in relation to three functions of culture: perception, communication, and stratification. The remaining four functions are culture as identification, as criteria of evaluation, as motives of behavior, and as a system of production and consumption. These functions need more space than is available in a single essay. For the time being, let us merely introduce them in relation to the influence of Western education and its tertiary extensions within Africa. Stratification is basically a ranking of social groups. But each group has an identity of its own and the interaction between these groups has its rules. Perhaps the most elaborate of the rules of stratified identities occur in caste-societies. On balance, the impact of Western education on such caste-systems has been progressive since it has created doubts about the legitimacy of caste as a mode of categorizing people. This has certainly been true of India, though the problem is still acute. It is also true of those few African societies that have something approximating caste. Chinua Achebe captures these dilemmas in his second novel, *No Longer at Ease*.

In Achebe's novel, Obi's education in the West creates doubts in his mind about the legitimacy of the status of Osu (the Ibo's equivalent of the Harijan or untouchable caste). And yet, tradition is too strong, and Obi himself is too weak to resolve the issue in a manner compatible with his affection for Clara, the Osu girlfriend. The old rules of interaction between castes are still compelling, but doubts have been created by Western education and the Ibo mind is "no longer at ease" on this issue. Also strained partly as a result of the Western impact are the residual caste relations between the Hutu and the Tutsi in Burundi. Things have indeed been "falling apart" since the old traditional rules of authority and deference in what was known as "Ruanda-Urundi"(now Rwanda and Burundi) was eroded by the challenge of a new normative order from the West. The clashes of identity between the Hutu and the Tutsi are reflected in other ethnic tensions elsewhere in Africa.

Rules of interaction between the sexes in Africa have also been in the process of modification because of Western education. Specially striking is the status of African women with university degrees. Women's liberation in Africa, as in most other parts of the world, is at best an aspiration rather than an accomplished fact. But among the factors that are facilitating it is the emergence of women graduates from African universities, asserting a greater independence than they might have done had they not received higher education in the Western idiom. In this instance the cultural dependency, which has come with the Western impact on Africa, is having the paradoxical side effect of facilitating greater independence for African women. A third area of identification, which has been affected by higher education in the Western idiom, concerns relations between age groups in African societies, including societies that have age-grades. Western education has eroded deference for elders, and made it difficult to maintain solidarity between age peers. The fourth and most comprehensive area of rules of interaction in relation to salient identification goes deep into political ideology. Universities in Africa are producing both defenders of Western liberalism and civil liberties and critics of such liberal rules. Is the individual the proper and ultimate unit of identity? The universities are also producing both the egalitarian radicals of the new Left in Africa and their ideological adversaries. Is social class the proper and ultimate unit of identity? The rules of the game in Africa are still in a state of flux, partly because of considerable cultural fluidity in this period of transition. African universities are major contributors to that cultural fluidity.

Culture as a set of rules is in fact inseparable from culture as a set of standards. This is where criteria of evaluation come into being. Western education has helped to change taste, morals, and other values. Western criteria of good and bad, ugly and beautiful, have won many African converts. Even the evil side of the Western demonstration effect has had a considerable impact on Africa. Some might even say that Africa has in reality been readier to imitate the evil side of the Western example than the good side! Nevertheless, there is little doubt that African concepts of what is proper or improper, just or unjust, attractive or repulsive have now been profoundly influenced by that system of education of which the university is the pinnacle. As Loweno has lamented about her westernized Acholi husband:

> You trembled [once upon a time]
> when you saw the tattoos on my breasts
> And the tattoos below my belly button;
> And you were very fond
> Of the gap in my teeth...
> My husband [now] says
> He no longer wants a woman
> With a gap in her teeth
> He is in love
> With a woman
> Whose teeth fill her mouth completely
> Like the teeth of war-captives and slaves.[3]

For better or for worse, Acholi concepts of beauty and adornment in Uganda are gradually giving way to Western culture. It is symptomatic of a deep normative change that Africa is experiencing, sometimes smoothly, sometimes convulsively. Western education is only part of the agony of transition. But it is a major factor in this tumult of change. Values in turn affect another aspect of culture: motives for behavior and conduct. The pursuit of private advantage, which in some parts of Africa has been aggravated by the impact of Western individualism and the erosion of traditional restraints, has sometimes led to a reckless ethos of "get rich quick" and an escalation of corruption and greed. Part of the cultural change is due to an interaction between the money economy (which is new in many parts of Africa) and Western notions of individualism and private profit. African universities cannot be blamed for these reckless acquisitive excesses in contemporary African society. The Universities are simply caught up in the contradictions between old rules and new motives, old impulses and new norms. Sometimes even genuinely constructive changes like a greater concern for the value of time and the need for punctuality can erode older motives for courteous behavior and social responsibility. Again, Loweno is eloquent on this issue:

> Time has become
> My husband's master
> It is my husband's husband.
> Like a small boy,
> He rushes without dignity.
> And when visitors have arrived
> My husband's face darkens,
> He never asks you in,
> And for greeting
> He says
> "What can I do for you?"...
> Listen
> My husband
> In the wisdom of Acholi
> Time is not stupidly split up
> Into seconds and minutes...
> It does not get finished
> Like vegetables in the dish
> A lazy youth is rebuked,
> A lazy girl is slapped,

A lazy wife is beaten,
A lazy man is laughed at
Not because they waste time
But because they only destroy
And do not produce.[4]

As for culture as this system of production and consumption, African universities have played a part in producing high-level personnel for important areas of African economies. But on balance, the universities have contributed more to African bureaucracies than directly to the productivity of African economies. The bureaucratic bourgeoisie that wields considerable political power in most African countries is overall a product of Western education. The impact of this class of people on patterns of consumption in African countries is sometimes greater than their impact on levels of production. But the centrality of their position in African political systems has in many cases made them custodians of the highest levels of economic policy in their countries.

Towards Decolonizing the African University

We have sought to demonstrate that the African university is part of a chain of dependency that continues to tie Africa to the Western world. African perspectives, models of communication, structures of stratification, rules of interaction, standards of evaluation, motives of behavior, and patterns of production and consumption have all been undergoing the agonies of change partly under the disturbing impact of Western culture. African universities have been the highest transmitters of Western culture in African societies. The high priests of Western civilization in the continent are virtually all products of those cultural seminaries called "universities." On balance, the African university is caught up in the tension between its ambition to promote genuine development in Africa and its continuing role in the consolidation of cultural dependency. If genuine development has to include cultural decolonization, a basic contradiction persists in the ultimate functions of an African university. It may generate skills relevant for modernization and development. But it has not even begun to acquire, let alone to transmit to others, what is perhaps the most fundamental skill of them all: how to promote development in a post-colonial state without consolidating the structures of dependency inherited from its imperial past. If development for Africa means the decolonization of modernity, then three major strategies are needed for African development, two of them capable of rapid implementation, and the third for slower but sustained introduction. The first strategy concerns the domestication of modernity: the bid to relate it more firmly to local cultural and economic needs. The second strategy is paradoxical. It involves the wider diversification of the cultural content of modernity. Under this approach, the foreign reference-group for an African institution becomes not only the West but also other non-African civilizations. The African university is thus to be transformed from a multinational to a multicultural corporation. The third strategy is perhaps the most ambitious. It concerns an attempt by the African continent as a whole to counter-penetrate Western civilization itself.

Dependency: The Therapy of Domestication

Let us take each of these strategies, beginning with the imperative of domestication in relation to education. Until now, there has been no doubt that African educational systems have entered deeply into the life-styles of local societies. In the very process of producing educated manpower, creating new forms of stratification, accelerating Westernization and modernization, African educational institutions have been major instruments through which the Western world has affected and changed the continent. In order to shift this balance, African societies must be allowed fundamentally to influence the educational systems themselves. It is not enough for an African university to send a traveling theatre to perform a play by Shakespeare or even by the Nigerian playwright, Wole Soyinka, before rural audiences in different villages. This type of endeavor is indeed required, and helps to deepen the life experiences of folk communities in the villages. But the traveling theatre of a university is only one more form of the university's academic impact on the wider society. It does not by itself constitute a reverse flow of influence. Similarly, extra-mural departments and even extension services are valuable methods of increasing skills and expanding social awareness among rural communities. Like a number of other professors at Makerere University in Uganda, I travelled many miles on hard roads to address village schools and assemblies on the implications of public policies in Uganda and the nature of the political system of the country. That kind of commitment was a way of reaching out to the isolated groups of the African countryside. But once again, it was much less an exercise in being affected by the society than an exercise in reaching the society. The social impact was still one-sided.

The first task, then, in decolonizing modernity is to enable the influence of the local society to balance that of the Western reference group. But how is this process to be realized in the universities? Four major areas have to be examined afresh: the requirements for admission of students, the content of courses throughout the educational system, the criteria for recruitment of teachers and other staff, and the general structure of the educational system. University admission requirements should be reformed in the direction of giving new weight to certain subjects of indigenous relevance. Social and cultural anthropology ought to become a secondary school subject, rigorously examinable, and required for entry to university. This should help promote considerably more interest in African cultures in primary and secondary school. Secondly, admission to a university should include a requirement for a pass in an African language.

There were times when many African universities required some competence in Latin for entry into some faculties; the African university of the future should require competence, formally demonstrated in an examination, of at least one African language regardless of the subject that the student proposes to study once admitted. African dance and music should be given a new legitimacy in all primary and secondary schools, regardless of the sensitivities of the authorities in power. Investigation should be undertaken into whether dance and music should be competitive, and in what way the ethnic diversity of musicological experience can be made creative rather than disruptive in an African school. These problems are far from insurmountable, and could add a new richness to the African aesthetic experience alongside the imported recreations of sports and athletics. Progress has already been made in the teaching of African history and literature. Further progress can be made, including more effective utilization of oral literature, duly transcribed, as an introduction to the pre-literate aesthetic creativity of African societies. The university in turn should re-examine the content of its courses, permitting indigenous culture to penetrate more into the university, and non-Western alien contributions to find a hearing at African universities.

Recruitment of faculty will in turn be affected by these considerations. Must all teachers at an African university have formal degrees from Western or Western-type educational institutions? Or should there be areas of expertise where lecturers or even professors could be appointed without the degree requirement so characteristic of Western institutions? Okot p'Bitek once compared the recruitment requirements for a university with the electoral requirements for an African parliament. African parliaments have insisted on competence in either English or French before an African could become a member. A candidate could speak ten African languages, and still be ineligible for parliament, if he did not speak the imported metropolitan language. Conversely, a candidate could speak only English or French, and no African language, not even the language of his immediate constituents, and still be eligible for parliament. Okot p'Bitek saw the linguistic and formal requirements of university appointments in terms similar to the formal requirements for a parliamentary career in Africa:

> You cannot become a member of *their* parliament unless you can speak English or French... You may be the greatest oral historian but they will never allow you anywhere near *their* University... Our universities and schools are nests in which black exploiters are hatched and bred, at the expense of the taxpayers, or perhaps heartpayers.[5]

The question that arises is whether there are specialists of oral history in African societies who can be appointed to university faculties without having a formal degree. Presumably, this might be difficult if these oral historians are unable to read or write. A compromise situation would be one in which only those oral historians who can in addition read and write might be regarded as eligible. Admittedly, literary skills are still a departure from ancestral ways in many African societies, but even readiness to acknowledge competence regardless of formal Western-type degrees would be revolutionary in African universities.

A related area is that of African languages. There are specialists in African languages who not only know how to use an African language, but also understand how the language behaves. Some of these are superb teachers at university level. I know of at least one who spent many years in an American university, teaching Kiswahili with sophistication unmatched by many of those who have actual degrees in the subject and in Bantu linguistics. Yet, in the United States, he could never hope to have a proper tenure appointment or even formal rank since he did not possess a degree. The same university would be quite prepared to appoint a distinguished British Swahilist from the London School of Oriental and African Studies, with a less intimate knowledge of certain African languages than the Kenyan. There is a case for broadening the criteria for recruiting academic staff to include both formal degrees and, where appropriate, indigenous traditional skills adequately demonstrated and capable of being effectively utilized on both teaching and research at the university level. Clearly a hybrid of cultures is at play here, and staff recruitment could reflect this dualism. Departments of sociology could have indigenous specialists in oral traditions; departments and faculties of medicine and preventive medicine could include specialists in indigenous herbs, and might even examine the medical implications of sorcery and witchcraft as part of the general training of a rural doctor in Africa. Departments of history, literature, musicology, philosophy, and religious studies could all allow for the possibility of recruiting skills on a different set of criteria from that which has been honored in Western institutions.

But in addition to reforms encompassing student admission requirements, curricula, faculty recruitment, there must be a broader structural transformation that relates general social needs to the educational system, and that reduces the tendency toward a pyramid educational structure with the university at the top, and everything below that being no more than a step toward the pinnacle. What is needed is a major change involving a diversification of the content of the curricula of each institution. At the university level, should studies continue to be organized according to conventional Western disciplinary categories? Or is there a case for having on the one hand a School of Rural Studies, encompassing agriculture, anthropology, preventive medicine in rural conditions, and the like, and on the other, a School of Urban Studies, examining the rural-urban continuum, labor migration, ethnic associations, criminology, and relevant preventive medicine? Other possible schools could include

Oral Tradition and Historiography, Languages and Oral Literature, and Religion and Witchcraft. Informing all these reforms would be a concept of relevance domestically defined, and which related to both the economic and cultural needs of the society as a whole.

Dependency: The Therapy of Diversification

The second strategy of development is that of diversifying the cultural content of modernity. This approach rests partly on the assumption that just as economically it is a greater risk to be dependent on one country than on many, so in culture one foreign benefactor is more constraining than many. To be owned by one person is outright slavery; but to be owned by many masters, who can be played against each other, may be the beginning of freedom. The African university has to move from being a multinational corporation to a multicultural corporation. From what we have discussed, it is clear that in spite of the fact that African university systems have grown up with structural or other links with metropolitan universities in Europe and North America, the African university has continued to be heavily unicultural; it has been more a manifestation of Western culture in an African situation than an outgrowth of African culture itself. For as long as the African university remained a multinational corporation in this sense, it denied itself the wealth of its own society. But in order to become a multicultural corporation it is not enough to combine African traditions with the Western heritage. It becomes more important than ever that African universities should take seriously the cultures and experiments of other civilizations. The educational system should not simply talk about European history, combined increasingly with African history, but in addition it should pay attention to Indian civilizations, Chinese civilizations and most immediate of all, Islamic civilizations. Although Arabic is the most widely spoken language in the African continent, the language has received very little acknowledgment in the educational syllabi of Africa south of the Sahara. It has not even received recognition from countries bordering Arabic-speaking areas, or with large numbers of Muslims among their own citizens. The Muslim community in Nigeria runs into millions, and the bordering countries contain millions more, yet Nigeria's universities once favored Latin and Greek rather than Arabic studies. As for Chinese studies, there is at most some interest in Mao Tse Tung in political science departments these days, but still no interest in Confucius. Chinese Civilization is relevant not only to ideology and economic organization, but also to intermediate technology, medicine, and new methods of agriculture. A conscious effort to learn more about what has been done in China since Mao, and an attempt to see how much of it is relevant for African needs could help add technical richness to cultural pluralism. A multicultural corporation requires not only a revival of interest in African indigenous traditions, but also a cultural diversification of the foreign component in African curricula. A twin process is then underway: increased Africanization, as the society is permitted to reciprocate the impact of the university; and increased internationalization as the foreign component ceases to be Eurocentric and attention is paid to other parts of the total human heritage.

An important subject that should be introduced into African secondary schools is the history of science. It is possible that the dependency complex among young African school children arises partly out of their being overwhelmed by Western science. The prestige of the Western world, in a continent that is very conscious of the power of prestige, derives disproportionately from Western leadership in science and technology. So great has that leadership been in the last 300 years that Westernism and science are sometimes regarded as interchangeable. In reaction to this Western scientific pre-eminence, some Africans have sought refuge in

Négritude as glorification of a non-scientific civilization. The leader of *Négritude* as a romantic movement in Africa, Léopold Senghor, former President of Sénégal, has defined it as "the sum of African cultural values" informed by their "emotive attitude toward the world."[6] Other Africans have sought answers in Marxism, partly because it seems to offer Africans the chance of rebelling against the West without ceasing to be scientific. After all, was not the Marxist heritage a scientific critique of the West? These two responses symbolize wider forces at work in Africa. The Négritudist rebels against the scientific West by idealizing his own heritage; the African Marxist rebels against the West by embracing an alternative scientism. Some African radicals have denounced Léopold Senghor, a cultural nationalist, as an intellectual primitivist who has tried to reduce African modes of knowledge to pure emotion and has turned the history of Africa into the story of the Noble Savage. But Senghor denies that he has deprived the African of the capacity to reason and innovate technologically:

> It is a fact that there is a white European civilization and a black African civilization. The question is to explain their differences and the reasons for these differences, which my opponents have not yet done. I can refer them back to their authorities. "Reason has always existed," wrote Marx to Arnold Ruge, "but not always under the rational form."[7]

Senghor then proceeds to quote Engels, whom he regards as even more explicit on this question in his work "preparatory to the *Anti-Dühring*":

> Two kinds of experience... one exterior, material; the other interior, laws of thought and forms of thinking. Forms of thinking also partly transmit-

ted by heredity. A mathematical axiom is self-evident to a European, but not to a Bushman or an Australian aboriginal.[8]

This debate between African cultural nationalists and African scientific socialists is likely to continue. What the two groups have in common is a rebellion against the West and the inferiority complex that had been created by Western scientific pre-eminence. The curriculum in African schools should at some stage reflect these disagreements. But at least as fundamental as the question of whether African culture was traditionally scientific or whether Marxism is a science is the issue of how much Western science owes to other civilizations. From the Indus Valley to ancient Egypt, from imperial China to medieval Islam, the West has found intellectual and scientific benefactors over the centuries. Yet very little of this is communicated to young children in schools in Africa. The cultural pluralism that lies behind the scientific heritage is lost to these young minds, as they continue to be dazzled at a formative period by Western civilization alone. Secondary school curricula in Africa must therefore put science in its proper historical context, reveal the diversity of the human heritage, and break the dangerous myth of Western scientific pre-eminence.

Another major change that would need to be introduced into primary and secondary schools concerns the teaching of languages. Each African child should learn a minimum of three languages: one European, one Asian, and one African. The era of learning multiple European languages—some ancient and some modern—while other linguistic heritages of the world are ignored should come rapidly to an end. Because of the colonial legacy, some African students in former British Africa will need to learn French and some francophone Africans will continue to learn English. Pan-Africanism will need the teaching of an additional European language for a minority of students. But any addi-

tional European language has to be a fourth language, chosen instead of, say, geography or fine art, but certainly not at
the expense of either an African language or an Asian one.
These linguistic requirements are partly based on the assumption that access to a culture is considerably facilitated
by knowledge of its language. At the university level, language requirements should continue in a modified form.
Each undergraduate, regardless of the field of study, should
take either an African or an Asian language at an advanced
level. In addition, all students should take a course on a non-
Western civilization, preferably, but not necessarily, linked
to the language of their choice. But perhaps the most fundamental of all reforms must be a change in attitude in all departments in African universities away from excessive Eurocentrism and toward a paradoxical combination of increased
Africanization and increased internationalization of the content of each department program. It is only in this way that
the African university can evolve into a truly multicultural
corporation.

Dependency: The Therapy of Counter-Penetration

But domestication of modernity and the diversification of its cultural content will not achieve final fulfillment
without reversing the flow of influence back into Western
Civilization itself. There are reformers in Africa who urge
only domestication and some of them would go to the extent
of espousing cultural autarky. This is a strategy of withdrawal from world culture, the outcome of which would be
the continuing marginality of Africa in global affairs. In a
world that has shrunk so much in a single century, there will
be many decisions made by others that are bound to affect
the world as a whole. For Africa to attempt a strategy of
withdrawal or total disengagement would be a counsel not
only of despair but also of dangerous futility. Modernity is
here to stay; the task is to decolonize it. World culture is

evolving fast; the task is to save it from excessive Eurocentrism. The question that needs to be addressed is how this task is to be achieved.[9] This is where the strategy of counter-penetration is relevant. If African cultures have been penetrated so deeply by the West, how is Western culture to be reciprocally penetrated by Africa?

The West has not, of course, completely escaped Africa's cultural influence. It has been estimated that the first piece of carving made by an African to reach modern Europe arrived on a Portuguese trading ship in 1504. African workmanship in leather and probably gold had a much older presence in Europe:

> However, African art burst upon the awareness of the Western world only in the turn of the nineteenth century. Army men like Pitt-Rivers and Torday brought back large collections with good ethnographic description... No one should jump to the idea that Picasso's women who look two ways at once, or anything else about his work, is a copy of something he discovered in African art. There was little direct, stylistic influence, although some can be discovered by latter-day critics. Rather, what happened was that with the discovery of African and other exotic art, the way was discovered for breaking out of the confines that had been imposed on European art by tradition—perspective, measured naturalism, and anti-intellectual sentimentality.[10]

At least as important as this artistic counter-penetration has been Africa's indirect influence through its sons and daughters exported to the New World as slaves. Africa's impact on jazz and related forms of music has already been documented. So has the influence of African tales on the literatures of other lands, particularly of the Southern

United States and the Caribbean. Africa's cultural influence on the West has been far more modest than the West's influence on Africa. This asymmetry will continue for at least some time, but the gap in reciprocity can be narrowed. To achieve this, Africa will need allies. The continent's most natural allies consist of the Black Diaspora and the Arab World. The Arabs share a continent with black people. Indeed, the majority of the Arabs are within Africa; so is the bulk of Arab land. Black and Arab African states share the Organization of African Unity (OAU). This organization and the Arab League have overlapping membership. There are possibilities of exploiting this relationship to the mutual advantage of both peoples. The Arab oil-producers have already started the strategy of economic counter-penetration into the West. This ranges from buying real estate in England and elsewhere in the West, to controlling banks in the United States and in Europe, and to acquiring considerable shares in multinational corporations. The whole strategy of recycling petrodollars is full of possibilities of economic counter-penetration. As a result, the West is at once eager for the petrodollars and anxious about its long-term consequences for Western economic independence.[11]

But alongside this risk is an opportunity for a new Third World alliance to counter-penetrate the West. Once again, economic power and cultural influence might be linked. The Organization of Petroleum Exporting Countries (OPEC) is heavily Muslim in composition, and includes the largest Muslim country in the world, Indonesia. The largest oil-exporting country is Saudi Arabia, where the spiritual capital of Islam, Mecca, is to be found. The second largest oil-exporter is Iran. Nigeria, another OPEC member, contains all three parts of the soul of modern Africa: the Euro-Christian, the Islamic, and the indigenous religious traditions. All three are vigorous, and Islam is already the strongest single rival to Westernism there. The rise of OPEC in world affairs, however transient, may herald the political resurrection of Islam. By the end of this century, African Muslims will probably outnumber Arab Muslims and will be making a strong bid for shared leadership of Islam. But at least as important as Arab money for African cultural entry into the West is the black American population. The second largest Anglophone black nation in the world (second only to Nigeria), Black America is situated in the middle of the richest and mightiest country of our times. At the moment, Black American influence on America's cultural and intellectual life is much more modest than, say, the influence of Jewish America. But as the poverty of Black America lessens, its social and political horizons widen, and its intellectual and creative core expands, Black American influence on American culture is bound to increase. A central task for African universities will therefore be to reach Black America, and, by influencing the most powerful country of the Western world, to reach the rest of the West as well. African universities would do well to encourage more Black Americans to gain part of their education in the African continent, north or south of the Sahara. Later, Brazilian, as well as Caribbean Blacks, might be encouraged to follow suit.

However, counter-penetration as a third strategy required for effective decolonization of African modernity is a longer term endeavor than either domestication or diversification, requiring conditions which make it possible for Africans to innovate sufficiently to teach others a thing or two. This counter-penetration by the whole African continent into the mainstreams of cultural and intellectual skills elsewhere might begin with influence from outside into the African rural area, followed by a balancing influence from the rural areas on educational systems in Africa, stimulated by foreign cultural, intellectual and technical skills. But the full maturity of African educational experience will come when Africa develops a capability to innovate and invent independently. Full reciprocal international penetration is a precondition for a genuinely symmetrical world culture. As Africa first permits its own societies to help balance the weight of Western cultural influence, then permits other non-Western external civilizations to reveal their secrets to African researchers and teachers, and then proceeds to transform its educational and intellectual world in a manner which makes genuine creativity possible, the continent will be on its way toward not only decolonizing modernity, but also helping to recreate modernity anew for future generations.

NOTES

This chapter is a revised version of an essay entitled "The African University as a Multinational Corporation: Comparative Problems of Penetration and Dependency," originally published in *Harvard Educational Review*, Vol. 45, N⁰ 2, May 1975, pp. 191-210, and in *Education and Colonialism*, edited by Phillip G. Altbach and Gail P. Kelly, London and New York: Longmans, 1978, pp. 331-352. It was later revised, in 1992, and was published, under the title "Towards Diagnosing and Treating Cultural Dependency: the Case of the African University," in *International Journal of Educational Development* (London), Vol. 12, N⁰ 2, 1992, pp. 95-111. This essay and its earlier versions are indebted to previous work by the author on cultural dependency, including research done in collaboration with the late Omari H. Kokole and with B.E. Kipkorir.

1. Refer to Chapter 5 in this volume entitled "Africa Between the Meiji Restoration and the Legacy of Atatürk: Comparative Dilemmas of Modernization."

2. Pyle, L., "Engineering in the Universities and Development," paper presented at the Conference on "The Future Relationships Between Universities in Britain and Developing Countries," held at the Institute of Development Studies, University of Sussex, England, March 17-20, 1978, pp. 2-3.

3. P'Bitek, Okot, *Song of Lawino* (Nairobi: East African Literature Bureau, 1966), part 4.

4. Ibid, part 7.

5. P'Bitek, Okot, "Indigenous Ills," *Transition*, No. 32, August/Spetember 1967, p. 47.

6. See *Senghor: Prose and Poetry*, edited and translated by John Reed and Clive Wake (London: Oxford University Press, 1965), p. 34. The emphasis is original.

7. Ibid.

8. Engels as cited by Senghor, ibid., p. 33

9. Aspects of the Eurocentrism of world culture are also discussed with passion and insight by Chinweizu, *The West and the Rest of Us: White Predators, Black Slavers and the African Elite* (New York: Random House, 1975). Chapters 14 to 16 are particularly relevant from the point of view of this article. Consult also Mazrui, *World Culture and the Black Experience* (Seattle: University of Washington Press, 1974).

10. Paul Bohannan and Philip Curtin, *Africa and Africans*, American Museum of Natural History (New York: The Natural History Press, 1971 edition), pp. 97-98.

11. This is argued more fully in Mazrui, "The New Interdependence: From Hierarchy to Symmetry," in James Howe (ed.), *The United States and the Developing World: Agenda for Action, 1975* (Washington, D.C.: Overseas Development Council, 1975).

TWO

IDEOLOGY AND AFRICAN
POLITICAL CULTURE (1992)

Throughout most of the twentieth century, under both colonial and postcolonial conditions, Africans have responded more to socio-cultural ideologies than to socio-economic ideologies. Socio-cultural ideologies focus on issues of identity, ancestry, sacredness, and social values. Socio-economic ideologies concentrate on solidarities of class, economic interest, and economic transformation. In Africa's experience, the most relevant socio-cultural ideologies have been ethnicity and its belief-system, race and its solidarities, religion and its value-systems, and nationalism and the structure of its aspirations. This paper will address issues of ethnicity, race, and nationalism, but not of religion.

Socio-economic ideologies attempted in Africa have included labor movements, different varieties of African socialism, and Marxism-Leninism. Some of these socio-economic ideologies captured political power and became the ideologies of the state. In similar ways to the sixteenth century European doctrine *cuius regio, eius religio* (loosely translated as "the religion of the King becomes the religion of the state"), the ideology of the president became the ideology of the state in postcolonial Africa. Socio-cultural ideologies have exerted greater influence, however, when the grassroots have been able to express ideological preferences. Behind this phenomenon lies the resilience of certain African values and cultural habits despite of all the imperial disruptions of the twentieth century. The study of African political thought has been excessively a prisoner of the categories of European thought and European ideologies. There has been excessive effort to make Africa's ideological experience conform to the European ideological categories of liberalism, conservatism, capitalism, socialism, Marxism, fascism, and the rest. In the twentieth century, there has of course been considerable overlap between African ideological orientations and Western categories. But just because two systems overlap, that need not mean that they are identical. Students of African thought should pause and re-examine the categories of their own subject matter. African intellectuals have spent a lot of energy rejecting the concept of "tribe" for Africa. Why? Mainly because African intellectuals have known that most Europeans despised "tribes." Was that a good enough reason for rejecting the concept? If Africans joined Western contempt for "tribes," are Africans also joining Western contempt for Native Americans who classify themselves as "tribes"? Do we join the general arrogance towards indigenous peoples and tribal societies worldwide? Perhaps, it is time to save the word "tribe" from excessive political correctness. What is needed is not stopping the use of the word "tribe" for Africa but reviving the use of the word "tribe" for the European experience. Against the background of the primordial outbreaks of conflict in the former Yugoslavia, it is clear that "tribalism" can as easily wear a white face as a black one.

In this essay, we use the more unusual word "tribality." We regard this concept as encompassing a set of beliefs and attitudes which, taken together, could be regarded as an ideological construct in its own right. For those who still insist on avoiding any reference to "tribe," we offer the alternative word of "ethnicism" for this ideological construct. Behind it all is the simple preposition that European colonialism destroyed structures rather than attitudes, undermined traditional monarchs rather than traditional mores. Despite the destruction of indigenous empires, tribality triumphed. What is the secret of the story? This essay clings to the premise that colonialism succeeded in destroying most of Africa's traditional political institutions while it fell considerably short of annihilating African traditional political values and ideas. In spite of British "Indirect Rule," the organized indigenous instruments of authority and rule did atrophy in much of Africa. However, normative African approaches to politics have revealed more resilience than might at first been thought possible. One of the major problems confronting the imported institutions and Western-style systems in Africa is precisely this cultural lag.[1] Where does tribality fit into this?

Clearly, such governmental organizations and instruments as the Western civil service, the cabinet system, the legislative council and important aspects of the judicial system were essentially alien to Africa. Nevertheless, two or three millennia of African traditions and experience could not be eliminated by a single century of European intrusion onto Africa. This substantial cultural resilience has had both benefits and costs for the survival of some of the post-colonial institutions. In an attempt to capture the essential elements of cultural continuity in African politics, we have grouped together a number of normative elements under different traditions. We propose to demonstrate that Africa's political experience in the post-colonial era is still being influenced by one or more of the following tribal or ethnicist traditions: (i) the elder tradition; (ii) the warrior tradition; (iii) the sage tradition; and (iv) the monarchical tendency.

There is a tendency in the study of African political thought to rely almost entirely on political ideas captured in writing. A major underlying assumption is that thought is not thought unless it is also written. Because of this assumption, there has been relative disregard of the oral tradition in political thought, and an almost complete obsession with political writers and with the written speeches of political leaders. But there are three major sources for the student of political thought in Africa: the oral tradition, the written word, and the political behavior of Africans. We will call these the oral, written, and behavioral expressions of political ideas. In this essay, we investigate and interrogate six major traditions of political thought in Africa. First, there is the tribal tradition, with its emphasis on continuity rather than change. Second, there is the dignitarian tradition responding to race. Third, there is the nationalist tradition, stressing collective solidarity and opposition to foreign rule and external control. Fourth, there is the liberal capitalist tradition, with its emphasis on property, production, and individualism. Fifth, there is the socialist tradition, sensitive to the morality of equality and opposed to class-based privileges. The sixth tradition is democracy with its concern for accountability, participation, and openness.

Principles of Tribality and Ethnicism

In this section, we begin with tribality in African political culture. Let us first identify some of its main characteristics as a conservative tradition, before we relate it more directly to Africa's political experience. An important initial premise of African tribality or ethnicism is the sacredness of one's ancestry. The tendency to treat ancestry with deference and deep respect is a characteristic of the conservative ethnicist turn of mind.[2] The tribal or ethnicist African takes ancestry so seriously partly because continuity is an important principle. Because continuity between the past and the present is important, continuity between the dead and the living is also important. Revering ancestors is a form of respect for the past. Kofi Busia's scholarly studies on the Ashanti of Ghana and Jomo Kenyatta's *Facing Mount Kenya* (1938) dealing with the Kikuyu of Kenya were works that validated and dignified ancestry.[3] In that way, a conservative ethnicist might prefer continuity to change; he or she would not be opposed to all kinds of change.[4] Where change is necessary, all that a conservative ethnicist would insist upon is gradualism. A profound distrust of either sudden or fundamental change is part of the tribal tradition in any political culture. Busia and Kenyatta after independence belonged to that tradition.

A related characteristic of African tribality or ethnicism is a reliance on experience rather than on rationalism or theory. This again is part of the logic of respecting the past. What has been tried out and has seemingly withstood the test of time is to be preferred to what is let out as a theoretical blueprint for social transformation. An understanding of history is regarded a better guide to political action than the knowledge of ideology. Also arising out of this empirical emphasis is the tribal preference for the specific, for the concrete, as opposed to the general and abstract. Rights and duties are viewed as belonging to specific societies rather than in generalized terms such as human rights. An Anglo-Irish political philosopher of the conservative tradition, Edmund Burke, was sympathetic with the thirteen American colonies in their anti-colonial rebellion against George III. But Burke felt that while the Americans had a good case, they worded it wrongly. Burke regarded the American "founding fathers" primarily as Englishmen. When they demanded the right of representation before they would obey the duty of taxation, they were demanding the rights of Englishmen rather than "the rights of man."[5] This Burkean approach was typically conservative and almost tribal, stressing specific rights that had developed out of the history of a specific society, rather than focusing on an abstract universal morality. Burkean philosophy later influenced the culturally relative British policy of "Indirect Rule" in Africa.[6]

Partly related to this aspect of social specificity, and partly because of the sacredness of ancestry, the tribal tradition takes kinship loyalties seriously, just as it idealizes family virtues. In Black Africa, this ethnicism may take the form of "tribal" solidarity, both black and white. Among the Afrikaners of South Africa, "tribalism" may take the form of Afrikanerdom, the unity of the *Volk*.[7] Sometimes kinship solidarity can be a metaphor for right-wing nationalism in Europe or Latin America. The sacredness of shared ancestry in Africa creates its own pull in favor of oneness based on kith and kin. Alongside this pull of kinship in the ethnicist tradition is the pull of religion. The conservative tribal tradition mistrusts "excessive" secularization and rationalization. Faith is often valued as a cardinal tribal virtue, emphasizing the links between the natural and the ultimate, between the secular and the sacred, between the mundane and the divine, between the temporal and the spiritual.[8] Partly for this reason, Léopold Sédar Senghor has described atheism as fundamentally alien to African culture.

Partially because of its link with the past, the tribal tradition in Africa is in many ways the most authentically indigenous of all the legacies of political thought. It concerns itself not just with the immediate colonial past but also with pre-colonial antiquity. The sacredness of ancestry is taken seriously—sometimes literally—to the mythical founding fathers of each particular "ethnic identity," be it Kintu for the Baganda, Gikuyu and Muumbi for the Kikuyu, or Gboro and Leme for the Lugbara.[9] The principle of continuity includes the doctrine of shared loyalties between the living, the dead, and the unborn. The dead in turn in many African societies exist in two stages. The first stage is when the dead are still remembered as specific individuals by those still alive, and the second stage is when the dead really do recede into oblivion. The Kenyan philosopher and writer on African religions, John Mbiti, has termed the stage when the dead are still being remembered by the living the *Sasa* stage, and the stage of complete oblivion the *Zamani* stage.[10] African interest in large families has sometimes been due to a desire to prolong the *Sasa* stage for parents. On the one hand, begetting many children is an insurance against the losses of infant mortality. But on the other hand, having many children who might remember their parents after they are dead and pass on that memory to their own children could be a passport to the immortality of the parents as they remain in the *Sasa* stage of death, maintaining contact with the living.

The manifestation of the tribal tradition in African political culture continues either through the oral tradition or through the political behavior of African societies, in spite of alien post-colonial constitutions. The preference for kinship solidarity as against theoretical ideology has manifested itself behaviorally in many African elections. The late Chief Obafemi Awolowo in Nigeria was sometimes the most prominent voice of the Left in his country. He articulated socialist rhetoric, trying to reach the disadvantaged of Nigeria regardless of ethnic origin. But whenever an election took place, and the Chief looked to see who was following him, he discovered that his followers were almost invariably fellow Yoruba regardless of social class, rather than the disadvantaged of Nigeria, regardless of ethnic origin.[11] In East Africa, Oginga Odinga was the Awolowo of Kenya. Again, he often articulated the rhetoric of the Left in Kenya. But apart from a few intellectuals and academics, those who responded to Odinga's trumpet-call were not the disadvantaged of Kenya regardless of ethnic group but rather Oginga Odinga's ethnic compatriots, the Luo, regardless of social class.[12] What this evidence reveals is the preference of the electorate in countries like Nigeria and Kenya for concrete kinship solidarity as against ideological theory, a preference for shared sacred ancestry as against commitment to radical change.[13] Thus, conservative tradition in Africa is manifested and expressed behaviorally, rather than in written texts.[14]

To that extent, the ethnicist tradition in Africa tends to have invisible authors, a body of thought without attribution to specific individual thinkers. Ethnicism and tribality tend to be collective political culture rather than a theoretical masterpiece from one individual mind. Tribality is captured in the accumulation of specific attitudes across generations, rather than in a specific text from a particular pen. Because African tribal conservatism is captured so cumulatively, it is almost by definition collectivist. It is a body of thought resting on a cumulative consensus, linking the past with the present and the future. The behavioral resilience of tribal conservatism has emerged in related sub-traditions. One is the elder tradition in African politics, conceding deference to age on the assumption that the older are wiser.[15] If experience is indeed the ultimate teacher, those who have lived longer have experienced more. Ernest Hemingway's statement that "experience is the name everyone gives to their mistakes," means that elders may guide youngsters from repeating the mistakes of their seniors. The elder tradition is at the pinnacle of this pyramid of analysis. Let us explore these cultural continuities more closely.

Tribal Theories of Leadership in Post-Colonial Africa

The elder tradition is a combination of patriarchal and gerontocratic elements. The patriarchal factor focuses attention on a single father figure commanding general allegiance and respect. Gerontocracy is a concession to age rather than to a single paternal symbol. Gerontocracy is, after all, an early form of government in many societies.[16] It used to be at one time a system in which the old men of the community were the rulers because of their presumed wisdom, special powers, and prestige.[17] The elder tradition in Africa did indeed include this reverence for age. In post-colonial Africa, a particularly striking illustration of the elder tradition at work was the role of the late President Jomo Kenyatta after independence. His affectionate national title, *Mzee* Kenyatta, meant "old gentleman Kenyatta" or "father-figure Kenyatta," or "Kenyatta, the Elder." The late President Félix Houphouët-Boigny of Côte d'Ivoire, and former President Ngwazi (conqueror) Hastings Kamuzu Banda of Malawi also qualified as elders in this special sense. Tunisia's former President, Habib Bourguiba, played the elder for so long that eventually he was forcefully retired when he became senile.[18]

The elder tradition can be either interventionist or permissive. When it is interventionist, the father figure demands almost constant scrutiny of the behavior and the performance of the other members of the society, and seeks also to be almost constantly involved in decision-making. But where the patriarch like Kenyatta is permissive, he may prefer to let the system make the most of what the patriarch regards as less fundamental decisions. He might withdraw behind a cloud of silent authority, commanding allegiance more by his presence than by utterance, compelling reverence more by what he is than by what he says. It is possible in some situations to distinguish the elder tradition from the patriarchal tradition. It is arguable that the elder tradition should in fact be oligarchic, rather than autocratic, involving a collectivity of aged wisdom rather than the authority of single person. As the saying goes: "The elders sat under a tree and talked until they agreed."[19] In this essay, we merge the patriarchal and the elder themes together to facilitate our analysis of post-colonial African politics.

In places like Kenyatta's Kenya or Banda's Malawi, the elder tradition does have characteristics that could make it difficult for a legislature to survive with vigor. The tradition puts a high premium on deference and reverence to the father *guru*. Politically, this often can translate itself into affirmations of loyalty. The elder tradition also puts a high premium on at least the appearance of consensus, "family unity" or "national solidarity." The warrior tradition, on the other hand, prefers discipline to consensus, enforced agreement rather than a quest for compromise. The warrior tradition also prefers obedience to reverence, the salute of a soldier to the filial salutation of a child towards his parents. Obedience is a response to orders and instructions; reverence is a response to customary devotion and hallowed dignity and traditional respect. The warrior tradition also thinks of itself as action-oriented, seeking to achieve results by physical exertion or the threat of physical action.[20] Partly because the warrior tradition is heavily action-oriented, it tends to have a pronounced distrust of wordmongers—orators, politicians, and intellectuals. Wordmongers are the specialists in verbal gymnastics, putting a special premium on verbiage as against valor, speech as against spear, wit as against war.

Clearly, the warrior tradition defined in these terms has all the makings of hostility towards a Western-style legislature. For what is a Western-style legislative assembly if it is not at its best an arena for wordmongers, for speech and wit, for argument and analysis as against armed bravery? In Anglophone Africa, a particularly intriguing—although transient and tyrannical—instance of the resurrection of the warrior tradition in African political cultures was the rise of Idi Amin Dada in Uganda in the 1970s. Amin symbolized the rugged, rustic warrior from the culture of the countryside, empowered suddenly with a modern army and with a state that was already a member of modern international organizations and a modern diplomatic system. Those aspects of the warrior tradition which were action-oriented, disciplinarian, anti-intellectual, distrustful of verbal skills based on analysis and argument, and partial to the skills of force and violent assertion, played their part in sealing the fate of legislative and quasi-legislative institutions in Amin's Uganda.[21] Other African states under military rule suffered a similar fate.

The sage tradition conceptualizes political leadership not in terms of child and father, nor in terms of soldier and military commander, but in terms of student and teacher. The sage tradition gives political leaders the role of mentor in the skills and comprehension of politics, instructors to the general population about political virtue and political vice, a guide to the nation through the intricacies of interpreting the present world and preparing for the national future. If the warrior tradition is, at least ostensibly, distrustful of word-mongers, the sage tradition at its best often encourages a good deal of discussion and analysis, provided these are within the terms of the lessons given by their national teacher. At its best, the sage tradition does not only avoid anti-intellectualism, it even attempts to promote general intellectual vigor. China under Mao Tse Tung was in part a case of the sage tradition. The debates that accompanied certain major modifications in the Chinese political orientation under the late Mao illustrated this tendency by the sage for vigorous argument and discussion.[22] In Francophone Africa, a particularly impressive sage was Léopold Sédar Senghor, a poet, a philosopher, as well as a statesman. In East Africa, an interesting example was Julius K. Nyerere of Tanzania. Nyerere, a great admirer of Mao Tse Tung, was referred to affectionately by his people as the *Mwalimu* (the teacher or mentor). His style as president had indeed included this inclination to transform the whole nation into a classroom. As for the texts that were used in this national classroom, Nyerere himself wrote some while others were written in collaboration with his colleagues. In modern terms, the sage tradition has often gone alongside documentary radicalism, a desire on the part of political leaders to produce documents of reform or revolution. In Tanzania's experience, such documentary radicalism has ranged from the *Arusha Declaration* to the *Mwongozo*, from the terms of reference that led to the setting up of a one-party state to Nyerere's document, *Education for Self-Reliance.*[23]

Another great sage was Gamal Abdel Nasser of Egypt, in power from 1952 until his death in office in 1970. In Nasser's Egypt, what was the impact of the sage tradition on the legislature? To some extent the legislature was indeed overshadowed by the great teacher of the nation. On the other hand, Egypt's political party, the Socialist Union, still enjoyed considerable rights of debate.[24] The sage tradition was not entirely distrustful of wordmongers, but gave them new arenas of disputation and word play. Modern forms of the sage tradition have recognized that the nation as a whole cannot conceivably be an alternative classroom without the necessary organizational structure to get the lessons across to the different parts of the country. As the modern version of the sage tradition gets radicalized, it finds it important to have a political party that can reach some of the remotest corners of the population. A radicalized sage tradition seeks to strengthen the party structure, partly to ensure that the nation is indeed an attentive classroom that can respond to guidance and direction, and partly to aid in unifying the artificial state, although not always successfully.[25] Julius Nyerere tried to convert the old Tanganyika African National Union (TANU) into a viable party of national attentiveness and collective response. In 1976, TANU at last merged with the Afro-Shirazi Party of Zanzibar, to make penetration across both parts of the United Republic of Tanzania easier through a single revolutionary party, *Chama cha Mapinduzi* (CCM).[26]

The monarchical tendency often characterizes all three traditions so far mentioned. The monarchical tendency in Africa need not be an independent tradition but could be a recurrent conditioning factor on the elder tradition, the warrior tradition, and the sage tradition. It is even arguable that the monarchical tendency is patriarchal basically, and should be married to an analysis of patriarchal tendencies. In this interpretation, one would therefore be inclined to remove patriarchy away from the umbrella of the elder tradition and define it instead as a variant of the monarchical principle. We define this monarchical tendency in terms of at least four elements of political styles. There is, first, the quest for aristocratic effect. In post-colonial Africa, this takes the form of social ostentation. More specifically, it means a partiality for splendid attire, for large, expensive cars, for palatial accommodation, and for other forms of conspicuous consumption. Ministers and Members of Parliament in African countries have been particularly prone to this kind of ostentation and are susceptible to corruption on a grand scale.[27] Another factor that goes towards making a monarchical style of politics is the personalization of authority. On its own, this factor could be just another type of personality cult. But, when combined with the quest for aristocratic effect, or with other elements of style, it takes a turn towards monarchism. Sometimes the personalization goes to the extent of inventing a special title for the leader and, occasionally, the title is almost royal literally though it can sometimes be "sacred" in another sense. Nkrumah's title, the *Osagyefo* (or Redeemer) was one such title. Hastings Banda, President of Malawi, has adopted a neo-regal title, the *Ngwazi* (Conqueror). Bokassa took the monarchical tradition to its literal extreme, complete with an extravagant neo-Napoleonic coronation in the Central African Empire. And Idi Amin had a string of titles before and after his name as part of his official identity.[28]

This linkage between royalty and sacredness brings us to the third element in the monarchical political style, the sacralization of authority. As we indicated, sometimes linked to the process of personalizing authority, but this need not be. The glorification of a leader could be in non-religious terms. On the other hand, what is being sacralized need not be a person but could be an office or an institution. The institutional form of sacred authority is, however, rare in new states precisely because those institutions are so recent and weak. Legitimacy for the office of the president or for a Parliament was in most cases rather feeble. The fountain of legitimacy had not yet begun to be politically sacralized. The fourth factor in the politics of monarchism, especially in Africa, has been the quest for a royal, historical identity. This phenomenon arises out of a vague feeling that national dignity is incomplete without a splendid past. And the glory of the past is then conceived in terms of ancient, kingly achievement.[29] As for literal monarchical systems in post-colonial Africa, those that have collapsed since the 1950s include the Royal houses of Egypt, Rwanda, Burundi, Zanzibar, Buganda, and Ethiopia. The most resilient surviving monarchies include those of Ashanti, Morocco, and Swaziland.

On Race and Dignitarianism

That aspect of Africa's socio-cultural preoccupation concerned with race might be called dignitarianism. This is a much more accurate term for it than the word "nationalism," although many authors (including this one) have often confused dignitarianism with nationalism. Nationalism is concerned with either the defence of, or the quest for, nationhood and its socio-cultural attributes. Digitarianism, on the other hand, is a defence of collective dignity in the face of a hostile or condescending environment. The African people may not be the most brutalized people in modern history, but they are almost certainly the most humiliated. The most brutalized people in modern history include the indigenous peoples of the Americas and of Australia, who were subjected to genocidal attacks by white invaders. Also among the most brutalized in more recent times were the Jews and the Gypsies in the Nazi Holocaust. On the other hand, no other groups were subjected to such large-scale indignities of enslavement for several centuries in the millions, as were the Africans. No other groups experienced to the same extent such indignities as lynching, systematic segregation, and well-planned apartheid as were the Africans. It is against this background that Africa's dignitarian impulse was stimulated. A deep-seated African rebellion against humiliation was aroused. It has been a misnomer to call this rebellion "nationalism." This has not been an African quest for nationhood. At best, nationhood has been just the means to an end.

The real deep-seated African struggle has been a quest for dignity—human and racial.

Africans have been accused of being a people without a history of their own. This stereotype has denied Africans historical dignity. In the notorious words of the then Regius Professor of Modern History at Oxford University, Sir Hugh Trevor-Roper:

> Maybe in the future there will be African history, but at the moment there is none. There is only the history of the white man in Africa. The rest is darkness—and darkness is not a subject of history.[30]

Africa's dignitarian response has been partly rhetorical and partly in terms of concrete historical research. The rhetorical reply has been in terms of repudiating Trevor-Roper's argument with counter-arguments. The response by research has resulted in more research by African historians themselves into the realities of the Black experience across time. The eight volumes of the *UNESCO General History of Africa* are part of the research answer to Trevor-Roper's breed of historical detractors of Africa.

It was out of dignitarianism that the earliest forms of Pan-Africanism were born. A sense of racial aspiration and cultural deprivation among Blacks in the Diaspora led to the Pan-African Congresses, the most famous of which was the one held in Manchester, northwest England, in 1945. Future historical figures like Kwame Nkrumah, Jomo Kenyatta, and Hastings Banda as well as W.E.B. DuBois were among the participants. Five different levels of Pan-Africanism subsequently evolved. These levels were Trans-Atlantic, Trans-Saharan, Sub-Saharan, West Hemispheric (or Trans-American) and Global. Trans-Atlantic Pan-Africanism was a movement of solidarity among people of African descent in both Africa and the Western Hemisphere. It was this level of

Pan-Africanism that gave birth to the Congress in 1945 and the preceding four Congresses, dominated by Diaspora Africans. The Trans-Atlantic version of Pan-Africanism was fundamentally dignitarian. Also dignitarian was West Hemispheric (or Trans-American) Pan-Africanism, a solidarity of Blacks in North America, the Caribbean and Latin America. Organizations that have fostered such Western hemispheric solidarity and have included the movement called "the Caribbean African American Dialogue." Also dignitarian are festivals like the African American *Kwanzaa*, celebrated from December 26 to January 1 every year on the basis of seven principles (*nguzo*) which are expressed in the Swahili language: *umoja* (unity), *kujichagulia* (self-determination), *ujima* (collective work and shared responsibility), *ujamaa* (economic familyhood and cooperation), *Nia* (purpose and will), *Kuumba* (creativity) and *Imani* (faith). These seven principles and the festival of *Kwanzaa* (meaning "first fruit") were first formulated by Maulana Karenga, an African American scholar, in 1966.

Aesthetic dignitarianism has helped to sponsor Pan-African Festivals of Arts and Culture that have been held in Lagos, Dakar, Accra and in parts of the African Diaspora. These festivals have brought together Black poets, singers, dancers, painters, orators and writers from Brazil, the United States, the Caribbean, Europe as well as Africa and elsewhere. To call such festivals "nationalistic" occasions would be a misnomer. They were in fact artistic expressions of African dignity. They were in that sense aesthetic manifestations of dignitarianism. Global Pan-Africanism continues to be essentially inspired by this quest to reassert African or Black dignity. This level of Pan-Africanism seeks to envelope not only Africans and the Diaspora in the Americas, but also Black people in Europe, the Arab world, and even the indigenous peoples of Australia and Papua New Guinea. In no sense can these diverse peoples scattered across the world be searching for a sense of shared nationhood. The bonds that hold them together at festivals are not bonds of nationalism but ties of dignitarianism. Sometimes dignitarian offense has been caused to these peoples by the school of thought that has portrayed Africans as a people without achievements in science and technology, without accomplishments in scholarship and philosophy. The African response has taken one of three forms: romantic primitivism, romantic gloriana and the realist school of African historiography.

Romantic primitivism celebrates what is simple about Africa. It salutes the cattle-herder rather than the castle-builder. On the other hand, romantic gloriana celebrates Africa's more complex achievements. It salutes the pyramids of Egypt, the towering structures of Aksum, the sunken churches of Lalibela, the brooding majesty of Great Zimbabwe, the castles of Gondar. Romantic gloriana is a tribute to Africa's empires and kingdoms, Africa's inventors and discoverers, great Shaka Zulu rather than the unknown peasant. Both forms of Pan-African cultural dignitarianism were a response to European imperialism and its cultural arrogance. Europeans said that Africans were simple and invented nothing. That was an alleged fact. Europeans also said that those who were simple and invented nothing were uncivilized. That was a value judgement. Romantic primitivism accepted Europe's alleged facts about Africa (i.e. that Africa was simple and invented nothing) but rejected Europe's value judgement (that Africa was therefore uncivilized). Simplicity was one version of civilization, Romantic primitivism said, in the words of Aimé Césaire of Martinique: "Hooray for those who never invented anything; who never discovered anything." Romantic gloriana, on the other hand, rejected Europe's alleged facts about Africa (that Africa was simple and invented nothing) but seems to have accepted Europe's values (that civilization is to be measured by complexity and invention). The same country in Africa can produce both types of Pan-African dignitarianists. Sénégal's Léopold Senghor has been a major thinker and poet in the *Négritude* school associated with romantic primitivism. Senghor's most hotly debated statement is: "Emotion is black... Reason is Greek." On the other hand, the late Cheikh Anta Diop, Sénégal's Renaissance Man who died in 1986, belonged more to the gloriana school. He spent much of his life demonstrating Africa's contributions to global civilization. And he was most emphatic that the civilization of Pharaonic Egypt was a Black civilization. This was all in the grand Pan-African tradition of romantic gloriana. What about the realist school of African historiography? It is based on the reality of Africa. It recognizes a fusion of the simple and the complex, the cattle-herder and the castle-builder. It sees Africa as more than romantic primitivism and romantic gloriana. Future Pan-Africanism must in turn go beyond the quest for dignity and attempt to deal with Africa's other problems.

In the future, the Pan-Africanism of economic integration will be led by Southern Africa under the Southern African Development Community (SADC). The success of this economic sub-regional integration will be partly because one member of the new economic fraternity is more equal than the others: the Republic of South Africa. A pivotal state often helps to assure the success of regional integration, but a shared sense of Africanity will also be needed to sustain SADC. The old European Economic Community (EEC) created in 1958 survived partly because some members were equal more than others. The Franco-German axis under Charles de Gaulle was more "Franco" than German. But German economic might has restored the balance in the new European Union (EU). However, a shared European culture also was needed all along to sustain unification. Similarly, Southern Africa has the advantage of having one member indisputably, "the first among equals"—the Republic of South Africa. The pivotal power is the premise of regional survival, but a regional identity has to be culturally strengthened to sustain long-term unity. Pan-Africanism of lingo-cultural integration will probably be led by East Africa with its good fortune of a region-wide indigenous language: the role of Kiswahili binding Tanzania, Kenya, to some extent Uganda, Somalia, and potentially Rwanda, Burundi, and the eastern parts of the Democratic Republic of the Congo (formerly Zaire). Northern Mozambique and Malawi are also feeling Swahili influence. Kiswahili is spoken by more people than any other indigenous language of Africa and will hit its first 100 million people early in the 21st century. It is expanding more rapidly than any other *lingua franca* in the continent. Pan-Africanism of political integration will probably be led by North Africa. There is already a kind of economic cooperation fraternity binding five countries: Libya, Tunisia, Algeria, Morocco and Mauritania. The economic cooperation has been limping along but Egypt may soon be joining this movement towards greater North African regional integration. The sub-region is still a long way from political integration, but it is the best placed in Africa for such an adventure since it shares a religion (Islam), a language (Arabic), a culture (Arabo-Berber) and a substantial shared history across centuries. Part of the stimulus for North Africa's integration will be European integration. The economies of North Africa and Southern Europe are to some extent competitive. The deeper integration of countries like Spain and Portugal and Greece into an enlarged European Union is ringing economic alarm bells in North Africa. This could help Pan-Africanism in Arab Africa. Pan-Africanism of military integration is likely to be led by West Africa, with the precedent set by the Economic Community of West Africa's Monitoring Group (ECOMOG) under the Economic Community of West African States (ECOWAS). In spite of the difficulties encountered by ECOMOG in Liberia, the effort has been a major pioneering enterprise in the history of *Pax Africana*.[31]

Within Pan-Africanism, dignitarianism can link up not only with nationalism but also with nation building and with the quest for development. But distinct as dignitarianism has been in Africa's ideological history, it has not of course kept out nationalism proper from Africa's experience. On the contrary, African nationalism has sometimes evolved out of African dignitarianism. What had previously been a cry of rebellion against racial indignities developed into wider territorial or cultural forms of nationalism. It is even arguable that nationalism in Africa developed from two very different parents: ethnicism, on one side, and dignitarianism, on the other. Ethnicism had contributed a tradition of collectivism and assertive solidarities rooted in indigenous culture. Dignitarianism had contributed race-conscious defensiveness and new Pan-African solidarities. Out of tribe-conscious ethnicism and race-conscious defensiveness and the new Pan-African solidarity, modern forms of nationalism in Africa were born. Let us examine this force of nationalism more closely.

Nationalism: Ideology and Policy

What is nationalism? We define it in this paper as a defensive or militant loyalty to one's nation, country or culture, real or presumptive. The term is similar to the idea of patriotism except in degree of militancy. Nationalism is quite often a more militant form of patriotism.[32] Nationalism can have a different focus, depending upon circumstances. For example, it can focus on the issue of language. Language has an emotive and unifying political effect.[33] Among the peoples of Africa, the Somali are particularly nationalistic about their language, feeling a strong sense of loyalty and pride towards it. It is also a form of ethnicism. In Canada, the French-speaking Canadians have developed a form of nationalism with a linguistic focus, partly because many believe that French-speaking Canadians are disadvantaged in a country with an English-speaking majority, which also borders the US.[34] This is also a form of ethnicism.

But nationalism in other places can also be focused on religion rather than language. Jewish nationalism or Zionism, for example, is primarily based on a cultural allegiance founded on religious ancestry. Loyalty to religion, especially when uniquely shared among a group of people, or perception of a threat to the religion, can have a powerful effect on nationalism.[35] In the Sudan, the Mahdist revolt against foreign rule in the last quarter of the nineteenth century was partly inspired by a form of nationalism with an Islamic focus. The Sudanese religious and nationalist struggle continued until Britain re-established control under the doctrine of the Anglo-Egyptian Condominium in 1899.[36] Militant ethnicism was also involved. Likewise in 1899, a Mahdi (or Islamic reviver) was proclaimed among the Somali, who then organized raids on British and Italian Somaliland. In 1900-1904, there were four British expeditions against this new adversary, "the Mad Mullah, Seyyid Muhammad Abdilleh Hassan." Since then Somali nationalism has continued to have a religious component, as well as its traditional linguistic focus. Nationalistic and ethnicist Mahdist movements have also appeared in West Africa from time to time. But Islam is not the only religion in Africa that has influenced the history of nationalism and ethnicism. Indigenous African religions have also played their part. Sometimes indigenous religious beliefs have been mobilized almost as weapons against the colonial order. The original primary resistance of African peoples against the incoming Europeans often invoked the support of supernatural forces against the white conquerors, sometimes with disastrous consequences. This is particularly true of such nationalistic and ethnicist resistance movements as the Maji Maji rebellion in Tanganyika against the Germans from 1905 to 1907. The African fighters believed in the protective power of suitably blessed water.[37] Alas, the water was not enough of a shield to protect African warriors from German bullets: the warriors fell in the thousands. Nevertheless, the Maji rebellion is widely regarded in Tanzania as the fountainhead of modern nationalism in the country.

In addition to language and religion, nationalism can sometimes be based on race as a foundation. This is particularly widespread in Africa since the Second World War and is especially linked to dignitarianism. Racially conscious African nationalism is partly a response to the arrogance of white rulers and white settlers in colonial Africa. Because the rulers were so concerned with issues of racial differences, the colonial subjects in time became equally concerned about racial dignity. Out of this defensive consciousness emerged a whole movement of dignitarian Pan-Africanism, especially that version which emphasized the solidarity of Black peoples.[38] In the first half of the century the leadership of the dignitarian versions of the Pan-African movement was in fact held by people of African ancestry in the western hemisphere: among the founding-fathers of Pan-Africanism were Marcus Garvey of Jamaica, George Padmore of Trinidad, W.E.B. DuBois of the United States. As alluded to earlier, from 1900 onwards, there were Pan-African meetings to emphasize racial solidarity and organize for the struggle against discrimination and in pursuit of racial dignity for Black peoples both in Africa and in the western world. It was not until 1945 that the leadership of the Pan-African movement passed from Blacks of the Americas to Blacks of Africa. This was the aforementioned fifth Pan-African Congress held in Manchester, England in 1945. The Africans at the conference were still slightly overshadowed by some of the giants of Black nationalism from the Americas, but nevertheless 1945 signifies the re-Africanization of Pan-Africanism, the passing of the torch from Diaspora people of African ancestry abroad to citizens of African countries. As a result of the Manchester conference, a slightly different focus from race entered the universe of Pan-Africanism. The new focus involved territory, of re-establishing control of the sovereignty of African lands. Dignitarianism became more nationalistic. In a sense territory became a more prevalent focus for nationalism than language, religion, or race. In Africa, territory-based forms of nationalism had at least two levels: statewide and continent wide. African nationalism was either concerned with liberating each African country in turn or concerned with the liberation of a whole region in Africa or the African continent as a whole. In our sense, regionally inspired nationalism went beyond the focus of a single country and may have encompassed all of West Africa, all of East Africa, or all of North Africa. When it encompassed the African continent as a whole, both north and south of the Sahara, it became Trans-Saharan Pan-Africanism. While the Trans-Atlantic variety of Pan-Africanism emphasized the solidarity of people with a Black skin, the Trans-Saharan version of nationalism emphasized the solidarity of the African countries, both Black and Arab. The Organization of African Unity (OAU), established in May 1963, was primarily based on the principle of Trans-Saharan Pan-Africanism, urging a unity based on the mystique of the African continent.[39]

The fifth focus of nationalism (after language, religion, race and territory) takes us back to ethnicity and ethnicism. In Africa this takes the form of what used to be called "tribal" solidarity. There is a good deal of debate as to whether the Mau Mau movement in Kenya from 1952 to 1960 was a nationally-inspired Kenyan nationalist movement or whether it was an ethnically inspired movement led by the Kikuyu. The movement was a struggle against land hunger among the peoples of central Kenya and against European monopoly of the best agricultural land in the country. Mau Mau was also a struggle for political and cultural liberation.[40] The religious symbolism used by the African fighters in the war was borrowed primarily from the religious heritage of the Kikuyu and related ethnic groups. This heritage was used as a basis for oathing ceremonies, to sanctify commitment to the movement and discourage treachery and subversion within the movement. The Mau Mau fighters were preponderantly drawn from Kikuyu, Meru and Embu ethnic groups. Can such ethnicism be nationalism? Both the fighters and the religious symbols of the movement were ethnic. But were the political goals of the movement national notwithstanding? If the answer to the second question is yes, then the Mau Mau movement was a war of liberation carried out by the Kikuyu and related small "ethnic groups" but on behalf of the wider African political community within Kenya. Similarly, Mugabe's army in Rhodesia (the Zimbabwe African National Liberation Army—ZANLA) two decades later consisted mainly of Shona ethnic compatriots, but the goals of the movement made it a liberation struggle for Zimbabwe as a whole. In short, it is possible for the composition of a movement to be ethnic while its political goals remain national or even transnational. At the initial point of colonization the distinction between national and ethnic resistance did not in any case make much sense. The ethnic groups of Africa resisted as autonomous societies against encroaching European penetration. Until the Europeans drew the colonial boundaries and created new proto-nations, any fighting by the Shona and the Ndebele was in each case both national and ethnic. Similarly, the struggles of the Banyoro in Uganda, or the Hausa-Fulani and Yoruba in Nigeria, involved political communities where ethnic boundaries substantially coincided with ancient national boundaries. It was the colonial mapmaker who disrupted this congruence between "tribal" and "national" identities.[41] Following colonialism, nationalism and ethnicism were often at loggerheads.

Capitalism: Ideology and Policy

Political ideas are not only linked to culture and history. They are also profoundly affected by economics. Production and values are inseparable. Most of the debates about African policy options fail to draw a simple distinction between restoring African economies to market forces and entrusting them to private ownership and private control. It is true that the liberal doctrine, at least since Adam Smith, has tended to assume that the market comes into relatively independent play when the pursuit of wealth is left to private initiative. What we now call privatization was deemed the only viable approach to the triumph of the market. Privatization was the means; marketization was the end. But in reality an economy could be in private hands and not subject to the free market because of factors downplayed or ignored by liberal thinkers. Or it could be under state-ownership and still respond to market forces and to the laws of supply and demand. The imperatives of re-structuring African economies have all too often assumed that the only route to the free market is through privatization. Indeed, economic reformers concerned with Africa have equated privatization with marketization. Is it time to take another look?[42] The free market in Africa can be constrained or inhibited by a number of factors which have very little to do with the state *per se*. A notorious inhibition on the free market in Africa is the simple fact that the whole market can be cornered or monopolized by an ethnic group.

Nigeria underwent the trauma of a civil war partly because the Igbo had been perceived in the North as monopolizing certain economic areas of activity—and the nation had no "anti-Trust legislation" for dealing with ethnic specialization and monopoly. Unfortunately, neither ethnic specialization nor counter-ethnic resentment ended in 1970, when large-scale fratricide ended in Nigeria. The civil war was concluded, but the precise cultural differences between the ethnic groups did not end. By the 1980s, the Igbo were once again a little too visible for their own safety in the North of the country in certain areas of trade and industry. We use the Igbo in this analysis purely as an illustration of ethnicity as a constraint on the market. In the 1980s in Nigeria there was more recognition of the need for ethnic "anti-Trust legislation" to prevent or to break up "tribal monopolies." Sometimes the euphemism for this description in favor of the disadvantaged is called "the federal character of Nigeria." This is Nigeria's nearest equivalent of the principle of Affirmative Action in the US—though in both countries the restoration of ethnic balance is rather haphazard and sometimes in conflict with other democratic values. Is it not Igbo success in certain economic activities (or Yoruba success in others) a case of the free market finding its own equilibrium of efficiency? This would partly depend upon whether Igbo (or Yoruba) preponderance is due to the unencumbered free play of relevant market factors. In reality there is devout ethnic solidarity and nepotism at play, and these ensure the success of some Nigerian entrepreneurs and severely handicap the efforts of others. The considerations of Igbo monopoly in the trade of car parts and other spare parts are not all rational elements of Igbo efficiency. Igbo success includes as one of its pillars Igbo nepotism. The same is true of Kikuyu success in Kenya in the late 1960s and 1970s. It is part of the reality of African conservatism in allegiance.

In addition to ethnic nepotism as a constraint on the market in spite of privatization, there is also the all-pervasive constraint of the prestige-motive in Africa's economic behavior. Traditional Western liberal doctrine had often taken for granted the psychology of the profit motive (later identified as the maximization of returns). African economic behavior, on the other hand, is often inspired more by the pursuit of prestige than by the quest for profit. Precisely because African cultures are more collectivist, members of the society are more sensitive to the approval and disapproval of the collectivity. On the positive side, the prestige motive serves as a device of income distribution. Those who are financially successful often desire renown for generosity. Obligations towards wider and wider circles of kinsfolk are fulfilled. Word gets around to relatives far and wide: "Our son has killed an elephant. There is more than enough meat for us all to chop." Those who succeed share their rewards with many others. Here too is cultural continuity. On the negative side, the prestige motive in African economic behavior encourages ostentatious consumption and self-indulgent "aristocratic" and "monarchical" exhibitionism. The Mercedes Benz has become the symbol of Africa's ostentatious indulgence—but in some places in Nigeria the expensive fleet of cars often goes with a palace or two, sometimes a private plane and a helicopter, and a loud way of life, all for a single family! While the profit motive in classical economic theory was supposed to lean towards greater production, the prestige motive in contemporary African economic behavior leans towards greater consumption. What is more, because they often have to be imported, consumer products commanding the most prestige require foreign exchange. Privatization on its own does not make an African economy produce more. The prestige motive operates both privately and at the state level, eating away into the resources of the country ominously. When Westerners call upon African countries to privatize, they are expecting the profit motive to be given a free play. However, in fact, the problem in most of Africa is not simply how to liberate and activate the profit motive, but also how to control and restrain the prestige motive. Arguably, the latter crusade is even more urgent than the former. Indeed, the ultimate crusade may well turn out to be how to tap the prestige motive in such a way that it serves the goals of production and not merely the appetites of consumption. Can we make creativity more prestigious than acquisition? Can we make production more prestigious than possession? Should we take a closer look at the problem of incentives in Africa? How can we be more precisely sensitized to the African equilibrium between prestige and profit?

A third major private constraint on the market (after ethnic nepotism and the prestige motive) is the general problem of bribery and corruption prevalent in post-colonial Africa. Corruption can clog up procedures and substantially paralyze production and distribution. Again, corruption can be both in the public sector and in the private; it can be bureaucratic or omnipresent. Privatization of the economy may simply mean the privatization of corruption, and sometimes this is more contagious in the wider society than the corruption of officials and bureaucrats. Capitalism has come to Africa but without the "Protestant ethic" of work and frugality. The white man in Africa himself set a dangerous example. He never washed his own clothes, or cooked his own food, or polished his own shoes, or made his own bed, or cleaned his own room, or washed his own dishes or even poured his own gin and tonic! The luxurious aristocratic life of the white settler as he played master to the African servant was detrimental to the spirit of capitalism. Africa's own prestige motive—which had been sociable in its original indigenous versions—was now transformed by the aristocratic lifestyles imported by the white man. Africa's prestige motive was given the colonial incarnation of expensive European consumer culture complete with huge houses, domestic servants and "garden boys." If the ideology of entrepreneurship simply meant acquisitiveness, this has now arrived in a big way in much of Africa. Indeed, those who do not take advantage of their opportunities to become wealthy, and to help their kinsfolk, are sometimes despised.

The challenge is partly about the means used to acquire wealth. Is the wealth created or simply obtained? Acquiring wealth from a prosperous farm is a creative process. Acquiring wealth as either a middleman on behalf of external interests or through corruption may not be creative at all. Can we transform the acquisitive instinct in Africa into something more directly productive? If the means of acquiring wealth need to be creative, the ends of acquiring wealth also need to be healthy. Ostentatious consumption is not usually among the healthier ends of economic success. In short, the African ideology of entrepreneurship needs a fundamental reform of both the means and the end of the pursuit of wealth in society. Until that happens, privatization of African economies—far from being the best way of achieving a healthy and free market—may itself be detrimental to the marketplace. For those who are sufficiently attentive, the African experience demonstrates that privatization is not necessarily the best protection for the free market in all cultures. But modern capitalism in Africa has often been almost inseparable from socialist aspirations and sentiment. It is to the complexities of Africa's socialist experience that we must now turn.

Socialism: Ideology and Policy

As a generalization, we might say that the intellectual climate for socialism in Africa has been quite good, but the sociological and material soil has not been fertile enough for socialism. Let us explore this twin proposition more fully. As to the reasons why the intellectual climate for socialism in Africa has been good, these reasons include once again basic historical continuities and discontinuities. For one thing, many Africans both north and south of the Sahara have conceptually associated capitalism with imperialism. In reality, you can have socialism accompanied by imperialism. Indeed the Chinese used to protest against "socialist imperialism" and "Soviet hegemony." It is also possible to be a capitalist country without being an imperialist country—Switzerland and Sweden might be considered by some as good illustrations of non-imperialist capitalism. But in Africa's historical experience it is indeed true that modern capitalism came with imperialism. Kwame Nkrumah was very sensitive to this linkage.[43] The enemy of imperialism is nationalism; the enemy of capitalism is socialism. If there is indeed an alliance between capitalism and imperialism, why should there not be an alliance between African nationalism and socialism? Such a paradigm of intellectual and ideological convergence has been found attractive in many parts of Africa. Leaders like Sékou Touré and movements like the Front for the Liberation of Mozambique (FRELIMO) became socialist for nationalistic reasons.

A second consideration that has contributed to the favorable intellectual climate for socialism in Africa concerns the accumulation of frustrations with efforts to develop Africa through Western patterns of economic growth. Many Africans are seeking alternative strategies of social and economic improvement out of a sheer sense of desperation at the inadequacies of the first decades of independence. In reality, socialist experiments in post-colonial Africa so far have not yielded any greater improvement for the masses than other experiments. On the contrary, sometimes the social costs of socialism in Africa have indeed been rather high. It is arguable that while there were relatively successful petty capitalist experiments in countries including Kenya, Malawi, Tunisia, and the Côte d'Ivoire until the early 1980s, Africa as a whole has yet to produce a significant improvement in the material conditions for the masses. The nearest socialist success story until the 1980s was perhaps Algeria. But socialist Algeria needed to sell oil to the capitalist world to buttress socialism. In spite of these contradictions, however, many Africans were so disenchanted with the first decades of capitalist independence that they did not mind experimenting with socialist approaches to social transformation.

The third factor that predisposed many Africans in favor of socialism was the rampant corruption among the immediate post-colonial rulers of the continent, all the way from Egypt to Zimbabwe. Again, corruption is by no means a peculiarity of capitalism, as many of those who have traveled in socialist countries will testify. But there is no doubt that social discipline can at times be more difficult to uphold in conditions of laissez-faire economic behavior than in conditions of relatively centralized planning and supervision. On balance, it is indeed arguable that the socialist ethic in Robert Mugabe's own personal socialism is, almost by definition, more opposed to "kick-backs, goodwill bribery," and even profit itself, than the ethic of acquisitive individualism in his comrades.

The fourth factor that contributed to the favorable intellectual climate for socialism in Africa was the widespread belief that traditional African culture was basically collectivist, and "therefore" socialist. There have been claims from quite early, by some African leaders including Senghor, Nyerere, and Mboya that the morality of sharing in traditional Africa, the ethic of responsibility for the young, for the old, and the disabled, and the imperative of collective ethic were akin to socialism.[44] Because of this broadly favorable intellectual climate, most African governments soon after independence paid some kind of lip service to socialism. Even regimes like that of Jomo Kenyatta and Habib Bourguiba managed to adopt in the initial years of independence a partially socialist rhetoric. Regimes that opted for the one-party state route were particularly tantalized by socialist symbolism. After all, the presumed centralizing tendencies of socialism helped justify a one-party monopoly of power. Prospects for socialism in the first decade of African independence did seem bright. Nasser, Nkrumah, Sékou Touré, Julius Nyerere, and Boumedienne were seen as architects of a new socialist Africa. From the 1970s, countries like Ethiopia, Angola, Congo, and Mozambique went all the way to Marxism-Leninism. In spite of the power of socio-cultural solidarities, was a socio-economic ideology taking root in Africa, after all?

This is what brings us to the barrenness of the sociological soil for socialism, in spite of the favorableness of the intellectual climate. One obstinate sociological factor against socialism was simply the primacy of ethnicism in Africa as against class-consciousness. Most Africans are members of their ethnic group first and members of a particular social class second. When the chips are down, Igbo peasants are more likely to identify with the Igbo bourgeoisie than they are with fellow peasants in Yorubaland. Socialism has confronted ethnicism. On balance, it can be legitimately argued that whenever there has been a neat confrontation and competition between the forces of ethnicism on one side and the forces of class-consciousness on the other side, ethnicism has almost invariably triumphed in Africa. This is one primary factor behind the infertility of the sociological soil for an ideology like socialism. Ethnicist conservatism is stronger than socialist theory. Socio-cultural forces are still stronger emotionally than socio-economic ones.

A related factor is the strength of cultural elites in Africa as against economic classes as such. The new elites especially have emerged out of the womb of Western imperial acculturation. It has not been the possession of wealth necessarily that opened the doors to influence and power, but the possession of Western education and verbal skills. To be sure, the initial political establishment of post-colonial Africa was disproportionately composed of a westernized and semi-westernized core. This galaxy of westernized stars included names like Nkrumah, Nyerere, Senghor, Kaunda, Ferhat Abbas, Obote, Houphouët-Boigny, Boutros-Ghali, Mandela, Banda, Bourguiba, Mugabe, Nkomo, Sadiq el-Mahdi, Machel, Neto, and others. This created a basic sociological ambivalence on the African scene. On the one hand, it seemed that the most opposed to imperialism rhetorically, and the ones most likely to link it to capitalism, were precisely the elites produced by the West's cultural imperialism in Africa. Even when these elements became truly revolutionary, there was a basic contradiction. After all, Karl Marx had expected the most revolutionary class to be the least advantaged class in the most advanced societies. This was deemed to be the proletariat in industrial Western societies. But when you look at the former revolutionary leaders in Angola, Tanzania, Guinea (Conakry), or Zimbabwe and examine the Western credentials of the leaders, you may be inclined to conclude that the most revolutionary of all classes in those societies were the best advantaged. In other words, westernized Third World bourgeois intellectuals were the most likely to produce the dream of socialist transformation. Therefore, it is not the least advantaged social class in the most advantaged society (the proletariat in the West) but the best advantaged social group in the least advanced societies (the westernized bourgeois intelligentsia in Third World countries) who have been the true agents of revolution in the last quarter of the twentieth century.

It is still a socio-linguistic impossibility for an African to become a sophisticated Marxist without being at the same time substantially westernized. This is partly because the process of becoming a sophisticated Marxist requires considerable exposure to Marxist literature, both primary and secondary. Access to that literature for the time being is only minimally possible through indigenous African languages like Kiswahili, or Yoruba, or Amharic. Even in Arabic, Marxist literature is relatively limited. An African who wants to read many of the works of Marx, Engels, and Lenin has to have been substantially initiated into the literary culture of the West. Even Africans who go to communist China or went to the former Soviet Union needed to have been previously Europeanized. Scholarships to China and the former Soviet Union were not normally offered to rural rustics untouched by Western schools or their equivalents. The nature of elite formation in Africa can therefore be counted as an aspect of the uncongenial sociological soil that socialism has to confront in African conditions.

A third factor of this barrenness of the soil concerns Africa's organizational capabilities in the present historical phase. Many hastily assume that a tradition of collectivism in a traditional setting is a relevant preparation for organized collective efforts in a modern setting. Unfortunately, much of the evidence points the other way. Collective effort based on custom and tradition and kinship ties leaves Africa unprepared for the kind of organized collectivism that needs to be based on command rather than ritual. If socialism requires a rational, efficient command structure that is not based on custom, ethnic empathy, or ritual, the present stage of social change in the African experience is still inhospitable to socialist transformation.

The fourth aspect of the infertility of Africa's sociological soil for the socialist plant would take us back to issues of historical continuity. Many African economies have already been deeply integrated into a world economy dominated by the West. African countries that go socialist domestically find that they are still integrated in the world capitalist system. The rules of that system are overwhelmingly derived from principles evolved in the history of capitalism. In international trade, countries seek to maximize their returns. The rules of business and exchange at the international level, the banking system that underpins those exchanges, the actual currencies used in money markets and in meeting balance-of-payments, are all products of the capitalist experience. Countries like Vietnam, Angola, and even Cuba discover soon enough that their best economic salvation is to gain international legitimacy by Western standards and it is part of their ambition to begin receiving Western currency markets as well. What all this once again means is that Third World countries can make their internal domestic arrangements socialist while remaining deeply integrated in the international capitalist system at the same time. It is even arguable that a country like Tanzania became more dependent on the world capitalist system after it inaugurated its neo-socialist experiment under the Arusha Declaration in 1967.

Finally socialism in Africa suffered in the 1990s because of the collapse of communist governments in Europe, which had previously supported regimes like the self-declared Marxist ones of Angola, Ethiopia, Mozambique and elsewhere. The sharp decline and disgrace of European communism was a blow to socialism in Africa. This then is the configuration of factors that on one side reveals that intellectually, post-colonial Africa has been ready for socialism and, on the other side, warns us that the material conditions for genuine socialist experimentation in Africa are not yet at hand. The intellectual climate was promising; the sociological soil was forbidding. Once again, a socio-economic ideology has failed to take root in Africa.

In Search of Democratic Stability

Finally, let us turn to Africa's struggle to establish democracy without further loss of stability. We define democracy as a political system which makes rulers accountable, assures the citizens participation and choice in electing their rulers, guarantees openness in public affairs and civil liberties for the people, has checks against arbitrary use of power, and is committed to the pursuit of justice. Every African government has continued to walk that tight rope between too much government and too little government. At some stage, an excess of government becomes tyranny; at some other stage too little government becomes anarchy. Either trend can lead to the collapse of the state, to death and to a large-scale displacement. Somalia under Siad Barre was a case of tyranny finally leading to the collapse of the state; the Belgian Congo (later Zaire) in 1960 was a case of anarchy nearly destroying the new post-colonial state.

A major unresolved dilemma lies in civil-military relations. Perhaps in everybody's experience military rule often leads to too much government—almost by definition. On the other hand, civilian rule in countries like Nigeria and Sudan has sometimes meant too little government, with politicians squabbling among themselves and sometimes plundering the nation's resources. If military regimes have too much power, and civilian regimes have too little control, countries like Nigeria and Sudan have to find solutions for the future, otherwise destruction and displacement loom threateningly. Dr. Nnamdi Azikiwe, the first president of independent Nigeria, once proposed a constitutional sharing of power between the military and civilians: it was called diarchy, a kind of dual sovereignty. At the time that Dr. Azikiwe proposed the dual sovereignty idea (part military, part civilian) in 1972, he was roundly denounced, especially by intellectuals and academics who were against military rule. But the dilemma has still persisted in Dr. Azikiwe's own country, Nigeria, and elsewhere in Africa: how to bridge the gap between the ethic of representative government and the power of the military. Has Egypt quietly evolved a diarchy since the 1952 revolution, a system of government of dual sovereignty between civilians and soldiers? Has Azikiwe's dream found fulfillment in Egypt—however imperfectly? Or is the Egyptian system still in the process of becoming a diarchy but has not yet arrived there? Starting as a military-led system in 1952, has it become increasingly civilianized—yet still in the process of change towards full power sharing?

Another dilemma concerning too much government versus too little hinges on the party system. There is little doubt that one-party states tend towards too much government. This has been the case in most of Africa. On the other hand, multiparty systems in Africa have often degenerated into ethnic or sectarian rivalries resulting in too little control. This tendency was illustrated in the 1980s by Ghana under Hilla Limann, Nigeria under Shehu Shagari and the Sudan under Sadiq El-Mahdi. The state was losing control in all three cases. If one solution to the civil-military dilemma is diarchy (the dual sovereignty), what is the solution to the dilemma between the one-party state and the multiparty system? Uganda may have felt its way towards one solution to the dilemma: a no-party state. Concerned that a multiparty system would only lead to a reactivation of Uganda's ethnic and sectarian rivalries, President Yoweri Museveni lent the weight of his name, office, and prestige to this principle of a Uganda without political parties for at least five years. In an election held in March 1994 to choose members of a Constituent Assembly, candidates in favour of a no-party Uganda seemed to have won a majority of the seats. Under both Idi Amin (1971-1979) and the second administration of Milton

Obote (1980-1985), Uganda experienced some of the worst excesses of both tyranny and anarchy at the same time. Although the state did not actually collapse, it lost control over a large part of the territory and was unable to perform many of the basic functions of the state. Thousands of people were displaced or escaped into exile. Champions of a "Uganda without political parties" hope that their new party-less approach to politics may avert the type of situation that brought Idi Amin into power in the first place. There are other possible solutions to the dilemma between multiparty anarchy and one-party tyranny. One possibility is a no-party presidency and a multiparty parliament. This could give a country a strong executive with extensive constitutional powers, but one who is elected in a contest between individuals and not between party-candidates. Parliament or the legislature, on the other hand, could remain multiparty. The president would not be allowed to belong to any political party. A system of a presidency without a political party may indeed give undue advantage to Africa's millionaires or billionaires. That may be the price to pay for a no-party presidency in a multiparty society.

All of the above are situations where the state succeeds or fails in relation to the nature of the political institutions (military or civilian, multiparty or one party or other). However, in reality a state succeeds or fails in relation to wider societal configurations as well. In post-colonial Africa ethnicity continues to be a major factor conditioning success or failure of the state.[45] Yet here too mother Africa presents its contradictions. The road to state-collapse or state-displacement could be either through having too many groups in the process—or, paradoxically, too few. Previous failures of the state in Uganda were partly due to the very ethnic richness of the society: the striking diversity of Bantu, Nilotic, Sudanic and other groups, each of which was itself internally diverse. The political system was not yet ready to sustain the immense pressures of competing ethno-cultural claims. Lives were lost; thousands were displaced. Ethiopia under Mengistu Haile-Mariam also drifted towards state-failure partly because the system was unable to accommodate its rich cultural and ethnic diversity. Mengistu's tyranny did not foster free negotiations, or compromise, or coalition building among ethnic groups. But how can a state fail or collapse because it had too few ethnic groups? At first glance, it looks as if Somalia has been such a case. George Bernard Shaw said that the British and Americans were a people divided by the same language. It may be truer and more poignant to say that the Somali are a people divided by the same culture. The culture legitimizes the clans that are among the central bases of discord. The culture legitimizes a macho response to inter-clan stalemates. The culture legitimizes inter-clan feuds. Inter-clan rivalries among the Somali would decline, if the Somali themselves were confronting the competition of other ethnic groups within some kind of plural society. The Somali themselves would close ranks if they were facing the rivalry of the Amhara and the Tigre in a new plural society. It is in that sense that even a culturally homogenous society can have major areas of schism, if wise answers are not found for them. In any case, Somalia even on its own could be studied as a plural society of many clans rather than of many "tribes." The single culture of the Somali people may be a misleading indicator. The pluralism of Somalia is at the level of sub-ethnicity rather than ethnicity. That disguised pluralism of Somalia was exploited by Siad Barre to play off one clan against another. Siad Barre's tyranny lasted from 1969 until 1990. It turned out to be the high road to the destruction of the Somali state. The Somali became more than nomads: they became refugees.

There is clear evidence that the people of Africa are tired of dictators. In one African country after another there have been riots and protests against dictators. There is genuine desire for democracy, but the capacity to democratize needs to be strengthened. The democratic spirit may be willing, but the political flesh is weak. In the course of the 1990s much of Africa continued to demonstrate a solid desire for democracy. What has yet to be tested fully is Africa's capacity to democratize. The desire for democracy has manifested itself in a variety of ways: from pro-democracy street demonstrations in Togo to the Muslim riots at the Kenya Coast, from the political tug-of-war between soldiers and civilians in Nigeria to the electoral fall of Hastings Banda's tyranny in Malawi. But are Africa's will and capacity to democratize strong enough? This capacity requires not only the urge to throw out one particular unpopular regime, but the determination to institutionalize legitimate political succession indefinitely. The will to democracy also requires readiness to permit an unpopular but legitimate government to govern without hindrance and complete its electoral term of office without being overthrown.

Ghana elected Kofi Busia in 1969, and the Ghanaian army overthrew him in 1972, before he completed his first electoral term. In 1979, Ghana elected Hilla Limann, and again the Ghanaian army overthrew him in 1981, before he completed his first term. Even more astonishing, popular opinion in Ghana cheered both military coups. The Ghanaian will to democracy was not strong enough yet. In 1992 a new situation arose: Flt. Lieutenant Jerry Rawlings, formerly a military dictator, resigned his military commission and stood for election as a civilian. According to international observers, Jerry Rawlings won the 1992 election. Had he won it because the register of voters was unfairly incomplete? Or did he win because of actual vote rigging during the election? Or were the opposition parties simply bad losers? Whichever of the above suppositions was the truth, it constituted evidence that Ghana's democracy was not fully consolidated. The evidence that Jonas Savimbi and his National Union for the Total Independence of Angola (UNITA) were bad losers in Angola is probably clearer. Former United States' protégé Jonas Savimbi was prepared to plunge the country into renewed civil war rather than accept even the first round of the presidential elections, which had gone against him. That Angola's will to democracy was weak was not surprising. The country had been ruled by one of the least democratic of all European colonial powers in Africa, Portugal. In the last decade of colonial rule, Angola was more accustomed to multi-army politics than to multi-party politics. The democratic tradition in Portuguese-speaking Africa had either been destroyed by the whole Portuguese domineering style or never arrived because Portugal ceased to be part of the European mainstream, and its colonies were ignored or brutalized as a result. The will to democratize is sometimes compromised by an unwillingness to accept the triumphant ideology in a contest. This was most dramatically illustrated in Algeria. The pluralistic experiment was not, in reality, ready to accept the triumph of the ideology of the Islamic Salvation Front (FIS). Elections were held but then aborted when the winner was not acceptable to those who were able to command military support to frustrate the democratic process. Algeria is now plunged in a "no win" situation as the democratic secularists seek to neutralize the majoritarian Islamists.

One of the major dilemmas confronting the new African democracies is whether economic liberalization should have preceded political liberalization. Should Africa have reduced the role of the state in the economy before Africa increased the role of the people in the political process? Would that have strengthened Africa's will to democratize? Experience in Asia seems to lend support to that strategy. South Korea embarked on vigorous capitalism before attempting liberal democratization. On the whole, this approach has also been true of Taiwan, and of most members of the Association of South East Asian Nations (ASEAN). Successful Asian capitalist countries have pursued the legacy of Adam Smith before they have paid any attention to the legacy of either Thomas Jefferson or the Jacobins. An even more dramatic case is that of the People's Republic of China since Mao Tse

Tung's death. The giant of Asia has definitely been moving towards greater economic liberalization, while remaining impeccably opposed to political liberalization. The Tiananmen Square suppression of 1989 was a measure of opposition to political liberalization, but China's commitment to economic liberalization has remained unabated. The Chinese people have a desire for democracy, but not yet the will to force the aging elite to provide it. On the other hand, Mikhail Gorbachev attempted political liberalization (*glasnost*) before any systematic economic liberalization (*perestroika*). The result in the former Soviet Union was rapid political disintegration without meaningful economic transformation. It was not only the Soviet empire of Eastern Europe, which disintegrated in the wake of *glasnost*; it was also the bicontinental body politic of the Soviet Union itself. The Chinese are justified in seeing Gorbachev as the man who destroyed the country that had made him its leader, the former USSR.

In Africa, Ghana has from time to time explicitly faced the dilemma as to which should have first priority: political recovery or economic recovery. Ghana's founder-president, Kwame Nkrumah, opted for the primacy of politics. He declared in the 1950s: "Seek ye first the political kingdom and all else will be added unto you"[46] Did Nkrumah mean that political independence for an African country would bring "all else added unto you?" Or did he mean the liberation of the whole of Africa (including the Republic of South Africa) was a precondition for Africa's "political kingdom?" Or was his concept of "political kingdom" a combination of both Africa's liberation and Africa's unification into a united country on a continental scale? Clearly political independence for individual African countries has never "added all else unto you." For individual African nations, Nkrumah's emphasis on the state as the primary actor in Africa's development has been invalidated.

Thirty years after Nkrumah's dictum of "seek ye first the political kingdom" another Ghanaian leader seemed to have drastically revised the dictum. Flight-Lieutenant Jerry Rawlings' politics from the mid-1980s until 1992 seemed to be based on the dictum: "Seek ye first the economic kingdom and all else will be added unto you." Jerry Rawlings, in spite of left wing rhetoric, submitted his Ghanaian government to the rigors of structural adjustment and related discipline of the World Bank and the International Monetary Fund (IMF). It was not until 1992 that Jerry Rawlings' government—under both domestic and international pressures—at last conceded political democratization. A timetable was more firmly announced for multi-party elections. Political liberalization was at last catching up with economic liberalization in the new Ghana. Was "the economic kingdom" about to demonstrate that it would have "all else added unto you?" At least for Ghana, the question is still wide open.

The fate of both political and economic liberalization hinges on cultural variables that have too often been underestimated. We may need to grasp the cultural dimension before we can fully gauge the scale and durability of social change in Africa. Every constitution needs to be culturally viable. Every development project needs a cultural feasibility study. History does not wait for historians. History has its own momentum. In many African countries, political liberalization has been taking place without either a cultural feasibility study or an economic stock taking. Liberal democratic activism has been under way from Madagascar to Mali, from Marrakesh to Maputo, from Dar es Salaam to Dakar. The scale of activism has varied from country to country, but a liberal, pluralistic contagion has been spreading across the continent. Yet the question persists: Is it only a desire for democracy or is there a real will and capacity to democratize? We pose a wider scenario: "Seek ye first the cultural kingdom and all else will be added unto you." This third scenario requires understanding the cultural pre-conditions of both political will and economic competence. Africa needs planned democracy, preceded by a feasibility study to ascertain the cultural viability of any proposed economic or political system. Slogans like "privatization" and "democratization" need to be accompanied by a cultural manual specific to the society or to the region. Africa's desire for democracy has reached significant proportions. Devising a culturally inspirational agenda for the future may transform that democratic desire into a powerful democratic will.

Conclusion

Colonial rule enclosed together people who previously lived separately and divided people who were once united. Ethnic tensions are conflicts of values. They have also become the greatest threat both to Africa's stability and to African democracy. The answer lies in purposeful national integration and a shared experience in ideas and values. Africa is in search of a creative ideology. When multiple cultures confront each other within the same national boundaries, their relationship can be at varying degrees of social depth. The minimum stage of relationship is that of co-existence, when and where two cultural communities barely know about each other. Each may have its own conservative paradigm of thought, grounded on ethnic exclusivity. Indigenous conservatism can reign supreme at this level. The second degree of relationship is that of contact, when and where two groups either begin to trade with each other, or participate jointly in the job-market, or become members of the same political party, or listen to each other's music. Above all, the contact must include sharing ideas and evolving shared priorities. Traditions of the elder, the warrior, and the sage may interact between ethnic cultures. The third degree of inter-ethnic relationship is that of competition, when and where these contacts result in rivalry for resources, for power, or for social and economic opportunities. Debates about ideology and policy are part policy are part and parcel of this competitive stage of nation building. Capitalism may conflict with socialism in the political arena. The fourth relationship between two ethnic cultures is that of conquest, when and where one of the ideologies or cultures begins to get the upper hand. One ideology, for example, may become more influential than others. Or the newly dominant system of values may successfully claim a disproportionate share of power, resources or socio-economic opportunities. Nepotism could prevail even under socialism. The fifth stage of relationship between cultures is that of compromise, when and where the competing ideologies, political values and traditions find a *modus vivendi*, an acceptable formula of conflict-resolution and a viable basis of social partnership. The sixth stage of relationship is that of coalescence, when and where the values and identities of the political groups begin to merge, and their boundaries become less and less distinct. The cultures, values, ideologies, and even language intermingle and a larger sense of identity starts to emerge. That enlarged identity could be national consciousness. A national ideology may be evolving.

In some African countries, ideological divisions are also affected by race relations and by economic factors. But it should be borne in mind that race and economics are often integrative as well as divisive. The balance varies from society to society. The struggle for national integration and state building in Africa is still in its infancy. Ideological intercourse and cultural interaction are part and parcel of the evolution of dignitarianism, ethnicism, nationhood and the consolidation of collective identity in the post-colonial era.

NOTES

This chapter is a revised version of an earlier paper, presented under the same title, at the Eighth World Congress on Comparative Education, Prague, Czechoslovakia (now Czech Republic), July 8-14, 1992. This essay is greatly indebted to previous joint work and consultations with the late Omari H. Kokole from Uganda, who died in 1996.

1. Indeed, the ethno-religious wars in the Balkans, racial unrest in the United States and Europe, and religious and ethnic conflict in Africa and South Asia, are testimony to the enduring nature of primordial cultural allegiances. On cultural factors' role in world politics, see, for instance, Morris Dickstein, "After the Cold War: Culture as Politics, Politics as Culture," *Social Research* 60 (Fall 1993): 531-544; Kay B. Warren (ed.), *The Violence Within: Cultural and Political Opposition in Divided Nations* (Boulder, CO: Westview Press, 1993); Ali A. Mazrui, *Cultural Forces in World Politics* (London and Portsmouth, NH: J. Currey and Heinemann, 1990); and Emile Sahliye (ed.), *Religious Resurgence and Politics in the Contemporary World* (Albany: SUNY Press, 1990).

2. Ancestor worship is practiced in several different parts of the world, from Asia to South and Central America, not just in Africa; consult, for instance, Kris Jeter, "Ancestor Worship As An Intergenerational Linkage in Perpetuity," *Marriage & Family Review* 16, 1-2 (1991): 195-217, for a cross-cultural study of ancestor worship.

3. See, Kofi A. Busia, *The Position of the Chief in the Modern Political System of Ashanti: A Study of the Influence of Contemporary Social Changes on Ashanti Political Institutions* (London: Frank Cass & Co. Ltd., 1968) and Jomo Kenyatta, *Facing Mount Kenya: The Tribal Life of the Kikuyu* (London: Vintage Books, 1938). Also see, Josiah Mwangi Kariuki, *"Mau Mau" Detainee* (Oxford: Oxford University Press, 1963).

4. Conservatism's meaning, like all ideologies, appears to be different across time and space; consult, for instance, Brian Girvin (ed.), *The Transformation of Contemporary Conservatism* (London and Newbury Park, CA: Sage, 1988)—although it is confined to Europe and North American conservatism—and Roger Scruton, *The Meaning of Conservatism*, 2nd ed. (London: Macmillan, 1984).

5. Consult, for Burkean views on the American Revolution, Edmund Burke, *Speeches on the American War, and Letter to the Sheriffs of Bristol* (Boston: Gregg Press, 1972, [c.1891]). Also refer

to Chapter 13 in this volume entitled "Edmund Burke and Reflections on the Revolution in the Congo."

6. On this kind of governance in Africa, consult A. E. Afigbo, *The Warrant Chiefs: Indirect Rule in Southeastern Nigeria, 1891-1929* (London: Longman, 1972); H. F. Morris, *Indirect Rule and the Search for Justice: Essays in East African Legal History* (Oxford, UK: Clarendon Press, 1972); and Ntieyong Akpan, *Epitaph to Indirect Rule: A Discourse on Local Government in Africa* (London: Cass, 1967).

7. See David Harrison, *The White Tribe of Africa: South Africa in Perspective* (Berkeley and Los Angeles: University of California Press, 1981), especially pp. 84-102.

8. See, for instance, Randall Collins, "Liberals and Conservatives, Religious and Political: A Conjuncture of Modern History," *Sociology of Religion*, 54 (Summer 1993): 127-46.

9. See John Middleton, *Lugbara Religion* (London: Oxford University Press, 1969).

10. John S. Mbiti, *African Religions and Philosophy* (New York and London: Doubleday and Heinemann, 1970).

11. For a collection of essays on Awolowo, see Olosope O. Oyelaran (ed.), *Obafemi Awolowo: The End of an Era?* (Ile-Ife, Nigeria: Obafemi Awolowo University Press Ltd., 1988).

12. For a biography of Odinga, see the series of interviews between him and H. Odera Oruka in H. Odera Oruka, *Oginga Odinga: His Philosophy and Beliefs* (Nairobi: Initiative Publishers, 1992).

13. On the influence of ethnicity on modern African politics, see, for instance, Henry Bienen, Nicolas Van de Walle, and John Londregan, "Ethnicity and Leadership Succession in Africa," *International Studies Quarterly*, 39 (March 1995): 1-25; Julius O. Ihonvberre, "The 'irrelevant' State, Ethnicity, and the Quest for Nationhood in Africa," *Ethnic and Racial Studies* 17 (January 1994): 42-60; and Kenneth Ingham, *Politics in Modern Africa: The Uneven Tribal Dimension* (London and New York: Routledge, 1990).

14. For one report on an instance of conservatism in African politics, see Athumani J. Liviga and Jan Kees van Donge, "The 1985 Tanzanian Parliamentary Elections: A Conservative Election," *African Affairs*, 88 (January 1989): 47-62.

15. See, for example, Kwasi Wiredu, *Philosophy and An African Culture* (Cambridge and New York: Cambridge University Press, 1980), pp. 8-24.

16. For a cross-cultural analysis of the links between age and leadership, consult Angus McIntyre (ed.), *Aging and Political Leadership* (Albany, NY: SUNY Press, 1988); for a specific study see Paul Spencer, *The Samburu: A Study of Gerontocracy in a Nomadic Tribe* (Berkeley: University of California Press, 1965).

17. For this brief definition, we are indebted to the *Dictionary of Anthropology*, edited by Charles Winick (Totavia, New Jersey: Littlefield, Adams and Co., 1966 edition), p. 230.

18. For one of the rare English-language works on Bourguiba, consult Norma Salem, *Habib Bourguiba, Islam and the Creation of Tunisia* (London & Dover, NH: C. Croom Helm, 1984).

19. This formulation is often attributed to Julius K. Nyerere.

20. Consult, on the warrior tradition, Ali A. Mazrui, "The Warrior Tradition and the Masculinity of War," *Journal of Asian and African Studies*, 12, 1-4 (Jan-Oct 1977), pp. 69-81 and Ali A. Mazrui (ed.), *The Warrior Tradition in Modern Africa* (The Hague and Leiden, The Netherlands: E. J. Brill, 1978).

21. For those who are interested in reading more about Uganda under Idi Amin, a useful guide may be Martin Jamison, *Idi Amin and Uganda: An Annotated Bibliography* (Westport, CT: Greenwood Press, 1992); for an early treatment, see James H. Mittelman, *Ideology and Politics in Uganda: From Obote to Amin* (Ithaca, NY: Cornell University Press, 1975).

22. One of the foremost experts on China and Mao is the Australian Ross Terrill; for an accessible account of the "Great Helmsman," see Terrill, *Mao: A Biography* (New York: Harper & Row, 1980).

23. See the periodical published by the Eastern African Centre for Research on Oral Traditions and African National Languages and the International Fund for the Promotion of Culture, *Studies and Documents* (EACROTANAL, 1980).

24. For a recent biography of Nasser, consult Peter Woodward (London and New York: Longman, 1992); generally, on Nasser and Egypt, see P. J. Vatikiotis, *Nasser and His Generation* (New York: St. Martin's Press, 1978), and R. Hrair Dekmejian,

Egypt Under Nasir: A Study in Political Dynamics (Albany, NY: SUNY Press, 1971).

25. Consult, on this subject, James S. Coleman, *Political Parties and National Integration in Tropical Africa* (Berkeley: University of California Press, 1964).

26. Information on these parties in Tanzania, and other political parties in Africa may be obtained in Roger East and Tanya Joseph (eds.), *Political Parties of Africa and the Middle East: A Reference guide* (Harlow, UK and Detroit, MI: Longman and Gale Research, 1993).

27. On the spread of corruption, see, for instance, Robert Williams, *Political Corruption in Africa* (Aldershot, UK and Brookfield, VT: Gower Pub., 1987).

28. His Excellency, Al-Hajj, Dr. Field Marshall Idi Amin Dada, VC, DSO, MC, and Conqueror of the British Empire.

29. For an earlier treatment of this royal theme, consult Ali A. Mazrui, "The Monarchical Tendency in African Political Culture," *The British Journal of Sociology*, Vol. XVIII, No. 3, Sept. 1967. Reprinted as chapter 10 in Mazrui, *Violence and Thought: Essays on Social Tensions in Africa* (London and Harlow: Longmans, 1969), pp. 206-230.

30. These frequently quoted remarks were made in a broadcast on British television in 1968. They were part of the first lecture in a series on *The Rise of Christian Europe* by Sir High Trevor-Roper reprinted in *The Listener* (London): 28 November 1968, p. 811.

31. See Guy Martin, "Francophone Africa in the Context of Franco-American Relations" in John W. Harbeson and Donald Rothchild (eds.), *Africa in World Politics: Post-Cold War Challenges* (Boulder, CO and Oxford: Westview Press, 1995) pp. 163-188.

32. Some of the earlier discussions of nationalism as a theoretical concept may be found in Louis Leo Snyder, *The Meaning of Nationalism* (New York: Greenwood Press, 1968) and Hans Kohn, *Nationalism, Its Meaning and History* (Princeton: Van Nostrand, 1965); for recent treatments, see, for instance, Ernest Gellner, *Encounters with Nationalism* (Oxford, UK, and Cambridge, MA: Blackwell, 1994); John Breuilly, *Nationalism and the State*, Rev. ed. (Chicago: University of Chicago Press, 1994); Liah

Greenfeld, *Nationalism: Five Roads to Modernity* (Cambridge, MA: Harvard University Press, 1992); and Anthony H. Birch, *Nationalism and National Integration* (London and Boston: Unwin Hyman, 1989); and for a postmodern view, see Lewis D. Wurgraft, "Identity in World History: A Postmodern Perspective," *History and Theory* 34, 2 (1995): 67-85.

33. On these connections, see, for example, Colin H. Williams, *Called Unto Liberty! On Language and Nationalism* (Clevedon and Philadelphia: Multilingual Matters, 1994).

34. A recent historical treatment on Québec's separatist movements is Guy Laforest, *Trudeau and the End of A Canadian Dream* (Montréal: McGill-Queen's University Press, 1995). In October 1995, the Québec separatists were narrowly defeated in a referendum.

35. Relatedly, consult Mark Juergensmyer, *The New Cold War? Religious Nationalism Confronts the Secular State* (Berkeley: University of California Press, 1993); and John Langan, "Notes on Moral Theology, 1994: Nationalism, Ethnic Conflict, and Religion," *Theological Studies* 56 (March 1995): 122-136.

36. Consult Michael Barthrop, *War on the Nile: Britain, Egypt and the Sudan, 1882-1898* (Poole, UK: Blandford Press, 1984).

37. Belief in specially sanctified water is by no means peculiar to indigenous African religions. In Islam there is the Zam water of the well of Medina. In Christianity there is the holy water of Lourdes and the legacy of Saint Bernadette in France. This is quite apart from the Christian doctrine of sanctified water or baptismal water at christening.

38. Readers interested in Pan-Africanism's history might find the following useful: P. O. Esedebe, *Pan-Africanism: The Idea and Movement, 1776-1991* (Washington, DC: Howard University Press, 1994); Imanuel Geiss, *The Pan-African Movement: A History of Pan-Africanism in America, Europe, and Africa* (New York: Africana Pub. Co., 1974); and Adekunle Ajala, *Pan-Africanism: Evolution, Progress, and Prospects* (New York: St. Martin's Press, 1973).

39. This inevitably has its effect on internal and external politics; see Tukumbi Lumumba-Kasongo, *Political Re-mapping of Africa: Transnational Ideology and the Re-definition of Africa*

in *World Politics* (Lanham, MD: University Press of America, 1994) and *Nationalistic Ideologies: Their Policy Implications and the Struggle for Democracy in African Politics* (Lewiston, NY: E. Mellen Press, 1991).

40. The following may be consulted on the Mau Mau revolt: Wunyabari O. Maloba, *Mau Mau and Kenya: An Analysis of A Peasant Revolt* (Bloomington, IN: Indiana University Press, 1993); Robert B. Edgerton, *Mau Mau: An African Crucible* (New York and London: Free Press and Collier Macmillan, 1989); and David Throup, *Economic & Social Origins of Mau Mau, 1945-53* (London and Athens, OH: J. Currey and Ohio University Press, 1987).

41. This has of course led to a lasting problem in modern African nations' political integration. Consult, for instance, Kenneth Ingham, *Politics in Africa: The Uneven Tribal Dimension* (London and New York: Routledge, 1990); Donald Rothchild and Victor A. Olorunsola, *State Versus Ethnic Claims: African Policy Dilemmas* (Boulder, CO: Westview Press, 1983); and John N. Paden (ed.), *Values, Identities, and National Integration: Empirical Research in Africa* (Evanston, IL: Northwestern University Press, 1980).

42. Some alternatives to structural adjustment have been explored; see, for example, Kidane Mengisteab and B. Ikubolajeh Logan, *Beyond Economic Liberalization in Africa: Structural Adjustment and the Alternatives* (London; Atlantic Highlands, NJ; and Cape Town: Zed Books and Southern African Political Economic Series, 1995); for a World Bank view on adjustment, see its *Adjustment in Africa: Reform, Results, and the Road Ahead* (Washington, DC: World Bank, 1994).

43. See, Kwame Nkrumah, *Neo-Colonialism: The Last Stage of Imperialism* (London: Heinemann, 1968).

44. See, for instance, Julius K. Nyerere, *Ujaama:Essays on Socialism* (Dar es Salaam, Tanzania: Oxford University Press, 1968) and L. S. Senghor, *On African Socialism*, trans. and introduced by Mercer Cook (New York: Praeger, 1964).

45. See, for example Naomi Chazan et al, *Politics and Society in Contemporary Africa* (Boulder, CO: Lynne Rienner, 1988), especially pp. 101-125.

46. See Kwame Nkrumah, *Ghana: The Autobiography of Kwame Nkrumah* (New York: International Publishers, 1957), p. 164.

THREE

AFRICA IN THE SHADOW OF A CLASH OF CIVILIZATIONS
FROM THE COLD WAR OF IDEOLOGY TO THE COLD WAR OF RACE (2000)

In discussing the clash of civilizations in the new millennium, there is a risk of mistaking symptoms of the disease for the disease itself. The deadly conflict in the year 2000 between Muslims and Christians in Kaduna, Nigeria, is a symptom of the disease. The genocide perpetrated by the Hutu against the Tutsi in Rwanda in 1994 was a symptom of the disease. The rival African armies shooting at each other in the Democratic Republic of Congo in the new millennium are also symptoms. The disease is Africa being at the bottom of the global heap, with the Western world at the top. Africa has the largest percentage of poor people, the largest number of low income countries, the least developed economies, the lowest life expectancy, the most fragile political systems, and is the most vulnerable continent to HIV and AIDS (whatever relationship there might be between HIV and the collapse of immunity systems in Africa). The Western world, on the other hand, is triumphant at the top of the global caste system. What is more, the Western world created the international caste system that reduced Africans to the "Untouchables" or Harijans of global injustice. Africa has mineral wealth that is exploited for the benefit of others, fertile land that is under cultivated, rich cultures that are being destroyed, and brain power that is being "drained" to other parts of the world. At the centre of this calamity is the role of the West in creating an international system that reduced proud Africans to the lowest caste of the twentieth century. How will Africans get out of this condition in the twenty-first century?

Partly because of Africa's history and the experience of Black people generally, African perspectives on global security have been strongly influenced by fear of enslavement, imperialism, and suspicion of racism in the world-system. There is a sense in which the African paradigm of the world-system is race-centric, identifying race and ethnicity as major definers of identities and major stimuli behind group behaviour. Starting from those premises there is a school of thought that sees a new Cold War of race replacing the Cold War of ideology. This does not mean that there were no racial divisions in the world-system before the collapse of the Warsaw Pact and the dissolution of the Soviet Union.[1] It simply means a new realignment of racial forces is now identifiable on the world scene. W.E.B. DuBois, the African-American crusader against racism, stated quite early in the twentieth century that the central issue of the century was going to be "the problem of the color line."

Where do we stand now as the century comes to a close? This paper will first put forward the historical case for a racial paradigm of world order. Has modern history consisted of waves of racio-cultural confrontations? The racial paradigm of world order will be related to the Huntingtonian debate about the clash of civilizations, examining the convergence and divergence between the two approaches. We shall then address Africa's preferred world of security, a regional capacity for peacekeeping (regional self-reliance) and a global agenda of interdependence. But given that this paper is especially focused on the racial paradigm of world order, we shall address the often neglected aspect of African economic aspirations—a Marshall Plan for Africa, which needs to be launched partly in response to the imperative of reparations for hundreds of years of damage to the African people. The case for Africa's Marshall Plan is not charity, but compensation for past and continuing damage to the African peoples in the history of boundaries of exploitation.[2]

Between Culture and Race

In 1993, Samuel Huntington of Harvard University sparked off an international debate with an article about the cultural consequences of the end of the Cold War. In the influential American journal *Foreign Affairs*, Huntington argued that conflicts after the Cold War would be less and less between states and ideological blocs and more and more between civilizations and coalitions of cultures. A few major issues arise with regard to Samuel P. Huntington's original formulation of his thesis about a clash of civilizations.[3] Is there a factual fallacy at the basis of Huntington's formulations? Conceivably, it may not be factually true that the main lines of conflict of the future following the Cold War will be lines of clash among civilizations. Conflicts could arise among states or economic blocs. Can one find a conceptual fallacy in what Professor Huntington puts forward? Could what he identifies as "civilization" be something else? Huntington himself asks "if not civilization the what?"[4] Could what he describe as a clash of civilizations be the third stage of racial conflicts in world history?

We may have to confront the role of racism in world affairs. If so, this is the third round of racial devastation. The first round of modern racial catastrophes led to genocide in the Americas and the trans-Atlantic slave trade.[5] This was the era of the West on the ascendancy. The second round of modern racial catastrophes was the period of colonialism and imperialism. This was the era of the West triumphant:

from the Berlin conference, where Africa was divided up,[6] to the emergence and consolidation of Western-dominated international financial institutions. Both these rounds were hot wars of race, rather than cold wars. As for what is now unfolding, it could be the third round of modern racial catastrophes. It is the period of the racism inherent in the marginalization of the weakest (like Rwandans, people of Gaza, and the Black underclass in the USA); the racism inherent in military containment of the darker races (nuclear whites YES; nuclear non-whites NO); and the racism inherent in the creation of a global economic pyramid with the West at the top and Africa at the bottom. This would be the era of the West in hegemony.

Where people share culture but not race, is race more salient? Are Filipino Catholics that much closer to Italian Catholics across the racial divide? Jamaicans may have more in common with white Americans than do white East Europeans. Do white Americans nevertheless feel more at home with Hungarians than with Jamaicans? Indeed, is the race of Samuel P. Huntington itself one of the factors that lie behind the extraordinary impact of his article worldwide? Is there an African American scholar who could write an article in the same magazine, *Foreign Affairs*, and have the same kind of impact worldwide? Was it enough that Huntington was personally distinguished and based at Harvard? Was it not also relevant that Huntington was a member of the white establishment? Huntington has since developed his thesis more extensively in a book.[7] Is the relevant twinning that of concepts civilization plus ethnicity (Huntington) or that of race plus ethnicity?

Does Huntington's thesis also suffer from a temporal fallacy? Even if we do have to be concerned about clashes of civilizations, are we talking about what is coming, or what was in the past, or what has always been there? Have clashes of civilizations been more the rule than the exception in the last four hundred years? For the 20th century, the great African-American macro-sociologist W.E.B. DuBois did indeed prophesy a recurrent problem of what he called the color-line. For the 21st century, Huntington is prophesying a recurrent problem of what might be called the culture-line. It is important to ask whether the color-line is fundamentally different from the culture-line. Could a "clash of civilizations" be a euphemism for a "clash of the races"—in its third round? At a more practical level, DuBois's concept of the color-line is now captured in the concept of an emerging "global apartheid" following the end of the Cold War.[8] With the big ideological divide in the white world ending, is there a new racial realignment on the world stage—the White races at the top, the Yellow races of Confucian East Asia and South-East Asia second, the Brown races of South Asia next, Latin Americans and the Arabs fourth, and the Blacks last? Is it really a clash of civilizations to which we are headed or a third round of a clash of the races? Or is the difference in perception itself culturally determined? Perhaps the worst mistake which Huntington made in his 1993 article was in assuming that the clash of civilizations lay in the future when it had, in fact, been generating tensions between Europe and the rest of the world for at least four to five hundred years. The clash of civilizations had produced not just the Crusades of nine centuries ago but, combined with racism, it has also generated the more recent trans-Atlantic slave trade and the European colonization of much of the world.

Clash of Civilizations as the Norm

The true picture is therefore as follows: the West has been a cultural aggressor against other races and civilizations for hundreds of years. This has been the norm rather than the exception. But the West was often inspired by a racial paradigm. In the Americas, this resulted in the wanton destruction of Native American civilizations—north, south, and center—by war, by bacteriological genocide and by cultural erosion.[9] In Africa, the West's cultural aggression and racial arrogance produced the most extensive slave trade in human history: the trans-Atlantic slave trade. Western consumption patterns, Western production techniques, Western definitions of racial identities, and a new stratification were all at play. Black African slaves were preferred to Native American slaves because the white man had concluded that Black culture had a higher work ethic than "Indian" culture. Blacks could be made to work harder without collapsing. In Africa, Asia, Latin America and the Caribbean the West's cultural aggression and racial paradigm had later resulted also in imperialism and colonization. Imperialism and colonialism forcefully modified the perceptions, standards of judgment, springs of motivation, bases of stratification, modes of communication, and the very identities of subject peoples as well as their means of production and patterns of consumption. Quite often, all these seven functions of culture were turned upside down by racism, being imperialist or colonialist.

Then three intra-civilizational wars in the Western world began to break the spell at long last. There was the First World War that was a civil war within Western civilization. The First World War helped to perpetuate the intra-civilizational conflict both from the left (with the Russian Revolution of 1917) and from the right (with the humiliating Treaty of Versailles which aroused German Nazism). World War II played a more significant role in weakening Europe's hold on its empires. While the Second World War destroyed Europe, it liberated Asia and Africa. The war helped to stimulate anti-colonial movements more speedily than would otherwise have been the case. And the impact of the war on the European imperial powers speeded up the actual attainment of independence for Africa. The third intra-civilizational war was the Cold War from the late 1940s until the late 1980s. It was a Cold War between Eastern European governments led by the Soviet Union and mainly Western European governments led by the United States. The Cold

War was a conflict between primarily white countries whose populations were brought up primarily in the Euro-Christian tradition. One side said it was Marxist and the other side said it was capitalist and democratic, but in the final analysis, the Cold War was a conflict between white folks at different stages of secularization from Christianity.[10]

It is said that the word "slave" originates from the word "Slav." In the 20th century, the Slavs were allies in the crusade for the most enslaved race in modern history: the Africans. The Cold War, while it was indeed an intra-civilizational war, was a real truce in the war between North-South civilizations. White Russians armed black liberation fighters against white minority governments. White Soviet pilots helped Egyptian nationalists run the Suez Canal in the face of white European hostility towards Egypt. Many of the conflicts during the Cold War were not between civilizations in the North-South sense, but within the Northern civilization itself. Briefly, the Slavs helped to arm those who had once been targeted as slaves. The liberation of Southern Africa might have been delayed by another generation without Soviet and Warsaw Pact arms to liberation fighters in Zimbabwe, Angola, Mozambique, Namibia and South Africa. The Cold War between ideologies was at least a cold truce between civilizations. Now that the ideological Cold War is over, is Huntington right that we are heading back for a "Clash of Civilizations" or are we witnessing the coming of "Global Apartheid"? The European Union is opening its doors to a wider white solidarity with the North Atlantic Treaty Organization (NATO) becoming the most powerful alliance of the white world. Racism is rising in Europe, affirmative action is under attack in the United States, and Africa is getting more deeply marginalized than ever. This may not be a hot war of race this time around, but is it a cold war of race? Doors of political asylum in the West for Blacks, Asians and other people of color are closing.

In the context of this cold war of race, we still have to face the challenge of creating a world with greater military and economic security for the most vulnerable. Militarily Africa would be best off in a world in which regions were, on the whole, enabled to develop their own peace-keeping and peace-enforcing capabilities. The United Nations would come in only if things got out of hand in a region. For Africa this would be a policy of *Pax Africana*. The intrusion of other races and other states in African affairs would be reduced. On the other hand, the optimum policy economically for Africa would not be simply regional self-reliance (as in military matters) but global interdependence (by the yardstick of enlightened human solidarity).

Culture Conflicts Among Africans

In regional military security, a start has been towards *Pax-Africana*. Stronger African states have started policies of benevolent intervention in weaker states that are in trouble. If critics of Pan-Africanism have not recognized the trend in the role of Uganda and Rwanda in the overthrow of the Mobutu regime in Zaire (now Congo), those critics have been less than fully alert. We shall return to this *Pax Africana* theme more fully later but first, let us examine whether there are clashes of civilizations between Africans themselves regardless of external influence. One ancient divide among Africans is between lovers of land and lovers of animals. African lovers of land are cultivators; African lovers of animals (cattle, camels, and horses) are pastoralists. Lovers of land are invariably settled in agriculture; lovers of animals may be nomadic.

At their most elaborate, lovers of land build states; lovers of animals are often stateless. Nevertheless, pastoralist Fulani (lovers of animals) conquered cultivating Hausa (lovers of land) and created a new empire of the Hausa-Fulani. Similarly, pastoralist Tutsi (lovers of animals) conquered cultivating Hutu (lovers of land) and created Ruanda-Urundi (today's Rwanda and Burundi). Lovers of land (cultivators), including the Yoruba and the Igbo, converted early to the exchange economy and acquired leadership in the cash economy. Should lovers of animals (pastoralists) convert to the cash economy directly or should they first become lovers of land? It is arguable that the Hausa-Fulani were left behind in the Nigerian economy less because they were Muslim and more because the dominant Fulani value-system was historically descended from valuing animals (cattle and horses) rather than valuing land and extensive cultivation. It is also arguable that the Hausa-Fulani elite tried to take a shortcut to the cash economy without a prior conversion to loving the soil. With regard to the Tutsi in the Great Lakes region in the 1990s, they took a shortcut to territorial ambitions rather than to the cash economy. In 1986, Yoweri Museveni, descended from the Tutsi culture of loving animals, captured power in Uganda. He helped to train the Tutsi of Rwanda who also descended from lovers of animals. In 1994, the Ugandan-trained Rwandan Patriotic Front crossed the border into Rwanda, ended the anti-Tutsi genocide, and established a new Tutsi-led regime.[11] In the Democratic Republic of Congo in the year 2000, soldiers who were descendents from lovers of animals—from Rwanda, Congo and Uganda—fought soldiers who were descendents from lovers of land—from Congo, Zimbabwe and Angola. And within Zimbabwe, black lovers of land turned upon white lovers of land in a historic struggle for land ownership and legitimacy—although there were some suggestions that these struggles were linked to Prime Minister Robert Mugabe's electoral troubles.[12]

Throughout Africa, pastoralists (or lovers of land) are on the defensive. The great majority of Africans are cultivators; but the majority of the pastoralists of the world are in Africa. The pastures for the pastoralists have been shrinking rapidly and their way of life is being decimated by the encroachments of the cultivators, the cash economy, and Westernization. "If you cannot beat them, should you join them?" The Hausa-Fulani tried a shortcut to the cash economy without adequate roots in the soil of entrepreneurship. The Tutsi have tried a shortcut to the territorial imperative without adequate tutelage in the cash economy. Their respective struggles have been inconclusive. Africans who are cultivators have responded faster to capitalism and Westernization. The cultivating Kikuyu have got more rapidly westernized than the pastoralist Maasai. The Yoruba and Igbo have moved faster towards Adam Smith, Keynes and Western education than have the Hausa-Fulani elites. Whether getting westernized faster, or getting deeper into capitalism, is a good thing for Africa is a matter for further cost-benefit analysis. While lovers of animals may be struggling to learn the culture of loving the soil, lovers of land are rapidly moving towards the stage of loving hard income. While animal-lovers are becoming engaged in shy land-flirtations, are land-lovers engaged in naked cash-romance in the new Africa? Colonialism had distorted African priorities, and created silent clashes of civilization among Africans themselves.

Who is to keep the peace when conflicts break out among Africans themselves, be it pastoralists against cultivators or across some other divide? Africans are now beginning to assert control over their unruly neighbours and to establish some kind of regional security: from Uganda's assistance of the Tutsi in reasserting control over Rwanda in 1994, to the support of Laurent Kabila's overthrow of Mobutu in the Democratic Republic of Congo (formerly Zaire) in 1997, to the role of ECOMOG in ending the Liberian civil war and to the Nigerian army intervention in Sierra Leone, both in 1997. The idea of creating a Pan African emergency force is also gathering momentum since the 1990s. The British-sponsored Blue Eagle Project in Southern Africa involved training the troops of at least eight African countries to be in readiness for special responsibilities in situations of political crisis. Much of the training occurred in Zimbabwe. The Blue

Eagle could develop into the ECOMOG of Southern Africa, but with more appropriate training for a peacekeeping role. The Clinton Administration in the United States championed a rapid crisis response African force. It has also been involved in training troops from countries like Sénégal and Uganda for peacekeeping roles. I believe that the Pan African Emergency force should be accountable to Africa itself—and not to the Security Council of the United Nations as preferred by the United States—through such revised institutions of the OAU as Africa may be able to devise. Alternatively, accountability should be towards relevant sub-regional organizations in Africa: to ECOWAS in West Africa, to SADC in Southern Africa, and to a newly evolving Eastern Africa Community. Only such an Afro-centered accountability would save *Pax Africana* from becoming a mere extension of *Pax Americana*.

While militarily Africa needs regional peacekeeping and self-reliance, economically Africa needs enlightened global interdependence: trade, investment and aid are familiar issues. In the context of the racial paradigm of world order, however, one additional economic issue needs to be addressed. Is there a debt of compensation that the Western world owes to the African peoples for some of those earlier waves of racial confrontations, especially the wave of the Atlantic slave trade and the wave of European imperialism? The year 1997 was distinctive for race-relations in the United States partly because, for the first time, the issue of a white apology for Black enslavement was discussed as an idea at the highest level. In his tour of Africa in 1998, President Clinton came quite close to apologising for the trans-Atlantic slavery. But the issue of apology and reparations is not only a matter for African-Americans; it concerns Global Africa as a whole. We define "Global Africa" as the continent of Africa plus, firstly, the Diaspora of enslavement (descendants of survivors of the Middle passage) and secondly, the Diaspora of colonialism (the dispersal of Africans which continues to occur as a result of disruptions of colonization and its after-math).

Reparations: An African Marshall Aid

While the abolitionist movement in the 18th and 19th centuries was mainly inspired by benevolent changes in the Western world, the reparationist movement in the 20th century has been partly inspired by malevolent continuities in the Black world. The benevolent changes in the West, which had once favoured the abolitionist movement, were partly technological and partly socio-normative. Innovations like the cotton gin made slave labour less and less necessary and less efficient for Western capitalism. The abolitionist movement found a more responsive political establishment as slave-labour became technologically more anachronistic.[13] In addition, the values of the Western world were in any case getting more liberalized in other fields—such as the extension of the franchise to the working classes in the nineteenth century, and the beginnings of movements for women's rights. The convergence of more efficient technologies and a more liberal ideology helped to boost the abolitionist movement in Europe and the Americas. These were the benevolent changes in the West whose cumulative impact favoured the abolition of the slave trade and subsequently of slavery itself. Even the political emancipation of Roman Catholics in Britain was a cause that William Wilberforce championed just a decade before he was converted to the more radical cause of abolishing the slave trade and slavery.[14] The consequences of colonization are not merely research topics for scholars, but are also horrendous civil wars and a normative collapse in places like Liberia, Angola and Somalia. Here are the malevolent continuities of colonialism. The consequences of both enslavement and colonization are not merely themes for plenary lectures at African Studies conventions, but are also the malfunctioning colonial economies in Africa and the distorted socio-economic relations in the African Diaspora.

On the other hand, the inspiration behind the reparation movement was not change but continuity. It was the persistence of deprivation and anguish in the Black world arising directly out of the legacies of slavery and colonialism. The consequences of enslavement and colonization are not chapters in history books but pangs of pain in the ghettoes of Washington, D.C., and the anti-Black police brutalities in the streets of Los Angeles, Rio de Janeiro, London, and Paris. These are some of the malevolent continuities of racism. While the most historically visible heroes of the abolitionist movement were disproportionately white, the emerging visible heroes of the reparationist movement are disproportionately Black.[15] Perhaps one of the more basic cultural returns to the past concerns the issue of collective compensation. In ancient times, if a member of one tribe was killed by a member of another tribe, a debt was immediately created, owed by the tribe of the killer to the tribe of the victim. This debt was not subject to any statute of limitation. The debt stood until it was paid. It could be paid with heads of cattle—or with blood. If the debt was not paid, there was a serious risk of a long festering feud between the two tribes. Because responsibility was collective, individuals in each community could be unnecessarily at risk for a killing for which they were themselves not directly responsible—they were indirectly culturally responsible. The civilized way out was to pay the debt in cows and goats. In other words, the civilized response was to pay reparations. This whole issue of reparations has, as we indicated, re-emerged in Black politics in both Africa and the United States: these reparations are for hundred of years of Black enslavement, colonization, and racial victimization. A debt is outstanding between the West and the Black world, a debt that is not subject to statutes of limitations.

We do believe that the damage done to Black people is not a thing of the past, but is here and now. It lies in the disproportionate Black faces in the jails of America, the disproportionate Black infant mortality rates in the United States, and the ease with which a Black man in police custody in London (like a certain Mr. Lumumba) or in Paris (like a 17 year old Zairean boy) can get killed by the police. It lies in the cheapness of Black lives from the sadistic streets of Rio de Janeiro to the masochistic streets of Soweto in South Africa. The damage is here; and the debt has not yet been paid. And the debt is not just moral but also economic.[16] How are the reparations to be paid? There are at least three alternative modes—modern versions of ancient heads of cattle from one tribe to another:

a) Capital transfer from the West to the Black world—comparable to the grand precedent of the Marshall Plan to Europe.

b) Skills transfer in the form of a major international effort to help build the capacities and skills of Africa and the rest of the Black world.

c) Power-sharing by enabling Africa to have a greater say in global institutions, such as having more effective representation in decision-making in the World Bank and the International Monetary Fund, not because Africa is rich but because it has been systematically enfeebled. Furthermore, why should all the permanent seats of the United Nations Security Council be given to countries that are already powerful outside the UN? Is there not a case for giving Africa a permanent seat with a veto, not because Africa is powerful but because it has been rendered powerless across generations?

In the 1960s, the United States invented the concept of affirmative action, an effort to make allowances for historic disabilities whenever minorities applied for jobs or sought other opportunities. It was a progressive step towards racial equity and socio-economic justice. We now need to make a transition from affirmative action to a more comprehensive redeeming action in the form of reparations. It is in fact the logical next step after affirmative action. Conservatives believe that the next step after affirmative action should be a free play of market forces. But the bondage of history and residual racism impede market autonomy. We have to move beyond affirmative action to the redeeming action of Black peoples the world over. There is a primordial debt to be paid to Black peoples for hundreds of years of enslavement and degradation. Some of the causes of global apartheid lie deep in that history. It may take a generation to win the crusade for reparations but a start has to be made. This will be one. more aspect of reverse evolution back to ancient ways of settling moral debts between tribes. The damage is here. It is time to mend.

Conclusion

Partly because African history and the Black experience were profoundly affected by racism and imperialism, African perspectives on the world-system are influenced by a fear of imperialism and a profound suspicion of racism. The paper has tried to indicate how this has given rise to a race-centric worldview and a racial paradigm of world order. Western racism had reduced Africans to the untouchable caste. In the African experience, as in the Irish experience, the past is part and parcel of the present. The day-before-yesterday is part of today. Samuel Huntington is wrong in affirming that the clash of civilizations is something to confront after the end of the Cold War. The Western world has made sure there have been clashes of civilizations for the last four hundred years, inspired by Western racism.

We have identified the following waves: the first wave

of racio-cultural confrontation involved the peopling of the Americas in a manner that required large-scale decimation of Native American populations, followed by the trans-Atlantic slave trade resulting in the enslavement and export of millions of Africans to the so-called New World. For many Africans, this awful past lives on in the present. This history has been an impediment to Black military and economic security. The second wave of racio-cultural confrontation involved Europe's colonization of much of the rest of the world: Asia, Africa, Latin America and the islands of the sea. This was the era of the West triumphant. The colonial past is central to the post-colonial present. Once again history is an impediment to economic and military security. The third wave of racio-cultural confrontation is the present one of military discrimination and economic stratification. In this arrangement, white countries may have nuclear weapons but darker races should be stopped from acquiring them. Israel may have weapons of mass destruction but Muslims in the Middle East may not. The United States may use chemical weapons and napalm against Vietnam and use nuclear weapons against Japan in World War II but Middle Eastern countries may not develop either weapons. The greatest economic victims of the new racial Cold War are Black people; the greatest military victims are Muslims. More than a million Muslims have been killed by Westerners since 1980. These have been Iraqis, Lebanese, Palestinians, Iranians, Libyans. Many Iraqi babies were killed by the Anglo-American sanctions.

Curiously enough, the two world wars of the twentieth century were initially intra-civilizational, starting as European civil wars. But they coincided with a period of history when Europe was calling the tune in most of the rest of the world. In reality two factors turned European civil wars into world wars: the involvement of European empires and the co-optation of the United States. But for Africa, World War II was also a positive development. It weakened the European powers, stimulated anti-colonialism and set the stage for genuine decolonization and independence. For Africa, World War II was, on balance, a liberating experience—terrible as it was for Europe and parts of Asia. The Cold War was also liberating and a trans-racializing experience. White Russians were supporting black liberation movements against white minority governments in Southern Africa. Karl Marx and V.I. Lenin, two white men, were the icons of millions of people of color. Oppression and liberation were deemed to be race-neutral. The liberation of Portuguese Africa and Southern Africa might have been delayed for a generation if there had been no armed struggle. And armed struggle was made possible by an alliance between Black nationalist fighters and white socialist governments who provided them with arms. The Chinese were also major allies of Black liberation fighters in Southern Africa. Yes, the Cold War was a trans-racializing experience.

The end of the Cold War has threatened those trans-racializing tendencies. Russia is too weak to be a major player in North-South relations. Western moral commitment to Africa has drastically slackened. Racism has increased in Western Europe and has re-emerged in Eastern and Central Europe. Affirmative action and other civil rights gains are under threat in the United States. The shadow of global apartheid hangs over the world-system with a structure in the form of a racial pyramid with white-ruled countries at the top and Blacks at the bottom. And yet the solution preferred by Africa is not "leave us alone!" The solution has three parts. To avoid further imperialism from outside, Africa should police itself more efficiently. A system of *Pax Africana* needs to be developed with stronger African states coming to the rescue of weaker ones. This involves partial racial sovereignty as a principle. Therefore, on the issue of military security, the preferred option is regional self-reliance. On the issue of economic security, Africa has to sell its minerals and its agricultural products. It does not want to opt out of the world economy. It simply wants a fairer basis for global economic interdependence. If a motto was needed for this strategy for Africa, it would be "Military Regionalism and Economic Globalism." On the whole, regions should sort out their own military problems at the regional level. Lovers of land should learn to love lovers of animals—and vice versa. But in economics, the scale has to be global.

On the issue of racial rehabilitation, Africa demands compensation for hundreds of years of enslavement, exploitation, especially because: 1) Jews were compensated for the Holocaust; 2) Japanese internees in World War II in the US were compensated; 3) Kuwait was compensated for Iraq's invasion; 4) steps towards making it up to the Aborigines of Australia are beginning to be taken. The options for reparations include the following: capital transfer (like the Marshall Plan); skills transfer (to transform the educational and skill capacities of the Black people); and power-sharing (giving Africa access to such citadels as permanent membership of the Security Council, weighted membership on governing bodies of the World Bank and the International Monetary Fund and the like). If we are building tribunals to try Africans in Sierra Leone and Rwanda for atrocities and crimes against humanity today, we should also construct financial courts to extract reparations from slaving nations and imperial powers of yesterday. Today's offenders against humanity deserve to be dragged before international tribunals for trial and punishment; yesterday's slaving and imperial offenders against humanity should be made at least financially accountable. The past is now and it casts a shadow on perspectives of world security and on the search for enduring solutions.

NOTES

This chapter is a revised version of a presentation made under the auspices of the Center for Black African Arts and Civilization, Abuja, Nigeria, on June 22, 2000.

1. In 1977, I had begun drawing the importance of these racial boundaries. See, for example, Ali A. Mazrui, *Africa's International Relations: The Diplomacy of Dependency and Change* (London: Heinemann, and Boulder: Westview Press, 1977), pp. 7-8.

2. Various economic and political studies have been done on Black reparations. See, for example, Clarence J. Mumford, *Race and Reparations: A Black Perspective for the 21st Century* (Trenton, NJ: Africa World Press, 1996) and Robert S. Browne, "The Economic Basis for Reparations to Black America," in *The Review of Black Political Economy* 21 (Winter 1993), pp. 99-110.

3. Samuel P. Huntington, "The Clash of Civilizations" in *Foreign Affairs* Volume 72, Number 3 (Summer 1993), pp. 23-49.

4. Samuel P. Huntington, "If Not Civilizations What?" in *Foreign Affairs* Volume 72, Number 5 (November/December 1993), pp. 186-194.

5. For one study of the impacts, see Joseph E. Inikori and Stanley L. Engerman (eds.), *The Atlantic Slave Trade: Effects on Economies and peoples in Africa, the Americas and Europe* (Durham, NC: Duke University Press, 1994). For the connection between slavery and capitalism, consult Barbara Solow, "Capitalism and Slavery in the Exceedingly Long Run," in *Journal of Interdisciplinary History* 17 (Spring 1987), pp. 711-737.

6. On the Berlin conference and the colonization of Africa, see R. J. Gavin and J. A. Bentley (comp. eds.), *The Scramble for Africa: Documents on the Berlin West African Conference and Related Subjects, 1884-1885* (Ibadan, Nigeria: Ibadan University Press, 1973).

7. Samuel P. Huntington, *The Clash of Civilizations and the Remaking of World Order* (New York: Touchtsone, 1997).

8. I have expanded on this argument in "Global Apartheid: Race and Religion in the New World Order," in Tareq Ishmael and Jacqueline Ishmael (eds.), *The Gulf War and the New World Order: International Relations of the Middle East* (Gainesville, FL: University Press of Florida, 1994), pp. 521-535, reproduced below, with revisions, as Chapter 10.

9. Some have termed this a "holocaust." See David E. Stannard, *American Holocaust: Columbus and the Conquest of the New World* (New York: Cambridge University Press, 1992).

10. For an overview of the Cold War, consult Michael Kort, *The Columbia Guide to the Cold War* (New York: Columbia University Press, 1998).

11. For articles on the Rwanda crisis, see *Africa Today*, Volume 45, Number 1 (January 1998), pp. 3-61.

12. See *The New York Times* (April 20, 2000), p. 5.

13. An overview of the Abolitionist movement may be found in David Eltis and James Walvin (eds.), *The Abolition of the Atlantic Slave Trade: Origins and Effects in Europe, Africa and the Americas* (Madison, WI: University of Wisconsin Press, 1981).

14. For a biography, see Oliver Warner, *William Wilberforce and His Times* (New York: Arco Pub. Co., 1963).

15. Among African Americans, Congressman John Conyers and Randall Robinson have been in the forefront of the "reparationists." Also consult Clarence J. Mumford, op. cit.

16. See Robert S. Browne, op. cit., and Randall Robinson, *The Debt: What America Owes to Blacks* (New York: Dutton, 2000), for the economic debts owed to Black Americans alone.

PART II

AFRICA AND OTHER CIVILIZATIONS

FOUR

THE DUAL UNIVERSALISM OF WESTERN CIVILIZATION
THE ETHNOCENTRISM OF "PROGRESS" AND OF WESTERN SOCIAL SCIENCES
(1988)

Never has the concept of "progress" been more influential than it has been in the twentieth century. One version of it, Marxism, is in serious trouble in most parts of the world. The other twentieth century version of the concept is "developmentalism." That version is alive and well in most of the Third World, and is embedded in relations between the industrialized Northern hemisphere and the so-called "developing" countries. Institutions like the World Bank and the International Monetary Fund are centrally involved in the doctrine of progress, precisely because they are involved in the ideology of developmentalism. In this essay we start from the premise that the doctrine of progress presupposes a concept of universalism. Marxism and developmentalism in the 20th century have rested on teleological assumptions, and these in turn have been universalist in either scope or aspiration. On the other hand, both Marxism and developmentalism have needed an image of an ideal society. Marxism has regarded Western capitalism as an intermediary stage to an ideal society. Developmentalism has tended to regard liberal capitalism as the final fulfillment—what Francis Fukuyama called "the end of history."[1]

We need hardly argue in this essay that the choice of the West as role model or ideal society is ethnocentric, while the idea that all societies are evolving towards the same destination is universalist. The concept of progress is caught in the dialectic between the universalism of process and the ethnocentrism of destination. In this essay, we are critiquing Western and Judeo-Christian teleological thought, partly from the perspective of the so-called "developing world." We propose to argue in this paper that Western theories of progress have been a meeting point of two universals, one religious and the other scientific. Universalism in Western religion has affected the normative foundations of theories of development and progress, and sought to convert the world to Western culture. Universalism in Western science has transformed that cultural self-assurance into a technological expansionism. Theories of development in all the social sciences are a fusion of religious faith and scientific rationalism. This is part of what we mean by "the dual universalism of Western civilization."

If Western culture is so universalistic in scope, how can it be ethnocentric at the same time? Its universalism is one of the causes of its ethnocentrism. The Jews taught the world about the one universal God, and then identified themselves as the "chosen people." Similarly the West told the world about the universalism of both science and the Gospel of Jesus, and then the white man of the West put himself forward as the chosen breed. He saw himself as the role model of humanity. In the hands of Europeans, the Jewish concept of the chosen people was racialized. Without using the phrase itself, Europeans developed a racist concept of themselves as the chosen people. What had been a religious doctrine of Jewish ethnocentrism became a principle of arrogance in European racism. The concept of "the White

Man's burden" was born. Let us look at these historical developments more closely.

Westerners tend to trace their civilization to two cultural fountains, each of which is in turn mixed. These fountains are the Graeco-Roman heritage and the Judeo-Christian tradition. If there is a division of labour between the two ancestries, it is one that makes the Graeco-Roman legacy the ultimate mother of the scientific spirit and the Judeo-Christian tradition the mother of Western morality. Both Western science and Western religion do indeed start from universalist premises. Western social science in the twentieth century has consciously modelled itself after the spirit, the method, and the universalism of natural science. At least as profound an influence on Western social science is the universalism of Western social science. It is often the religious universalism, rather than the scientific, that has fed Western theories of progress and of development.

Underlying the tendency has been the *de facto* Western self-conception as the new chosen people. Just as Western Christian missionaries believed that people of other faiths should be converted to the Christian Gospel and "rescued" from other creeds, so Western social scientists have often believed that Africans and Asians could be "rescued" from their cultures and converted to the Western gospel of development and progress. "Development" especially has become the equivalent of a new religion rather than a new technology. Developmentalism shares with Christianity many characteristics, such as: 1) they are both creeds that seek to convert the whole of humankind, and they have different interpretations of their own respective Gospels (The Gospel according to Matthew or to Adam Smith); 2) they each have an underlying premise of a unilinear route to ultimate salvation: Christianity and developmentalism are both deeply rooted in Western teleological culture and values; and, 3) the Western world is the global leader of both, with a disposition towards usurping the role of the "chosen people."

The Doctrine of the Chosen People

The idea that the Jews are the Elect of God has been a recurrent theme in Jewish liturgy: "For thou art an holy unto the LORD thy God, and the LORD has chosen thee to be a peculiar people unto Himself, above all the nations that are upon the earth."[2] Is being chosen a matter of superior moral qualities and racial sensibilities? Or is it, on the contrary, a matter of heavier burdens of responsibility and greater accountability? By being called upon to reveal, preserve, and transmit the word of God, were the Jews also called upon to aspire to higher standards of ethical and spiritual performance?

There have been Jews who have "modernized" the concept of the chosen people. They have made it a vehicle of progress. Nachman Krochmal was neo-Hegelian in his vision of the Jewish people as the bearer of the historical process. What Hegel saw in Prussia Krochmal saw in the Jews. But Krochmal had added a cyclical dynamic to history. The Jews were the only nation to arise again and again, re-invigorated after every decline. The Jews alone had a direct link with the Absolute Spirit. The Jews were therefore a source of special creativity, for each ascent was to a higher level of self-realization. Moral progress was at work; spiritual renewal and human creativity were the raison d'être of the Jews as the Elect of both God and History.[3] Reform Jews in the contemporary era have de-emphasized nationality and have focused on the more positive aspects of the Diaspora. The concept of the chosen people has been demoted in the theology of Reform Judaism—but remains triumphant in more preponderant Conservative and Orthodox circles round the world.

Perhaps the transfer of the concept of the chosen people to Christians began with St. Peter. He applied to Christians the Old Testament reference of Israel as "a kingdom of priests and a holy nation" (Ex. 19:6), implying that the followers of Jesus were the new elect of God: "But ye are a chosen generation, a royal priesthood, an holy nation, a peculiar people."4 Peter was setting the stage for what became, nearly two millenia later, "The White Man's Burden." He was inaugurating the new era of Imperial Christianity dedicated to imperialism as an engine of progress. The first Christians had in fact been Jews. In the beginning, there was no distinction between the two concepts of the chosen people. Christianity therefore began as a sect of Judaism. Jesus had not come to "destroy" but to convert Jews to a new perspective of their own traditions. Early Christians even circumcized their young sons, obeyed the laws of Moses, and observed the Jewish Sabbath. The conversion of Paul was the first major step towards the universalization of Christianity—a case of spiritual "progress." From then on the Christian Gospel was preached to Gentiles as well as to Jews. Paul declared that there was no distinction between them or between slave and free man.

The marriage between the Graeco-Roman heritage and the Judeo-Christian tradition came with the conversion of Roman Emperor Constantine I (280-337 A.D.). That constituted another major step in the universalization of Christianity—a second stage in Christian "progress." Over time, it meant the conversion of much of the Roman Empire, and certainly most of Europe. A new concept of the chosen people was being born, and with it the supreme self-confidence of Europe. Much later yet, another stage in the universalization of Christianity was the settlement of the Americas by Europeans. Again, it looked as if God had "chosen" Europeans to populate and control the New World. The fourth major stage in Christian universalization was modern European imperialism, especially in Africa and Asia. This latest phase of Europe's role as the chosen people gave itself the slogan of "The White Man's Burden." Europeans traversed the world in search of gold and glory—and to serve God. Africa was a particularly attractive area for Christian missionary activism.

Indigenous African creeds were not regarded as worth respecting, let alone saving. The crusade against African "heathenism" went unimpeded. African sacred belief-systems were not called "religions" at all until the second half of the twentieth century.

Just as Black Africa had once been virgin territory for the spread of the Christian Gospel, so it was later to be regarded as virgin area for experiments in developmentalism and modernization theories. The Gospel according to Matthew sometimes joined forces with the Gospel according to Adam Smith. In post-colonial Africa, the Gospel according to Mark sometimes gave way to a new Gospel according to Marx. In all of them, a basic dual universalism has persisted. Somewhere between Mark and the Bible on one side, and Marx and his successors on the other, lies Charles Darwin, author of the momentous work *On the Origin of Species*, and originator of an entirely new school of the chosen species of evolutionary teleology. It is one of the ironies of history that when Karl Marx wanted to dedicate to Darwin the first volume of Capital, the British biologist declined the honour. In 1860 Marx had written to F. Engels, after a month spent nursing his sick wife: "During my time of trial, these last four weeks, I have read all sorts of things. Among others Darwin's book on natural selection. Although it is developed in the crude English style, this is the book which contains the basis in natural history for our views." Marx elaborated this point elsewhere, arguing that in place of a war of nature he provided a theory of the "fierce strife of classes." Engels, in his funeral oration over Marx's grave in 1883, said: "As Darwin discovered the law of evolution in organic nature, so Marx discovered the law of evolution in human history." A new teleology had arrived, and the dual universalism of Western civilization entered a new phase.[5] The doctrine of progress was unfolding.

From Racism to Ethnocentrism

Charles Darwin's *On the Origin of Species* was published in 1859. It was soon to have long-term repercussions both for the study of biology and for the study of social science. Racists could now proceed to demonstrate, by the utilization of the theory of natural selection, that major differences in human capacity and human organization were to be traced to biological distinctions between races. But to some extent this theory was much older than Darwin. What Darwin added was the dynamism of converting mere classification of beings into a process. The static version of the theory was religious and went back to the ancient idea that God had so organized the world that the universe and creation were arranged in a "Great Chain of Being"—that all creatures could be classified and fitted into a hierarchy extending "from man down to the smallest reptile, whose existence can be discovered by the microscope."[6] Those at the very top of this hierarchy were the chosen people.

In other words, it was not just those of the lower species who were so classified. Even within the highest species created in the Almighty's image, there were in turn other divisions. Theories of the great chain of beings assumed that the Almighty, in His wisdom, did not want a big gap between one type of creature and the next. Therefore, there had to be intermediate categories between orangutans and the white man. As early as 1713 naturalists began looking for the "missing link" between men and apes and apparently speculated on the possibility that Hottentots and orangutans might be side by side in the "scale or life," separated only by the fact that orangutans could not speak.[7] What Darwinism helped to refine into specific theoretical form was the element of motion in this process, the idea that the backward people might be on the move towards a higher phase, and those in front further still. Progress was activated at last.

The link between racism and ethnocentrism is not difficult to see. Even for the earliest racist theories, there had been no difficulty about deciding where to place the white man in the chain of being. As Phillip D. Curtin puts it in discussing these early biological theorists:

> Since there is no strictly scientific or biological justification for stating that one race is 'higher' than another, the criteria of ranking has to come from non-scientific assumptions. All of the biologists... began by putting the European variety at the top of the scale. This was natural enough if only as an un-thinking reflection of cultural chauvinism. It could be held to follow from the assessment of European achievements in art and science... it was taken for granted that historical achievement was intimately connected with physical form—in short, that race and culture were closely related.[8]

The dynamic element in ethnocentric theories of evolution inevitably led to assumptions about white leadership in the whole process of historical change. Progress was social selection if not natural selection. And within the white races themselves, specific leadership was assumed to come from the "tougher" of the European stock. For example, in his inaugural lecture as Regius Professor of Modern History at Oxford in December 1841, Thomas Arnold gave a new lease of life to the ancient idea of a moving centre of civilisation. Arnold argued that the history of civilisation was the history of a series of creative races, each of which made its impact and then sank into oblivion, leaving the heritage of civilisation to a greater successor. What the Greeks passed on to the Romans, the Romans bequeathed in turn to the Germanic race and of that race the greatest civilizing nation was England.[9] In many cases, this was seen as part of God's grand design— for emperors and kings were God's anointed.

Notions of leadership very often led to notions of the right to rule the less developed. Even that prophet of liberalism, John Stuart Mill, could still argue that despotism was "a legitimate mode of government in dealing with barbarians, provided the end be their improvement..."[10] In Mill also there began to emerge the notion that Western democratic institutions constitute the ultimate destination of much of socio-political development. And the capacity to operate democratic institutions was already being regarded as an index of political maturity and institutional stability. Mill even seemed to share some of the reservations held by current modernization theorists about the possibility of operating liberal institutions in multi-ethnic situations. To use Mill's own formulation, "free institutions are next to impossible in a country made up of different nationalities."[11] Here, then, is the essential assumption of some of the current theories of integration that preach a process towards the fusion of nationalities within a single territory into a new entity capable of sustaining the stresses of a more liberal polity. At least one major approach in theorizing about political modernization in our own day has rested on what Robert A. Packenham describes as "the idea that political development is primarily a function of a social system that facilitates popular participation in governmental and political processes at all levels, and the bridging of regional, religious, caste, linguistic, tribal and other cleavages."

Packenham goes on to argue that one form that this particular approach has taken today is to assess the social correlates of democracy. Are these the new criteria of the chosen people? These correlates are supposed to include relatively high "scores" on such sociological variables as an open class system, literacy and/or education, high participation in voluntary organizations, urbanization and communication system.[12] Much of this analysis assumes that the highest of modern institutions must inevitably be those devised in the West. The Darwinian evolution toward modernity is evolution towards Western ways. Edward Shils seemed to be expressing his own view of the matter as well as the views of some members of the Afro-Asian elite when he said: "Modern means being Western without the onus of dependence on the West." Much of the rest of Shils' theorizing on the process of development bears the stamp of ethnocentric preference for "a regime of representative institutions" of the Western kind.[13] The concept of "the chosen people" has now been democratized.

There have been models of theorizing about developments that have gone as far as to classify political regimes in the world in terms of first, the Anglo-American type; second, the continental European types; third, totalitarian types; and fourth, the types that one found in Africa and Asia.[14] The concept of the chosen people has found a liberal guise. Evidently, this ethnocentrism has strong links with older theories of Anglo-Saxon leadership as a focus of a new wave of civilization. Theories of evolutionary change culminating in the pre-eminence of a single nation had major philosophers of the West among their disciples. Not least among these philosophers was Hegel, for whom the entire process of change in the universe had for its ultimate human culmination the emergence of the Prussian state and the Germanic genius. Hegel, too, was in a sense, a pre-Darwinian social Darwinist, both in his notion of a creative tension between thesis, antithesis, and synthesis and in his notion of a powerful evolution towards the emergence of a high species.

More recently, there have been historians who have seen human evolution in terms of a progressive rise to the pre-eminence of their own nation or group of nations. William H. McNeill interpreted world history in such a way that he might easily belong to this tradition.[15] McNeill challenges in part the Spenglerian pessimism of a Western decline and the whole conception of history as a collection of separate civilizations, each pursuing an independent career. For McNeill human cultures have had a basic interrelationship and their history has been leading to a global pre-eminence of Western civilization.

In the field of sociology, Talcott Parsons has talked about "evolutionary universals" in terms that indicate a belief that development is ultimately in the direction of greater comparability with the political systems of the Western world. Parsons argues that the existence of a definitive link between popular participation and ultimate control of decision-making is crucial for building and maintaining support for the political-legal systems, and for its binding rules and decisions. Therefore, in so far as large-scale societies are concerned, the "democratic association" is an "evolutionary universal." In defense of this proposition against anticipated criticism, Parsons prophetically declares:

> I realise that to take this position I must maintain that communist totalitarian organisation will probably not fully match "democracy" in political and integrative capacity in the long run. I do indeed predict that it will prove to be unstable and will either make adjustments in a general direction of elective democracy and a plural party system or "regress" into generally less advanced and politically less effective forms of organisation, failing to advance as rapidly or as far as might otherwise be expected.[16]

A similar prophetic ethnocentrism is evident in the approach of J. Roland Pennock to the study of political development. Pennock enumerates principles like "justice according to law," "the rule of law," and "due process" as among the political goods that are delivered when a society attains a certain degree of political development. Pennock declares in a long footnote,

It might be objected that modern totalitarian dictatorships may not subscribe to the standards of justice according to law outlined above. Are we then to call them less "developed" than modern constitutional regimes?—I would be quite happy to say that to this extent they are in fact less developed, less fitted to fulfill the needs of men and society.[17]

Later in the same article, Pennock discusses political development in ethnocentric terms, affirming that the history of human evolution is towards the type of institutions and ideals cherished in the Western world. This is a new type of ethnocentric universalism since Pennock does not describe such ideals as "Western" but refer to them as associated with a "world culture." Nonetheless, the inclination to discern an upward movement of human evolution towards Westernism is recurrent, as expressed in the concluding sentence of his article:

It is common today to compare or rank states by the degree of party competition, or their adoption and use of the major devices of representative government, or their social mobilization. It is my suggestion that, to see a more nearly complete picture and to make more highly discriminating judgments, anyone who is concerned with political development in any way involving measurement of comparison should take full account of some of the measurable elements of the political goods of security, justice, liberty, and welfare.[18]

By the time of our current theories of modernization and Fukuyama's "end of history," the racist element in theories of human development had considerably declined, at least within the ranks of scholarship. The racial component was what had given social Darwinism a continuing biological feature borrowed from Darwin's *On the Origin of Species*. In fact, in the heyday of racial theories, it was by no means clear where biological Darwinism ended and social Darwinism began. But in the modern theories of development and modernization, Darwinism is substantially debiologized. It is no longer pure racial bigotry that is being invoked to explain stages of political growth. What is invoked is at the most mild racial arrogance or ethnocentric cultural pride on a universal scale.

Evolution and Optimism

The shift from biological explanations of human backwardness to cultural explanations of that factor had important implications. Biological differences imply a slower rate of mutation of character. The African thus could not help lagging behind for many generations simply because he could not help the biological traits he had inherited from his own sub-species. There is a quality almost of immutability, of being retarded, when a lack of development is attributed to hereditary characteristics within the race. But as ideas on social evolution took a turn toward cultural determinism, the notion of a backward people catching up with more advanced people was at last brought within the bounds of feasibility.

The shift from biological determinism to cultural determinism had its transitional moments. Let us take W.R. Greg as a case of intellectual transition in this field of theorizing. Greg inherited the leadership of Anglo-Saxon ethnocentrism from Thomas Arnold. At any rate, upon Arnold's death Greg speculated further in the *Westminster Review* on the whole destiny of human evolution, discussing Africa specifically. He noted that some "backward races" elsewhere were becoming extinct while the "Negro race" seemed to retain a striking resilience. Figures from North America indicated that Blacks could continue in healthy persistence even when they were transplanted from Africa to the very different environment of North America, and to the very different experience of constant contact with Europeans. Greg was of the opinion that Africans were intellectually devoid of the possibilities of ultimate originality, but they had one very important characteristic from the point of view of successful acculturation: Africans were endowed with a significant imitative genius. They could therefore assimilate what the West could bequeath to them. This had implications for the whole notion of progress for Greg was, to some extent, a precursor of theories of "demonstration-effect." Human progress was possible because the more backward of the races had at least the ability to imitate. European achievements could, therefore, be grafted unto the African stock.[19]

Some of these notions were to last into the period of colonial expansion in Africa and were used to legitimize individual colonial policies. The whole paraphernalia of ideas of French "assimilationist" policies in the colonies had great intellectual affinity with the kind of tradition to which Greg belonged—the perspective that conceded to the African the capacity to emulate without permitting him the capacity to innovate. The policy of attempting to Gallicize Africans was firmly within the flow of this historical stream of ethnocentric universalism. With independence, theorists in the Anglo-Saxon world discussed for a while the feasibility of upholding some of the inherited institutions from colonialism. The argument of whether Ghana could sustain the "Westminster model" or not was also part of this tradition; it was in fact concerned with the potential imitative capacity of African political man. Gradually, theories of political development attained a sophistication that sharply differentiated them from simple biological explanations of whether or not there was an important emulative genius within the African subspecies. The Ghanaian capacity to maintain the Westminster model, or the ability of Nigeria to cope with inherited federal and Westminster institutions, became more firmly associated with varied constraints and pre-conditions with which the

Western World had already managed to cope but that the rest of the universe had yet to evolve.

Nevertheless, there was a firm conviction that the direction of universal change would be towards a greater approximation to Western achievements. In the meantime, political science as a discipline embraced more fully the comparative ethos and with it the idea that different cultures could be compared in terms of what was being accomplished in the political process. Almost any two political systems could be a subject of comparison—exemplified by comparisons between Ghana and Spain, Mexico and Uganda, Tanzania and the Soviet Union. The comparative dimension in political science has been both a manifestation and a further reinforcing factor for the acceptance of cultural relativism and toleration of major differences. To some extent, then, the Darwinian evolutionary tendency achieved a high level of cross-cultural accommodation when the structural-functionalists in political science began to discern comparable functions, performed by different agents and structures, between varied societies. But side by side with this toleration and indulgence was the conviction that progress was almost inevitable for the more backward societies. The direction of that progress was towards greater similarity of values, norms, and structures of the Western world.

In discussing the processes of change explained in the varying contexts of the five geographical areas reviewed in the influential book, *The Politics of the Developing Areas*, the late James S. Coleman asserted that the consequences were by no means uniform and yet "in general the changes have brought the countries concerned nearer the model of a modern society." What is a modern society? Coleman's own view as expressed elsewhere is more detached and less ethnocentric, but in that early book that he edited with Almond, he derived a definition of a "modern society" from Almond's introduction and from Shil's model of a "political democracy." On the basis of the systemic characteristics enumerated thus, Coleman concludes: "it is clear from this list of attributes that the Anglo-American qualities most closely approximate the model of the modern political system..."[20] Could Africa and Latin America be democratizing in that modernizing direction? Does political science have intimations to convey to us about the future? And how do those intimations relate to religious prophecy on one side and scientific prediction on the other? Let us turn to these areas of convergence now.

On Prophecy and Teleology

Prophecy and foretelling the future were for a long-time part of the validation of religion, especially among the Semites (Arabs and Jews). With the new social sciences in the twentieth century, Western world prediction replaced prophecy as a measure of credibility. As the social sciences have claimed greater affinity to science, they attempted greater proximity to predictive power. But once again what appears to be an effort to marry social studies to the scientific method is, at least in part, a case of resurrecting an older religious tradition. Predictive power as a validation of science is sometimes another version of prophetic power as a validation of religion. Social studies are caught in-between.

This tendency inaugurates a different kind of universalism, the universalism of time—as contrasted with the universalism of space that we have discussed so far. Spreading the Gospel to different parts of the world is a conquest of space; identifying the future is a conquest of time. Western social science has claimed the universalism of time, as well as of space, while remaining ethnocentric. In the earlier phases of classical political theory, a major pre-occupation was to validate the present by reference to the past, rather than forecasting the future by reference to the present. The state of nature in Thomas Hobbes and John Locke was partly derived from *Genesis* and the Garden of Eden. Hobbes preferred the idea of "original sin" and man's basic fallibility. Locke preferred the concept of man as Adam before the fall.

The whole tradition of the "social contract" as a basis of political obligation rested quite often on assumptions about the past of man. It is true that later contractual theorists more systematically regarded the contract idea as a logical device rather than an historical assertion about man's first entry into society. But could it also have been a theological device? As a logical device, the state of nature that preceded the contract was simply a way of trying to assess what man would have been like if all the effects and implications of living in society were to have been withdrawn. The attempt here was to get to the residue of essential humanity by trying to isolate the factors attributable to living in a community. But the concepts of the "Garden of Eden" and the "original sin" were also logical devices, as well as theological postulates. On the other hand, the historicity of the social contract remained part of the debate in political theory for quite a while. When Hobbes equated the state of nature with the state of war he felt he had to defend himself against those who were skeptical of the reality of such a state. In Hobbes' own words:

> It may peradventure be thought there was never such a time nor condition of war as this, and I believe it was never generally so over all the world; but there are many places where they live so now. For the savage people in many places of America, except the government of small families, the concord whereof depends on natural lust, have no government at all and live at this day in that brutish manner as I said before. Howsoever, it may be perceived what manner of life there would be where there were no common power to fear by the manner of life which men that have formerly lived under a peaceful government use to degenerate

into in a civil war.[21]

Locke's concept of the social contract also had elements of historicity in its assumptions and, certainly, the 1688 Glorious Revolution in England rested much of its philosophy on the presumed historical understanding between king and people. When Edmund Burke criticized the French Revolution, later, it was in part because the French Revolution was not adequately guided by a look into the past before attempting to push into the future. A lack of sensitivity to the past could, in Burke's estimation, lead to a reckless disregard of the real interests of future generations. For "people will not look forward to posterity who never look backward to their ancestors."[22]

Yet, the move from theology and traditionalism to the rationalism of the eighteenth and nineteenth centuries is in part a move from a backward-looking orientation of values to a futuristic orientation in norms. John Plamenatz, the late Oxford political theorist, asserted that man cannot help but see himself as a traveller, and cannot know that he is alive, without looking back to a past and forward to a future. But the political philosopher in the earlier period spent more time in trying to understand the past than in attempting to discern the shape of the future. In Plamenatz' words:

> From the beginning the philosophical student of politics has been interested in the course of social change. Aristotle imagined the *polis* growing out of the village, and the village growing out of the family; and, since he called man a political animal, a creature whose nature it is to create a political community and to realise itself in so doing, he saw the movement from family to *polis* as a movement in a desirable direction, as progress. But he imagined nothing better than the *polis* and did not ask himself what might come after it to

take its place.[23]

Religious thinkers saw man not as a traveller but as a pilgrim. The journey was a slow process towards salvation. Liberalism as a tradition was perhaps intermediate between the older forms of political philosophy with their grounding in custom, religion, and history on the one hand, and the militant scientism of some of the rationalist schools of political theory later in the nineteenth century. But liberalism itself was in the nineteenth century part of the whole phenomenon of widespread belief in progress. This involved a belief that history was moving in a desirable direction, or could at least easily be helped to move in that direction. The belief in progress was perhaps the real origin of the lure of prediction in some of the social sciences in the modern period. But was it different from the belief that history was moving towards the Second Coming and the final opportunity for salvation?

The idea that history had a purposeful direction was older than the form it took in the eighteenth and nineteenth centuries. E.H. Carr argued that it was the Jews, and after them the Christians, who made it a sound postulation of their thought that there was a goal towards which the historical process was moving—the teleological view of history. History was permitted to acquire a meaning and a purpose, but it was desecularised in the process. The attainment of the goal of history would automatically mean the end of history. This view of history converted history into a theodicy. Carr goes on to assert, however, that the Renaissance restored the classical view of an anthropocentric (homocentric) world and of the primacy of reason. For the pessimistic classical view of the future the Renaissance substituted an optimistic view derived from the Jewish Christian tradition. Gibbon, perhaps the greatest of the enlightenment historians, found it possible to record what he called "the pleasing conclusion that every age of the world has increased, and still increases the real wealth, the happiness, the knowledge, and perhaps the virtue of the human race."[24]

Of the liberal exponents of the belief in progress, Lord Acton also ranks high. He regarded history as a record of progress and the study of history as "a progressive science." For him history, as the course of events, was a continual expansion of liberty—though he was writing before the Afro-Asian struggles for independence:

> It is by the combined efforts of the weak, made under compulsion, to resist the reign of force and constant wrong, that, in the rapid change but slow progress of four hundred years, liberty has been preserved, and secured, and extended, and finally understood.[25]

Hegel brings us back to European images of the chosen people. Hegel too, had conceived of history as purposeful, but, unlike Marx, he seemed incapable of seeing beyond the emergence of the Prussian monarchy. He had an image of the chosen state rather than the chosen people. For Hegel the end of progress was the emergence of the Prussian state. Marx, however, was more future oriented than Hegel; his conception of the purpose of history and its direction bore a comparison with that of the liberal Acton. Both Marx and Acton, in a sense, looked at history as being in the direction of an ultimate maximization of human freedom. Their conceptions of intermediate freedom were vastly different, but their image of the ultimate freedom of the future was more in common. Liberalism and Marxism have both shared a profound distrust of the state as an instrument of coercion. For Marx the state is basically an instrument of class oppression; for liberals it is all too often a threat to individual liberty. Yet the vision of the classless society in Marxism, projected into the future, does postulate a highly autonomous individual, unencumbered by the state machinery or by the demands and constraints of economic need. This Marxist utopia is one in which the individual would at last be able to "hunt in the morning, fish in the afternoon, rear cattle in the evening, criticize after dinner... without ever becoming hunter, fisherman, shepherd or critic."[26] Such a vision of an autonomous individual is a profoundly liberal heaven. Acton and Marx differed in all stages of freedom prior to this ultimate form; but perhaps they could share the vision of this final destination of history as a maximization of human freedom.

When normative political theory predicts certain forms of human behavior, there is often room for self-fulfilling prophecies. Marx believes neither in the chosen people nor in the chosen state; he believed in the chosen class. His predictions of proletarian or neo-proletarian revolutions have sometimes approached fulfillment in situations where sufficient numbers of underprivileged people have believed in themselves as a revolutionary class. To act and behave as if Marx was right is sometimes a way of making Marx right. Marxist universalism, while still ethnocentric, has succeeded in producing rebels against other versions of Western hegemony. Liberalism too has at times opened doors for self-fulfilling prophecies. An assertion, for example, that where elections are denied, and freedom of expression suppressed, people will revolt could all too easily fulfill itself if enough people in such a situation believed in the inevitability of such a response. The American Declaration of Independence did in part rest on a belief that human nature revolted against illiberal regimes. Some of the agitation in Greece after the military coup in 1967 was an attempt to vindicate a view of the Greeks as a freedom-loving people. The patriotic British assertion that "Britons never, never, never shall be slaves," when it is believed by enough Britons, has been known to inspire them into resisting attempted repression or invasion.

Yet these are usually assertions that are colored by patriotic self-conceptions. On balance, British political culture has not been quite as convinced about the predictability of human behavior as have some of the less traditionalist and more rationalist cultures elsewhere. Teleology has been diluted in Anglo-Saxon conservatism. On balance, in fact, it might be said that the lure of prediction in normative theory is more characteristic of radical schools of thought than of conservative ones. The radical schools are closer to religion and to teleological theology. Indeed, it is almost a defining characteristic of conservatism to distrust the plannability of social change and political direction; the conservative normally distrusts faith in progress. In Michael Oakeshott's famous metaphor:

> In political activity then, men sail a boundless and bottomless sea; there is neither harbour for shelter nor floor for anchorage, neither starting-place nor appointed destination. The enterprise is to keep afloat on an even keel; the sea is both friend and enemy; and the seamanship consists in using the resources of a traditional manner of behaviour in order to make a friend of every hostile occasion.[27]

Progress and Laws of Regularity

In the more futuristic and rationalistic schools of normative political theory there has been a high component of determinism in the assumptions made. The echoes of religious fatalism are strong. Determinism in turn presumes certain laws of causality. In Marxism, there is an explicit doctrine of economic determinism placed within a broader conception of a materialistic system of causality. Sometimes one can hear echoes of John Calvin's doctrines of predestination. Perhaps the most extreme form of determinism is that which is captured in the poet's words:

With Earth's first Clay They did the Last Man's knead,
And then of the Last Harvest sow'd the Seed:
Yea, the first Morning of Creation wrote
What the Last Dawn of Reckoning shall read.[28]

The determinism of Marx sometimes approaches the assertion that the final dawn of reckoning will inevitably be the first stage of real socialism, and this was predictable from the first morning of primitive communism in the cradle of history. Yet, Marx is much less crude and naive than he may sometimes sound. For our purposes here what needs to be grasped is that determinism is the belief that, to use the words of the mathematician Laplace, "the present state of the universe [is] the effect of its antecedent state and the cause of the state that is to follow." Laplace himself believed that if one could comprehend that which is before today, one could foresee what will happen tomorrow.

An intelligence, who for a given instance should be acquainted with all the forces by which Nature is animated and with the several positions of the entities composing it, if further his intellect were vast enough to submit those data to analysis, would include the one and the same formula the movements of the largest bodies in the universe and those of the slightest atom. Nothing would be uncertain for him; the future as well as the past would be present to his eyes.[29]

Although scientific determinism has links with theological predestination, both can sometimes be greatly diluted or disguised in variant language. Eddington suggests that the basic wish of the determinist is to "base on our ordinary experience of the sequence of cause and effect a wide generalization called the Principle of Causality."[30] The religious pre-determinist believes in the laws of God; the scientific determinist believes in the laws of Nature. A disguised form of neo-determinism might be a quest for regularities of human behavior which could then be attributed, either explicitly or by implication, to certain laws governing human responses to given situations. It is these subtle assumptions of regular patterns of human response that provided a bridge linking rationalist normative theories like Marxism, the scientific political theory of more recent times, and the approaches and methods of the natural sciences. David Easton, in itemizing the characteristics that describe one preeminent school of the new political science, cited as the first attribute the search for regularity. Easton defined this as an assumption that "there are discoverable uniformities in political behavior. These can be expressed in generalizations or theories with explanatory and predictive value."[31]

Mulford Q. Sibley takes the discussion further and argues that scientific prediction would appear to be as feasible in politics as in physics. In both realms, the quest is for "scientific prediction: that is to say, we endeavour to state the several possibilities of future experience and the limits within which such alternatives must lie." Science can be looked to for information as to what cannot happen under specified conditions or, as Karl Popper puts it, the "lawfulness of phenomena" can be expressed by asserting that such and such a thing cannot happen, that is to say, by a sentence in the form of the proverb: "You cannot carry water in a sieve."[32] Sibley emphasizes categorically that scientific prediction is not to be confused with forecasting the future, which is more blatantly prophetic. He accuses Marx and Engels of having done the latter. He also cites Harold Lasswell as a modern analyst who often appears to confuse scientific prediction with overall forecasting. Nor was Lasswell alone in this; several others associated with the behaviouralist mode appeared to follow in this forecasting trend.[33]

Sibley defines the distinction between scientific prediction and forecasting by saying that the behavioral scientific prediction is an "if-then" proposition and therefore hypothetical; whereas the forecast insofar as it exists

> must be unhypothetical or unconditioned, else it ceases to be a forecast. Thus, one can perhaps predict what Congress will do about a proposed piece of legislation under carefully assumed conditions and contingencies. But one cannot—at least scientifically—purport to forecast what it will do. One can conceivably predict what the population of the world is likely to be twenty years hence if trends *yex* continue under conditions *zoa* and *bbm*. But one cannot—behaviorally—forecast what the population of the world will be twenty years hence, period. Any forecast of this kind would be guesswork based on overall "hunches" and could never be classified as "scientific."[34]

According to the school of thought to which Sibley belongs, the boundaries of prediction then, if they are to be regarded as scientific, lie within two areas of capability. First, scientific forecasting is feasible only negatively, as one asserts what cannot happen. This is like Popper's example of the proverb "you cannot carry water in a sieve." The second area of scientific prediction may be positive, but hypothetical. It consists of "if-then" propositions. The behavioral scientist is thus expected to be able to suggest how, under precisely formulated conditions and circumstances, men would behave in the future, "and he will provide us with statements of limits beyond which, under a specified and controlled environment, they would probably not act."[35]

Perhaps one major difference between prediction based on observed regularity and a forecast based on prophetic vision is that the former lends itself more easily to conscious interference in order to avert what is forecast. Even for the determinist, human consciousness could sometimes make a difference. Marx relegated human consciousness to the superstructure, arguing that it was the reflection of social factors more fundamental than itself. But Lenin, in reviving the role of ideology into a conscious instrument of change rather than a mere reflection of class awareness, reinstated human consciousness into the domain of active factors in history. Man can himself transcend his own original sin. The Supreme Being for Man is at last Man. The chains of predestination are broken at last.

Conclusion

We have attempted to explore, in this paper, the interplay between Western ethnocentrism and the dual universalism of Western civilization in relation to progress and development. We have argued that Western social science is, to a large extent, a product of two universals: natural science and the Judeo—Christian tradition. But like the Jews who taught us about the Universal God while proclaiming themselves the chosen people, Westerners have instructed the world about the universalism of both science and Jesus while declaring that the white man is God's chosen breed. In other words, both the Jews and the Europeans revealed a genius for marrying genuine universalism with real ethnocentrism. We have argued that Europe borrowed the Jewish religious concept of the chosen people and racialized it. The underlying ethnocentrism has affected Western academic paradigms.

Contemporary theories of development and modernization have been especially distorted by the conflict between Western ethnocentrism and the dual universalism of Western civilization. The scientific leg of the dual heritage entered a new phase with the biological findings of Charles Darwin and his impact on social theories. The religious leg of the dual universalism was in turn profoundly affected by the ideological impact of Karl Marx. Especially persistent in the theories has been a teleological tendency. There was a time when religion validated itself by demonstrating a capacity to prophesy. More recently, branches of science have tried to establish their credentials by demonstrating a capacity to predict. The new methodologies of the social sciences of the West have often been caught between claims of forecasting and claims of predicting. A look into the future has been one of the meeting points between religion and science throughout the history of the West. Mastering the future is a universalism of time; conquering the world is a universalism of space. Doctrines of progress are often implicit in both.

It is by no means rare for major schools of intellectual analysis to have significant antecedents in earlier traditions. Perhaps that is what intellectual history is all about: a succession of waves, or alternatively a long chain of moments of inspiration, linked together in a tradition of thought. We have attempted to demonstrate that current theories of development and modernization do have ancestral ties with earlier notions of social evolution and Darwinism. There have been dramatic changes in many of the postulates of this line of intellectual analysis. In fact, the change sometimes has been from racism to broad humanism. But it has often been a form of humanism that is animated by the self-confidence of ethnocentric achievement.

In many of the current theories of development and modernization, as indeed in old theories of social Darwinism, an optimistic outlook at the ultimate destination of human history has persisted. Such optimism believes that, although every birth eventually leads to death, there is a constant process of rebirth in the history of human societies. Hence the belief in creative tension that soothes the social anguish of new nations: out of upheavals, societies might indeed be uplifted, and out of the depths of despair, development might still be feasible. Darwin's ultimate gift to human knowledge might well have been the gift of an incorrigible scientific optimism. And the new developmentalism is often inspired by this optimism, ultimately rooted in precisely that dual universalism of the Western heritage as a whole.[36]

The idea of progress once justified classifying societies "from the primitive to the civilized." In the name of progress, the slave trade was once defended as a method of propelling the industrial revolution. In the name of progress, child labour has been exploited from factory to factory. In the name of progress, Rudyard Kipling celebrated race-conscious imperialism. The doctrine of progress can all too easily turn Machiavellian as harsh means are justified in pursuit of noble ends. Developmentalism is one such twentieth century version of the doctrine of progress, sometimes justifying the harsh means of "structural adjustment" by reference to the noble end of "economic recovery."

NOTES

This chapter is a revised version of a paper that was initially presented at the XIV World Congress of the International Political Science Association, August 28-September 1, 1988, Washington, D.C., under the title "Judeo-Christian Universalism and the Ethnocentrism of Western Social Science." The paper in question later appeared in a collection of essays entitled *Progress: Fact or Illusion?*, edited by Leo Marx and Bruce Mazlish (Ann Arbor: University of Michigan Press, 1996), pp. 153-174, under the title "*Progress:* Illegitimate Child of Judeo-Christian Universalism and Western Ethnocentrism: A Third World Critique."

1. See Fukuyama, *The End of History and The Last Man* (New York: The Free Press, 1992). In the book, Fukuyama goes beyond the thesis of his article "The End of History?" in *The National Interest*, 16 (Summer 1989), pp. 3-18.

2 *The Holy Bible*, King James Version, *Deuteronomy*, 14:2.

3. Convenient summaries of modern Jewish history and thought include Howard Morley Sachar, *The Course of Modern Jewish History* (1958); Joseph Blau, *Modern Varieties of Judaism*

(1966); and Nathan Rotenstreich, *Jewish Philosophy in Modern Times* (1968). Krochmal's own work on Jewish uniqueness was published posthumously in 1851 under the title of *More nevukhe ha-zman* ("Guide for the Perplexed of Our Time").

4. *The Holy Bible*, King James Version, *The First Epistle of Peter* 2:9. For a less exclusivist application of Christian doctrine to global affairs consult Alberto C. Coil,"Some Christian Reminders for the Statesman," *Ethics and International Affairs*, Vol. I (1987), pp. 97-112.

5. Cited by Edgar Hyman, *The Tangled Bank* (New York: Grosset and Dunlop, The Universal Library, 1966 edition), pp. 121-126. This part of the paper is greatly indebted to my earlier work on political development and modernization. See especially Mazrui "From Social Darwinism to Current Theories of Modernization: A Tradition of Analysis," *World Politics*, Vol. XXI, No. 1, October 1968.

6. See A.O. Lovejoy, *The Great Chain of Being* (Cambridge, MA: Harvard University Press, 1936). Also consult Anthony Appiah, "The Uncompleted Argument: DuBois and the Illusion of Race," *Critical Inquiry* (1) 1985.

7. Ibid., p. 233 and A.O. Lovejoy "Some Eighteenth Century Evolutionists," *Popular Science Monthly*, Vol. LXV, No. 4 (July 1904), pp. 238-251.

8. See P.D. Curtin, *The Image of Africa* (London: MacMillan and Company, 1965), pp. 38-39. I am indebted to Curtin's book for bibliographical guidance and for some insights.

9. See T. Arnold, *Introductory Lectures on Modern History* (New York: D. Appleton & Co., 1842), pp. 46-47, and consult Curtin, *The Image of Africa,* esp. pp. 375-377. See also Arthur Penrhyn Stanley, *Life and Correspondence of Thomas Arnold* (London: Ward, Lock and Company, 1845), esp. pp. 435, 438. This notion of a moving center of civilization is also discussed in my Inaugural Lecture *Ancient Greece in African Political Thought* (Nairobi: East African Publishing House, 1967), reproduced in this volume as Chapter 11.

10. J.S. Mill, *Representative Government*, R.B. McCallum [Ed.] (Oxford: Basil Blackwell, 1946). Consult also Joseph Ike Asike, "Culture, Development and Philosophy," *Africa and the World*, Vol. I, No. 3, April 1988, pp. 20-25.

11. Ibid. Carl G. Rosberg Jr., for example, makes a similar point, when he argues that "the dangers to stability presented by ethnic and other parochialism are magnified in most African states by a lack of that fundamental of common values and widely shared principles of political behaviour generally termed "consensus." Typically, the terms of a consensus prescribe that the pursuit of group interests be conducted peaceably and within established institutions of the constitutional framework." See Rosberg, "Democracy and the New African States," in Kenneth Kirkwood (ed.), *St. Antony's Papers on African Affairs*, No. 2 (London: Chatto and Windus, 1963), p. 26. Comparable arguments abound in the literature on democracy in new states.

12. See Packenham, "Approaches to the Study of Political Development," *World Politics*, Vol. XVII, No. 1, October 1964. For subsequent additional insights I have benefited from conversations with Gwendolen Carter, the late William O. Brown and the late James S. Coleman.

13. See esp. Shils, *Political Development in the New States* (The Hague: Mouton and Co., 1965), pp. 10 ff. See also David Easton, "Political Science in the United States: Past and Present," *International Political Science Review*, Vol. 6, No. 1, 1985, pp. 133-152.

14. Gabriel Almond has shared such a vision of political development, especially in his earlier work. A more cautious but related formulation is Eisenstadt who says: "Historically, modernization is the process of change towards those types of social, economic, and political systems that have developed in Western Europe and North America from the Seventeenth Century to the Nineteenth and have then spread to other European countries and in the Nineteenth and Twentieth Centuries to the South American, Asian, and African continents." See Eisenstadt, *Modernization: Protest and Change* (Englewood Cliffs: Prentice Hall, 1966), p. 1. Consult also the series of books entitled "Studies in Political Development" sponsored by the Committee on Comparative Politics of the Social Science Research Council of the United States. Of special interest as a study of value-systems is Lucian W. Pye and Sidney Verba (eds.), *Political Culture and Political Development* (Princeton, N.J.: Princeton University Press, 1965).

15. See McNeill, *The Rise of the West* (Chicago and Lon-

don: University of Chicago Press, 1963). For a more ambivalent work see J.M. Roberts, *The Triumph of the West* (London: British Broadcasting Corporation, 1985).

16. Parsons, "Evolutionary Universals in Society," *American Sociological Review*, XXIX (June 1964), p. 356. See also in the same issue of the journal S.N. Eisenstadt, "Social Change, Differentiation and Evolution."

17. James Roland Pennock, "Political Development, Political Systems, and Political Goods," in *World Politics*, Vol. XVIII, No. 3 (April 1966), p. 424.

18. Ibid., p. 434. Pennock cites an appendix in Gabriel A. Almond and James S. Coleman (eds.), *The Politics of the Developing Areas* (Princeton, 1960), and Phillips Cutright, "National Political Development: Measurement and Analysis," in *American Sociological Review*, Vol. 28, No. 2 (April 1963), pp. 253-264. Another discussion by Almond of some of these issues is in his article "A Development Approach to Political Systems," *World Politics*, Vol. XVII, No. 2 (January 1965), pp. 183-214.

19. W.R. Greg, "Dr. Arnold," *Westminster Review*, Vol. 39, No. 7 (January 1843), pp. 1-30.

20. Conclusion in Gabriel A. Almond and James S. Coleman (eds.), *The Politics of the Developing Areas,* op. cit., pp. 536, 533. In his introduction to *Education and Political Development* (Princeton, N.J.: Princeton University Press, 1965), Coleman defines political development more neutrally in terms of enhancing "political capacity." See especially pp. 15-16.

21. *Leviathan* (1651). See The Library of Liberal Arts edition of *Leviathan, Parts I and II*, edited by Herbert W. Schneider (New York and Indiana: The Bobbs-Merrill Company, 1958), p. 108.

22. For an attempt to relate this to the problem of tradition and shifting loyalties in a new state in Africa see Mazrui, "Edmond Burke and Reflections on the Revolution in the Congo," *Comparative Studies in Society and History*, Vol. 5, No. 2, January 1963, reproduced in this volume as Chapter 13.

23. John Plamenatz, *Man and Society*, Vol. 2 (London: Longmans and Green, 1963), p. 409. See also Jacques Barzun, "Is Democratic Theory for Export?," *Ethics and International Affairs*, Vol. I, No. 1, 1987, pp. 53-72. Consult also Ekkehart, "The Domi-

nance of American Approaches in International Relations," *Journal of International Studies, Millenium*, Vol. 16, No. 2, Summer 1987, pp. 207-214.

24. Gibbon, *The Decline and Fall of the Roman Empire*, Ch. XXXVIII; the occasion of the digression being his discussion of the downfall of the Western Empire. Cited by E.H. Carr, *What is History?* (London: MacMillan & Company 1961), pp. 104-105.

25. John E.E.D. Acton [Lord Acton], *Lectures on Modern History* (London and New York: Macmillan, 1906), p. 51.

26. Marx and Engels, *German Ideology* (1846). Consult the edition edited by R. Pascal (New York: International Publishers, 1963), p. 22.

27. Oakeshott, An Inaugural Lecture delivered at the London School of Economics. See his *Rationalism in Politics* (London: Methuen and Co. 1962), p. 127.

28. Edward Fitzgerald, *The Rubaiyat of Omar Khayyam of Naishapur*.

29. Cited by Arthur Stanley Eddington, "The Decline of Determinism," in *Great Essays in Science*, edited by Martin Gardner (New York: Pocketbooks, 1957), pp. 246-247.

30. Ibid., p. 256. Consult also *The Science of Science*, Maurice Goldsmith and Alan Mackay [eds.] (Harmdsworth: Penguin, 1964).

31. David Easton, *A Framework for Political Analysis* (Englewood Cliffs, N.J.: Prentice Hall, 1965), p. 7.

32. Karl Popper, *The Poverty of Historicism* (Boston: Beacon Press 1957), p. 49. Mulford Q. Sibley, "The Limitations of Behaviouralism," in *Contemporary Political Analysis*, James C. Charlesworth [ed.] (New York: The Free Press, 1967), p. 60.

33. Sibley, "The Limitations of Behaviouralism," p. 64. The works he cites as illustrations of the tendency by modern social scientists to equate scientific prediction with forecasting include Lasswell and A. Kaplan, *Power and Society* (New Haven: Yale University Press, 1950); Louis H. Bean, *How to Predict Elections* (New York: Knopf, 1948); Stuart Dodd, "Predictive Principles from Polls—Scientific Method in Public Opinion Research," *Public Opinion Quarterly*, Vol. 15 (1951—1952), pp. 23-24; R.A. Dahl, "The Science of Politics: New and Old," *World Politics*, Vol. VII, No. 3 (April 1955), pp. 479-489; and David Apter, "Theory and the

Study of Politics," *American Political Science Review*, Vol. 51, No. 3 (September 1957), pp. 747-762.

34. Sibley, "The Limitations of Behaviouralism," pp. 64-65.

35. Ibid., p. 51. See also "Norms and Values: Rethinking the Domestic Analogy," *Ethics and International Affairs*, Vol. I, 1987, pp. 135-162.

36. See also Richard L. Rubenstein, "Religion and Cultural Synthesis," *International Journal of the Unity of the Sciences*, Vol. 1, No. 1 (Spring 1988), pp. 99-118.

FIVE

AFRICA BETWEEN THE *MEIJI* RESTORATION AND THE LEGACY OF ATATÜRK
COMPARATIVE DILEMMAS OF MODERNIZATION (1981)

Approximately half a century separated the Meiji Restoration of 1868 in Japan and the rise of Mustafa Kemal Atatürk in Turkey. Involved in those two events were two distinct paradigms of modernization that are of relevance to non-occidental societies elsewhere. Of special relevance in this paper will be the dilemmas of African societies. What is at stake is the process of modernization, with its baggage of science and technology from the Renaissance to the post-industrial age. Can a non-Western society embrace this heritage of knowledge and modernity without committing cultural suicide? Are we still bedeviled as to whether a society can ever modernize without westernizing? Post-Meiji Restoration Japan and Turkey in the wake of the Kemalist Reforms gave two separate answers to this question. The Japanese after 1868 operated from the conviction that it was possible to embark upon economic and military modernization without simultaneously undergoing cultural Westernization. The economy and the military transformed the body of the state; the soul of the state, however, lay in the values, mores, and spiritual culture of the society. Although Shintoist doctrine is less dichotomous than Christian theology, the Japanese did seem to distinguish between the outer functions of the state and the inner spirit of the society. But in order to perform its functions, the state could indeed borrow specific military or industrial techniques from other societies. The slogan of "Western technique, Japanese spirit" captured the deliberate selectivity of the Japanese approach to modernization at that moment in time. Economic and military modernization began with the assumption that Japanese culture could be constant.

Fifty years later, Turkey faced comparable dilemmas, although the origins of those dilemmas went even further back than the period of the Meiji Restoration. After all, the Ottoman Empire had periodically agonized between Islamic authenticity and Western technical efficiency. These dilemmas among the Turks went back not only to the Young Turk Revolution but also to the *Tanzimat* and beyond. The moment of ultimate testing came, however, when the Ottoman Empire disintegrated and Turkey faced the realities of being a distinct and separate nation-state. The Atatürk Revolution took place at a moment of historic decision-making; Turkey was at the crossroads between Empire and Republic. Would Turkey choose the road of industrial and military modernization combined with cultural authenticity, as the Japanese had done? Or would Turkey decide that the economic and military body could not be modern if the cultural soul was still traditionalist? On the whole, the Kemalist doctrinal assumptions leaned towards the latter. Kemal Atatürk was more inclined to equate modernization with Westernization than the Meiji reformers in Japan. Another fifty years later societies in yet a third part of the world were confronting similar agonizing choices. In this paper, we are focusing especially on societies in Africa south of the Sahara. Can these societies modernize without westernizing? Should they adopt

Atatürk's doctrine that technical modernization was impossible without cultural Westernization? Or should they listen to the nostalgic music of a Japanese slogan in the last quarter of the nineteenth century: "Western technique, Japanese spirit"? Let us now turn to the African arena of these historic psychological conflicts.

Is Westernized Africa Pre-Modern?

In some respects, former colonial territories are fundamentally different from either Turkey or Japan. Far from being a former colony, Turkey after World War I became a former imperial power, an empire that had shrunk into a smaller republic. Japan in 1868, on the other hand, was a potential empire, and soon became an empire-in-the-making. Turkey modernized in the wake of territorial shrinkage; Japan modernized in anticipation of territorial expansion. Nationalism, in part, inspired both Turkey and Japan. Both sought modernization partly for defensive purposes: to strengthen themselves against the danger of being dominated by others. The history of Turkey after the modernization was a history of trying to abstain from the domination of others. The history of Japan after the Meiji Restoration was for a while a history of enhanced appetite for dominion over others.

Africa is of course different from both those historic situations. Much of the continent was indeed colonized by outsiders including the Turks. In North Africa the impact of the Ottoman heritage was considerable, but it also extended to the Horn of Africa. Indeed, the influence of Islam in Africa during the Ottoman Empire inevitably included an Ottoman component since the Ottoman Empire was at the time the political heartland of the Muslim world. From the second half of the nineteenth century it was Western Europe that gained the ascendancy in controlling the fortunes of the African continent. Britain, France, Portugal, Belgium, and others established varying empires in the African continent. Part of the legitimisation for empire building was best rendered by Rudyard Kipling's concept of the white man's burden. This included the commitment to "civilize" other societies, which in those days was approximately the equivalent of "modernize." To this extent, Africa had less of a choice as to which direction to take than either Turkey or Meiji Japan. The Western European powers in Africa chose the directions of social, economic, and political change. They also chose the main instrumentalities of change, from missionary schools to multinational corporations. Africa was deprived of both the industrial innovativeness of the Meiji reformers and the revolutionary interpreters of Kemalist Turkey. The Africans were not captains of their own destiny. They were not invited to look at historic charts to determine whether they could sail towards modernity without traversing Westernism.

Yet there is a residual fundamental question that we need to ask. Normally, the pertinent question has been whether one can modernize without westernizing. The converse has seldom been tackled. Can one westernize without modernizing? Part of the answer lies in the African experience. The pace of Westernization in Africa has been faster than the pace of modernization. In some areas of social change, there has therefore been Westernization without modernization—the transmission of culture without a transmission of skill. The question that now arises is under what circumstances can Westernization take place without modernization. In the African context, a number of discordant processes form part of this basic anomaly.

One anomalous process is urbanization without industrialization. In Western Europe urbanization gained momentum because industrialization was well under way or because large-scale agrarian plantations were forcing peasants into wage labor. In Africa, on the other hand, there was no agrarian revolution forcing subsistence farmers into wage labor. The sons of farmers moved to the cities for drastically different reasons. Within the cities themselves there was no expanding industrial revolution devouring the workers from the countryside. Industrial change in African cities was relatively modest, and was in any case overwhelmingly in the control of alien hands and under the management of alien skills. Whatever it is that generated urbanization in some important centers, it was neither large-scale rural productivity of the kind attained by England during her agrarian revolution nor was it expanding factory productivity that devoured labor from the countryside. Urbanization was fatally disjointed from industrialization in Africa. Urbanization helped foster Western tastes, dress, and ghetto lifestyles, but cultural urbanization was not accompanied by real, autonomous, and sustained industrialization.

The other discordant note in the African experience was scientification without secularization. The Western impact fostered the ideology of scientism, a religious belief in the supremacy of science. In the African context, the anomaly arose out of the paradoxical role of Christian missionaries. On the one hand, missionaries were in Africa to propagate a new gospel, asking Africans to exchange old beliefs and traditional religions for the Bible. On the other hand, the same Christian missionaries helped to build schools where Isaac Newton's theories were taught and where mathematics competed with Shakespeare. Out of this paradox of missionary schools, propagating a scientific culture emerged the deeper paradox of converting Africans to the ideology of scientism while at the same time capturing their souls for an alternative religious order. The outcome of it all was precisely the process of shallow scientification of African attitudes and values without their translation into technology.

Closely related to this anomaly is the anomaly of education without training. Much of the education in African colonial schools was a process of transmitting values without transmitting skills, acculturation without training. There were indeed differences among the imperial powers. For example, Belgium in the Congo was widely credited with emphasizing training rather than acculturation. Vocational training in the Belgian Congo had a higher premium than in either the British or the French colonies. Schools in Africa were more instruments for transmitting values and lifestyle than for transmitting skills and techniques. Quite often this meant transmitting to African societies some elements of European traditions, rather than elements of European modernity.

This element compounded the other anomaly of urbanization without industrialization. African schools seemed preeminently designed to produce rural misfits. An African who completes the equivalent of the Cambridge School Certificate examination, or in some areas the Higher School Certificate examination, is regarded as no longer suitable for residence in the rural areas. The young person's own parents may feel betrayed if the child with such a level of education insisted on remaining in the village. People assumed that sacrifices for higher and higher levels of education ultimately were to facilitate urban accomplishments rather than rural performance. Parents who have sacrificed a lot towards their children's secondary education, paying fees in societies without free education, would regard themselves as deeply betrayed if their educated offspring opted for the rural life instead of seeking fortunes in the urban areas. Had the schools been designed more for training (e.g., farming) instead of acculturation (e.g., Shakespeare and the Bible), education in Africa would not be quite as incompatible with rural development as it has tended to be. Once again, Westernization has triumphed over modernization.

Yet, another anomaly in the African situation is the promotion of capitalism without entrepreneurship. The profit motive and the quest for maximization of returns are indeed vigorous and widespread in African societies. Nonetheless, genuine entrepreneurship is still relatively rare. Sometimes, new wealth mitigates precisely against the spirit of entrepreneurship. For example, oil wealth in Nigeria hovers on the borderline between near-capitalism and innovative entrepreneurship. The Nigerian civil war generated innovation in Biafra as the beleaguered community engaged in major areas of self-reliance and inventiveness to cope with their own deprivation. One did hope that the civil war would at least have one beneficial effect because necessity fosters inventiveness. Unfortunately, Nigeria missed the opportunity of learning the techniques of creativity from the agonies of destruction, of learning innovation from the deprivations of war. The Nigerian situation was one in which oil wealth succeeded a civil war. While the civil war created a predisposition towards innovation, the oil wealth in the 1970s created a predisposition towards lethargy. A considerable diffusion and dilution of human energy took place in Nigeria in the aftermath of petro-energy.

These then are the major anomalous processes of Westernization in Africa, devoid of modernization. In reality, the picture is drawn a little too sharply. Some modernization, of course, has taken place in Africa. A modest level of industrialization has taken place alongside disproportionate urbanization. A modest level of technology has occurred alongside exaggerated secularization. As for education in Africa, it has disproportionately involved acculturation without training, the transmission of Western culture without necessarily transmitting Western skills and technique. How does this African predicament relate to the comparative scenarios of Atatürk's Turkey and the Meiji Japan? Meiji Japan was a case of attempted modernization without Westernization. The African colonial experience has been so far a case of Westernization basically without modernization. The case of Turkey under the legacy of Mustafa Kemal Atatürk has been a case of modernization through Westernization. Three scenarios are confronting the judgment of historiography. Are there ways of going beyond these traditional dilemmas of modernity and Westernism? Is there an escape from this paradigm of dilemmas ranging from the Meiji Restoration to the reforms of Kemal Atatürk, from the fortunes of former empires to the destinies of former colonies, from the power of political systems like those of Turkey and Japan to the fragility of ex-colonial states? The quest for a new paradigm may require regional specificity. A preliminary solution may have to be region-by-region, rather than global in scale; modernization as against Westernization; the struggle for authenticity as against the imperative of change.

Modernization in a Foreign Idiom

There is a more pervasive reason as to why the Western impact on Africa resulted in more Westernization than modernization. This involved the role of European languages in the whole process of acculturation in the African colonies. To understand the implications of this linguistic factor more fully, it is important first to confront the issue of modernization. We have already referred to processes like urbanization, industrialization, and secularization. These are accompanying characteristics of modernization rather than its defining attributes. These are the outer signs of modernization rather than its inner dynamic. In our terms, modernization is change in the direction which is compatible with the present stage of human knowledge, and which does justice to the potentialities of the human person both as a social and as an innovative being. This definition gives three attributes to modernization. One is compatibility with science and know-how. Second, modernity involves expanding social horizons and expanding frontiers of sympathy. Allegiance to clan and tribe is less modern than allegiance to nation; allegiance to nation is less modern than allegiance to continent; allegiance to continent is less modern than sensitivity to the needs of the human race. The second attribute of modernization in terms of doing justice to the human person as a social being carries with it the logic of constant effort to touch the global village. The third defining attribute of modernization is acceptance of innovativeness, encouragement of the spirit seeking improvement through exploration. Modernization becomes to some extent a readiness to applaud inventiveness, a readiness to encourage discovery.

The outer manifestations of this trinity of modernization can encompass processes like industrialization. Inventiveness and innovation can accelerate the application of science and technology to the tasks of economic productivity. When industrialization results in urbanization, the ties of clan, tribe, and village loosen, and social horizons expand. Ultimately modernization is partly measured by its proximity to current levels of awareness and knowledge, ranging from medical science to military capabilities. Secularization can be an outer manifestation of this deepening scientific sophistication. To an outside observer, Turkey since the Kemalist Revolution has sometimes mistaken the outward trappings of modernization for the inner essence, and has sometimes mistaken effect for cause. For example, should Turkey invite science in, or should it simply take religion out? The pursuit of science is a defining characteristic of modernization; but the discouragement of religion is an outer trapping, an accompanying characteristic of modernization at the most. The legacy of Atatürk has not always been clear: is it pursuing science or simply diluting the role of religion in society? Major reforms in the Kemalist tradition seem to be obsessed with such trappings as dress and vocabulary as ways of reducing the visibility of religion in Turkish society. The flamboyant trappings of religion were either discouraged or torn asunder; but the essence of science was not necessarily pursued.

In contrast, Japan after the Meiji Restoration focused on the pursuit of technique and know-how rather than the dilution of religion. On the contrary, religious symbolism was mobilized to lend greater legitimacy to the aggressive pursuit of technical efficiency. The religious outlook of the

Japanese had varied aspects. The most national was of course the Shintoist tradition, but this was moderated by two other traditions. One had its ancestry in India, Buddhism. The other had its ancestry in China, encompassing both Buddhist and Confucian elements. A synthesis of some kind, or at least a *modus vivendi* among the different traditions, had evolved over the centuries. The Japanese decision to add a Western component to that diverse heritage did not begin with a decision to secularize Japan. It began with a decision to industrialize Japan, not by destroying the Gods of religion but by lighting the fires of science.

Another contrast between Turkey and Japan concerns the issue of expanding social horizons as a defining characteristic of modernization. The Atatürk revolution in Turkey occurred, as we indicated, in the wake of territorial shrinkage. The Ottoman Empire had been disintegrating and Turkey was shrinking to the size of a solitary republic. In contrast, the Meiji Restoration was to some extent a prelude to an imperial role. Initially the primary ambition of Japan, as of Turkey after World War I, was simply protection against an external threat. In the words of Josefa M. Sanial:

> Modernization was Japan's response to the nineteenth century challenge caused by the threatened military and economic aggression from abroad at a time when continued unrest beset Tokugawa Japan. After the fall of the *Tokugawa bakufu*, modernization was a response to the challenge of continued infringement of Japan's sovereign rights by "extra-territoriality" and "uniform tariffs" provisions of her "unequal treaties" with Western powers—for as long as Japanese feudal institutions persisted.[1]

Then Japan became expansionist, looking for a global imperial role. Yet, for quite a while she was frustrated by the prior rivalry of Western powers. As Michael Edwardes put it:

> When Japan felt the impetus of imperial expansion herself—the natural consequences, Marxists would maintain, of her Western capitalist structure—she was continually frustrated by the old colonial powers unless it suited the immediate advantage of imperial rivalries. Japan's position was that of an uninvited guest arriving late at the banquet, only to find that the choicest food was reserved for others.[2]

What is clear from these trends is that Japan's industrialization gradually led to the expansion of social horizons, with all their frustrations at that stage. On the other hand, shrinking social horizons accompanied Turkey's Westernization as the legacy of an imperial order gave way to the parochialism of a solitary republic. Japan's expanding social horizons might have aided her capacity to modernize in substance instead of only westernizing in trappings. Turkey's social shrinkage might have made it more difficult for her to embark on an adequate "takeoff."

In the period immediately following the Meiji Restoration, the Japanese became economically strong mainly because they wanted to be militarily strong. The impetus for industrialization was, at least in the initial stages, the imperative of national defense. But then came World War II, Pearl Harbor, and the disasters of Hiroshima and Nagasaki. The American occupation followed and one product was the constitution of Japan, eventually forbidding Japan from arming itself beyond minimal local defense. A second Japanese miracle occurred. Whereas the Meiji industrialization was the achievement of a militantly militarized Japan, the new industrialization seemed to be the achievement of militantly pacifist or at least demilitarized Japan. In the first half of the century the industrial might of Japan was partly attributed to its war-like determination; in the second half of the twentieth century, Japanese achievements were sometimes attributed to the fact that she spent less money on her own defense and let the United States assume ultimate responsibility for the military protection of Japan. By the 1980s, pressures were mounting on Japan to spend more on her defense to get her to reduce her exports to the United States and Europe. These pressures were particularly conspicuous in policy statements from Washington. In other words, there was a feeling among Japan's Western friends that Tokyo should become more militarily aggressive and less economically aggressive. Tokyo should spend more money on her military preparedness against the Soviet Union and devote less energy towards capturing economic markets in Europe and North America.

In either case, Japan could not but have her global horizons broadened, with commensurate performance in her productive capabilities. Even without repealing the relevant clause in her constitution that limits her expenditure on defense, Japan's military capability was already among the top seven in the world when calculated in terms of expenditure and industrial prowess. The three defining characteristics of modernization—responsiveness to know-how, expanding social horizons, and deepening innovation—all seem to be supremely realized in the Japanese miracle. What was often lacking was the moral underpinning of expanding social horizons, a moral empathy with other people beyond mere understanding of the behavior of their markets and the dynamics of supply and demand in their societies.

What Turkey and Japan did have in common was the effort to modernize through their own national languages. This was in sharp contrast to colonial situations where educational and scientific change was disproportionately in the imported idiom of the imperial power. There were indeed differences between Turkish attitudes and Japanese attitudes to language. Both the Turks and the Japanese wanted to make their languages more flexible in order to accommodate both the richness and the specificity of modern scientific discourse. But whereas the Japanese decided to do it mainly through borrowing new words, the Turks decided to do it both through borrowing new words and through destroying old usages. The Japanese welcomed such specific Western concepts as *baransu*, meaning "balance," a concept that has had considerable influence in both Japanese economic policy and technological thrust. But the Japanese have also permitted their linguistic heritage to fare for itself in the new industrial age. The Turks, on the other hand, have not limited themselves to adopting new Western phrases and concepts; they have at times systematically attempted to purge Turkish of certain older and Arabic derived concepts. Again, in vocabulary as in lifestyle, the Japanese insisted on introducing new things, and letting new things affect the destiny of older ways. The Turks, on the other hand, have sometimes insisted on destroying older ways in the hope that the ashes would be fertile for the growth of new things.

But where does Africa lie as between these two paradigms? The most basic factor to grasp in the African situation is the massive impact of alien languages in precisely those areas regarded as central to modernization. For the time being, it is a socio-linguistic impossibility for an African to be a sophisticated physicist without at the same time being fluent in a European language. It is indeed a socio-linguistic impossibility for African physicists to sit together and discuss professional issues in an African language. The business of physics, chemistry, and biology must be conducted almost exclusively in European languages. The path to scientific modernization in an African context is, for the time being, inevitably through linguistic Westernization. African universities are special arenas for Western acculturation. Outside Arab Africa, the medium of instruction in all departments is a European language, although most first year undergraduates have still a rather limited command of the imperial medium. In the specific area of political modernization, we once again have to bear witness to the striking role of Western languages. In many African countries that have competitive parties and parliamentary systems, the medium of electoral and parliamentary discourse is a European language, understood only by a limited number of the citizens. Is the prominence of the imperial language an aid or a hindrance to keeping up with the present state of human knowledge? In the short run, it is indeed an aid. Mastery over French or English enhances the modernization of the elite in African societies. On the other hand, equating modernization with competence in English or French slows the modernization of the masses in the African context. Modernizing through the imperial language gains speed at the relevant level of elitist change, but it slows down the involvement of the masses in the modernizing process.

The masses in Japan have been more speedily involved in the technological age than they would have been had they needed first to learn a European language. The technical modernization of the Japanese language was in part a process of technological democratization—making it possible for more and more Japanese to enter the process of modernization without having to learn an entirely alien linguistic universe. Kemal Atatürk inaugurated a similar process in Turkey, helping the Turkish language to acquire technological competence, and thereby enabling the Turkish masses to be initiated into the technological age sooner than they might have done had they been forced to learn another language before becoming modern.

The imperial language in ex-colonial states might appear to enhance the capabilities of the elite to expand their social horizons and to understand the wider world. They do indeed understand the wider world; but do they cease to understand their immediate environment? Do the elites of Africa understand London, Paris, and New York more readily than they understand their own villages? If that is the case, there is no real expansion of social horizons; there is only a substitution of alien horizons for indigenous ones. Once again, the African predicament is one of faster Westernization than modernization. The illusion of linguistic acculturation also sometimes hampers innovation. Because Africans are learning new things through their new language, they sometimes think they are learning original things. Very often, what is being transmitted is secondhand and sometimes banal, but it is being transmitted in impeccable French. The romance of the French language is mistaken for scientific originality. Once again, modernization lags behind Westernization in Africa.

Towards Modernizing Westernized Africa

Given that Africa is for the time being sentenced to the apparent paradox of Westernization without modernization, what is the way out of this fate? And what lessons can be drawn from the experience of the Meiji Restoration and the reforms of Mustafa Kemal Atatürk? In an ex-colonial state the first imperative for modernization in the face of prior Westernization is, paradoxically, the imperative of indigenization. Westernization has linked the local psyche, especially among the elite, with the distant world of Europe and North America. In order to transform cultural substitution into cultural expansion, a connection has to be reestablished with the local scene. The imperative of indigenization seeks to localize resources, personnel, and effective control. The Atatürk Revolution did include a substantial indigenization. The Meiji Restoration began with the indigenous and proceeded toward mating the indigenous with the stimulus of the alien. The strategy of indigenization in Africa requires that in situations where African rivers could be converted into hydroelectric power, this should be regarded as more important than establishing instrumentalities of energy that require imported oil or imported uranium. Indigenization is partly an exercise in selecting what is indigenously available and giving that priority over what is exogenously imported.

A second struggle in the pursuit of modernization as against Westernization is the strategy of domestication. In this latter sense, what we are looking for is not resurrection or utilization of the indigenous it is closer to the effort of making the foreign more relevant to the local scene. In Africa, one of the more obvious examples is the African university itself, ostensibly a carrier of modern labels of knowledge and sophistication, a measurement of one of the defining characteristics of modernity. The strategy of domestication means making these institutions much more responsive to the imperative of local needs.[3]

A third strategy for going beyond Westernization involves the strategy of cultural diversification. The effort to learn from more than one culture, to respond to the stimulus of creative diversity, is itself a process of minimizing the Western impact while at the same time responding to the impact of modernity. Diversification also aids expansion of social horizons, educating Africans to take seriously not simply what the West has to teach the world, but also what China, Japan, Islam, India and other civilizations have to contribute to the broad arena of both human understanding and human skills. This degree of diversification to some extent has been deficient in both the examples of Turkey and of Japan. On balance, both the Kemalist and the Meiji reforms focused on an immediate marriage between the indigenous and the Occidental heritages. In the African condition, the diversification needs to go further, linking the African not only with the West, but hopefully also with the Turkish and with the Japanese and with other heritages beyond. The beginnings of cultural freedom lie in cultural diversification, responding to the full impact of external plurality combined with national singularity.

Deeply related to this particular thrust is what I have called elsewhere the strategy of horizontal interpenetration. This is the mutual penetration of otherwise less privileged societies or otherwise less autonomous cultures. The Japanese had at least a prior synthesis of this kind of interpenetration, ranging from the legacy of India to the legacy of China at a time when Japan was about to experiment with the legacy of Europe. It is arguable that Turkey did not permit itself to be as culturally promiscuous. Turkey under Atatürk mistrusted the demands of the Islamic heritage but was at the same time fascinated by the promise of Western civilization. Modernization under Kemal Atatürk was in part a quest for civilization. In the conclusion of his monumental *Six-Day Speech* of 1927, Kemal reasserted his creed that "we make use of every means solely and exclusively for one purpose: to bestow upon the Turkish nation that position which is its due within the civilized world."4 Atatürk's formulation has already been traced to the 1914 decree in Turkey abolishing the capitulations in reviewing the nineteenth century reform efforts:

> The Ottoman Empire ... continues to march in the path of renaissance and reform which it entered upon [with the *Tanzimat* Decree of 1839] ... in order to assure for itself the place which was due to it in the family of the civilized peoples of Europe.5

Ultimately modernization requires responsiveness to more than Western civilization. Neither Turkey with the Atatürk legacy nor Japan in the aftermath of the Meiji Restoration were able to go beyond responsiveness to Western culture as an additive to what had already been accumulated indigenously.

A fifth strategy of conversion from Westernization to modernization involves what I have had reason to call elsewhere counter-penetration. This involves penetrating the citadels of power, and exerting some leverage over those powers in defense of Third World interests. Japan has been the most decisive instrument of economic counter-penetration in history. Its ability to enter into the citadels of Western economic power, and create consternation in those citadels, has been something almost unequalled in the history of the Western world's relations with the rest of the universe. Japanese counter-penetration has led to screams for the control of Japanese imports from Detroit to Birmingham, from Minnesota to Munich. Yet, when Japan's economy is in recession the world holds its breath nervously. Turkey's economic performance since the Atatürk Revolution has been far less impressive than Japan's performance since the Meiji Restoration. The comparison is less than fair to Turkey since no other country has equaled Japan's industrial miracle. Africa's capacity for counter-penetrating the Western world in the future would depend on three possible trends: the stabilization and Pan-Africanization of Nigeria, the more complete liberation of the Republic of South Africa,[6] and the politicization and sophistication of Black America.[7]

Counter-penetration helps to make dependence mutual. To that extent, it is the logical conclusion of genuine modernization. We did indicate earlier that modernization is in part a process of expanding social horizons and expanding empathy. Those who are loyal only to their clans and tribes are less modern than those loyal to some wider human entity. The most modern of all are the few who are beginning to perceive the world as a global village. These may regard humankind as a whole as their clan to help defend and protect without being "clannish." Reciprocal penetration between societies on terms that are fair and equitable can become the foundations of genuine human interdependence. The expanding horizons and empathy that would in time result from such equitable interdependence could be the ultimate consummation of the process of modernization. Today one cannot travel around Africa without witnessing a little bit of the Western world from one African country to another. Perhaps one day it might be true that one cannot travel within the Western world without witnessing a little bit of Africa from one Western society to another. Before that fully happens, Africa would have to catch up in two areas of modernization: enhanced sensitivity to new levels of knowledge and enhanced capacity for innovation. These two would help facilitate that third process of modernization mentioned earlier—expanding social horizons and empathy. By that time, Africa will have learnt not to mistake Westernization for modernization, not to pursue the trappings of Western cultures at the expense of the substance of modernity.

Conclusion

This paper has attempted to disentangle some of the central dilemmas of modernization and social change that have faced many societies in the last hundred-and-fifty years. We have focused especially on two paradigms of purposeful change: Japan's industrialization after the Meiji Restoration and the reforms of Kemal Atatürk in Turkey after the First World War. We have sought to demonstrate that, in at least earlier phases of modernization in Japan, the ambition was to hold a substantial part of Japanese culture constant while the Japanese economy and military modernized. It was believed that technique could be distinguished from essence. Japanese culture was the soul of the society while the economy, the state, and the military were the equivalent of physical limbs. The limbs could be made stronger with exercise and a change of diet, but ultimately the soul had to remain loyal to itself. Hence the old Japanese slogan: "Western technique, Japanese spirit!"

The Atatürk reforms in Turkey, on the other hand, started from the premise that neither the state nor the economy could effectively modernize unless Turkish culture itself modernized. The soul of the nation had to be converted to a new allegiance before the limbs of the nation could perform their tasks effectively. In theory, the Atatürk approach seemed the more coherent. Society was an integrated phenomenon, and no easy distinction could be made between culture and economy, between the state and the collective soul. In practice, the Japanese effort involved a greater transformation and a higher level of performance than anything attained by Turkey since Atatürk. However, the reasons for the difference in performance are complex and cannot be attributed solely to the distinction between modernizing without westernizing (the Meiji way) and modernizing through westernizing (the Atatürk way). In the case of Africa, the trend has been more like westernizing without modernizing. The trappings of Western culture have gained ascendancy rather than the real substance of modernization. It is time for Africa to go back to the drawing board.

NOTES

This chapter is a revised version of a paper presented, under the same title, at an international symposium on Atatürk, held from May 17 to May 22, 1981, and subsequently published in *The Bankasi International Symposium on Atatürk* (Ankara: Turkiyi is Bankasi Kultur Yayinlari, 1983), pp. 359-394.

1. "The Mobilization of Traditional Values in the Modernization of Japan," in Roberts N. Bellah (ed.), *Religion and Progress in Modern Asia* (New York: The Free Press, London: Collier-MacMillan, 1965), pp. 124-125.
2. Michael Edwardes, *Asia in the European Age, 1498-1955* (New York: Frederick E. Praeger, 1962), p. 278. Consult also Robert A. Scalapino, "Ideology and Modernization: The Japanese Case," Chapter III, in David E. Apter (ed.), *Ideology and Discontent* (New York: The Free Press of Glencoe; 1964), p. 94.
3. For a more detailed discussion of various means of modernizing and decolonizing the African university, refer to my article entitled "Africa and Cultural Dependency: the Case of the African University," reproduced as Chapter 1 in this volume.

4. *Nutuk*, 1934, Edn. II, p. 336.

5. Cited in J.C. Hurewitz, *Diplomacy in the Near and Middle East* (Princeton, N.J.: Van Nostrand, 1956), Vol. II, p. 2.

6. Political apartheid has substantially ended, but economic apartheid is still intact. The best lands, the best mines, the best jobs, the best economic and commercial opportunities are still under white control.

7. For a fuller discussion of these aspects, please refer to Chapter 1 in this volume.

SIX

ISLAM IN AFRICA
AN OVERVIEW (1991)

The history of Islam in Africa is almost as old as the history of the religion itself. There is reason to believe that Islam arrived in Ethiopia before the beginning of the Islamic calendar itself, that is to say, before the *Hijrah* when the Prophet Muhammad migrated to Medina. A few believers, persecuted in Mecca, finally crossed the Red Sea and found their way to the "Habash" of Abyssinia in search of asylum. Ethiopian records claim and celebrate that event to the present day. Islam's earliest conversion of an African probably took place in the Arabian peninsula itself. It seems probable that Bilal, the slave who was freed as a result of the Prophet's intervention, was the first great African convert to Islam. Bilal became the first outstanding *muezzin* in Islamic history. As a person he was one of the Prophet Muhammad's favourites. While in sub-Saharan Africa Islam first arrived as a victim in search of asylum, in North Africa Islam first arrived as a victor in search of new worlds to conquer. The Arabs conquered Egypt from Byzantium in the year 639 A.D. The victors then moved further west, conquering more and more of North Africa.

Cultural Diffusion: Religion and Language

With the Arab conquest of North Africa two processes were set in motion that were of relevance for Africa into the modern period: the processes of Islamization and Arabization. Islamization was the gradual transmission of the Islamic religion, as more and more of the conquered peoples embraced the faith. Arabization was the transmission of the Arabic language, as more and more North Africans became native-speakers of Arabic over the centuries. Arabization in North Africa took much longer than Islamization. But when North Africans became native speakers of Arabic, it was only a matter of time before they would see themselves as indeed Arabs. It was not just their language; it was also their very identity. Up the Nile Valley the twin processes of Islamization and Arabization continued. The two processes together constituted the making of new Arabs along the valley of the great river. More and more Northern Sudanese not only converted to Islam, but also increasingly saw themselves as part of the Arab world. The Arabic language became their mother tongue, long after the Islamic religion had indeed become their faith.

The establishment of British control under the so-called "Anglo-Egyptian condominium" in the Sudan (1877 to 1955) slowed down the processes of Islamization and Arabization further South. Indeed, Southern Sudan was effectively insulated from the Arabized North because of British imperial policy. Christianization was encouraged in the South, while Islamization was banned, to all intents and purposes. The foundation of a religious apartheid system was being laid under British control. These policies of ethno-religious compartmentalization had devastating consequences after Sudan's independence in 1955. Perceived widely as a war between the Arabo-Muslim North and the Christian-animist South, the first Sudanese civil war lasted from 1955 until 1972. The second Sudanese civil war broke out in 1983 and was partly in protest against President Jaafar Numeiry's decision to make Islam a state religion and the *Shari'a* the law of the land. The southern military leader, John Garang, continued to rebel against the North in spite of the overthrow of Numeiry and the succession of other regimes in Khartoum. Far from ceasing to be the religion of the state, Islam was further consolidated politically under the government of General Umar Hassan Ahmad al-Bashir.

Despite the war, however, the Arabic language continued to spread in Southern Sudan. Indeed, Southern Sudan was probably the only part of sub-Saharan Africa where Arabization was proceeding much faster than Islamization. In all other parts of sub-Saharan Africa where Arabic and Islam were important factors, it was the religion rather than the language that was making the most inroads into African life and society. Islam in North Africa as a whole arrived as a victor; Islam in southern Africa, and especially in South Africa, arrived as victim. The importation of Muslim Malay slaves into South Africa in the eighteenth century created a distinct setting for the religion in subsequent generations. While the Arabs brought and promoted Islam in Northern Africa, Islam in southern Africa was partly a legacy of South-East Asians and South Asians. In North Africa, Muslim majorities lived alongside a deepening level of Westernization. In Southern Africa, Muslim minorities lived alongside what later became an even more rapid degree of Westernization.

For North Africa, as we indicated, Islamization (the spread of the religion) was followed by Arabization (the linguistic assimilation of the people). For Southern Africa, there was Islamization without any significant degree of Arabization. East Africa and West Africa also present contrasting models of Islamization. Basil Davidson has argued that Islam in sub-Saharan Africa owed "nothing to Arab conquest but much to Berber influence." The trans-Saharan trade went back to pre-Phoenician times, and had resulted in the settlement of Berber communities in parts of West Africa.

But now the difference was that Islam could more effectively bind all these communities together, whether in the Western Sudan, among the oasis relay stations of the desert country, or in North Africa.[1]

Davidson does concede that there were two major Moroccan military invasions. These were the destructive Almoravid raids of the eleventh century and the Moroccan invasion of Songhay in 1591. These incursions from the north did not help Islam in West Africa and, according to Davidson, might even have undermined it. Of longer-term significance was the quiet spread of Islam as a result of Berber settlements, trans-Saharan trade, and the broader historical intercourse between the Berber peoples and their southern neighbours. It was not the sword of the Arabs but the socializing of the Berbers that laid the foundations of Islam in West Africa.

Where Basil Davidson is over-reaching himself is when he extends this thesis to the whole of sub-Saharan Africa. It works for West Africa, but it most certainly does not work for East Africa. Partly because of the proximity of the Arabian Peninsula, and partly because of the special role of Muslim Egypt, the Arab factor has been pronounced in the arrival and expansion of Islam in this Eastern sub-region from the earliest days into the twentieth century. *Qadis*, *Walis*, and other religious leaders were overwhelmingly people who claimed Arab descent, if not descent from the Prophet Muhammad himself. One adverse consequence of this Arab leadership of East African Islam was that it prolonged the image of Islam as a "foreign" religion—in contrast to Islam's rapid indigenization in West Africa. A related adverse consequence in East Africa was that Arab leadership inhibited the emergence of dynamic indigenous African Muslim leaders—again in contrast to the towering role of local African leaders in West African Muslim affairs.

Perhaps in direct consequence, Islam in West Africa continued to expand numerically and geographically even under the dominion of Christian imperialist powers. On the other hand, the spread of Islam in what are today Tanzania, Kenya, and Uganda was arrested because the foundations of the religion in the hinterland had not yet been adequately Africanized. In earlier centuries, Islam in both West Africa and East Africa had been a major spur in state-formation. In West Africa, these included the imperial states of Kanem-Bornu (thirteenth to nineteenth centuries), Mali (thirteenth to fifteen centuries), and Songhay (fourteenth to sixteenth centuries). In East Africa, the Swahili city-states of Kilwa, Pate, and Mombasa, lasted until they were undermined by the Portuguese following Vasco da Gama's circumnavigation of the Cape of Good Hope. Zanzibar under the Omani Sultanate later fell under so-called British "protection" until 1963. In January 1964, a revolution by indigenous Africans (mainly fellow Muslims) overthrew the Arab Sultanate. What all these experiences and upheavals demonstrated was that Islam was an important factor in the history of state-formation in both East and West Africa. It was also a major force in the history of urbanization. In ancient Mali and Songhay the social tensions were sometimes between the Islamized towns and the far less Islamized countryside. Monarchs were sometimes known to play the forces of the countryside against the towns in a bid for ancient checks-and-balances. Sunni Ali, ruler of Songhay, was one such ruler who tried to manipulate Islamized townsman against animist peasant, and vice versa, in a perpetual game of political intrigue in the last third of the fifteenth century.

Agents of Islamic Expansion

Underlying the whole saga about religion and society are the five modes by which Islam has spread in Africa. The most spectacular mode is expansion by conquest. Paradoxically, this affects mainly Arab Africa in the north of the continent, which was Islamized initially by the sword. Sub-Saharan examples of Islamization by conquest are few and far between. Some conquests did take place, as in the case of the Almoravid's devastating incursions into West Africa from 1052 to 1076. Ibn Khaldun confirms that the conquerors did force Blacks to become Muslims. But today's historians affirm that since Almoravids did not maintain a continuing presence, their short-term atrocities harmed the image of Islam rather than helping it. Such invasions were therefore not relevant for explaining the spread of Islam. Subsequently, people converted despite the memory of the Almoravids.

The second agency for the expansion of Islam was Muslim migration and settlement in non-Muslim areas. Arabs from Yemen and Oman settling in East Africa were among the co-founders of the Swahili civilization in what is today Tanzania and Kenya. The rapid Islamization and Arabization of North Africa was not only achieved through conquest, but also through migration and settlement. Doctrinally, this mode of transmission of the Message goes back to the *Hijrah* itself. As we indicated earlier, the migration may sometimes be of victims rather than victors. This is true of the Malay slaves and labourers imported into South Africa. Islam arrived in chains in what later became the land of apartheid. These ex-slaves (counted among the "Coloreds" of South Africa under apartheid) have kept the flame of Islam burning in South Africa for three hundred years.

The third agency for the spread of Islam was trade. By far, the best illustration is the trans-Saharan trade. The camels that crossed the great desert carried varied commodities in each direction. Perhaps the greatest commodity of all was cultural diffusion, the spread of Islam from North Africa to Western Africa especially. Today countries like Guinea, modern Mali, Sénégal, and Niger are overwhelmingly Muslim in population. Arab and Swahili traders in Eastern, Central and Southern Africa also played a part in carrying Islam to parts of what are today Uganda, Zaire, Malawi, and Mozambique. The commodities involved in the trade included ivory, copper, gold, manufactured goods from abroad and, tragically, slaves.

The fourth agency for the spread of Islam was actual purposeful missionary work or *D'awa*. In the earlier centuries this took the form of travelling *imams*, healers, and teachers. Muslim healers acquired such a reputation that to the present-day a large proportion of their patients in Africa are non-Muslims, including Christians. Their healing techniques have included the use of verses of the Qur'an, including the popular prescription of writing out the verse in washable ink on a slate, then washing it into a bowl and having the patient "drink the sacred verse." Grateful patients sometimes converted to the faith. Recently, Islamic missionary work has included material for use in *madrasa* and schools. Special books or pamphlets have been written in African languages to explain the religion not only to students, but also to non-Muslims. Pamphlets in the Swahili language have poured fourth from Zanzibar, the Kenyan Coast, and the Coast of mainland Tanzania. And in the twentieth century, the Qur'an was at last translated into Kiswahili, first by the controversial Ahmadiyya movement, and later by Sunni scholars from Tanzania and Kenya. As the twentieth century was coming to a close there were three different Swahili editions of the Qur'an, though the third one was published only in part. Some Muslims believed that translations of the Qur'an into other languages were a form of sinful imitation of the Holy Book. The chief Muslim jurists of East Africa have given *fatwas* contradicting that doctrine. They have argued that if it was not sinful to translate the Qur'an orally in a sermon in a mosque, it was not sinful to translate it into writing.

In parts of Africa, the most active missionary group for Islam has indeed been the Ahmadiyya movement, founded by the nineteenth century religious militant in British India, Mirza Ghulam Ahmad. But the movement is widely regarded as "heretical" by most African Muslims, and has had a hard time gaining legitimacy in countries like Nigeria. The main bone of contention is that members of the Ahmadiyya denomination do not regard the Prophet Muhammad as the last of the prophets; they only acknowledge him as the greatest. Mirza Ghulam Ahmad was, to his followers, a prophet in his own right—but not as great as Muhammad. In Nigeria, in the twentieth century, the Ahmadiyya have sometimes been denied foreign exchange privileges to enable them to make the pilgrimage to Mecca— because they were not recognized as Muslims. The Saudi authorities also wanted the Ahmadiyya to be controlled, if possible. The movement continues to be one of the most active missionary forces on behalf of Islam evident in Africa.

Sunni and Shiite missionary work entered a new stage in the second half of the twentieth century with the arrival of petro-wealth in Saudi Arabia, Iran, Libya, and other parts of the oil-producing Muslim world. In Africa, schools could be built as well as mosques. Clinics were subsidized and scholarships offered to study abroad. On the whole, the petro-wealth was used not so much to attract new converts into the Muslim fold as to support the welfare and well-being of those who were already Muslims. There were reparations favouring new conversions. Sunni Islam is still by far the main beneficiary of such conversions. Although itself Shiite, Iran has sometimes been ready to subsidize Sunni missionary work in Africa in a spirit of Muslim unity. As for the Ismaili movement under the leadership of the Aga Khan (more Shiite than Sunni), it sometimes explicitly committed its missionaries to the propagation of Sunni Islam rather than to its own denomination. The rationale was that "expanding the size of the Muslim *ummah* in Africa is more important than creating more followers for His Highness the Aga Khan."

In examining the agencies for the spread of Islam in Africa, we have so far examined conquest, migration, trade, and missionary work. The fifth agency in Africa's historical experience has been periodic revivalist movements. These sometimes take the form of an internal "morally purifying *jihad*," or are under the leadership of a "*Mahdi*." Among the most spectacular of these revivalist movements were those that unleashed the *jihad* led by Uthman dan Fodio in what is today Nigeria. Until this upheaval, the Hausa states were at best an informal and loose confederation—sometimes allies, sometimes rivals. Katsina, Gobir, Zaria, and Kano vied with each other from about the fourteenth century. The north-south trade across the Sahara was at the core of much of their rivalry. It was in the nineteenth century that the revivalist *jihad* led by Uthman dan Fodio, partly inspired by a glorified vision of the Abbasid dynasty centuries earlier, burst onto the stage of West African history. Was it merely revivalism or was it conquest? In reality it was both. The long-term consequence was the relative unification of much of Hausaland under a single over-arching sovereign. Uthman's son, Muhammad Bello, became the first *Amir al Mu'minin* of Hausaland, the "Commander of the Faithful." Islam expanded as the Hausa integrated.

At least as spectacular was the movement in Eastern Sudan led by Muhammad Ahmad Ibn Abdullah. This Muslim Reformation in Eastern Sudan started in 1881 in the wake of many years of Turco-Egyptian rule, compounded by British manipulations. Unlike the *jihad* of Uthman dan Fodio, that of Muhammad Ahmad was also a struggle for national independence. Religious revivalism intertwined with political nationalism. Muhammad Ahmad went further than Uthman dan Fodio. The Sudanese leader declared himself the *Mahdi*, appointed by God to re-unite the Muslim *ummah*. His vision extended well beyond his own ancestral Sudan. In a sense, he wanted to fuse Pan-Islam with Pan-Africanism and Pan-Arabism. His dream was too big for his base, and too vulnerable to the new European imperialism and he was defeated. But Islam did make one more step forward in Sudanese history. To the present day the *Mahdi*'s religious and political legacy lives on in the political configuration of the Sudan. Indeed, the country's last elected prime minister of the 20th century was Sadiq al-Mahdi, his grandson.

In Africa since independence two issues have been central to religious speculation: Islamic expansion and Islamic revivalism. Expansion is about the spread of religion and its scale of new conversions. Revivalism is about the rebirth of faith among those who are already converted. Expansion is a matter of geography and populations; it is a search of new worlds to conquer. Revivalism is a matter of history and nostalgia; it is a search of ancient worlds to re-enact. The spread of Islam in post-colonial Africa is basically a peaceful process of persuasion and consent. The revival of Islam is often an angry process of re-discovered fundamentalism. In Arab Africa there is little expansion taking place, although some Egyptian Muslim fundamentalists regard the Coptic Church as a historical anachronism which ought to end. For North Africa as a whole, Islamic revivalism is the main issue. It probably cost President Anwar Sadat his life in 1981 and it has been at war with the ruling regimes of Algeria and Egypt under Mubarak. For a while after 1969, Libya carried Islamic revivalism further as an official policy than any other ruler in Africa. Jaafar Numeiry as ruler of Sudan, before his overthrow in 1985, also attempted a full-fledged revival of Islamic law (*Shari'a*), with severe additional strain on the North-South divide in the country. Once proclaimed, it became difficult for Numeiry's civilian successors to repeal *Shari'a*, the Islamic code. Sadiq al-Mahdi continued the search for a formula that would enable the Sudan to retreat from what he describes as "Numeiry's September laws." But the succeeding regime of al-Bashir became more militantly Islamic.

Outside Arab Africa the central issue concerning Islam is not merely its revival; it is also the speed of its expansion. Unrealized though it may be, there are more Muslims in Nigeria than there are Muslims in any Arab country, including Egypt. Muslims in Ethiopia are not a small minority; they are nearly half the population. Islam elsewhere in Africa has spread, however unevenly, all the way down to the Cape of Good Hope. Islam in South Africa is three hundred years old, having first arrived not directly from Arabia but from South East Asia with Malay immigrants, as we indicated. The largest countries in Africa in population are Nigeria, Egypt, Ethiopia, and the Congo (Zaire). Between them, these four countries account for well over 120 million Muslims—with the Islamic part of the Congo (Zaire) being mainly in the east. Virtually half the population of the continent is now Muslim. But Islam in Africa does not of course exist in isolation. The world of religious experience in Africa is rich in diversity. Let us look at Islam in this wider religious context.

Indigenous Ecumenicalism
and Semitic Competitiveness

Of the three principal religious legacies of Africa (Indigenous, Islamic, and Christian) perhaps the most tolerant is the indigenous tradition. It is even arguable that Africa did not have religious wars before Christianity and Islam arrived. Precisely because these two latter faiths were universalist in aspiration (seeking to convert the whole of human kind), they were inherently competitive. In Africa, Christianity and Islam have often been in competition for the soul of the continent. Rivalry has sometimes resulted in conflict. Indigenous African religions, on the other hand, are basically communal rather than universalist. Like Hinduism and modern Judaism, and unlike Christianity and Islam, indigenous African traditions have not sought to convert the whole of human kind. By not being universalist in that sense, the African traditions have not been in competition with each other for the souls of other people. The Yoruba do not seek to convert the Ibo to Yoruba religion, or vice versa. Nor do the

Yoruba or the Ibo compete with each other for the souls of a third group like the Hausa. By not being proselytizing religions, indigenous African creeds have not fought with each other. Over the centuries, Africans have waged many kinds of wars with each other but hardly ever religious ones before the universalist creeds arrived. What has this to do with contemporary Africa? The indigenous toleration today has often mitigated the competitiveness of the imported Semitic religions (Christianity and Islam). Let us illustrate with Sénégal, a country that is over eighty per cent Muslim. The founder president of this predominantly Islamic society was Léopold Sédar Senghor. He presided over the fortunes of post-colonial Sénégal for two decades, in basic political partnership with the Muslim leaders of the country, the Marabouts. His successor as President (partly sponsored by him) was Abdou Diouf, a Muslim ruler of a Muslim society. But the tradition of ecumenical tolerance continued in Sénégal. The first lady of the country, Madame Elizabeth Diouf, was Roman Catholic. And several of the Ministers of the new President were Christian. Senegalese religious tolerance has continued in other spheres since then. What in other Islamic countries elsewhere in the world might be regarded as provocative is tolerated in Sénégal. There have been occasions when Christian festivals (like those celebrated after the First Communion) were publicly held in Dakar right in the middle of the Islamic fast of *Ramadan*. And the Christian merry-makers have been left undisturbed.[2] To summarize the argument so far, predominantly Muslim countries south of the Sahara have been above average in religious toleration. The capacity to accommodate other faiths to some extent may be part of the historical Islamic tradition in multi-religious empires. But far more religiously tolerant than either Islam or Christianity have been indigenous African traditions, especially since these do not aspire to universalism and are not inherently competitive. In Black Africa, this indigenous tolerance has often moderated the competitive propensities of

Christianity and Islam.

As President of Uganda in his first administration Milton Obote (a Protestant) used to boast that his extended family in Lango consisted of Muslims, Catholics, and Protestants "at peace with each other." Obote's successor, Idi Amin Dada, himself a Muslim, also had a similarly multi-religious extended family and even once declared that he planned to have at least one of his sons trained for the Christian priesthood. And as we have indicated, the new Muslim president of Sénégal, Abdou Diouf, had a Roman Catholic wife. Tanzania has had a Muslim plurality that is not an overall majority. Yet Roman Catholic Julius K. Nyerere did bestride the country's narrow world like a colossus. He was president from 1961 to 1985, with no challenge to his religious credentials. His successor as President, Ali Hassan Mwinyi, is a Muslim. But Nyerere remained head of the ruling party, *Chama cha Mapinduzi*, for a while. A truly ecumenical Tanzania was forged where a Muslim head of state worked, hand in hand, with a Christian head of the ruling party. Once again the competitive proclivities of Christianity and Islam were moderated by the more tolerant tendencies of indigenous African culture.

But there are situations in Africa when even indigenous culture fails to ameliorate religious divisions between Christians and Muslims. This is particularly so when religious differences coincide with ethnic and linguistic divisions. This is true of the North/South divide in Sudan, with an overwhelmingly Muslim and Arabized North and a Christian-led Black Southern region. The religious difference between North and South has simply re-enforced other historical, cultural, and racial fractures. When Christianity and Islam sharpen such other differences, religion itself can be divisive in Black Africa. Similar ethno-religious cleavages in post-colonial Africa have manifested themselves from time to time in Ethiopia, Chad, and Nigeria. When the Christo-Islamic divide coincides with ethnic frontiers, the competitiveness of Christianity and Islam overwhelms the natural ecumenicalism of indigenous Africa. Using Nigeria as a case study, we shall explore these contradictions more fully.

In his book, *Consciencism*, Kwame Nkrumah, Ghana's founder-president, traced the genesis of the contemporary African heritage to these three forces: indigenous traditions, Islam, and what Nkrumah called the "Euro-Christian impact." It was the synthesis of these three forces that Nkrumah called "Consciencism." These three forces are sometimes mutually supportive, sometimes mutually antagonistic, and sometimes independent parallel lines in a nation's history. But how strong are these three forces in Africa's life? Here one must distinguish between Western religious impact on a country like Nigeria, which has taken the form of Christianity, and Western secular impact, which ranges from capitalism to the triumph of the English language. Let us consider the religious domain first.

What is the balance between Muslims, Christians, and followers of African traditional religions in Nigeria? Actually, the hardest figure to estimate is the third one. This is partly because African traditional religion can combine with either Christianity or Islam. Can one be both a Christian and a follower of an African indigenous religion? Millions of Nigerians are. Can one be both a Muslim and a follower of an African indigenous religion? Millions of Nigerians are. Can one be both a Christian and a Marxist? Many Nigerian intellectuals sympathize with Kwame Nkrumah's affirmation when he declared: "I am a Marxist-Leninist and a non-denominational Christian and I see no contradiction in that." Can one be both a Muslim and a Marxist? Post-colonial Muslim countries like Guinea, Algeria, Iraq, and Somalia have produced such hybrids. Some people would describe the Nigerian scholar Bala Usman as such a combination. But can one be both a Muslim and Christian? Here lies the rigid line of mutual exclusivity. Although Christianity and Islam are much closer to each other than to either Marxism or to African traditional religion, in reality, the two Semitic religions of the Middle East tend to be mutually exclusive.

The Triple Heritage at Work: The Case of Nigeria

Jesus is a major figure in Islam: Muslims recognize the virgin birth of Jesus; Muslims accept many of the miracles he performed on earth to cure the sick and the disabled; Muslims also accept the bodily ascent of Jesus to heaven upon the completion of his earthly career. But although theoretically Islam does encompass a version of Christianity, in reality no Muslim is likely to describe himself as a Christian—and vice versa. On the other hand, African traditional religions combine easily with other creeds. That is a major reason why it is difficult to quantify the followers of this indigenous tradition in Africa's religious experience. As for the number of Christians and Muslims in post-colonial Nigeria, the most reliable percentages recognized by the outside world were based on the 1963 census: 47% of Nigerians were Muslim and 35% were Christian, according to that census. Since l963, we have had no reliable figures to indicate whether the gap between Muslims and Christians narrowed or widened. Nonetheless, the end of colonial rule in Africa slowed down the spread of Christianity without necessarily slowing down the spread of Islam. Colonial rule was a favourable condition for Christian expansion. Therefore, the end of colonial rule was bound to be costly to Christianity, at least in the short run. The factors that slowed down the spread of Christianity after independence included:

1) The post-colonial decline of the prestige of Western civilization in Africa and the decline of Nigeria's fascination with it. Western civilization was deemed to include its most important religion, Christianity.

2) The post-colonial decline of the influence of Christian missionaries within Nigeria, including the reduced role of mission schools in Nigeria's education.

3) The post-colonial change of focus of Christian missionary work in Africa as a whole: the shift from the mission of saving souls to the mission of saving bodies, from commitment to salvation in the hereafter to commitment to service in the here and now.

4) Post-colonial atheists in Africa are more likely to be former Christians than former Muslims. This is partly because atheism is itself an alternative form of Westernization.

5) The post-colonial prosperity of oil-rich Arab countries has given Islam resources for missionary work in Africa that are unprecedented in modern Islamic history. Islam is beginning to be economically competitive with Christianity in the rivalry for the soul of Africa.

6) With regard to the natural increase of population, the figures are hard to interpret. But at least at the level of elites, Christian elites in Africa are more likely to favour smaller families than Muslim elites.

What then can one infer or conclude from all of these considerations? If in 1963, "47% of Nigerians were Muslim and 35% were Christian", the balance since 1963 is unlikely to have shifted in favour of Christianity. On the contrary, the percentage of Muslims is likely to have increased. While in Nigeria Islam may be winning in the competition between Islam and Christianity, Islam is probably losing in the competition between Islam and secular Westernization—for the time being, at least. The greatest threat to Islam is not the Passion on the Cross, but the ecstasy of Western materialism; it is not the message of Jesus but the gospel of modernity; it is not the church with a European face but capitalism in Western robes. As young Nigerian Muslims are mesmerized by disco music and the nightclub, their faith is endangered more than when they listen to a Christian preacher reaffirming love and the resurrection. Western materialism is a greater threat to African Islam than Western Christianity.

It is arguable that the strongest and most resilient indigenous culture in West Africa may well be Yoruba culture.

It is certainly the most durable of the three major ones of Nigeria. On one side is Ibo culture which has been all too ready to be westernized. On the other side is Hausa culture which has been all too ready to be Islamized. But Yoruba culture has absorbed both Westernization and Islam and still insisted on the supremacy of the indigenous. Christianized Yoruba are usually Yoruba first and Christians second. Islamized Yoruba are usually Yoruba first and Muslims second. No system of values in Nigeria has shown greater indigenous resilience than the Yoruba legacy. The best illustration in Nigeria of Islam triumphant is among the Hausa-Fulani. The best illustration in that country of Westernization triumphant is among the Ibo. But the best illustration in Nigeria of the triple heritage at work, with the indigenous as the first among equals, is the entire Yoruba experience. Only Yorubaland is capable of producing distinguished westernized scientists with startling facial ethnic marks. Only Yorubaland is capable of producing the most remarkable commodities for "Juju" traditional medicine, with sorcery sold alongside both the Qur'an and the Christian Bible in the streets of Ibadan. On the other hand, if Nigeria had consisted of only the three major groups (Yoruba, Ibo, and Hausa-Fulani), the Islamic factor would predominate more clearly. The alliance between Hausa-Fulani Islam and Yoruba Islam would have overwhelmed any alliance between Ibo Christianity and Yoruba Christianity in the post-colonial era. The numbers would have favoured the Islamic configuration. But among the smaller minority "tribes" the balance tilts in favour of Christianity and indigenous African religions. The small ethnic groups were once the least alienated of all the groups, but were also among the most exposed to Christian missionaries. The minorities exhibit some of the purest forms of Africanity and some of the most westernized. The three forms of power in Nigeria have been: a) economic and educational power, held for a while by Ibo and Yoruba; b) political power, held for a while by Northerners under

Hausa-Fulani leadership; c) military power, held subtly and sometimes unknowingly by minority groups.

The first to recognise their own power were the Ibo and Yoruba. Well before independence, the Ibo and Yoruba saw that they stood a chance of inheriting the earth in Nigeria because of their economic skills and Western educational qualifications. The Hausa-Fulani were slower in recognizing their own political power numerically. On the eve of independence, the Muslim North was so nervous about Southern power that there was a strong separatist sentiment among the Hausa-Fulani. The Ibo were not first tempted by secession; it was the Muslim North. Nnamdi Azikiwe and Chief Obafemi Awolowo began to worry that Nigeria was going to be another India, partitioned along religious lines. These Nigerian leaders, and even Kwame Nkrumah in Ghana, began to condemn what they called "Pakistanism." What all this meant was that Southerners in Nigeria were very self-confident, while Northerners were insecure and nervous about independence. Within a few years, the boot of self-confidence was on the other regional foot of Nigeria: the North became increasingly self-confident while the South was frustrated and insecure.

Some writers have attributed this reversal of fortunes to the brilliant regional leadership of Ahmadu Bello, the Sardauna of Sokoto. The former editor of *West Africa* magazine, David Williams, once put it in the following terms:

> When the Sardauna of Sokoto entered party politics in 1951 at the age of 42, the leading politicians of Nigeria's then northern region were convinced that their own region, although covering two thirds of the country's area and containing over half its people, was threatened by political and even economic domination by the two Southern regions. When he was assassinated in 1966, the politicians in the southern regions were denounc-

ing political domination by 'the north.' It was the towering personality and political skill of the Sardauna, first and only premier of the northern region and leader, though not founder, of the Northern People's Congress, which produced this reversal.[3]

Before long separatist sentiment became a characteristic of the South rather than the North. Southern separatism took its most tragic form in Biafra's bid to secede. Half a million to a million lives were lost, seemingly in vain. Captured in the latest version of Southern separatism is the debate about conferdation, a looser form of Nigerian union. The ghost of "Pakistanism" has been changing shape. The South was still self-confident and strong economically and educationally but it has become insecure politically. The last groups to discover their power are the minorities of Nigeria, the smaller ethnic groups. This self-discovery began during the civil war under Yakubu Gowon's administration. The process of self-discovery gathered momentum during the 1970s. Self-discovery is sometimes a dangerous process; it can result in precipitate acts of self-assertion. That is one possible interpretation of events that resulted in the assassination of Murtala Muhammed in 1976. Without realizing it, the minority had been a sleeping giant. The new awakening has had brief moments of danger, but the power is getting tamed and domesticated.

Islam in Post-Colonial Africa: Between Revivalism and Expansion

Islamic revivalism in post-colonial Africa has had contradictory causes. Sometimes it arises out of economic disadvantage and desperation, almost echoing Karl Marx's portrayal of religion as "the sigh of the oppressed creature and the soul of soul-less conditions." At its most dramatic, Islamic revivalism has emerged out of famine and drought, as if the physical barrenness of the soil has given rise to spiritual fertility. In the words of Susan MacDonald's account of Sénégal and the Sahel:

> Now Islam is consolidating its position as people turn to the strict Muslim moral code to give them a sense of direction... Persistent drought and the spreading desert have caused poverty, misery, and hardship. This diversity has created a favourable terrain for increased religious fervour.[4]

Islamic revivalism in Muslim Ethiopia and Somalia was, at one time, one of the consequences of drought and famine. While in the 1960s and 1970s Somali poets sang about the ravages of "amputation" (lamenting the political fragmentation of the Somali nation and dreaming about re-unification), the poets and writers of the 1980s have lamented the agonies of hunger and deprivation, as well as the curse of domestic tyranny. Problems of political refugees and of refugees of economic deprivation have merged.[5] By the 1990s the poets lamented anarchy and banditry in Somalia. In Sudan, Islamic revivalism has also drawn sustenance from social and economic deprivation. Numeiry's declaration of the *Shari'a* was partly in response to new hardships in the country in the 1980s and to the regime's need for new allies among orthodox Muslims. The Bashir regime subsequently took the crusade of Islamization even further. On the other hand, Islamic reformers in search of new interpretations were more vulnerable to fundamentalists than ever. The most dramatic martyrdom of an Islamic reformer in Sudan was the execution of Mahmoud Muhammad Taha in 1985. His unusual modernizing ideas for Islam got him into trouble with the more orthodox *ulemaas* (learned ones). He was accused of apostasy under Islamic law and was subsequently executed under Numeiry. Islamic fundamentalism had clashed with Islamic reform and Taha was the most dramatic martyr of the reform movement.[6]

But while revivalism in the Horn of Africa and the Sahel was in part the product of hardship and desperation, revivalism in Libya was partly the product of new wealth and its attendant self-confidence. It was the outcome of a convergence of oil-wealth and the threat of Western hegemony. While Somalia and Sudan were two of the poorest countries in the Muslim world, Libya was one of the best endowed. In the former model, Islamic revivalism grew out of desolation; in the case of Libya, revivalism grew out of the hazards of newly acquired oil wealth. In the Sahel, people were returning to Islam in the aftermath of shortage of water; in the Sahara (Libya and to a lesser extent Algeria), a return to Islam was often a response to the new abundance of oil. Muslims were rediscovering their faith either in desperation or in renewed self-confidence. But the self-confidence is only relative. Underlying both forms of Islamic revivalism is the constant threat of Western cultural hegemony. The fear of Western imperialism is one of the resilient inspirations behind Islamic fundamentalism. American imperialism radicalized the ayatollahs in Iran. The threat of both Western imperialism and Zionism radicalized Qaddafi. Economic deprivation, economic wealth, and the threat of cultural disruption from the West have all played their part in sustaining the new wave of Islamic revivalism.[7]

As for the geographical expansion of Islam, it is more modest in Eastern Africa than in Western Africa. The reasons are both colonial and post-colonial. European colonization of West Africa earlier in the century never really arrested the spread of Islam, although it did considerably help the spread of Christianity. Both Semitic religions expanded at the expense of indigenous creeds, though not at the expense of each other to any great extent. By contrast, the advent of European colonial rule, as we indicated, seriously harmed Islam in Eastern Africa. Why did Islam have such a different fate in the two sub-regions of Africa in the face of the joint adversary of European imperialism? We have mentioned that during the European colonial period Islam in Eastern Africa continued to be Arab-led, whereas the leadership of Islam in West Africa had already been deeply indigenized. In Eastern Africa, it appeared as if Arab missionary activity was in competition with European missionary effort, both being rival foreign forces. However, even the nineteenth century *jihads* in West Africa under Usman dan Fodio and others were entirely indigenous African phenomena. This degree of Africanization in West Africa sustained the Western region's Islam despite the challenge of European colonization. Another contributing factor was the fact that the image of the Arab slave trade hurt Islam in Eastern Africa, especially when Euro-Christian propaganda exploited that image during Western colonization. Colonial schools in Eastern Africa dramatized the Arab role in the slave trade and underplayed the Western role in the trans-Atlantic slave trade. East Africans emerging from colonial and missionary schools learnt far more about the Arab slave trade, and far less about the trans-Atlantic flow, than did young colonial West Africans. Islam in Eastern Africa therefore suffered more from anti-Arabism than did Islam in the West.[8]

After independence, Muslims in West Africa were strong enough numerically and politically to be able to inherit the reins of post-colonial power in countries like Mali, Guinea (Conakry), and Niger. In Nigeria, under civilian rule, Muslims were also triumphant from 1960 to 1966 and, to some extent, from 1979 to 1983. In Sénégal, as we indicated, a Roman Catholic rose to the presidency with Muslim support. In Cameroon, a Muslim individual, Ahmadou Ahidjo, rose to the top with Christian support and in Gabon, a Christian ruler, Omar Bongo, was converted to Islam. In Eastern Africa, Somalia and Sudan had Muslim majorities that inherited the reins of post-colonial power. But in Uganda, it took the military coup of Idi Amin Dada, a Muslim, to put Muslims in positions of supreme power. Islam was politically triumphant in Uganda from 1971 until 1979. The succeeding regimes in Uganda have politically marginalized Islam to levels below those it enjoyed before the rise of Idi Amin.

Tanganyika under Catholic Nyerere united with Zanzibar under Muslim Abeid Karume in 1964. From that year on the country had consistently a Christian President and a Muslim Vice-President until 1985 when Julius K. Nyerere stepped down as President while retaining the chairmanship of the Party. From 1985 onwards, both the President and the Vice-President have been Muslims. In the Congo (Zaire), Rwanda and Burundi, and in Southern Africa as a whole, the chances of a Muslim head of state in the foreseeable future appear remote. Kenya's Muslim population is estimated at about six million, about a quarter of the total population of Kenya, but its political influence is well below that proportion. The spread of Islam in Kenya may have been helped by two factors: the missionary activism of the Indo-Pakistani Ahmadiyya movement and the new financial aid given to Muslim institutions by the Muslim members of the Organization of Petroleum Exporting Countries (OPEC). But while the support of Libya and Iran to African movements may have helped the cause of Islamic revivalism among those already converted, the radicalism of Iran and Libya has sometimes caused political consternation and anxiety in countries like Kenya, and slowed down the cause of Islam's expansion into new ethnic and geographical areas.[9] When all is said and done, the dual destiny of Islam in post-colonial Africa remains ambivalent. In Africa, is Islam on its way towards greater geographical expansion or is it destined for a fresh historical revival? Are there new worlds for Islam to conquer on the ground or is the faith in quest of old glories to resurrect? Is Islam reaching out for new converts or is it searching in for old ancestors?

Islam in African Art

In architecture and in the verbal arts, the impact of Islam on sub-Saharan Africa has been that of a stimulus, opening up new horizons of creativity. In sculpture and in the performing arts, Islam has often been an inhibition rather than a stimulus in sub-Saharan Africa. In painting, the impact of Islam has been mixed: stimulating in some respects and stifling in others. In West Africa, one of the most important milestones in the Islamization of architecture came after the legendary pilgrimage to Mecca of Mansa Musa, emperor of ancient Mali (reigned 1312-1337). He travelled in wealth and golden splendor, through Cairo, to the holy cities of Islam, Mecca and Medina. The legend is tied to the wealth of this black pilgrim to Mecca. But more fundamental for the architectural future of West Africa was Mansa Musa's decision to bring back an architect from Arabia. New mosques rose with more impressive minarets and domes in Timbuktu. Mansa Musa also presided over the use of a revolutionary new building material, brick instead of *pisé* or pounded clay. The architectural civilization of Muslim West Africa changed probably forever. Timbuktu did itself become a major center of learning and the new mosques were at once places of worship and centers of scholarship. The architectural changes affected private homes also, many of them acquiring the style of a flat roof with a central dome. Subsequent influences from the Maghreb helped to stimulate local African innovations, culminating in subsequent centuries in such splendid creations as the Mouride mosque in Touba in Sénégal. In East Africa, the Muslim stimulus in architecture came from the Arabian Peninsula and the Gulf. That Muslim stimulus contributed to the rise of the Islamic city-states on the East African coast such as Kilwa, Mombasa, Sofala, and Pate. A deserted ancient city like Gedi on today's Kenya Coast preserves much of its Afro-Islamic authenticity in its very ruins. But while Islam was indeed a creative stimulus in African architecture, was it a stumbling block in African sculpture, the performing arts, and (in some respects) painting? It is to this inhibiting tendency of Islam that we should briefly turn.

Why is Islam in a more tense relationship with African sculpture than it is with African architecture? One reason why Islam has often militated against African sculpture is Islam's own uncompromising monotheism. It is so monotheistic that it regards the Christian concept of Trinity as a departure from monotheism. Partly because of that monotheism, some versions of Islam have become very wary about idolatry. And yet African sculpture is sometimes about deities or protection against magic. This tense relationship between Islam and the African art of masks and figurines can be traced back all the way to idolatry in pre-Islamic Mecca. Pre-Islamic Arabia had worshipped idols in the very places where Muslims today circumambulate the *Ka'aba* in Mecca. According to Islamic tradition, the Prophet Muhammad himself later destroyed some of those idols with his own hands. They were the Islamic equivalent of the graven images. In order to discourage the return of idolatry, art forms such as sculpture and painting became circumscribed in terms of what they could represent on canvas or in other plastic forms. In time, according to some schools of Islam, to paint an animal was regarded as an attempt to imitate God. So "organic art," in the sense of making art recreate living natural organisms, became increasingly taboo to at least some leading schools of Islam. Rather than creatures from nature, letters of the Qur'an decorated mosques. Islam was a stimulus to creative calligraphy but an obstacle to portraiture.

Islam therefore had a tense relationship with a variety of traditional African cultures that related to this type of representation of nature. Among the most important has been African sculpture. Islam's uncompromising monotheism has often militated against African masks and bronze figures. The rich tradition that produced the rich bronze work of ancient Benin and Ife, and that much later inspired such European artists as Pablo Picasso, was threatened by this particular school of Islam. Of course, some African Muslims did go ahead anyhow and mixed the cultures. In general, Islam's distrust of representational and organic art was derived from ancestral distrust of idolatry and it remained in a continuing tense relationship with particular forms of African art.

Islam also distrusts African dance for two principal reasons: first, the dance's apparent proximity to idolatry, and second, its apparent nearness to sexuality. *The Cambridge Encyclopedia of Africa* tells us:

> Dance is central to ritual, for example, when the Yoruba priests of the God Sango in Nigeria depict the thunder and lightening of their tempestuous deity through the dramatic intensity of their dance gestures. They restate the nature of his power to the worshippers who in turn pay homage with formal songs and dances.

In later centuries, even African governments that were not Muslim also tended to steer clear of celebrating indigenous gods. Today, almost all African countries celebrate some Christian festivals, certainly the great majority of them would celebrate Christmas, and some in the Anglophone tradition would celebrate Easter. African countries that are Muslim would celebrate festivals like *eid ul-Fitr, eid ul-Haj,* and sometimes the Prophet's birthday. Countries like Nigeria would celebrate all of those, Christian and Muslim, and a few secular ones. What no African country has really celebrated nationally in the twentieth century are the indigenous religious traditions. There is no day set aside to celebrate the gods of Africa's ancestors. Almost none of the African countries pay tribute at the national level to the gods of African ancestors the way they pay tribute to the one God of the Christians and Muslims. Fear or neglect of African indigenous ritual is not peculiar to Islam as a tradition: African governments themselves fall short of paying tribute even when they are not Muslim. Islam and missionary Christianity have also distrusted African dance for reasons unconnected with idolatry. They have distrusted it for presumed nearness to sexuality, and sometimes because some of the dances have a gender division of labour. Again, I quote *The Cambridge Encyclopedia of Africa*:

> The working movements of farmers and fishermen are formally stylized dances expressing their strength and virility of men while in some societies their wives and daughters use more restrained movements to express qualities expected of women. This contrast is clearly expressed in the vigorous dances of young Zulu men of South Africa and the more subtle foot patterns of Zulu women. Men and women have distinct dances.

Of course, in the case of Christian missionaries in Africa, the distrust of the dance sometimes resulted in strict westernized discipline in missionary schools, and the distrust of African patterns of dress did sometimes lead to special innovations to satisfy the rules of Christian modesty in dress. Islamic rules of dress have often been even more severe for women. On the dance floor and in sculpture and in painting, the Islamic aesthetic and the African aesthetic have therefore often diverged.

As for Islam and the aesthetic of words, the situation is quite different. On the issue of African languages and literature, Islam has played a more stimulating role, though sometimes dialectically. On the one hand, Islam appears to be linguistically intolerant. Formal prayer has to be in the Arabic language. The *muezzin* calls the believers to prayer in Arabic. On the other hand, Islam and the Arabic language have created whole new indigenous languages in Africa, or profoundly enriched indigenous tongues. Such Afro-Islamic languages include Kiswahili and Hausa, arguably the two most successful indigenous tongues of the continent. In the verbal arts of Africa, Islam has been a great creative stimulus. A fair question is whether indigenous African traditions of poetry have enriched interactions with other traditions of poetry. Has Islam enriched or inhibited African poetry? In range of subject matter treated by poets, Islam has sometimes been an inhibiting factor. Islamic values of discourse made certain topics sinful. On the other hand, in terms of depth of meaning and sophistication of the craft of versification, Islam has probably been immensely enriching. While the art of African fiction in indigenous languages has been greatly enriched by contact with the West, African poetry in indigenous languages has been more enriched by contact with Islam. African languages with the most complex poetic forms are probably disproportionately within cultures that have been in contact with Islam. The most astonishing African culture with a preoccupation with poetry is probably the Somali culture. Despite all of their political failings, the Somali developed an exceptional culture of oral and even instantaneous poetry. Their greatest modern national hero was Syed Muhammad Abdallah Hassan, the exceptionally sane *Mullah* (The British called him "the mad Mullah"). He was in fact a fusion of Winston Churchill and William Shakespeare, both savior of the nation and hero of the language. In Tanzania, many of the writers in Swahili are not Muslims but the Swahili traditions within which they operate are partly the product of contact with Islam. Julius K. Nyerere experimented, when he was president, with the task of making Shakespeare available in Swahili. Kiswahili, an African language in contact with Islam, was called upon to bear the burden of Shakespeare, the greatest poet in the English language.

Is there a tense relationship with Islam regarding the older art forms associated with songs? It probably depends upon the themes of the songs. There may be certain themes of songs in African culture that may appear immodest by Islamic criteria of propriety, even if not necessarily Islamic criteria of beauty. But songs are, of course, a major part of Islamic culture as well as of African culture. It probably got its respectability with one of the first great songs of Islam receiving the Prophet Muhammad on his arrival in Medina after his flight from Mecca:

> *Talaa al badr alaina*
> *min thaniyat il wida*
> *wajaba shukr alaina*
> *ma da alillah da'*

This song welcomed him as if he was a new crescent, a new dawn, and was rendered into music by the great Egyptian singer, the late Umm Kalthum.

To conclude, while in the aesthetics of words and of architecture, Islam has strengthened African culture, in the aesthetics of plastic and performing arts, Islam has often tended to militate against the African tradition. In more recent trends, there have been Muslim artists who have broken out of the confines of doctrine and painted people or sculptured animals, or drew living forests. These artists have seen themselves not as imitators of God but as sparks of the Almighty. Human genius at its best is but a spark of the First Cause.

NOTES

This chapter is a revised version of an unpublished paper that later contributed towards the article entitled "Islam and Sub-Saharan Africa" in *The Oxford Encyclopedia of the Modern Islamic World*, Volume 2 (New York and Oxford: Oxford University Press, 1995), pp. 261-271.

1.Basil Davidson, *Africa in History: Themes and Outlines* (New York and Oxford: Maxwell Macmillan International and Collier Books, 1991 edition), p. 134.

2. Consult Susan MacDonald, "Senegal: Islam on the March," in *West Africa* (London), No. 3494, August 6, 1984, page 1570.

3. David Williams, "A Towering Leader's Skill," in *Financial Times* (London), special supplement on Nigeria, February 24, 1986, page XVI.

4. Susan MacDonald, "Senegal: Islam on the March," op. cit., p. 1568.

5. Somalia's leading novelist, Nuruddin Farah, has addressed this merger in some of his work. See, for example, *Sweet and Sour Milk* and *Maps* (1986).

6. Consult Mahmoud Mohamed Taha, *The Second Message of Islam*, translated by Abdullahi Ahmed An-Na'im (Syracuse, NY: Syracuse University Press, 1987).

7. Consult also "The Impact of Islam," Chapter 8 in Basil Davidson, *The Story of Africa* (London: Mitchell Beazley, 1984), pp. 95-104.

8. For further background consult Omari H. Kokole, "The Islamic Factor in African-Arab Relations," in *Third World Quarterly*, Vol. 6, No. 3, July 1984, pp. 687-702.

9. Consult for background, Geoffrey Parrinder, "The Religions of Africa," in *Africa South of the Sahara 1986*, Fifteenth Edition (Europa Publications Limited, 1987), pp. 131-135.

SEVEN

AFRICA AND ASIA IN THE POSTCOLONIAL EXPERIENCE (1997)

This essay addresses the issue of Africa's relationships with Asia along four dimensions. These dimensions are comparative, competitive, cooperative, and conflictual. What emerges from these four areas of interaction is a picture of two continents that have been both political allies and economic rivals in the second half of the twentieth century. Let us look more closely at these dimensions and processes.

The Comparative Scale

When we look at Africa and Asia comparatively, we need to address both their similarities and differences. Most of the countries in both continents emerged from World War II with the shared experience of colonial rule. Territorially, almost the whole of Africa was colonized. By comparison, only about 60% of Asia endured the same experience. Of all the existing states in Africa, Ethiopia was the only country to remain out of Western colonial hands—apart from a brief period from 1935 to 1941—while in Asia, several countries managed to resist Western colonization successfully.[1] Temporally, on the other hand, African colonies were colonized for a much briefer period than Asian countries. Europeans had established several coastal settlements and some kind of political dominance in various parts of Africa since the end of the fifteenth century but, until 1815, European interests in Africa were limited to the exploitation of raw materials and slaves and as a way-station en route to Asia. As D. K. Fieldhouse put it:

> Before 1815, then, Europeans remained on the periphery of Africa, ignorant of its interior and uninterested in colonization.[2]

In contrast, many parts of India had been under different degrees of British control for hundreds of years before India's partition and independence in 1947. Between 1744 and 1816, Britain had effectively established its superiority over other European powers and local rulers in India.[3] Indonesia had similarly been under Dutch control for centuries. As early as 1619, the Dutch had established their supremacy in Indonesia and they had to finally give up control of it in 1949.[4] The British, French, and Dutch, who were the main players on the Asian continent, were quick to establish control over indigenous Asian regimes and held on to power for a longer period of time, while the main players in Africa, namely Britain, France, Belgium, and Portugal, were late to empire-building in Asia and were colonial masters for a shorter time.

This is where a paradox emerges, as disruption came much faster for African cultures and values, in spite of the brevity of their colonial experience—in comparison to that of Asia. Within less than a century, whole African societies were Christianized, whereas most Asians had resisted Christianization. Furthermore, African political and educational systems became more dependent on European languages than

Asian systems. We never refer to "English-speaking Asian countries" or "French-speaking Asian states" the way we discuss Anglophone Africa and Francophone Africa. About thirty African countries have European languages as the sole official language; about fifteen have both European and non-European languages; and only seven have non-European languages as the sole official language. In Asia, by contrast, almost twenty countries have non-European languages as their only official language, while six have both non-European languages and European languages.[5]

By religious, linguistic, and educational indicators, Africa seemed to be westernizing faster than most Asian countries. Why then was Africa soon to be left behind by Asia in economic performance? If Africa was culturally westernizing faster than Asia, why was Asia economically westernizing faster than Africa? What is the relationship between cultural Westernization and economic Westernization? We know that Western culture (including the Protestant ethic in Max Weber's sense) has been good for economic performance within the Western world but we still do not know if Western culture is good for economic performance outside the West. On the contrary, some Asian examples seem to demonstrate that the best approach is a combination of Western technique with indigenous culture. The Japanese, after the Meiji Restoration in 1868, asked themselves: "can we economically modernize without culturally westernizing?" They said "yes" and proceeded to adopt the strategy of what they called "Western technique, Japanese spirit." The first Japanese industrial miracle occurred, between 1868 and 1945, as Japan became a major industrial power while remaining culturally authentic.[6] In the 1920s and 1930s, the Turks under Mustafa Kemal Atatürk also asked themselves "can we economically modernize without culturally westernizing?" Their answer was "no, cultural Westernization is the only route towards modernization." They substituted the Roman alphabet for the Arabic in writing the Turkish language; they westernized the legal system; they outlawed the fez and, of course, they abolished the monarchy and the caliphate. Yet, in the final analysis, Turkey's pace of industrialization and economic transformation was far slower than that of Japan.[7]

As Africa emerged from colonial rule, she asked herself if she could actually modernize economically without culturally westernizing. In reality, Africa's answer so far has been to engage in "cultural Westernization without economic modernization." Africa has been in double jeopardy by, first, westernizing too fast and, second, by westernizing in the wrong areas of Western culture. Africa westernized in prayer, but not in production; in idiom but not in innovation; in costume but not in computer. Taiwan, South Korea, and Hong Kong adopted mainly the more productive elements of Western civilization, and linked them to their own methods of social organization and cultural modification. At the end of World War II, these three societies were not very different in level of modernization from those of the more prosperous parts of Africa such as Ghana, Kenya, and Southern Rhodesia (Zimbabwe), as exemplified by various categories of production and output.[8] One possible way of looking at economic performance is to examine the growth of real per capita Gross Domestic Product (GDP)—the total monetary value of all goods and services produced in a year, excluding payments on foreign investments—between 1965 and 1989 for three regions: East Asia, South Asia, and Sub-Saharan Africa. While Sub-Saharan Africa was indeed behind East Asia in the 1965-73 period, it was ahead of South Asia; by the 1973-80 period, it was behind the two regions; and in the last 1980-89 period, real per capita GDP actually declined for the African region. To illustrate a typical comparison between African and Asian economic development, let us look at Ghana and South Korea. When Ghana became independent in 1957, its per capita income was about the same as that of South Korea. Forty years later, Ghana has been left far behind economically. In a comparison of the two countries,

Werlin pointed that while, in 1957, Ghana had a per capita income of $490 and South Korea $491 (in 1980 dollars), by the early nineties, Ghana's income was only $400 while South Korea's had shot up to $6000.[9]

Yet, Ghanaians speak better English than South Koreans, and are more Christianized than South Koreans. They have universities that are more Western and Eurocentric than South Korean universities. Ghana has had one intellectual president who wrote about ten books (Kwame Nkrumah), one president with a distinguished Ph.D. in anthropology (Dr. Kofi Abrefa Busia), and one president who was a medical doctor (Dr. Hilla Limann). Every civilian ruler of Ghana has been a highly westernized intellectual. The most successful military ruler (Flt. Lieutenant Jerry Rawlings) was half-Scottish in parentage. Yet, these high profile Western cultural qualifications that Ghana has enjoyed failed to help Ghana keep pace with South Korea's relentless industrialization and economic performance. Ghana's greater cultural Westernization has not saved it from being left behind by South Korea in economic Westernization. The secret of economic development may not lie in culturally imitating the West; it may lie in combining Western innovation with local authenticity. East and South-East Asia may have found the secret of that combination of westernized innovation with indigenous authenticity. The African elite is still stifled by excessive Western imitation without adequate indigenous authenticity.

The Competitive Factor

While colonialism helped to turn African and Asian countries into political allies, that same colonial experience prepared the ground for their economic rivalry. The European powers created in the colonies economies based upon primary products. Let us consider a few illustrative examples. In rubber production, Nigeria was in competition with

Malaysia. In 1905, Nigeria produced 1.4 thousand metric tons of rubber while Malaysia only produced 0.1 thousand metric tons; by 1988, Malaysia produced 1,662 thousand metric tons while Nigeria only produced 68 thousand metric tons.[10] In 1949, Kenya produced 6 thousand metric tons of coffee while the Philippines produced 4 thousand metric tons; by 1988, the African country produced 125 thousand metric tons while the Asian country produced 142 thousand metric tons.[11] In some products, Africa clearly enjoyed a margin of advantage at one time. For instance, with reference to cotton exports, in 1900, Egypt was exporting 293 thousand metric tons to India's 182 thousand metric tons; in 1988, the North African country was exporting 80 thousand metric tons while the South Asian country was exporting 194 thousand metric tons.[12] Africa has historically been the area of major production for a few commodities. Therefore, items like palm oil, groundnuts (peanuts), and cocoa, became bigger exports from Africa than from Asia. Nigeria was the main exporter of palm oil and palm kernels, and groundnuts, while Ghana was a major source of cocoa.[13] By 1991, however, Malaysia produced more palm oil than Nigeria;[14] by 1988, Indonesia produced more cocoa powder than Ghana or Kenya.[15] Even in mineral production, where Africa traditionally led the way, it has lost ground to Asia in quite a few areas in the last decade. In the rare cases where Africa's production has increased, it has been slower than that of Asia.[16]

This is quite apart from the even more dramatic difference in pace of industrialization and mechanization between most African countries and most Asian countries. Outside the Republic of South Africa, Egypt, and the Maghreb, Africa is now way behind almost all Asian countries in industrialization. What could have enabled Asia to outperform Africa economically within less than three decades? We have already referred to two interrelated causes: that African societies attempted to westernize too fast, and that they were westernizing in the wrong areas. One result has been a peculiar process of "mal-modernization." Africa has experienced urbanization without industrialization, Western tastes without Western skills, capitalist greed without capitalist discipline, Western consumption patterns without Western production techniques, Western culture of letters without Western culture of numbers. To paraphrase the English poet, Alexander Pope:

> A little modernity is a dangerous thing,
> Drink deep or taste not the Western spring.[17]

Other factors have militated against African development as compared with Asia. Some sectors of labour costs in Africa have been higher than their counterparts in South Asia. Africa's counterparts in South Asia have less labour costs in some sectors. A 1989 World Bank report put the disparities in the following way:

> In most African countries at the beginning of the 1980s public sector wages, measured as a multiple of per capita income, were several times those of Asia. For instance official Tanzanian wages, which were relatively low for Africa, were more than double those of Sri Lanka.[18]

The gross neglect of the African infrastructure has also been very damaging to the wider strategy of development. Comparisons of Gross Domestic Investment (GDI)—the sum of gross domestic fixed investment and the changes in stocks—per capita figures for the sub-Saharan African, South Asian, and East Asian regions, from 1973 to 1993, reveal dismal disparities. Between 1973 and 1993, the GDI per capita in the African case fell from $150 (in 1987 US$) to $80 in 1993; in the South Asian case, it increased from $50 to $80; while in the East Asian case, it shot up from $50 to $200.[19] At least partially, the dismal state of infrastructure in

Africa is due to the fact that charges for infrastructure services in Africa are not only lower than economic costs but they are even lower than what is needed for infrastructure maintenance. The World Bank sub-Saharan report mentioned above has argued that: "moderate increases in financial terms would yield revenue equivalent to about 20 to 30 percent of current public revenues."[20] Such a strategy would be easy to implement, administer, monitor, and audit. Increased charges on electric power, water, roads (vehicle licenses), and telecommunications could improve maintenance and expansion. The price increases would be charges rather than taxes, hitting higher income groups rather than the poor. They may arrest the relentless decay of roads, railways, and equipment for telecommunications, electricity generation and water supply.

Improved infrastructure may help Africa narrow its growing developmental gap with most Asian countries, but Africa and Asia are also in competition as magnets for foreign investment. With the end of the Cold War, additional opportunities have emerged for Western investment not only among the former members of the Warsaw Pact but also among newly liberalizing Asian economies. In 1993, for example, it seems that Latin American countries received almost fifty percent of the total Foreign Direct Investment (FDI) and East Asian countries received about thirty percent of the total FDI while the sub-Saharan African region only received three percent of the total FDI.[21] Data on direct investment flows reveal shifts in investment toward South and East Asia and the Central and East European regions, with less or even declining attention paid to sub-Saharan Africa.[22] Take for example India, which has been suspicious of Western investment during much of its socialist years; it has now converted to the virtues of the market and has become extra receptive to foreign investors. It is quite understandable that, for foreign investors, India's population of over 900 million people constitutes a more attractive market than various African countries.

The Cold War had been an asset in creating a bond of political partnership between Africa and most of Asia: it made the Nonaligned Movement meaningful, as Asian and African countries sought solidarity in distancing themselves from the Warsaw Pact and the North Atlantic Treaty Alliance (NATO). On the other hand, the end of the Cold War has weakened the political partnership between Africa and Asia and heightened the economic rivalry. India became a rival for Western investment and became less of an ally in nonalignment. China became less a solicitor for political influence in Africa and more of a competitor for capitalist investment within its own borders.[23] And even Vietnam, for so long a pariah state under *Pax Americana*, emerged in the 1990s as a magnet for American business as well as for other Western investments.[24] The end of the Cold War definitely weakened the forces of political alliance between Africa and Asia and strengthened the prospects of escalating economic rivalry. This includes the area of foreign aid. On the other hand, the increasing prosperity of some Asian countries makes them less and less eligible for foreign aid. East and South-East Asia may soon become more aid-givers than aid-recipients. However, most parts of Africa and large parts of South Asia are still within the poverty belt of Planet Earth. The post-Cold War era is also witnessing the decline of foreign aid from the West. The question arises whether that aid is more likely to go to Laos than to Liberia, to Azerbaijan rather than Burkina Faso, to Bangladesh rather than Nigeria. Is Asia outstripping Africa as a magnet for foreign aid in the post-Cold War era?

The Cooperative Factor

Four inter-related political forces helped to bring Africa and Asia closer together in the twentieth century, at least for a while. One was the bond of being fellow victims of European racial and pigmentational arrogance, or racial solidarity. Second was the bond of being fellow victims of European cultural and civilizational arrogance, or cultural solidarity. Third was the bond of being fellow victims of actual and direct Western imperialism and colonization, or anti-imperial solidarity. Fourth was the bond of attempted disengagement from the Cold War while it lasted, or the solidarity of nonalignment. The first two bonds, those of racial and cultural solidarities, resulted in different Afro-Asian movements. The most famous was the Bandung Conference in Indonesia, in 1955, which brought together emerging leaders of the two continents in a shared struggle against Western hegemony.[25]

Clearly, racial and cultural solidarities were closely linked to the struggle against imperialism, the third foundation of Afro-Asian solidarity. In time, imperialism was defined not simply as old style territorial colonization and annexation by Europe but also as continuing Western hegemony and control, including the powerful and ominous shadow of the United States on other countries. But by this extended definition of imperialism, it was not merely Asia and Africa that had been dominated by the West; it was also Latin America. The concept of the "Third World" entered the vocabulary of international politics in the 1960s. The "First World" was the world of technologically advanced capitalist countries economically led by the United States, Germany, and Japan. The First World was politically led by the United States, Britain, and France. The "Second World" was the world of technologically advanced socialist countries, led or dominated by the Soviet Union at the time, but encompassing such healthier economies as that of Hungary and Czechoslovakia. The "Third World" was the world of developing countries in Africa, Asia, and Latin America—ranging from Brazil to Botswana, from Pakistan to Paraguay, from China to Chad. The People's Republic of China insisted on being regarded as part of the developing world rather than being associated with either the Warsaw Pact or with the status of a potential superpower. The extension of Afro-Asian solidarity to include Latin America had wide ramifications for the whole emerging paradigm of "North-South relations" in the global domain. It affected alliances in such United Nations fora as the United Nations Conference on Trade and Development (UNCTAD) and cooperation in the Uruguay Round, GATT and its successor, the World Trade Organization (WTO).[26]

The expansion of Afro-Asian solidarity to encompass Latin America was also part of the foundation of the Nonaligned Movement (NAM). However, it is worth remembering that the Nonaligned Movement included a European component right from the start. Its first conference was indeed held in Belgrade, Yugoslavia (September 1-6, 1961). Other European members since then have included Cyprus and Malta.[27] The purposes of the Nonalignment Movement were originally inspired by a concern about the arms race between the North Atlantic Treaty Organization (NATO) and the Warsaw Pact. The original 25 members of the movement aspired to influence the world towards both disarmament and increasing decolonization. Over the decades, the Movement has retained the ambition of pursuing "peace, achievement of disarmament, and settlement of disputes by peaceful means." It has also remained committed to self-determination and independence "for all peoples living under colonial or alien domination and foreign occupation." But it has also increasingly emphasized "sustainable and environmentally sound development," the promotion of "fundamental rights and freedom" and the quest for strengthening "the role and effectiveness of the United Nations."[28] Above all, the Nonaligned Movement has been advocating "a transition from the old world order based on domination to a new order based on freedom, equality and social justice and the well-being of all" as described in the Final Declaration of its 1989 Belgrade Conference.[29] Africa and Asia are still the senior continents in the movement and have hosted most of the conferences to date. Indeed, until the mid-1990s, only one conference had been hosted in Latin America—in Havana, Cuba, in 1979. Moreover, the largest country in Latin America, Brazil, has not been a member of the Nonaligned Movement. On the other hand, the Movement admitted in June 1994 Africa's most industrialized and potentially most influential state on the world stage, the Republic of South Africa. Just as the Afro-Asian solidarity movement suffered from a crisis of *raison d'être* as old style European colonialism came to an end, the Nonaligned Movement has been suffering from a similar crisis of ultimate purpose in the wake of the end of the Cold War. Some members have gone as far as to recommend the dissolution of the Movement now that the world is no longer endangered by East-West tensions. Other members, in response, have championed a refocus on North-South relations at the global level, asking the movement to seek three paramount objectives: first, greater and healthier economic cooperation between North and South; second, greater and more self-reliant cooperation between South and South; and, third, a more general reform of the world system towards greater social justice and international equity.

The Conflictual Factor

Conflictual relations between African and Asian countries also go back centuries, but some versions of conflict have mainly disappeared. An ancient form of conflict that is now rare is the slave raid. West Asia was extensively involved in the African slave trade almost a millennium before the trans-Atlantic slave trade began. The Indian Ocean side of Africa was either the raiding ground or the transit area for the slave trade conducted by West Asians. While this eastern slave trade was smaller in scale than the trans-Atlantic traffic of the seventeenth and eighteenth centuries, it was certainly a major cause of conflict between Asia and Africa. If murder can be first degree and second degree, can slavery be similarly graded in depth of evil? Our own answer is that slavery can also be subject to a moral calculus. Just as virtue is subject to measurement, so surely is vice. Just as some social systems are more virtuous than others, surely some social systems are more vicious than others. What is the status of the West Asian slave trade tradition?

We have reached the conclusion that the least evil of the slave-systems in Africa was the indigenous system. The indigenous slave system was the least commercialized and the most responsive to family values. We regard it as third-degree culpable slavery. This essay regards the West-Asian slave system as second in culpability. It probably has the highest record of upward social mobility—as exemplified by the Mamluks in Egyptian history, among others. If indigenous slavery was mono-racial (black slaves, black masters), West Asian slavery had been multiracial (slaves and masters could be of any race). Islam itself did not declare slavery an outright vice, but it did declare the emancipation of a slave an outright virtue time and again. One the whole, the West Asian system should be declared guilty of second-degree enslavement. The system had also been among the most racially assimilationist. As for the Euro-Christian trans-Atlantic slave-system, this was by far the most directly wedded to racism (white masters, black slaves). It was polarized across the color divide. The geography of slavery, involving the Middle Passage, was almost as devastating as the history of slavery. In terms of assimilating the slaves into the master race, this slave-system was the least integrationist and the least assimilationist of the three systems. In economic orientation, the trans-Atlantic slave-system was the most commercialized. In scale, it was by far the most extensive coerced movement of human beings across long distances in human history. While there are indeed differences among Portuguese, Spanish, and Anglo-Saxon slave systems, the general picture is irresistible. If slavery is subject to gradation of culpability, the architects and main offenders of the trans-Atlantic slave system were definitely guilty of first-degree slavery.

Let us now return to the contemporary scene of slavery on the Indian Ocean. In the 1990s, the situation in Sudan posed a number of interrelated factual and moral questions. Is there indeed a new slavery, as some Western journalists and observers have claimed? If so, is it a revival of war-inspired enslavement, rather than a commercially inspired traffic? If it is an outgrowth of the war system, is this a revival of Arab-Islamic slavery or of indigenous slavery? In the history of both Islam and indigenous Africa, war often resulted in prisoners and captives who were sometimes held in bondage. The war in Southern Sudan is not only between Arabs and Black Africans; it is also between southern ethnic groups and between factions of "tribes." If there is indeed slavery on any scale in Southern Sudan, it involves both Arab capturing Black and Black capturing Black, probably a partial revival of both Arab-Islamic and indigenous slavery. But is the government in Khartoum implicated? Evidence seems to suggest it may be guilty of sins of omission rather than of commission, by not doing enough to stamp out traffic in captives and their being held in bondage. A strong indication that the government is not involved in any slave trade is that so many Southern Sudanese regard Northern Sudan as a haven to run to for safety from the war in the South, as shown in figures of the United Nations High Commission for Refugees (UNHCR) on distribution of displaced persons within Sudan; they see the Khartoum government as their protector from the bloody consequences of war.

Outside Africa, it is mainly in Asia that newer forms of slavery are rearing their ugly heads. Child prostitution in countries like Sri Lanka, the Philippines, Thailand, Myanmar, and Cambodia is resulting in the sales of boys and girls, sometimes by their own parents. Western pedophile tourists are among the pillars of this new form of enslavement. Fortunately, some Western governments are beginning to take note of the atrocities of this new form of child enslavement. Tourists committing pedophile offences in far away Thailand may find themselves liable to prosecution on returning home to England or Australia. The moral calculus of slavery is looking for legal sanctions in the modern age. We are already setting up courts to try perpetrators of genocide. In the twenty-first century, there is a case for setting up international courts to try perpetrators of slavery—first, second, or third degrees of the crime of bondage. The African and the Asian connections are only part of that horrendous story.

More recent conflict situations include the racial relationships between Africans and South Asians in Eastern Africa. South Asians became commercially and financially successful in Eastern and Southern Africa, and generated a combination of class conflict and racial antagonisms. One of the more dramatic explosions was the mass expulsion of Asians by Idi Amin's Uganda in 1972, many of them merchants and professionals who were born in Uganda. There have also been periodic anti-Asian demonstrations in the streets of Nairobi, Kenya. On the other hand, South Africans of South Asian origin have long been part of the vanguard of the struggle against racism and apartheid, going back to campaigning by Mohandas Gandhi when he lived in South Africa at the beginning of the twentieth century. Many South Asians have since been among the leading activists of the African National Congress (ANC), including the woman who became the speaker in parliament, Speaker Jimwalla.

Large-scale war situations between Asia and Africa go back to many fluctuations in power between ancient Egypt and its Asian neighbours. Then came the momentous conquest of Egypt by the Arabs in the seventh century of the Christian era, followed by the Arab conquest of the rest of North Africa. A remarkable aspect of this historical saga was that many of those who were conquered by the Arabs became themselves Arabs. Over the centuries, Egyptians became not only Islamized in religion but also Arabized in language and identity. Egypt became the largest Arab nation in population, the most advanced in know-how, the best endowed culturally, and potentially the mightiest militarily. Al-Azhar University in Cairo became the most distinguished center of Muslim learning in the world, and one of the oldest. War can indeed lead on to creativity and innovation. This happened in North Africa after the Arab conquest. It happened in Zanzibar after the establishment of an Arab Sultanate. It happened in Ethiopia after centuries of interaction between Southern Arabia and the Horn of Africa. More recently, conflict situations between Africa and Asia included competitive territorial claims to islands between Eritrea and Yemen, nearly leading to war in 1996.

Conclusion

The Indian Ocean played an important role in African-Asian interaction. This interaction was both old and effective, and comprised various forces that contributed to shaping the respective histories of Africa and Asia. In culture, the relevant forces include Islamization, the birth and spread of new languages, and the impact of Indian music and cuisine. Politically, African-Asian interaction has included both friendship and conflict, and has ranged historically form the slave trade to the post-colonial Nonaligned Movement. The economic contacts between Africa and Asia go back to at least two thousand years, extending through the *dhow* trade on the Indian Ocean, and culminating today in such modern transactions as South Africa's arm sales to Asian countries. The great saga between Planet Earth's two largest continents is still unfolding. In the second half of the 20th century, African and Asian countries have been both political allies and economic rivals. As economic rivals Asia has been winning. As political allies both continents have been beneficiaries. We would like to conclude this essay with a number of paradoxes that characterize the experiences of Africa and Asia and their relationship as depicted along comparative, competitive, cooperative, and conflictual lines.

1) The Time-Space Paradox: Although Africa was colonized for a much shorter period than Asia, a much bigger percentage of African space was put under the colonial yoke than the percentage of Asian space. Less Asian territory was colonized but Asia was, on the whole, colonized for a longer period.

2) The Time-Change Paradox: Although Africa was colonized for a shorter period than were the colonized parts of Asia, African societies were changed and disrupted more fundamentally than were societies of Asia. Within less than a century, whole African societies were Christianized, whereas most Asians had resisted Christianization for hundreds of years. Furthermore, African political and educational systems became uniquely dependent on European languages.

3) The Culture-Economy Paradox: Although Africa seemed, by some indicators, to be westernizing faster than Asia, Africa was slower in economic modernization. Asian experience seems to indicate that, while thoroughgoing Protestant ethic and Western culture may be good for economic modernization in the West, they are not necessarily the best prescription elsewhere. Some Asian examples demonstrate that a combination of Western technique with indigenous culture is the secret of dramatic modernization and development—the Asian spirit for Asian development. Higher cultural Westernization in the Third World has not necessarily meant higher economic and developmental returns. As the Ghana-South Korea comparison shows, in reality, genuine development equals modernization minus dependency, especially cultural dependency.

4) The Paradox of Divisive Peace: Unfortunately, peace is divisive. Asian and African countries were greatest allies when they perceived shared dangers or common enemies. They were united against Western racism when the West was essentially bigoted (Afro-Asian racial solidarity). They were united in defense of non-Western civilizations when the West demeaned them (Afro-Asian cultural solidarity). Asian and African countries were certainly united against Western imperialism and colonialism (Afro-Asian anti-colonial solidarity). Asian and African countries were also united against the risks and dangers of the Cold War before it ended (Afro-Asian solidarity behind the Nonaligned Movement, joined by Latin America). The Afro-Asian movement got weaker and weaker as the struggle against direct racism and imperialism receded into history. The Non-aligned Movement has lost its original reason for existence with the end of the Cold War, so there is a gallant struggle to transform the movement from its historic East-West concerns to the more enduring North-South issues. Is East-West reconciliation bad for North-South relations? The end of the Cold War and the triumph of market ideologies are turning Africa and Asia away from the old political solidarities and more and more towards new economic rivalries. As Vietnam increases liberalization and the spirit of welcoming foreign investment, Vietnam becomes a rival to Africa for some of the investment and some of the aid. China is experimenting with market Marxism and has become a much more attractive magnet for many western investors than any part of Africa. India too is liberalizing, marketizing, and enticing foreign investment with greater vigor. With a population significantly larger than that of all the 50 African countries added together, the Indian market is very appetizing for many foreign investors.

5) *The Roots-Goals Paradox:* Every society seeks to develop two kinds of national myths: the myth of ancestry, in order to emphasize its heritage from the past, and the myth of purpose, in order to emphasize its reason for existence and its goals for the future. The myth of roots is tied to sense of history and identity; the myth of purpose is about sense of

social direction. Societies that totally lose a sense of their past have a hard time realizing their future goals. Western imperialism undermined Africa's own sense of ancestral heritage more seriously than it undermined Asia's sense of its own glorious past. African school children were taught to believe that they were a people without history. In Asia, China's cultural revolution under Mao involved a denial of roots and definitely resulted in damaged goals. Vietnam's communist experiment was for a while a denial of roots, with the consequence of damaging developmental goals. Both China and Vietnam have now retreated from an assault on their own ancestral heritage. The partition of India was a partial denial of the subcontinent's shared religious heritage (Hindu plus Muslim). It released passions and rivalries that heightened a sense of sectional heritages (Hindu versus Muslim). Goals suffered as a result for both India and Pakistan— and subsequently for Bangladesh, when it became separately independent. Mahatma Gandhi and the Nehru family in power tried to help India build a new myth of national purpose: "The Seven Pillars of a New International Indian Moral Order." The four domestic pillars were non-violence, liberal democracy, socialist development, and church-state separation. The three international pillars were: non-alignment in a world divided by ideology, the arms race, and military alliances; solidarity with the peoples of Asia and Africa and the dispossessed everywhere, in a search for a world without racism or imperialism; and a commitment to the United Nations system, including a struggle to liberate it from big power manipulation. These were the seven pillars of wisdom that independent India's founding fathers seem to have had in mind when constructing the post-colonial myth of national purpose for India. The question is: how many of those seven pillars of wisdom are still left standing? Have others been added? Are the pillars still enough to ensure India's special historic role as a leader in vision and a vanguard of international moral standards? Can the pillars effectively maintain India's role as a diplomatic bridge between the concerns of Asia and the aspirations of the African peoples?

6) The Cultural Paradox of Greed: Among the cultural casualties of the colonial experience was the underdeveloped nature of greed in Africa before the coming of the white man. Outside the Nile Valley, Great Zimbabwe, and a few other exceptions, there were hardly any African equivalents of the Taj Mahal, the Palace of Versailles, or the Temples of Cambodia. It takes a love of luxury, a pursuit of surplus, or a hunger for profit to produce a civilization of comparable monuments. It takes the exploitation of simpler people to build palaces, temples, and pyramids. Most precolonial African cultures were neither greedy enough nor exploitative enough. This underdeveloped greed was a casualty of European colonization and imperialism. Postcolonial African elites have learnt the attractions of luxury, surplus, and profit with a vengeance! They learned capitalist greed though not always capitalist discipline. Not all of Africa's problems require a culture change, and that culture change need not take too long. An Asian example is post-war Japan where, after a brief American occupation that brought a new constitution, Japan experienced a rapid and fundamental transformation in its political culture where a liberal competitive multiparty system took root. This just goes to show that fundamental culture change need not take too long. There is therefore hope for Africa too as the new century unfolds and globalization takes one more step forward.

NOTES

This chapter combines revised versions of two essays respectively entitled "Africa and Asia in the Postcolonial Experience: Political Allies or Economic Rivals" and "A Tale of Two Continents: Africa, Asia, and the Dialectic of Globalization." The first essay was presented at the sixth Indira Ghandi International Conference on the theme "The Post-Colonial World: Interdependence and Identities" held in Delhi, November 19-22, 1997. The second essay appeared in *Cooperation South* (a publication of the Special Unit for Technical Cooperation among Developing Countries, United Nations Development Programme), Number Two, 1998, Special Issue on Globalization, pp. 118-133. Both essays are indebted to previous work of the author on dependency and on African-Asian interactions.

1. See M. E. Chamberlain, *Decolonization: The Fall of the European Empires* (Oxford and New York: Basil Blackwell, 1985), pp. vi-ix, and D. K. Fieldhouse, *The Colonial Empires: A Comparative Survey from the Eighteenth Century* (London: Weidenfeld and Nicolson, 1966), pp. 226-241.

2. D. K. Fieldhouse, *The Colonial Empires*, p. 126.

3. Ibid., pp. 162-169.

4. Ibid., p. 151.

5. These figures are drawn from David Crystal (ed.), *The Cambridge Encyclopedia of Language* (Cambridge: Cambridge University Press, 1987), p. 357, and Arthur S. Banks *et al* (eds.), *The Political Handbook of the World, 1995-1996* (Binghamton: CSA Publications, 1996).

6. Consult, for instance, Donald H. Shively (ed.), *Tradition and Modernization in Japanese Culture* (Princeton, NJ: Princeton University Press, 1971).

7. For a discussion on the Turkish efforts at eliminating the influence of Islam and promoting secularism and modernization, see Javaid Saeed, *Islam and Modernization: A Comparative Analysis of Pakistan, Egypt, and Turkey* (Westport, CT: Praeger, 1994), pp. 157-196. Also refer to chapter 5 in this volume, entitled "Africa Between the Meiji Restoration and the Legacy of Atatürk."

8. See figures and tables to that effect in B. R. Mitchell, *International Historical Statistics, Africa, Asia & Oceania, 1750-1988*, second revised edition (New York: Stockton, 1993), especially pp. 476-489.

9. A number of other fascinating but depressing observations are made by Herbert H. Werlin in "Ghana and South Korea: Explaining Development Disparities," *Journal of African and Asian Studies* Volume 29, Number 3-4 (July/October 1994), pp. 205-225.

10. See Mitchell, *International Historical Statistics*, op. cit., pp. 255-257.

11. Ibid., pp. 226-232.

12. Ibid., pp. 332-333.

13. Ibid., pp. 627-631.

14. See United Nations, *Industrial Commodity Statistics Yearbook, 1993* (New York: United Nations, 1995), p. 189.

15. Ibid., p. 219.

16. Ibid., pp. 12-40.

17. See Alexander Pope, *Essay on Criticism* (1711) and *the Dunciad* (1728).

18. The World Bank, *Sub-Saharan Africa: From Crisis to Sustainable Growth* (Washington, D.C., November 1989), p. 29.

19. Drawn from World Bank, *World Tables 1995* (Washington and Baltimore, MD: World Bank and Johns Hopkins University Press, 1995), pp. 14-15.

20. Ibid., p. 163.

21. Jack D. Glen and Mariusz A. Sumlinski, *Trends in Private Investment in Developing Countries 1995: Statistics for 1980-1993*, International Finance Corporation Discussion Paper No. 25 (Washington, DC: The World Bank, 1995), p. 3.

22. OECD, *International Direct Investment Statistics Yearbook, 1995* (Paris, France: OECD, 1995), Table 6 of respective country tables.

23. A comprehensive survey of foreign direct investment in the Chinese economy may be found in Chung Chen, Lawrence Chang, and Yimin Zhang, "The Role of Foreign Direct Investment in China's post-1970 Economic Development," *World Development* 23 (April 1995), pp. 691-703.

24. Consult, for example, "Looking Outward," *Far Eastern Economic Review* 144 (April 27, 1989), p. 70; "Romance Meets Reality," *Far Eastern Economic Review* 157 (September 22, 1994), p. 72; and "Hanoi Names More Military Officers to Politburo," *New York Times* (July 2, 1996), p. 4.

25. On the Bandung Conference, see Richard Wright, *The Color Curtain: A Report on the Bandung Conference* (Cleveland, OH: World Pub. Co., 1956).

26. Relatedly, consult Robert A. Mortimer, *The Third World in International Politics*, second updated edition (Boulder, CO: Westview Press, 1984); Marc Williams, *Third World Cooperation: The Group of 77 in UNCTAD* (London and New York: Pinter

and St. Martin's Press, 1991); and Frans N. Stokman, *Roll Calls and Sponsorship: A Methodological Analysis of Third World Group Formation in the United Nations* (Leyden: A. W. Sijthoff, 1977).

27. A dated but still useful guide to the Nonaligned Movement may be found in D. R. Goyal (ed.), *Non-Alignment: Concept and Concerns* (Delhi: Ajanta Books International, 1986).

28. For an examination of the relationship between the United Nations and the Nonaligned Movement, see M. S. Rajan, V. S. Mani, and C. S. R. Murthy (eds.), *The Nonaligned and the United Nations* (New York and New Delhi: Oceana and South Asian Publishers, 1987).

29. See *Final Declaration*, Nonaligned Movement, Belgrade Conference, 1989.

PART III

AFRICA AND THE INTERNATIONAL ORDER

EIGHT

HUMAN OBLIGATION AND GLOBAL ACCOUNTABILITY FROM THE IMPEACHMENT OF WARREN HASTINGS TO THE LEGACY OF NUREMBERG (1993)

Two interrelated processes in world history have profoundly affected the fate of human rights and their emergence as a world order issue. One process involved Europe's territorial expansion, from Christopher Columbus to the scramble for Africa. The other process was the development of international accountability in upholding human rights. The transition of this second process extended from the impeachment of the eighteenth century British imperial administrator, Warren Hastings, to the Nuremberg trials of Nazis after World War II. These two processes of international territorial expansion and international moral accountability were interlinked. Europe's territorial appetite and material greed sealed the fate of the Americas as settler colonies. European expansionism also subjugated India, Africa, and much of the rest of the world. Yet, that very internationalization helped to shape new rules of conduct, and laid down the principles of wider international accountability.

As human symbols of Europe's territorial expansion, we have chosen Christopher Columbus, who helped open the new world, Warren Hastings, who pioneered British penetration of India, and Otto von Bismarck, the German statesman who hosted the European imperial conference of Berlin in 1884-85. As symbols of the evolution of international accountability, we have chosen the impeachment of Warren Hastings (1788-1795) in the House of Lords, London, on one side, and on the other, the Nuremberg trials (1945-1946) of German Nazis after World War Two.

Columbus and Africa: A Dialectical Relation

If Christopher Columbus in 1492 helped to open the gates of the colonization of the New World, Otto von Bismarck in 1885 helped to open the gates of the colonization of Africa. The voyages of Columbus in the fifteenth century put before Europe a whole new world to conquer. The diplomacy of Bismarck in the nineteenth century helped to present to Europe a whole new continent to colonize. Four centuries separated Columbus from Bismarck but both the European "discovery" of the Americas and the European "scramble" for Africa had enormous consequences for the Black race and for human rights.

One product of the legacy of Columbus was of course the United States of America. Black America was part of that product, with its meaning in the history of suffering. What is not often realized is that the triumph of Columbus was itself partly a product of Africa's impact on maritime history. Africa helped to produce Columbus, and Columbus in turn helped to produce the United States and Black America. If you asked me what forced Christopher Columbus to turn westward in search of a sea-route to Asia, my answer would be "Africa." Africa compelled his eyes to look to the West in his quest for the Orient. Africa's earliest impact on world history was simply by being there: a huge land mass with the Atlantic on one side and the Indian Ocean on the other, a vast island which resisted circumnavigation. It was a stubborn impediment to Europe's search for a sea-route to India and China. Columbus himself had his apprenticeship round the rough waters of North-West Africa. From Madeira Islands, he acquired sailing experience and may have reached as far south along Africa's coast as the Portuguese trading post of Mina on the Gold Coast.

Had Africa been easier to circumvent, Europe's interest in going West could have been delayed for another hundred and fifty years or more. For one thing, the later the Americas were discovered, the less extensive would have been Spain's and Portugal's share of it. "Latin" America might not have existed at all had the Americas been "discovered" after the decline of Spain and Portugal. By speeding up the discovery of the Americas, Africa might have spared the world an even larger British Empire than in fact existed. Africa denied the world an English-speaking South America. The Americas as we know them were thus born out of Europe's desperation. Asia was once the lure, Africa had been the decisive historical obstacle, and the diverse New World accidentally became the prize, culturally more varied than it would have been had it been discovered by an Anglo-Saxon equivalent of Christopher Columbus a century and a half later. On the other hand, a later discovery of the Americas by Europeans could have reduced the scale of genocide perpetrated against Native Americans.

Other contradictions developed in Africa's relations with the New World. While Africa's location had forced Columbus into "discovering" the Americas, the Americas in turn had their revenge on Africa. The Western hemisphere developed an enormous appetite for African slaves. Millions were transported all the way from the "dark continent" that had originally forced the New World to be "found" in the first place. A major African presence was established in the Americas, but it was a presence throbbing with pain. The slave trade inaugurated the process of Africa's political marginalization. The continent became almost powerless in global terms and an easy prey to colonization and further exploitation. This most central of all continents was pushed to the fringes of world affairs.

On the other hand, a reverse process was taking place in the New World. The Americas started off as both geographically and politically peripheral. Today, the New World is still distant from the main concentrations of human populations. Some eighty percent of the human race lives in Asia, Africa, and Europe, thousands of miles away from the Americas. But thanks partly to the Europeans for whom Columbus had blazed the trail, and partly to the African labour which came with slavery, North America by the middle of the twentieth century had become politically central in world affairs—though still geographically on the fringes of the populated world. Africa and the United States had become mirror opposites.

That particular disparity in power was worse than ever by the 1980s. The Reagan-Bush years were, by coincidence, a kind of centenary celebration of the years of Bismarck's high diplomacy. The history of the Black experience became a transition from the imperial politics of the 1880s to the hegemonic policies of the America of Reagan and Bush in the last decades of the twentieth century. But the impact of the United States on the world was much older than the administrations of its fortieth and forty-first presidents. The American war of independence had reverberations across the globe. When the news reached India in 1778 that General John Burgoyne of Britain had surrendered in Saratoga, North America, the previous year, a man called Warren Hastings wrote:

> [... I]f it really be true that the British arms and influence have suffered so severe a check in the Western world, it is the more incumbent upon those who are charged with the interest of Great

Britain in the East to exert themselves for the retrieval of the national honour.[1]

America's independence helped to seal the fate of India's sovereignty for the worse. In a sense, Calcutta served as historical compensation for the humiliation at Saratoga. And Warren Hastings was part and parcel of the Indian side of this British equation.

The Raj in the Making

Born in 1732 in Oxfordshire, Warren Hastings went to India at the age of 17 as a junior employee of the East India Company, one of the earliest multinational corporations of the Western world. In 1771 Hastings was put in charge of East India company affairs in Bengal as governor. He brought the Indian government in Bengal directly under British Control with himself first as governor and then as governor-general. He later got involved in political rivalries within the Company and in British politics, becoming more controversial at home. From 1774 to 1784, he also embarked on a number of expensive wars in India, which interfered with trade. Hastings' reputation in his own country was damaged when he returned to England in 1785. Three years later, he faced impeachment in the House of Lords, a prosecution by the House of Commons before the Lords.

Hastings was being held accountable for offenses including extortion, such as the requisitioning of the treasures of the mother and grandmother (Begums) of the Vizier of Oudh in India. He was also being accused of complicity in judicial murder in Bengal. The seeds of international accountability for violation of human rights were being sown, as Edmund Burke led the prosecution before the House of Lords. An idea was being born, a concept that was later to mature in the Nuremberg trials some one hundred and fifty years later. It was in February 1788 that the seven-year impeachment of Warren Hastings began. From 1772 to 1785, Warren Hastings had dominated Indian affairs. His was the longest and most eventful governorship of British India. Some would describe him as the virtual co-founder of British India, and perhaps the greatest of the British rulers in India. Broadly, three types of rights were involved in the impeachment of Warren Hastings at the time, although they were not framed in precisely those terms. They were: (a) the juridical rights of states; (b) the collective rights of groups and races; and (c) the individual rights of persons.

Hastings was accused of violating the rights of Indian states and principalities. He was accused of violating the rights of such groups as the Afghan tribe of Rohillas by hiring British troops to the Nawab of Oudh. He was also accused of violating the rights of individual Indians by extortion and corruption. In the fate of Raja Nandakumar (Nuncumar) perhaps all three rights were involved. Nandakumar had accused Hastings of bribery in 1775; Hastings accused him in turn of conspiracy. Then another Indian accused Nandakumar of forgery. A Court headed by Sir Elijah Impey, Hastings' contemporary at Westminster, tried him. On the charge of forgery, Nandakumar was sentenced to death. Hastings refused to commute the sentence and Nandakumar was executed.

Execution for forgery was virtually unknown to Indian society. From an Indian perspective, it was a barbaric punishment imposed by a foreign power. To that extent, it violated the rights of the cultural group to which Nandakumar belonged. And the whole British presence was in turn a violation of the juridical rights of Indian states and principalities. On the issue of forgery, Indian law and custom were more humane and less barbaric than the imported English law, but English law prevailed. Did Hastings conspire with Sir Elijah Impey to condemn Nandakumar or did he merely let his vendetta against the Indian go to the extent of refusing to reprieve him? The events of the 1770s in India took place against the background of another major convulsion thousands of miles away: the American war of independence. Warren Hastings saw himself as the redeemer of Britain's national honor. As Britain lost her Western empire, she proceeded to build her Eastern empire. As we indicated earlier, America's independence helped to seal the fate of India's. Hastings did see Calcutta as compensation for the humiliation of Saratoga.

After seven long years of an impeachment trial, Hastings was acquitted of all charges. But he could no longer hold public office and was in other ways more dishonored for his great lapses of conduct. Edmund Burke, the great Anglo-Irish thinker, was probably sincere in his outrage. He rejected Hastings' relativist argument that things that were wrong in Britain could be all right to commit in India. Burke retorted "this geographical morality we do protest against..." and he elaborated as follows:

> [Mr. Hastings] has told your Lordships, in his defence, that actions in Asia do not bear the same moral qualities which the same actions would bear in Europe... These gentlemen have formed a plan of geographical morality... as if, when you have crossed the equinoctial, all the virtues die, as they say some insects die when they cross the line... We think it necessary, in justification of ourselves, to declare that the laws of morality are the same everywhere. There is no action which would pass for an act of extortion, of peculation, of bribery, and of oppression in England, that is not an act of extortion, of peculation, of bribery, and of oppression in Europe, Asia, Africa, and all the world over.[2]

Burke's position was itself somewhat eclectic. He combined cultural relativism with moral universalism. He was enraged by Hastings' apparent insensitivity to the moral sensibilities of Indians. Yet Hastings in turn was a strange mixture. The man who sometimes violated Indian culture and custom also helped to promote a new legal system based on Hindu law by encouraging special translations from Hindu law books and by encouraging the study of Sanskrit by European scholars. Hastings himself knew Persian, Bengali, Urdu and some Arabic. He encouraged the founding of the Asiatic Society of Bengal in 1784, and founded a college of Arabic studies in 1781. But Edmund Burke felt that power was a divine trust and Hastings had abused that power. The profoundly conservative Edmund Burke was ahead of his time in the views that emerged in the course of the impeachment. The concept of imperial power as a trust had conditioned both Burke's view about America and his views about India. He defended the American colonies: they had a good case but bad arguments; theirs were not the rights of man but the rights of Englishmen. In India, the rights of the natives were not human rights either; they were the rights of Indians in the light of their own customs and civilizations. Burke was in many ways a prophet of self-determination as guided by a sense of history. "Men will never look forward to prosperity who never look backward to their ancestors," he had once said. He was more sensitive to the collective rights of groups and peoples than to individual rights of persons. He defended Bengalis, Afghanis, French Canadians, the Irish, and others. He attacked the French, but mainly because he thought the French Revolutionaries displayed collective amnesia, a loss of memory as to their identity and place in history.

The Burkean legacy of power as an imperial trust greatly conditioned the future course of British policies in the colonies. Lord Lugard's doctrine of indirect rule in Africa was in part descended from the impeachment of Warren Hastings. Lugard's guiding principle was: "If you have to rule other societies, try to respect their cultures as far as possible, and rule them through institutions they understand." But perhaps the most farsighted aspect of Burke's ideas is only beginning to emerge now. He felt that what we would today call "multinational corporations" should be subject to a code of conduct based on triple accountability: (a) accountability to the host societies in which they operate; (b) accountability to the rules laid down by the companies' own country of origin; and (c) accountability to a higher standard of equity, propriety, and justice. Thus, the impeachment of Warren Hastings was in part the trial of a multinational corporation, the East India Company, and unlike many capitalists today, Edmund Burke realized that human rights could be violated by companies as much as by states, by non-governmental forces as much as by governments.

From Bismarck to the Third Reich

In the years that followed Hastings' impeachment, economic imperialism entered a new phase. And yet the expansion of the British Empire coincided with new levels of British accountability. The campaigns to abolish first the slave trade and later slavery itself were new stages in the history of imperial ethics. Those who were colonized were protected from outright enslavement. The mighty were beginning to be morally answerable. Nonetheless, while the legacy of the impeachment of Warren Hastings did make Western imperialism more ethically restrained, it did not make it more geographically restricted. European domination of other societies was beginning to have rules of self-restraint. Europe's territorial appetite was still unabated. This is what brings us to the German statesman who hosted the Berlin conference of 1884-5. The conference was itself designed to help European powers agree on the rules of their own competitive scramble for Africa. The presiding presence was Otto von Bismarck. The venue was the city that was one day to become the headquarters of Nazi Germany. Perhaps the events that were one day to be put on trial in Nuremberg in 1945 had their origins in the imperial conference in Berlin in 1885, openly conspiring to annex and partition Africa. In the words of the nineteenth century novelist, Charles Dickens: "Think for a moment of the long chain of iron or gold, of thorns or flowers which would never have bound you but for the formation of the first link on one memorable day."[3]

Prince Otto von Bismarck lived from 1815 to 1898. He was involved in three European wars that helped foster German unification. The wars were with Denmark (1864), Austria (Seven Years' War, 1866), and France (1870). He was made Prince von Bismarck on March 21, 1871 and appointed Chancellor of the German Empire that same year. He then proceeded to govern the German Empire from January 1871 to 1890. Bismarck united the Germans and helped to divide Africa. He promoted basic human needs for Germans and helped in violating basic human rights for Africans. He was responsible for introducing state insurance in his country: for sickness in 1883, for accident in 1884, and for old age in 1889. He was an innovator in the history of the welfare state and of the satisfaction of at least some basic human requirements.

In 1884, Bismarck quarreled with Britain and within the course of a single year obtained the Cameroons, Southwest Africa, East Africa (Tanganyika, Rwanda, and Burundi) and part of New Guinea. The architect of the welfare state was also the designer of Imperial Germany. In 1889 Bismarck declared: "I am not a colonial man," but he brought Germany closer to a colonial role than any other modern figure with the exception of Adolf Hitler. In the history of human needs versus human rights one could consider the period from Bismarck to Hitler. To some degree, the link gives us half a century of Western ambition. Prince Otto von Bismarck was in power in Germany in the 1880s. Hitler was in power from 1933 to 1945. A second reason for looking at this period concerns imperial history. As we indicated, it was

Bismarck who convened the Congress of Berlin, a meeting of Western powers designed to set down the rules of the game in Europe's scramble for Africa. Another reason for bringing Bismarck and Hitler together is in relation to the dialectic between welfare and warfare. Bismarck was a titled aristocrat, a prince who had entered statecraft and the arena of politics. Such a background could afford the magnanimity of "noblesse oblige"—readiness to be generous but not necessarily humble—the result being the German welfare state. The years of Bismarck in 19th century Germany were also the years of daring social legislation committed to the health of the poor, the amelioration of the unemployed, the survival of the humble, and meeting other human needs. Hitler, on the other hand, was not a natural aristocrat. There was little of the "noblesse oblige" attitude among his supporters: insensitivity to basic human needs was their hallmark. And so, while Bismarck's Germany was decidedly innovative in social welfare, Hitler's Germany became socially demolitional. As he constructed a war machine, Hitler's casualties were millions of lives. But his militaristic politics also sacrificed such German social achievements as: (i) meals for school children; (ii) subsidies for urban renewal; (iii) benefits for the blind and disabled; (iv) charity for the poor; (v) social security for children whose parents had died; (vi) compensation for the unemployed; (vii) subsidies for the non-Nazi Arts and Humanities; (viii) subsidies for denominational schools; and (ix) support for higher education. What this means is that Bismarck combined the welfare state with the warfare state. His Germany linked social legislation with military discipline. The country provided bread for the poor and arms for the warrior. Hitler's Germany, on the other hand, glorified the warfare state and left the welfare state bleeding. Human rights were violated as basic human needs were increasingly denied. The shadow of the Swastika became the shadow of death. Genocide was at hand.

Reckoning at Nuremberg

At the end of World War II, the principle of international accountability was once again invoked. A tribunal was set up, under the signature of the victorious powers (Britain, the United States, the Soviet Union, and France). The great trial began in that old city of Bismarck and of the Imperial Conference on Africa of 1884-85. But in 1945, the presiding personality in Berlin was not a Prussian statesman but a Russian general, I.T. Nikitchenko. The opening date of the tribunal was October 18, 1945. The charges were numerous crimes against peace, against humanity, and in violation of conventional rules of war. The accused were specific Nazi personalities and specific Nazi institutions like the Gestapo and the Nazi Secret Police. From November 1945, the tribunal moved from Berlin to Nuremberg and the presidency passed to the British member of the tribunal, Lord Justice Sir Geoffrey Lawrence. The trial was conducted in four languages, an improvement on the single language of the impeachment of Warren Hastings. But from the global perspective of a world war it was perhaps unfortunate that all the four Nuremberg languages were European: English, French, German, and Russian. From the perspective of crimes against humanity, it would perhaps have been fitting to add either Hebrew or Yiddish as the fifth language at Nuremberg.

From the point of view of world culture, the subsequent trial of Japanese war leaders (1946-1948) was more representative. It is true that the Tokyo trial recognized only two languages instead of the four at Nuremberg, but the fact that the two languages at Tokyo were Japanese as well as English helped to break the mould of Eurocentrism. Even more significant was the fact that the tribunal of the Tokyo trials included justices from India, China, and the Philippines, besides European and American judges. Judge Delfin Jaranilla of the Philippines filed a separate concurring opinion at the conclusion of the trial. And Judge R.M. Pal of India dissented generally from the majority opinion. The trend towards wider global accountability as a principle took one more step forward at the Tokyo trials. The nature of accountability at the Tokyo trials made more allowances than at Nuremberg for what might be called juniority (as opposed to seniority). Being junior in a chain of command could be a mitigating circumstance by the rules of Tokyo, and obeying orders could mitigate the punishment. Legal minds in the two tribunals of Nuremberg and Tokyo were still grappling with the age-old philosophical problem of the limits of political obligation.

At Nuremberg three of the individual defendants were acquitted, twelve received the death sentence by hanging, three were to be imprisoned for life, and four got lesser prison sentences. The decision was unanimous, though General Nikitchenko would have preferred the death sentence instead of life imprisonment for Rudolf Hess. The Soviet member of the tribunal was also more logical than his Western counterparts in defining the boundaries of accountability. General Nikitchenko wanted the Reich cabinet itself to be declared a criminal organization, and not just the Gestapo and Secret Police created by the Cabinet. The Soviet member was also eager to have the Nazi High Command of the German armed forces declared criminally liable. The Western members disagreed. The logic of ultimate responsibility was perhaps on the side of Soviet reasoning on these particular details. At the Tokyo trials seven defendants were sentenced to death by hanging, sixteen to life imprisonment, and two to lesser terms. Two of the defendants died in the course of the trial, and one was declared unfit to plead. The trials that followed World War II have been on trial on moral grounds, from the outset. Were human beings being punished for acts that were not criminal at the time they were committed? This concern about ex-post facto accountability has been of serious ethical implications all along. Could the vanquished have a fair trial at the hands of the victors? Although the learned judges displayed more fair play than many of their critics had expected, it is still a matter of regret that the Nuremberg trials did not include justices from neutral nations. Since the victors also committed war crimes, and perhaps even crimes against humanity, the moral credibility of the Nuremberg trials was to some extent compromised by omitting to level charges against the victors. Much of the brutal allied bombing of Dresden or even Berlin would have qualified as both war crimes and crimes against humanity had the allies not been the sole definers of what constituted such "crimes."

Notwithstanding such concerns, progress was made at Nuremberg and at Tokyo towards a world of greater legal as well as ethical accountability. Precedents were set which may contribute towards even higher standards of political and moral conduct. As Justice Robert H. Jackson, the American member of the Nuremberg tribunal, said in his report to President Harry S. Truman:

> One of the chief obstacles to this trial was the lack of a beaten path. A judgment such as has been rendered shifts the power of the precedent to the support of these rules of law.[4]

But the very importance of Justice Robert Jackson at the Nuremberg trials signified a double shift that was taking place in the world. Nazi Germany had not only failed to become the ultimate super-power in the world, it had helped to confirm the United States as the alternative super-power of the post-war years. The United States emerged as the mightiest nation in the world and saw itself as a kind of global policeman or sheriff, holding the rest of the human race to a code of accountability.

The USA: Sheriff on Trial

The best illustration that there is no room for moral

complacency lies in the behaviour of the United States. The self-appointed custodian of the conscience of the world has vindicated Lord Acton's conviction that power does indeed corrupt. The war in Vietnam was the most dramatic illustration of this. Both war crimes and crimes against humanity were perpetrated in the American crusade against communism. The list includes the American use of napalm bombs, the impact of Agent Orange on food crops, the ruthless bombing of Hanoi and Cambodia, the mining of Haiphong Harbor, the undeclared war on the people of Vietnam as a whole—the entire litany of American violations of the spirit of Nuremberg during the Vietnam war. Yet American society did not take it lying down. The Vietnam war was the most unpopular in the history of the republic. A new domestic principle evolved during the demonstrations of American campuses and in American streets. Warfare itself was getting democratized as the demonstrator insisted on the principle of "warfare by consent." However, the moral principle of accountability was still struggling for acceptance as the legacies of Columbus and Bismarck converged in the role of the United States. Geographical expansion and moral accountability continued to be part of the dynamic of Western hegemony. How can the United States be a credible trustee of Nuremberg and the Rule of Law if in the 1980s Washington could violate international law in various instances, including the following?

1) The aggressive mining of the harbours of Nicaragua; 2) the summarily rejection of the jurisdiction of the International Court of Justice on the matter of Nicaragua's security; 3) the imposition of a trade embargo on Nicaragua in defiance of a World Court Order; 4) the violation of a 1958 Treaty of Friendship, Commerce, and Navigation between the USA and Nicaragua; 5) the skyjacking of an Egyptian civilian aircraft in pursuit of Palestinian suspects associated with the Achille Lauro incident; 6) the deliberate violation of Italy's territorial jurisdiction and airspace on the same issue;

7) the bombing of Libyan cities of Tripoli and Benghazi in retaliation for acts for which it now appears that Libya was not responsible; 8) the invasion of the small island of Grenada; 9) the violation of United Nations Charter obligations on payment of dues and seeking to expel or close down the mission of the Palestine Liberation Organization to the United Nations, in clear violation of international treaties that the US has ratified; 10) the refusal of a visa to Yasir Arafat who was supposed to address the General Assembly, in violation of America's 1947 legal obligations as host country to the UN.

An American International lawyer, Burns Weston, has asked: "If we say to the Secretary of State, the CIA, and the National Security Council that it's O.K. to bend the law because we don't like another country's ideology, can we rightfully expect that the Attorney General or the FBI will not [also] bend the law a little...? Can we legitimately expect to separate the standards that govern the way our government operates internationally from those that govern it internally?"5

In addition to the Nuremberg trials, the Second World War gave birth to the United Nations' system. The United States has become less interested in the United Nations precisely as the world body has become more representative of the world community. The United States pulled out of UNESCO, played havoc with its UN dues, put pressure on other UN Agencies, and sabotaged Africa's earlier chances of producing a Secretary-General of the UN. It is legitimate to ask how the United States can be a leader in democratic accountability when it does not respect majority opinion in the evolving parliamentary institutions of mankind. In Africa, the most basic contribution the United States can make to democratic aspirations entails respect for the principle of self-determination. Wasn't making the independence of Namibia dependent on the withdrawal of Cuban troops from Angola a denial of self-determination? Chester Crocker, US Assistant Secretary of State for African Affairs under the

Reagan presidency, is on record as having said: "we have no intention of waging economic warfare on South Africa and its people. On the contrary, we firmly believe that economic growth has been—and will continue to be—a principal engine of constructive change in all fields in that country." If economic warfare is wrong when waged against South Africa, why did the Reagan Administration wage it against Nicaragua and Panama? On the other hand, if it makes sense for the United States to lend direct support to UNITA in the fight for democracy in Angola, why has it not made sense for the US to contribute money to the African National Congress in the fight for democracy in South Africa?

Anti-colonial movements in Africa and the Civil Rights Movement in the United States were part of the same process of democratizing the Western world. Liberated Africa made . segregated America increasingly anachronistic. And yet the Reagan-Bush years still succeeded in pushing the imperial clock back a little.[6] When we look at the black man or black woman, we are looking at somebody the origins of whose exploitation go back not only to the world before Ronald Reagan but also to the world before Bismarck. What is the equilibrium between the West and the Black world across the centuries? How accountable is the West? Again the puzzle persists: Why should we pronounce Prince Otto von Bismarck in the same breath as Ronald Reagan? Our argument is once again summarized: a hundred years of Africa's relations with the West are consummated in the juxtaposition. The Conference of Berlin of the 1880s sought to establish the rules for the colonization of Africa and the end of Reagan's eight years in office became a dubious centenary celebration of such a scramble for Africa. Reagan presented dilemmas between the welfare state and the warfare state. Bismarck invented the welfare state without relinquishing the warfare imperative. In the early 1880s, this Prussian prince (Bismarck) exercised power over the German nation. In the early 1980s, a Californian film star (Reagan) exercised power over the American nation. One was a case of "noblesse oblige;" the other was a case of "nouveau riche." Somewhere in between was the Black predicament, caught between the white aristocracy (Bismarck) and the white bourgeoisie (Reagan). Human rights and basic human needs were often at stake. Bismarck helped to set the stage of the West's penetration of Africa. The Conference of Berlin helped to define the rules of annexation. The United States was similarly ambivalent. Germany and the United States lived to become peripheral to colonialism, but central to capitalism. The two countries built relatively small territorial empires, but against the background of considerable domestic development. Both countries touched the destiny of the Black world. The United States was a major factor in the history of slavery. Germany was a major factor in paving the way for the imperial scramble for Africa. As for the interplay between the warfare and welfare state, Bismarck's Germany had combined the two. Hitler's Germany tilted in favor of the warfare state. The post-war Federal Republic of Germany reversed the tilt in favor of the welfare state. The United States of America has never been in love with the welfare state. At best, she has occasionally flirted with the idea. But the Reagan Administration showed every sign of turning its back on major areas of welfare, while emphasizing the warfare aspects of the federal machine.[7]

Conclusion

The United States has been a major factor in the history of the slave trade, an even bigger factor in the history of capitalism, but a relatively minor factor in the history of colonizing the rest of the world. This last colonizing role was played out more extensively by European powers, partly facilitated in the 1880s by a German statesman called Otto von Bismarck. Historically Bismarck was crucial in the unification of Germany but he was also instrumental in the division of Africa. While Africa was being colonized, Blacks all over the Americas were being emancipated from slavery. The legacy of Bismarck created colonial chains for Africa, while the shackles of the legacy of Columbus were being loosened in the New World. The final act of the drama includes the future role of Black Americans. Together they constitute one of the largest black nations in the world. Black Americans are lodged in the most powerful country in the world, the United States. Will Black Americans one day become as effective and influential in shaping American policy towards Africa, as Jewish Americans are in shaping American policy towards the Middle East? There are twice as many Black Americans as there are Jews in the whole world added together. One day, the gap in influence between these two groups of Americans will surely narrow, hopefully to the advantage of human rights and equal human worth. What may then happen could be the final act of a momentous piece of historical theatre. The slave trade initiated the process of Africa's political marginalization in world power. Descendants of African slaves may begin the process of getting Africa back towards the center of the global scheme of things. The story of Africa's discovery of Columbus, and of Columbus' discovery of the Americas, may one day finalize a momentous dialectic in the history of racism and human rights.

Behind this racial dialectic have been two wider processes: the imperial expansion of the West and the internationalization of accountability in the world system. We have sought to demonstrate that two milestones in the history of global accountability are the impeachment of Warren Hastings (1788-1795) and the Nuremberg trials of the Nazis (1945-46). In the ringing words of Edmund Burke at the impeachment of Hastings: "Law and arbitrary power are in eternal enmity." But just as in the award of the Nobel Prize for Peace the judges are excessively Scandinavian, so in the proceedings against Hastings and the Nazis, the judges were excessively Western. The principle of global accountability has made progress since the East India Company was let loose on Bengal. But who decides what is a war crime? Who determines what is a crime against humanity? Accountability is getting globalized, but the rules are still overwhelmingly Eurocentric. Edmund Burke's prosecution of Hastings implied the accountability of a multinational corporation, the East India Company. The Nuremberg trials took the case of institutional accountability a stage further with its case against the Nazis. It was only a matter of time before the Third World would begin to make the state itself accountable, with the offending state of South Africa as the architect of apartheid. Out of the humiliations of Bengal and the concentration camps of the Nazis, out of the burnt bodies of Vietnam and the brutalities of apartheid, out of the legacy of Bismarck and the regressive tendencies of the Reagan years, the human race has nevertheless taken one more step forward in its search for restraint and global accountability.

NOTES

This chapter is a revised version of an essay that originally appeared under the same title in *The Constitutional Foundations of World Peace*, edited by Richard A. Falk, Robert C. Johansen, and Samuel S. Kim (Albany, New York: State University of New York Press, 1993), pp. 329-347.

1. Penderel Moon, *Warren Hastings and British India* (1947) and Keith Feiling, *Warren Hastings* (1954).

2. Burke, *Speech on the Speech of Warren Hastings*, February 16, 1788, *Collected Works*, Boston edition (1865-1867), Volume IX, pp. 446-459.

3. Dickens, *Great Expectations*.

4. See *Report of Robert H. Jackson, United States Representative to the International Conference on Military Trials* (1949).

5. Burns H. Weston, "The Reagan Administration vs. International Law," in *Journal of International Law*, Vol. 19, No. 3, Summer 1987, p. 300.

6. Michael Clough, *Critical Issues Beyond Sanctions: Reorienting US Policy on Southern Africa* (Council on Foreign Relations, 1988).

7. In terms of basic human needs, Reagan's apparent determination to dismantle the American welfare state had implications for American Blacks as well as Africans. In a similar fashion to Germany's policies under Hitler, Reagan's policies involved the reduction of unemployment benefits and free lunches for needy children, the elimination of various aspects of medicare, and the curtailment of social security benefits, of old age protection, as well as of legal services and legal aid for the aged and the poor. On the other hand, Reagan's reconstruction of the warfare state revealed trends towards an enhancement of the defense or war budget (the greatest in peace time), greater support for such regimes as El Salvador, elaboration of ideas like the Rapid Deployment Force in the Gulf, and warfare disguised as welfare in such schemes as: (a) aid to Zaire (now the Democratic Republic of the Congo); (b) aid to Kenya; and (c) aid to Somalia.

NINE

THE FRANKENSTEIN STATE AND THE INTERNATIONAL ORDER (1988)

The most compelling alarm bells against the sovereign state should have sounded with the rise of Hitler's Third Reich and the outbreak of World War II. Yet, by a strange twist of fate, World War II was not only a great indictment of the doctrine of state sovereignty but also a great disseminator of that doctrine to other cultures and societies. Nazi genocide against its own citizens disgraced the principle of domestic jurisdiction. The behaviour of loyal Nazis like Eichmann in carrying out orders of genocide disgraced the notion of limitless obedience to "the law of the land." The brutalities of aggression and war crimes, the obscenities and inhumanities against Jews and others, the sheer destruction of life, limb, and property from Leningrad to Hiroshima, all cried out for a new alternative to the state system. But the same international conflict that raised profound moral questions about sovereignty was at the same time instrumental in globalizing the state system. World War II aroused new political and national expectations in Asia and Africa, and strengthened Afro-Asian movements for independence and sovereignty. World War II also improved the chances of such movements by weakening European imperial powers, strengthening the anti-colonial policies of the Soviet Union and the United States, and transforming the international climate of opinion in favour of globalizing the state system. On the issue of sovereignty, World War II played out its ultimate paradox: it was itself an indictment of state sovereignty and of its genocidal and militaristic tendencies, while ate the same time helping to lay the foundations of a much more universal Westphalian system.

When in 1818 Mary Wollstonercroft Shelley bequeathed to the world the book *Frankenstein: Or the Modern Prometheus*, she little knew that she was creating the metaphor of the sovereign state. In the original story, Frankenstein was of course the creator of the monster rather than the monster himself. Frankenstein was a Swiss student of occult sciences who created an artificial monster out of parts of corpses and casualties of the past. Similarly, humankind created a dangerous artifice and anthropomorphized it. Humans created a monster in their own image, partly out of the dead limbs of other human beings. Homo Sapiens created the sovereign state, the ultimate Frankenstein's monster. Just as his own monster destroyed Frankenstein, so the sovereign state has enormous potential for destroying the human species that produced it. The state's capacity for such annihilation is expanding with its own escalating energies of violence. Planet Earth lies in the shadow of the Frankenstein state.

The Frankenstein State in Action

The new post-war world created a special setting of interaction between the First, Second, and Third Worlds. We define the First World in the usual way, as the world of advanced capitalist countries. We define the Second World as the world of advanced socialist industrial powers. We define the Third World as the world of the developing countries of Asia, Africa, and Latin America, and of related islands. Our first proposition is that successful attainment of state sovereignty in the Third World has so far been the burial ground, the graveyard, of other social movements. We use the term "attainment of state sovereignty" in the sense of national acquisition of political independence. The acquisition of that independence in most of the Third World has often resulted in a rapid shrinkage of the arena of social movements. Our second proposition is that socialism in the Second World has also been the burial ground, the graveyard, of most other social movements. This has been partly because socialism in the Second World has capitulated to the sovereign logic of the state system, and has itself interpreted liberation and revolution as the sovereign control of state power. The Frankenstein state is the monster that overwhelms even its own socialist creator. Our third proposition is that the First World of advanced capitalist countries is the mother of both the worst aspects of the human condition in the twentieth century and some of the best aspects. Those two aspects are also captured in the proposition that political and social movements are at their most diverse precisely in this First World of liberal capitalist democracy.

Let us take these three propositions in turn and examine the components that add up to this particular paradigm of state and sovereignty. In many Third World countries, the heyday of political diversity and the open society consisted of the last days of colonial rule and the first few years of independence. The last days of colonial rule witnessed a rich explosion of dissent and nationalist aspirations, an open defiance of those in authority, a candid challenge to the legitimacy of the colonial order. The first few years of independence included a shared euphoria among the different elements that had struggled for autonomy, an acceptance in the case of former British colonies of the Westminster model with its pluralist assumptions, an emphasis on civil liberties and human rights, a concession to the principle of limited government. The struggle for sovereignty and political independence generated a variety of movements: cultural and literary groups like *Négritude* in West Africa; labor movements like Tom Mboya's organized experiments in collective bargaining in East Africa; religious movements like the *Mahdiyya* in the Sudan; as well as a diversity of political parties and political organizations. Some of this rich pluralism survived into independence.

But after the first few celebrations of independence day, the rot in many Third World countries set in. The creative energies of anti-colonialism began to be diffused. It is partly because of this that political liberation has so often become the cemetery, the burial ground, of other social movements. Labor unions fell under stricter control in one former colonial country after another, where they were once part of the vanguard of opposition to colonial authority. Leaders of literary movements and editors of magazines were intimidated, detained, or forced into exile. Within Africa the mystique of the one party system helped to annihilate one opposition political party after another as power within the ruling party was consolidated, dissent discouraged, and political diversity forced to shrink. One fundamental reason for this clash between political liberation and political diversity is the very concept of "national liberation" disproportionately translated as indigenous capture of the sovereign machinery of the state. National liberation movements were inspired disproportionately by the lure of the sovereign state, dreaming of capturing it and using it. But the state in turn has its own logic. Max Weber's famous definition of the state emphasized its capacity to assert "the legitimate use of physical force" within a given territory. In order to assert a monopoly of the legitimate use of physical force, the state is all too often tempted to assert a monopoly of the legitimate use of intellectual power. Attempts by the state to monopolize instruments of coercion often include attempts to monopolize avenues of opinion. A desire for concentrated physical force leads on to a desire for orchestrated intellectual power. In such an atmosphere, independent social movements suffer as the state seeks to contain their activities and control their direction and orientation. There are of course occasions when the state does not succeed in asserting a monopoly of either physical force or intellectual power. We shall return to some of those occasions later in this essay. For the time being it is fair simply to note that the logic of the state is not simply to assert Weber's "monopoly of the legitimate use of physical force" but also to assert a monopoly of the legitimate uses of intellectual power. The demise of social movements in many parts of the Third World has been part of this logic of the state. Political pluralism has been among the first casualties of state formation in the Third World.

The Socialist State: A Contradiction in Terms?

It has not been merely in the Third World that social movements have suffered: it also has been in the Second World of advanced socialist countries. Just as successful national liberation in the Third World has often resulted in the shrinkage of pluralism, so has the establishment of socialist states in the Second World. Is the phenomenon of a "socialist state" a contradiction in terms? The triumph of the sovereign state in the socialist world has indeed been ironic. After all, a profound distrust of the state is manifest in both liberal thought and socialist thought. Both ideological traditions have in fact regarded the state as an instrument of oppression. Liberal thought has identified the state as a potential threat to the individual; socialist thought has seen it as a threat to the exploited classes. The classic liberals sought to reduce the oppressive nature of the state by arguing that the state should be involved in as few things as possible. Marxists, on the other hand, have theoretically sought to reduce the harm of the state by trying to ensure that it oppressed as few classes, or as few people, as possible. Liberals have focused on minimizing the activities of the state; Marxists have stressed the minimization of its victims. Lenin, like Engels, insisted that "while the state exists, there is no freedom." If that is the case, how could we ensure that the state harmed as few people as possible? By reducing the number of those who were on the receiving end of its oppression, and that, in turn, could be best realized by entrusting the state to the numerically superior class as per the *Communist Manifesto*:

> All previous historical movements were movements of minorities, or in the interest of minorities. The proletarian movement is the self-conscious, independent movement of the immense majority, in the interest of the majority.

Oppression by the proletariat in an industrial society will therefore be oppression against the bourgeois few. If there must be tyranny, let the tyranny be of the majority, a dictatorship of the proletariat. But must there be tyranny? The implicit Marxist answer is yes. The worker must first become a dictator before he or she becomes a free person. Society must multiply its tyrants before it can consist of liberated individuals.

These are some of the basic theoretical assumptions underlying Marxist and liberal attitudes to the state. What both ideologies have all too often overlooked is that the captives of the state are not only those on the receiving end of state oppression. Those in power are also held hostage to the logic of the state. In other words, whoever captures the state is captured by it. The Frankenstein state asserts its logic: it overwhelms and sometimes devours its own creators. When revolutionaries succeed in capturing the state, the leaders become converted to the state system itself, sometimes almost fanatically. When workers capture the state in the name of socialism, they soon develop state consciousness rather than class consciousness. They seek to protect the interests of the state that they now control rather than continue to struggle to realize the interests of the workers in whose name they captured the state in the first place. The bizarre example of the socialist state in Poland pitched against the workers was for a while only the most open of illustrations available in the Second World of advanced socialist countries.

Classical Marxism and orthodox Leninism have always envisaged "the withering away of the state" as a kind of ultimate utopia. Since the state has been seen ideologically as the instrument of the ruling class, it theoretically has been taken for granted that the withering away of classes would inevitably result in the withering away of the state. It is our contention in this essay that any capture of the state by the proletariat would be a Sisyphean exercise—a stone taken to the top of the hill, made to roll down the hill, only to be laboriously pushed back to the top of the hill for another rolling down, and so on and so forth repeatedly. Should any section of the working class ever capture the state, its class consciousness is often rapidly transformed into state consciousness, as we indicated. That is why preoccupation with the interests of the state often replaces preoccupation with class interests. It is because of this that we have concluded that whoever captures the state is captured by it. The conqueror's orientation changes. The survival of the state becomes the paramount aim even if it means repressing fellow workers, or fellow nationals. When workers capture the state, they commit class suicide. The Sisyphus absurdity arises because we first witness a section of the workers capturing the state in order to roll it down to its doom and redundancy. But before long those same workers become concerned with the "need" to preserve the state. They roll the stone of the state back upwards to the top of the hill. They may indeed be overcome by another set of workers or socialists or nationals later on bent on the same ambition. They in turn wish to roll the state downwards to its doom only to attempt a renewed ascendancy. Whoever controls the state is compulsively tempted to preserve it. If the controller was originally class conscious, he or she becomes state conscious, he or she becomes state conscious.

Where does this leave the Marxist-Leninist expectation concerning the withering away of the state? When socialist revolutionaries capture the state, socialism itself starts to wither away, not the state. The state corrodes socialism rather than socialism corroding the state. The state corrupts: the absolute state corrupts absolutely. A functional equivalent of the absolute state is the garrison state, a state geared toward militaristic self-preservation. A striking illustration of the corrupting power of the garrison state is in fact the state of Israel. Israel was born out of the womb of a social movement, the Zionist movement going back to Theodor Herzl and beyond. The ideals were rooted in compassion and a longing for national dignity and human worth. The Zionist political and social movement felt that it could best realize Jewish dignity and human worth through the creation of a Jewish state. At first the obstacles in the way of this Zionist movement were immense. Where would the movement find land without a people for use by a people without land? Though a return to Palestine was always the favorite aspiration of the Zionist movement, alternative homes were considered, including the famous offer of parts of Uganda and Kenya to the Zionist movement by Joseph Chamberlain, Britain's Colonial Secretary at the turn of the century. Curiously enough, it was the excesses of the Nazi absolute state that helped to assure the ultimate political victory of the Zionist movement. Hitler's policy of genocide against the Jews created what many Westerners regarded as a compelling moral case for the establishment of a Jewish state after the war. The excesses of Hitler's absolute state resulted in what was to become a Jewish garrison state. And just as Nazi absolutism corrupted the German state, so did Israeli militarism come to corrupt the Jewish state.

Israel was born out of the marriage between Judaism and the legacy of the Peace of Westphalia of 1648, which helped to inaugurate the modern system of the sovereign state. The legacy of Judaism had contributed enormously to the finer moral sensibilities of the international community as a whole; but the legacy of Westphalia came to corrode and corrupt those same sensibilities in the new Jewish state. By the time Israel invaded Lebanon in June 1982, it had already become the most arrogant sovereign state on the world scene since Nazi Germany. The state corrupts, and either absolutism or militarism could make it corrupt absolutely. Nazi Germany was of course both absolutist and militaristic; but the state of Israel is only militaristic. Within its own borders is the most open society in the Middle East, though the openness has been shrinking in recent years. But in relation to its neighbours, Israel has permitted itself to become the mini-bully of the Near East. In the occupied territories, the Israelis have become one of the worst colonial powers of the twentieth century. The establishment of the state of Israel in time created a counter social movement in the Arab world, especially from the 1960s onwards when Arab Palestinians converted themselves into an independent nationalist movement in their own right. The Palestinians gradually evolved a dream of either recreating a unified Palestine encompassing both Arabs and Jews (the two nations, one state, solution) or creating a separate Palestinian state of their own (the two nations, two states, solution). A Palestinian Diaspora had been created as a result of the establishment of Israel, and those dispersed Palestinians evolved the same kind of nostalgia and longing for a return to their homeland that the Jews had previously manifested in their own Zionist longings. Again, the solution was widely seen in terms of creating yet another state. If the Palestinian state, when it is established, becomes either absolutist or militaristic, it would display the same symptoms of spiritual and moral decay that the state of Israel has manifested in recent years. Once again those who capture the state will discover that they are captured by it. Those who seek to purify the world through the state system will discover in time that they are themselves polluted by the state system. The polluted by the state system. The Frankenstein state continues to proclaim its capacity to devour its own creator.

Uneven Sovereignty and the United Nations

This brings us to yet another great paradox of the postwar world, linked to the earlier paradox of sovereignty. This is the paradox of the United Nations. The world body, as we know it, is the child of two major historical forces of the twentieth century: World War II and the process of decolonization. As we intimated, World War II heightened the urgency for establishing a global body dedicated to the moderation of sovereignty in pursuit of peace. Decolonization, on the other hand, transformed the United Nations' composition and helped to universalize the principle of sovereignty. The world body symbolized the dialectic between confirming the sovereignty of its members and aspiring to put limits to that sovereignty. The United Nations system is part of the human ambition to evolve a parliament of the world. Nevertheless, each member of the world body is jealous of its sovereignty and would not willingly permit the collectivity to circumscribe it. The third paradox of the UN is that it claims equality for each of its members, and yet it is a grand arena for acting out the unevenness of sovereignty among states. At least outside the Security Council, the member states have equal voting power, but they do not really enjoy equal sovereign power. In no area of political experience is this better illustrated than in the relationship between the United Nations and the countries of Africa and Asia. In retrospect, we can now identify the wider patterns of that relationship.

Since its formation in San Francisco in 1945, the United Nations has played a number of conflicting roles in relation to the Third World. First, there was its role as a collective imperial power on whose behalf certain "dependent territories" were administered as "trusteeships." In other words, the UN inherited imperial jurisdiction over the former Mandates of the League of Nations. It is in that sense that the new world body, from 1945 onwards, played the role of an absentee imperial landlord, on whose behalf member nations like Britain and France administered "dependent territories" like Tanganyika (later Tanzania), Togoland (later Togo), Ruanda-Urundi (later Rwanda and Burundi), the Cameroons (later Cameroon), and South-West Africa (Namibia). Apart from the special case of Namibia, this role of the UN as an absentee imperial landlord ended in the beginning of the 1960s with the independence of all the administered territories. Even before its collective imperialism ended, the UN had also begun a role as an ally of the forces of liberation in the colonial world generally, over and beyond its own trusteeships. Both in the Trusteeship Council and in other institutions of the world body voices were increasingly in favour of the rapid granting of self-government to the colonies. The UN was combining the paradoxical roles of a benevolent collective imperial power, on the one hand, and an ally of colonial liberation on the other. The third UN role in relation to Africa and the rest of the Third World has been that of a partner in development. The world body has played this role in a variety of ways, ranging from the work of the UN Economic Commission for different regions to the wider policies and politics of the UN Conference on Trade and Development (UNCTAD), and ranging from preserving the territorial integrity of the Congo (Zaire) to the launching of the campaign for a New International Economic Order. The fourth role of the UN affecting the Third World is the organization's status as an empire of the Western world, one more arena for Western power and hegemony in global affairs. In this special sense, the United Nations was from the start "annexed" and "colonized" by the West. Like Africa before independence, the UN was itself a vast institutional dependency, and just as Africa was partitioned after 1885 in order to be subjugated, the United Nations was constituted after 1945 partly in order to be dominated. From this point of view, the United Nations was itself a victim of imperialism, a

United Nations was itself a victim of imperialism, a kindred spirit of the colonized world. More specifically, the world body and its specialized agencies have been under the hegemonic shadow of the United States, as if the United Nations was itself a vast "dependent territory" under *Pax Americana*. Uneven sovereignty characterizes those four areas of interaction between the world body and Africa: the UN as a collective imperial power; second, as an ally of liberation; third, as a partner in development; and finally as a fellow victim of Western imperial power.

Because the world body's imperial role ("absentee landlord") was so benevolent, it is not that easy to disentangle it from the world body's role as an ally of liberation. Unlike other imperial powers, the United Nations was keen to speed up the pace of decolonization. The UN therefore often clashed with those very colonial powers that were administering the Trusteeships on its behalf. Where the world body's role as a collective imperialist ended and its role as an ally of liberation began was not always easy to ascertain. As for the United Nations itself being an empire of the Western world, it has been one more domain of Western power and hegemony. In this special sense, the United Nations was itself colonized by the West almost like Africa's territory. The United States has played a special role in this particular experience of the world organization. The horrors of the Second World War made America much more receptive to the concept of a world body than it ever was in its attitude to the defunct League of Nations. For the new global body that was to succeed the League, the United States was even prepared to play host to its headquarters and accommodate the Secretariat in New York City. The motives were indeed honorable on almost all sides. The United States did wish to make the world a safer place through the United Nations. Then history played its ironic game once again. By a convergence of circumstances, the new world body became itself an American empire. Perhaps more by accident than by design, the

Americans colonized the United Nations. In previous epochs, single nations or individuals had indeed attempted to turn the whole world into an empire. Such attempts have ranged from those of Alexander the Great to those of Adolf Hitler. But only in the twentieth century has a single nation attempted to turn a truly global body like the United Nations into an empire of one of its members. This was a transition from colonizing global territory to colonizing a global institution.

It is important to emphasize that the United Nations became an American empire less as matter of design than as a matter of historical accident. Franklin Roosevelt and Harry Truman as two of the American founding fathers of the United Nations were genuinely concerned with the mission of saving the world from "the scourge of war" but then a number of factors tilted the global balance in America's favour. World War II resulted in the shrinkage of the power of Great Britain and France as global actors. Although these two countries were given veto power in the Security Council, Britain turned out to be almost continuously under American influence, while France was ambivalent between national independence and loyalty to the Atlantic Alliance. In general, the decline of Britain and France as global powers favoured the influence of the United States in the new global body. Africa got caught up in the twilight of the British and French empires. Another factor that favoured the United States was the defeat of Japan and the collapse and division of Germany. As it turned out, these two countries were the nearest rivals technologically to US pre-eminence after the war. Despite their technological revival after World War II, Japan and West Germany deliberately made themselves political and military dependencies of the United States. The division of Germany effectively prevented the Germans from becoming a political super-power in their own right. This also affected the configuration of genuine power in the Security Council of the United Nations.

The third factor that facilitated the transformation of the United Nations into the empire of *Pax Americana* was the political economy and the budget of the world body. The budget of the United Nations exaggerated the United States' share in the world economy. Although the United States is the most important single factor in the world economy, the United States should not be responsible for nearly a quarter of the total budget of the United Nations and most of its agencies. After all, the American economy, preeminent as it is, is far from being a whole quarter of the global output. American consumption of the world's output is more disproportionate than American production and it seems that consumption was the basis of the contribution by the United States towards the UN budget. The fourth factor that helped convert the United Nations into an American empire was the communist revolution in China. After the defeat of the Chinese Nationalists and their exile in Taiwan on the island of Formosa, the United States contrived a situation wherein the world's largest country in population was represented at the UN by the regime on the island of Formosa. This resulted not only in the disenfranchisement of mainland China until the 1970s but also added another dimension to the power of the United States in the Security Council. As long as the Chinese seat on the Security Council was represented by Taiwan, China's vote was almost invariably part and parcel of America's vote. Great issues concerning Third World liberation were compromised in this alliance. The fifth factor concerned the role of Latin American votes. Popular opinion in Latin America was hungry for a global transformation but the policies of most Latin American governments in power were always formulated with Washington in mind. The foreign policies of Latin American countries were particularly anxious not to diverge too far from the prescribed Washingtonian mainstream. Although Africa and Latin America were both part of the Third World, very few Latin American governments were prepared to risk Washington's overt displeasure within the politics of the United Nations.

The sixth factor that gave the United States undue leverage at the United Nations was the location of the headquarters of the world body in New York. Though indirect, this influence was multi-faceted. The American delegation at the UN had closer and more direct contact with American policy-makers than is possible for delegates from more distant lands. The lobbying process by United States officials on other delegations was greatly facilitated by the proximity of the State Department and the White House. The United Nations' Secretariat tended to feel the physical nearness of the most powerful member of the organization more directly and congressional opinion, often hostile to the UN, can almost be overheard at the UN Secretariat. All this is quite apart from the wider social and sociological environment, ranging from local American television to locally-recruited American ancillary staff of the organization, from the nearness of pro-Israeli or anti-Soviet "publics" in New York City to the use of American policemen for United Nations' security needs. The effects of an organization's location are often subtle, but the different elements can add up to a silent environmental influence upon that organization. These then are some of the factors that propelled the world body into the orbit of *Pax Americana*. The massive dependency of the world organization upon the American largesse made it particularly vulnerable to the changing moods of both Capitol Hill and the White House in Washington, DC. The United Nations Organization is also vulnerable to the concert of the Western alliance more generally and has been, quite often, under Western domination.

We examined the Third World's relationship with the United Nations earlier from the point of view of other areas of interaction. In its role as an absentee imperial landlord, the world organization served as a supervisory body over the administration of the former German colonies of Tanganyika, Ruanda-Urundi, Togoland, Cameroons, and South-West Africa (Namibia), all former Mandates of the League of Nations. In reality the Republic of South Africa, which was the administering authority of South-West Africa under the League, did not recognize the United Nations as a successor to the League and therefore refused to be accountable to the UN about the "dependent territory." It took a number of battles, both within the United Nations and at the International Court of Justice at The Hague, before the UN's jurisdiction over South-West Africa (later renamed Namibia by the liberation fighters) could at last be definitively confirmed, notwithstanding South Africa's continuing dissent. On balance, the UN's insistence on continuing jurisdiction in Namibia was motivated by a desire to free the country from South Africa's control. It has been a case of the UN insisting to be a collective imperial power over Namibia in order to serve as Namibia's ally in liberation—a UN desire to "reconquer" Namibia in order to free it. Apart from Namibia, the UN's role as a collective imperial power basically ended with the independence of the prize trusteeship of Tanganyika in 1961. The other trusteeships had gained independence earlier. The world body's role as an ally of liberation went beyond speeding up the independence of its own trusteeships. Especially after India's independence in 1947 and India's admission to the UN, voices against imperialism and colonialism in the chambers of the world organization gathered strength. In 1960, more than fifteen African countries joined the UN in a single year. Before long, the General Assembly passed resolutions condemning imperialism, colonialism, racism, and eventually Zionism, as moral offenses against a new international code of justice. The face of the international order was thus being transformed.

The United Nations' role as a partner in Third World development, though modest in relation to Third World needs, has nevertheless been significant. Rescuing the former Belgian Congo in 1960-61 from territorial disintegration was important not only for the future of the Congo (Zaire) but also for all other fragile states in Africa. Had Katanga's secession succeeded so early after Africa's independence, the demonstration impact on other separatist groups elsewhere in the rest of the continent could have put severe stress on the very principle of national cohesion all over Africa. But the UN's partnership in Africa's development has over the years taken other forms as well. Despite stresses and strains in its relationship with the Organization of African Unity, the UN Economic Commission for Africa has played a major role on matters that ranged from the functions of the African Development Bank to the formulation and promotion of the Lagos Plan of Action. Partnership in Third World's development has also included the contributions of the Food and Agriculture Organization of UNESCO, the World Health Organization, the International Labour Organization, and a variety of other specialized agencies of the UN family. As for the United Nations' *de facto* status as a dominion of the Western world, in a constant struggle to assert its own independence, it has turned out historically that the decolonization of the world body was, in part, dependent upon the decolonization of Africa. Africa's admission to the world body was not a sufficient condition for the decolonization of the organization—but it was a necessary condition. When the composition of the UN became almost one third African, Western domination of the organization became increasingly shaky.

What the world was witnessing in the 1980s was a new Western attempt to "re-colonize" the United Nations. The withdrawal of the United States and the United Kingdom from UNESCO, the Reaganite pressure on the budget of the UN in New York, the US pressures on the International Labour Organization from time to time, were all part of a coordinated effort to re-establish Western hegemony over the world body and its specialized agencies. The question for the future is whether the Third World states can stay unified enough to repay the two primary debts that they owe to the world body. Can the Third World now be counted as an ally in the liberation of the United Nations, just as the United Nations once served as an ally in the third World liberation? Just as the world organization and its agencies continue to be partners in Third World development, will Third World states become effective partners in the development of the world body in return? In some ways, the United Nations is as fragile as the African states it has particularly sought to serve. It needs stability and integrity in order to expand its own "per capita income" and to make its own "structural adjustment." Like Africa, the United Nations also needs to achieve all this without risking the trauma of "recolonization." The future may yet have its surprises: it may allow for a historic partnership between the world body and some of its poorest and weakest member states to achieve the miracle of their joint redemption in the coming international order. But while the United Nations may escape the controlling power of the United States, the world body remains hostage to the principle of sovereignty. The UN could remain hostage to the wider system of the Frankenstein state, a system thanks to which governments are prepared to go to war for the sake of inches of barren territory. Impossible as the task may be now, there is a compelling case for exploring both alternative world bodies and alternatives to this state. For the time being, however, we are prisoners behind the bars of Westphalia. We are lurking in the shadow of the Frankenstein state.

We are also prisoners of the capitalist world economy even when we declare our own society socialist. In a sense, socialist or communist states are prisoners of the world capitalist economy as much as non-socialist and non-communist sates. The global system operates on the basis of supply and demand, the classic logic of the dynamics of capitalism. Market forces often reign on the world arena, again reflecting capitalist preferences. The rules of international trade and exchange emanate from capitalist doctrine and history. The currencies of international exchange, the so-called "foreign exchange," are basically currencies of the leading capitalist countries of the world. The leading financial and banking institutions, for commerce and for development, are under the control of capitalist powers and subject to capitalist rules of the game. Countries in the Second World are as heavily in debt to the Western financial institutions as are countries in Third World. The announcement that a state has gone socialist or is under indigenous control does not liberate it from the prison walls of global capitalism. Both capitalism and the state system continue to be omnipresent

The Potentialities of the Feminization of the State

We have sought to demonstrate that the underprivileged groups and nationalities have attempted to capture the state and were captured by it instead. Nationalists of Asia and Africa sounded the knock of entry into the world system, and then became the high priests of the state system itself, both in the United Nations and outside. The Frankenstein state has so far been triumphant. The underprivileged classes have also sought to capture the state and, when they did, they were captured by it as well. Socialists and workers sounded the knock of exit from the capitalist system and at the same time sounded the knock of entry into the state system. Domestically, countries of the Second World have achieved some kind of socialist structure but, externally, the prison walls of the global capitalist system surround socialist countries as well as non-socialist ones. The underprivileged races and underprivileged classes have not yet made a difference to the fate of the two global systems. The question now arises whether the underprivileged sex or gender could hold the secret of global transformation. Women are for the time being fellow prisoners behind the bars of capitalism and Westphalia, but do women hold the key to an eventual es-

cape? There is one fundamental difference between oppressed races and oppressed classes on one side and the oppressed gender on the other. While an oppressed race or oppressed class might aspire to capture the state monopolistically for itself, there is no question of women capturing the
state instead of men. Indigenous liberation fighters may
want to capture the state and replace the foreigners; an underprivileged class might wish to capture the state and replace the privileged classes of the previous era; but the balance of probability is that women who may capture the state
would not be interested in replacing men. The feminist case
is in reality not substitution but balance, not replacement but
displacement, not control but parity. Women would not want
to capture the state monopolistically but to share it equally.
This is in stark contrast with other underprivileged groups.
National liberation fighters never seek to share equally with
foreigners after they have emerged triumphant in their liberation war. Socialist workers never seek to share equally
with the bourgeoisie after they have emerged triumphant
from the revolution. But in reality, women never ask for
more than equality, as their ultimate ambition is to establish
an egalitarianism that would be inclusive of men. But when
the state becomes androgynous will its nature change? We
cannot be sure. All we know is that until now the state has
been tied to patriarchy, including its central primordial principle of male dominance, à la Frankenstein.

If the Frankenstein state is an institutionalized monopoly of the legitimate use of physical force, and if women
are less physically inclined to violence than men, the very
concept of legitimate use of physical force may change when
the state becomes androgynous. The state's ultimate instruments of coercion have so far been disproportionately male-
dominated. The great majority of members of the armed
forces in one state after another have been men. The great
majority of the police in most states have been overwhelmingly men and the great majority of prison wardens have

been men. Those entrusted with the duties of execution have been almost exclusively men. The navies of the world and their air forces have been disproportionately men. In other words, the foundation of all the security forces and security services or power of the state has been highly masculine. But who in any case is likely to challenge the state's monopoly of the legitimate use of physical force? Once again, the ratio has been disproportionately male-oriented. The overwhelming majority of those who commit crimes of violence, in societies that are otherwise vastly different from each other, have been men. As for the world of political rebellion, military coups, and sheer terrorism, once again masculinity is, on the whole, the order of the day. There are indeed female guerrilla fighters and female "terrorists," but when all allowances have been made for great heroines and great female villains, the fact nevertheless defiantly remains that the game of physical violence involving direct spilling of blood has been more a heritage of the male of the human species than that of the female. To that extent, the inner gender of the state has been masculine.

What has happened in those situations where a woman has been at the pinnacle of the state, seemingly in control of its destiny? What has happened when there has been a Queen Elizabeth I, a Mrs. Golda Meir, a Mrs. Indira Gandhi, or a Mrs. Margaret Thatcher? In reality, in political systems that are primarily male-dominated, a single female at the top does not change the fundamental masculine dynamic of the structure. The women who make it in a male-dominated world have themselves to display male-derived perceptions of strength. Margaret Thatcher had to out-macho the Tory patriarchs over the Falkland issue if she was to survive the apparent "national humiliation" which was perceived as the outcome of the Argentinean invasion of the Islands. The female Prime Minister in London had to display all the toughness of masculinity if she was to remain credible in a male dominated political system. The question for the future is whether a real feminization of the state would reduce its propensity for violence. Is the female predicament unlikely to result in a mere substitution of who controls the state? Overall, it is arguable that the feminist movement has been seeking mechanisms for sharing rather than monopolizing power. It is arguable as well that feminism, given that men and women need each other more than races or classes do, might result in reducing polarization in the struggle for equality. Finally, it is also arguable that since femininity tends to be less militaristic than masculinity, the feminist struggle might help to minimize the militarization of ultimate utopias. Given those previous considerations, feminist styles and aspirations would help to minimize this game of post liberation violence.

The concepts for describing the different strategies have also to be differentiated: the struggle for national or racial utopia is indeed national liberation; the quest for a class utopia is usually class struggle; the new movement for a gender utopia is women's liberation. National liberation tends to be militarized eventually; revolutionary class struggle tends to be armed; but women's liberation can be basically agitational and mobilizational, without getting militarized. National liberation is obsessed with the state, seeking to capture it on behalf of the indigenous population. The quest for class utopia is in turn also enticed by the state, and is subsequently entrapped by the state. But the struggle for a gender utopia can be state neutral, seeking to realize the rights of women without monopolizing the power of the state. For those who seek to create the right condition for a nationalist struggle, one of the first phases of liberation lies in cultivating national consciousness. For those who seek to realize a dictatorship of the proletariat, one of the first phases of class struggle is the cultivation of class consciousness. For those who seek to realize a gender utopia, the basic aim lies in transforming gender consciousness rather than conquering or cultivating it. National liberation emphasizes the distinction between the alien and the indigenous; class struggle emphasizes the distinction between the alienated and the integrated; the struggle between the sexes transcends such distinctions.

If the Frankenstein state has always been masculine so far, what about Capitalism? What has been the gender of the capitalist animal in the world arena? Capitalism has become more masculine as it became more internationalized; it also became more masculine as it became more mechanized. In the earlier years of the pursuit of the profit motive, women were almost as active in producing as men. Certainly, in rural production in many societies, women were in control of basic cultivation, and sometimes they were in control of at least part of animal husbandry. In West Africa, women have been conspicuous in trade and marketing, sometimes overshadowing men's commercial activities, but all this was in relation to small-scale economic arenas. As the economic activities of West Africa assumed a greater international dimension, and as the transnational corporations entered the scene, the ratio of men and women changed. The greater internationalization of West African economies meant more men making decisions on boards of directors or assuming control in factories, overshadowing the market ladies of yesteryears. Greater internationalization of African economies meant greater masculine control. Similarly, greater mechanization of African economies has also resulted in diminishing the feminine share in those economies. Women are omnipresent in African agriculture, where the technology of cultivation is that of the hoe. But when the technology of cultivation becomes the tractor, the driver behind the wheel in African situations becomes primarily the male. Similarly, as industries move from soft to hard, the masculine share increases. The textile industry is more likely to consist of men and women than the steel mill and, certainly, industries like mining in Southern Africa are almost entirely masculine in composition of personnel.

To summarize the argument so far, the state has always been basically masculine in its inner dynamic, but the gender of Capitalism has been less constant. Capitalism at a primitive state is androgynous, involving both men and women in comparable productive capacities. But as Capitalism got more internationalized, it also got more masculine dominated. Similarly, as Capitalism got more mechanized and industrialized, it got more male-dominated. The gender of Capitalism is still more androgynous than the gender of the state system, but this is only a relative measurement. Both the state system and the capitalist global economy are major universes of the male of the human species awaiting fundamental reform through partial feminization. The destiny of the world may depend on those social and political movements that seek to increase the role of women in decisions about war and peace, the role of workers in decisions about production and consumption, and the role of oppressed political groups in decisions between tyranny and freedom. National, class, and gender utopias need to find some kind of equilibrium in the tempests of social change and global reform. Only then will the Frankenstein state either be destroyed or be transformed into something more nearly human.

Conclusion

Until reforms in power sharing are carried out among classes, nations, and genders, Mary Shelley's powerful warning of the Frankenstein monster will retain its ominous relevance for the sovereign state. A woman's imagination, back in 1818, provided the ultimate metaphor for the destructive tendencies of the most dangerous of all political creations, the sovereign state. It is one of the ironies of our projection in this essay that only the imaginative participation of women in decisions about war and peace stands a chance of taming this political monster in the coming international order. In the final analysis, the Frankenstein state needs to be either abolished or truly transformed. It is not enough to make this monster anthropomorphic; we need to make it more human. We have precedents of class revolutionaries and national liberation movements capturing the state. All the evidence so far demonstrates that the conqueror has always become the captive of the state; the state captures whoever conquers it and not the other way around. A new international order may require a gender revolution, but it definitely needs the corrective powers of new standards of equitable participation within countries, across countries, and in the evolving global institutions.

NOTES

This chapter is a revised version of an essay originally presented at a workshop on "The Coming Global Civilization: What Kind of Sovereignty? Problems of Interdependence, Integration, and Fragmentation," co-sponsored by the Soviet Political Science Association and the World Order Models Project, and hosted by the Institute of World Economy and the World Order Models Project, October 10-16, 1988, Moscow, USSR. That essay was subsequently published, under the title "The Frankenstein State and Uneven Sovereignty: The Multiverse of Democracy," in *Essays in Honour of Rajni Kothari*, edited by D. L. Sheth and Ashis Nandy (New Delhi: Thousand Oakes, and California and London: Sage, 1996), pp. 50-77.

.

TEN

GLOBAL APARTHEID
RELIGION AND RACE IN THE
NEW WORLD ORDER (1991)

Now that secular ideological divisions between East and West have declined in relevance, are we witnessing the re-emergence of primordial allegiances? Are we witnessing new forms of retribalization on the global arena? In Europe, two levels of retribalization may be discernible: micro-retribalization and macro-retribalization. In Eastern Europe, micro-retribalization is particularly strong and is mainly concerned with micro-ethnicity, involving such conflicts as those between Serbs and Croats, Russians and Ukrainians, or Czechs and Slovaks. On the other hand, Western Europe shows strides towards regional integration that can be described as macro-retribalization when it is race-conscious. Macro-retribalization in this case would consist of solidarity of white people, an arrogant Pan-Europeanism greater in ambition than anything since the Holy Roman Empire.

Now that apartheid in South Africa is disintegrating, is "Global Apartheid" in the process of formation?[1] With the end of the Cold War, will we see in the twenty first century a more united and potentially more prosperous white world presiding over the fate of a fragmented, and a persistently more indigent black world? In addition to the black-white divide in the world, Muslim countries may have special reason to worry in the era after the Cold War. Will Islam replace communism as the West's perceived adversary? In this paper, we will argue that Muslims are the frontline military victims of the New World Order while Blacks are the frontline economic victims of this emerging Global Apartheid. Muslims, especially in the Middle East, have felt the firing power of American guns and American-subsidized Israeli planes. Blacks have felt the deprivation of both economic exploitation and economic neglect. It is to these issues that we turn.

Religion and the New World Order: The Military Victims of Global Apartheid

In a sense, Western fears of Islam are centuries older than Western fears of communism. But in recent times, Western anti-Islamic tendencies had been ameliorated by the indisputable superiority in technological and military power that the West had. Western nervousness about Islam was also ameliorated by the West's need for Muslim allies in its confrontation with the Soviet Union and the Warsaw Pact. However, a few things have happened in the last quarter century that may have brought back Western fears of Islam. First, elements in the Muslim world learned that those who are militarily weak had one strategy of last resort against the mighty: terrorism. Some Muslims became convinced that terrorism was no worse than any other kind of warfare; if anything, it killed far fewer civilians than conventional warfare, let alone nuclear. If terrorism is the weapon of the militarily weak, nuclear weapons are for the technologically sophisticated. While some elements of the Muslim world were experimenting with terrorism and guerrilla warfare, other elements began to explore the nuclear option and other weapons of mass destruction. Ancient Western worries about Islam were re-kindled. In this context, Egypt must be bribed to sign the Nuclear Nonproliferation Treaty whether or not

Israel did so. Pakistan must be stopped from acquiring a nuclear capability. And Iraq must be given enough rope to hang itself over Kuwait, so that all Iraqi weapons of mass destruction could then be destroyed.

As the fear of communism receded in the 1980s, the West felt freer than ever to be tough about terrorism from the Muslim world. Libya was bombed and Syria was put into diplomatic cold storage. American ships went to the Persian Gulf to intimidate Iran in the midst of the Iran-Iraq war, and to protect Kuwaiti ships. In the process, the Americans shot down an Iranian civilian airline and killed all on board. A related reason for Western anxiety about Islam is the importance of Muslim oil for Western industry. Although Western technological power was still pre-eminent and undisputed, its dependence on Middle Eastern oil made it vulnerable to political changes in the Muslim world—changes of the magnitude of the revolution in Iran or of Iraq's annexation of Kuwait. Was the Gulf War against Iraq part of Global Apartheid? Aspects of the war were certainly ominous including Soviet submissiveness to the United States, Western hegemony in the United Nations, the attempted re-colonization of Iraq after the war, and Western insensitivity to the killing of over two hundred thousand Iraqi lives. The Gulf War was not really a war; it was a massacre. Admittedly, it was triggered off by Iraq's unforgivable aggression against Kuwait, but Bush, in turn, was more interested in saving time than saving lives: he refused to give sanctions enough time, even if it meant killing hundreds of thousands of Iraqis. The coalition against Iraq was multiracial but its leadership was decidedly and unmistakably white. Bush regarded the war against Iraq as the first major war of the New World Order. Perhaps one day we will also lament the Gulf War as the first major war of the era of Global Apartheid. Just when we thought apartheid in South Africa has ended, apartheid on a global scale seemed to rear its ugly head.

The military victimization of Muslims has taken either the direct form of Western bombing, as in the war against Iraq, or the surrogate Western aggression by heavily subsidising Israel without adequately criticising its repressive and military policies. The apparent demise of Soviet and East European anti-imperialism has also hurt the Muslim world in other ways. When a United States ship shot down an Iranian civilian airline over international air space, the new Soviet Union under Gorbachev did not attempt to rally the world against this act of manslaughter committed by Americans. Would the Iranian airline have been shot down if there were European passengers on board? Would Soviets have been silent if Soviet citizens were aboard? Moscow said it was deliberately not going to follow the accusatory precedent set by the United States in 1984 when Washington led the world in vigorously denouncing the Soviet Union's shooting down of a Korean civilian airline. When the Soviets shot down South Korea's Flight 007, the Cold War was still on. Many of the passengers killed were Westerners, including a US Congressman. At that moment, the United States seemed to serve as the conscience of the world. When a US battleship shot down the Iranian airline, the Cold War was ending. There was no reason to believe that any Westerners or Soviet citizens were on board. The USSR, therefore, refused to serve as the conscience of the world.

If there is Global Apartheid in formation, how will it affect the European and Asian parts of the former Soviet Union? One out of 5 citizens of the old USSR was a Muslim, and the Muslim pace of natural reproduction was much faster than that for non-Muslims. One possible scenario could be an alliance between the Russian Federation and the Muslim Republics. Indeed, the possibility of a Muslim President of the USSR was already in the cards—though with much reduced power. Even Gorbachev was already considering a Muslim Vice-President. No less likely is a scenario in which the European parts of what used to be the Soviet Union would get closer to the newly integrated Western Europe, while the Muslim parts of the former USSR found new relationships with the rest of the Muslim world and the rest of the Third World. Pakistan is seeking new markets in places like Uzbekistan and Turkey is seeking a new role in that part of the Muslim world. Such a trend would once again reinforce Global Apartheid. There is even a risk that the former Muslim republics would become Russian Bantustans, "backyards" with even less power than they had before.

But not all aspects of the newly emerging Global Apartheid may be detrimental to Muslim interests globally. After all, the new world order is predicated on the foundation of *Pax Americana*. An imperial system values stability and peace (hence the "*pax*"), even though on its own imperial terms. Objectively, the main obstacle to peace in the Middle East since the 1970s has been Israel. Will *Pax Americana* not only force Israel and the Arabs to the negotiating table but also compel them to consider exchanging land for peace? Before he went to war against Iraq, George Bush vowed that there was no linkage between the Gulf crisis and the wider Arab-Israeli conflict. Almost as soon as the war was over, Secretary of State Baker started a series of shuttle diplomacies in order to help start a peace process in the Arab-Israeli conflict. There was *de facto* linkage. Furthermore, Desert Storm temporarily made Bush so strong in domestic politics that he was able to stand up to the pro-Israeli lobby and defy the Israeli prime minister. Most commentators have focused on the political and economic losses that the Palestinians have sustained as a result of the Gulf War. Almost no commentator has noted that this is balanced out, at least to a small degree, by the political losses sustained by Israel as a result of a new US-Arab realignment and of the popularity of George Bush in the aftermath of the war. Bush's popularity was great enough to withstand the criticism of the pro-Israeli lobby, at least for one year. Israel's political decline in Washington, DC, modest as it was, may be due to two very different factors: the end of the Cold War and the new US Arab realignments following the Gulf War. The end of the Cold War reduced the strategic value of Israel to the United States. The Gulf War brought certain Arab countries closer to the United States.

The end of the Cold War has also reduced the strategic value of Pakistan to the Western world. Pressures on Pakistan to conform to Western prescriptions have already increased. Pakistan's nuclear credentials have become even more of an issue in its relations with the United States. As far as the West is concerned, Islam must on no account be nuclearized and that is why it proceeded to achieve the following objectives: to try to stop Pakistan from going nuclear; to destroy Iraq's capacity in weapons of mass destruction; to neutralize Egypt by getting it to sign the Nuclear Non-Proliferation Treaty; to co-opt Syria into pro-Western respectability; and to prevent Qaddafi from buying nuclear credentials.

One should not forget that the United States' conventional capability, while originally targeted at the Second World of Socialist countries, has in reality been used against the Third World. Under the administrations of Reagan and Bush, the United States bombed Beirut from the sea, invaded Grenada, bombed Tripoli and Bengazi in Libya, hijacked an Egyptian plane in international airspace, shot down an Iranian civilian aircraft in the Gulf and killed all on board, invaded Panama and kidnapped General Noriega, and bombed Iraqi cities as part of an anti-Saddam coalition. In all of these military acts, Muslim victims have been disproportionate. More than two thirds of the casualties of American military activity since the Vietnam War have been Muslims, amounting to at least a quarter of a million, and possibly half a million deaths. In the New World Order, Muslims are the first military victims of Global Apartheid. If the first military victims of Global Apartheid have been disproportionately Muslims, the first economic victims of Global Apartheid may be

Blacks.

Race and the New World Order:
The Economic Victims of Global Apartheid

In the struggle against old style narrow nationalism and the nation-state, Western Europe has been leading the way. The Treaties of Rome created the European Economic Community in March 1957, and set the stage for wider regional integration. 1992 saw an enlarged European Community achieve even deeper integration as further walls between the members came down. The former German Democratic Republic has now been re-united with the rest of Germany as part of this wider Europe. And the newly liberated Eastern European countries are seeking new links with the European Community, further eroding narrow nationalism and enlarging regional integration.

Even Yugoslavia and the former Soviet Union, torn by ethnic separatism as they are, still manifest in the European areas an eagerness to be accepted into the wider European fraternity. The decline of socialist ideology all over Eastern Europe has been accompanied by a resurgence of primordial culture. Marxism has either died or been de-Leninized, but a pan-European identity is re-asserting itself on a scale greater than the Holy Roman Empire. Marxism-Leninism, while it lasted, was trans-racial. It made European Marxists seek allies and converts among people of color. European identity, on the other hand, is by definition Eurocentric and increases the chances of Pan-Europeanism. The bad news is that Pan-Europeanism can carry the danger of cultural chauvinism and even racism. Anti-Semitism has been on the rise in Eastern Europe as an aspect of this cultural chauvinism. Racism and xenophobia in the re-unified Germany have reached new levels. Racism in France has taken its highest toll among North Africans. All over Europe there is a new sense of insecurity among immigrants who are of a darker hue than the local populations. An old dilemma has once again reared its head.

Then there is the racial situation in the United States, with all its contradictions. On the one hand, the country had changed enough to produce the first Black governor of a state (Virginia) and the first Black mayor of New York City. On the other hand, the state of Louisiana in 1991 produced a startling level of electoral support for David Duke, a former member of the Klu Klux Klan and former advocate of Nazi policies. Duke got a majority of the white votes that were cast but he lost the election because of the other votes. In April 1992, a mainly white jury in California found that beating and kicking a black suspect (Rodney King) while he was down was not excessive force. The verdict sparked off the worst riots in US history in which nearly sixty people were killed in Los Angeles.

George Bush had himself exploited white racial fears in the presidential election campaign of 1988. A television commercial of the Bush campaign had exploited to the utmost the image of a black convict, Willie Horton, who had been prematurely "furloughed" in Massachusetts and who killed again. The television commercial was probably a significant factor behind George Bush's victory in the presidential election of 1988. Meanwhile, the Supreme Court of the United States has been moving further and further to the right, endangering some of the inter-racial constitutional gains of yesteryears. The new right wing Supreme Court legalized atrocities that ranged from violence by prison wardens to kidnapping by US agents in countries like Mexico. The economic conditions of the black underclass in the United States are worse than ever. Poverty, drug abuse, crime, broken homes, unemployment, infant mortality, and now the disproportionate affliction by AIDS are a stubborn part of the black condition in America.

The holocausts of the Western hemisphere have continued to the present day to inflict pain and humiliation on Native Americans and descendants of African slaves. Ap-

Native Americans and descendants of African slaves. Approximately 40% of the prisoners on death row in the United States are African-Americans. The jails, mortuaries, and police cells still bear anguished testimony to the disproportionate and continuing suffering of American holocausts. In the United States today there are more male descendants of African slaves in prison than in college. Equally ominous on a continental scale is the economic condition of Africa itself. The continent still produces what it does not consume, and consumes what it does not produce. Agriculturally, many African countries have evolved "dessert and beverage economies," producing what are, at best, elements of incidental consumption in the northern hemisphere. These dessert-and-beverage economies produce cocoa, coffee, tea, and other incidentals for the northern dining table. In contrast, Africa imports the fundamentals of its existence from basic equipment to staple food. In addition, Africa is liable to environmental hazards that sometimes lead on to drought and famine in certain areas. The Horn of Africa and the Sahel have been particularly prone to these ecological deprivations.

The external factors that have retarded Africa's economic development included price fluctuations and uncertainties abut primary commodities, issues over which Africa has had very little say. The debt crisis in Africa is also a major shackle on the pace of development. Although as compared with what countries like Brazil and Mexico owe the debts of African countries are modest, it is important to remember that African economies are not only smaller but also more fragile than those of the major Latin American states. The West has shown more flexibility in recent times about Africa's debt crisis and some Western countries have been ready to extend debt forgiveness. Speedy action towards resolving the debt problem would be a contribution in the fight against the forces of Global Apartheid.

Just as African societies are getting more democratic, African states are having less influence on the global scene than ever. African people are increasing their influence on their governments just when African countries are losing leverage on the world system. As the African electorate is getting empowered, the African countries are getting enfeebled. Africa's international marginalization does include among its causes the absence of the Soviet bloc as a countervailing force in the global equation. A world with only one superpower is a world with less leverage for the smaller countries in the global system. Africa's marginalization is also due to the re-emergence of Eastern European countries as rivals for Western attention and Western largess. Africa is also being marginalized in a world of such mega-economies as an increasingly unified North America, an increasingly unified European Community, an expanding Japanese economy, and some of the achievements of the Association of South East Asian Nations (ASEAN). In the economic domain, Global Apartheid is a starker and sharper reality between white nations and black nations than between white nations and some of the countries of Asia.

In the United Nations and its agencies, Africa is also getting marginalized, partly because Third World causes have lost the almost automatic support of former members of the Warsaw Pact. On the contrary, former members of the Socialist bloc are now more likely to follow the American lead than join forces with the Third World. Moreover, the African percentage of the total membership of the UN system is declining. In 1991, five new members were admitted to the United Nations, none of them African (two Koreas and three Baltic states). The disintegration of Yugoslavia and the Soviet Union may result in at least ten more members. The numerical marginalization of Africa within the world body is likely to continue.

In the financial world, the power of the World Bank and the International Monetary Fund not only remains intact but is bound to increase in the era of Global Apartheid. Unfortunately, all indications continue to point in the direction of greater escalation of Africa's dependence upon such international financial institutions. On the other hand, the World Bank sometimes acts as an ambassador on behalf of Africa, coaxing Japan, for example, to allocate more money for African aid. The World Bank may help to persuade Western countries to bear African needs in mind even as the West remains mesmerized by the continuing drama in the former Soviet Union and Eastern Europe. At its best, the World Bank can be a force against the drift towards Global Apartheid. But at its worst, the World Bank is an extension of the power of the white races upon the darker peoples of the globe.

It is virtually certain that German money is already being diverted from Tanzania and Bangladesh towards the newly integrated East Germany and to compensate the former Soviet Union for its cooperation with German reunification. Western money before long will be going in larger amounts to Poland, Hungary, Czechoslovakia, and the newly independent Republics of Lithuania, Latvia, and Estonia. Western investment in former Warsaw Pact countries may also be at the expense of investment in Africa and Western trade may be re-directed to some extent. Now that white Westerners and white Easterners no longer have an ideological reason for mutual hostility, are their shared culture and their shared race acquiring more primary salience? Are we witnessing the emergence of a new northern solidarity as the hatchets of the Cold War are at last buried? Are Blacks the first economic victims of this Global Apartheid?

Conclusion

We have argued that if there is a New World Order, its first economic victims are Black peoples of Africa, the Americas, Europe, and elsewhere. We have also argued that the New World Order's first military victims are Muslims. Hundreds of thousands of Palestinians, Libyans, Iraqis, and

Lebanese have been killed by the West or by Western-subsidized initiatives since the Vietnam War. One advantage about the old East-West divide was that is was trans-racial and inter-racial. White socialist countries supported Black liberation fighters militarily against white minority governments in Africa. But now the former Socialist countries are among the least supportive of Third World causes. In the United Nations the former communist adversaries are often more cooperative with Washington than are some Western allies.

Long before the end of the Cold War, I had occasion to worry publicly about a "global caste system" in the making. I argued in a book published in 1977 that the international stratification did not have the flexibility and social mobility of a class structure, but had some of the rigidities of caste.

> If the international system was in the first half of the twentieth century a class system, it is now moving in the direction of rigidity. We may be witnessing the consolidation of a global caste structure... Just as there are hereditary factors in domestic castes, so there are hereditary elements in international castes. Pre-eminent among those factors is the issue of race... If people of European extraction are the brahmins of the international caste system, the black people belong disproportionately to the caste of the untouchables. Between the highest international caste [whites] and the lowest [blacks] are other ranks and estates [such as Asians].[2]

What prevented this global caste system from becoming Global Apartheid at that time was, ironically, the Cold War that divided the white world ideologically. Rivalry between the two white power blocs averted the risk of racial solidarity among the more prosperous whites. The white world was armed to the teeth against each other; the Brahmins were at daggers drawn. But there is now a closing of the ranks among the white peoples of the world. Pan-Europeanism is reaching levels greater than anything experienced since the Holy Roman Empire. The question is whether this new Pan-European force, combined with the economic trend towards a mega-North America, will produce a human race more than ever divided between prosperous white races and poverty-stricken Blacks. The era of Global Apartheid has coincided with the era of a unipolar world, a global system with only one superpower. The main military victims of this unipolar world have so far been predominantly Muslims while its main economic victims have been disproportionately Blacks. Race and religion remain potent forces in global affairs. Historically, race has been the fundamental divisive factor between Westerners and people of African descent almost everywhere. Religion has been the fundamental divisive factor between Westerners and people of Muslim culture almost anywhere. Was the collapse of the Berlin Wall in 1989 the beginning of the racial re-unification of the white world? Did the Gulf War of 1991 put the holiest places of Islam under the imperial umbrella of *Pax Americana*? Will the twenty first century unfold in ways that build on the new legacy of Global Apartheid? The trends are ominous, but let us hope that they are not irreversible.

NOTES

This chapter is a revised version of a paper presented at the 90th Anniversary Nobel Jubilee Symposium, on the panel on "The Changing Pattern of Global Conflict: From East-West to North-South Conflicts?" sponsored by the Norwegian Nobel Committee and the Norwegian Nobel Institute, Oslo, Norway, December 6-8, 1991. The paper was subsequently published, under the title "Global Apartheid? Race and Religion in the New World Order," in *Beyond the Cold War: New Dimensions of International Rela-*

tions, edited by G. Lundestad and O. A. Westad (Stockholm: Scandinavian University Press, 1993), as well as in *The Gulf War and the New World Order: International Relations of the Middle East,* edited by T. Y. and J. S. Ismael (Gainesville, FL: University of Florida Press, 1994) and in *Redefining the Good Society* (New Delhi and Bombay: Indira Ghandi Memorial Trust, 1995), pp. 106-122. The author is especially indebted to Professor Darryl Thomas of Binghamton University, SUNY, for stimulation.

1. Gernot Köhler did use the concept of "Global Apartheid" in a working paper published for the World Order Models Project. See Köhler, *Global Apartheid* (New York: World Order Models Project, Working Paper No. 7, 1978). His definition of apartheid did not require a fundamental solidarity within the privileged race. My definition does.

2. Ali A. Mazrui, *Africa's International Relations: The Diplomacy of Dependency and Change* (London: Heinemann, and Boulder, Colorado: Westview Press, 1977), pp.7-8.

PART IV

PHILOSOPHICAL AND LITERARY PERSPECTIVES

ELEVEN

ANCIENT GREECE IN AFRICAN
POLITICAL THOUGHT (1966)

In his first important publication in 1947, Kwame
Nkrumah suggested that the very idea of "European" expansionism originated with the Greeks and their immediate successors. The phenomenon of "Europeans" conquering each
other might have been older than the Greeks, but the phenomenon of a major "European" intrusion into another continent had its grand precedent in what Nkrumah called "the
idea of Alexander the Great with his Graeco—Asiatic empire."[1] If Nkrumah was exaggerating, his exaggeration was
academically respectable, for it is a respectable academic
tradition to be able to discover the Greek root of every important phenomenon of the modern world. It is usually safe
to say that "it all goes back to ancient Greece." This is often a
myth, but it is a myth with a capacity to fulfill itself. A
thinker starts suspecting that his thoughts have their roots in
ancient Greece, he turns to the Greeks to find antecedents of
his own thoughts and, before long, his thinking is indeed affected and stimulated by what he reads of Greek ideas. The
ideas of African nationalists have at times been influenced by
the tendency to refer themselves back to the Greeks. It is all
bound up with the place of the Greeks in the total mythology
of "European civilization" and the influence of this mythology on the course of African history.

The ambition of this essay is threefold. First, it aspires to throw some light on the nature of this classical mystique in Africa and the response of African nationalism to it. Second, we hope to define briefly the relation of Eastern Africa both to the mystique and to the African reaction. Third, we intend to pose the question whether ancient Greece was, in any meaningful sense, a European civilization. My own interest in these matters is not, of course, that of a historian. It is the interest of a student of social thought and political behavior. But social thought must often reflect on the findings of historians for new insights into man's image of himself. What we are reflecting upon are matters that do indeed have a bearing on the crisis of identity facing African nationalists. What must not be forgotten is that there is also a crisis of identity confronting every modern African university and the mystique of ancient Greece is at the heart of it.

Let us then first try to fathom the political meaning that this classical mystique has had in contemporary Africa. The first thing that needs to be noted is that, in an important sense, the mystique of ancient Greece contributed to the total cultural arrogance of Europe in relation to the rest of the world. At his inaugural lecture as Regius Professor of History at Oxford in December 1841, Thomas Arnold gave a new lease of life to the ancient idea of a moving center of civilization. Arnold argued that the history of civilization was the history of a series of creative races, each of which made its impact and then sank into oblivion, leaving the heritage of civilization to a greater successor. What the Greeks passed on to the Romans, the Romans bequeathed in turn to the Germanic race. And of that race, the greatest civilizing nation was England.[2]

Lord Lugard also came to share the vision of Britain as a successor to Rome. In his book, *The Dual Mandate*, Lugard asserted that Roman imperialism helped to transform the inhabitants of the British Isles into a civilized nation. Those islands then became a civilizing nation in their own right. To use Lugard's own words:

> As Roman imperialism... led the wild barbarians
> of these islands [of Britain] along the path of pro-
> gress, so in Africa today we are repaying the debt,
> and brining to the dark places of the earth... the
> torch of culture and progress.[3]

In more extremist hands than Lugard's, the Graeco-Roman heritage of the West was used for darker purposes. Biological explanations were sometimes advanced to show that it was right that the whites should have produced a Greek intellectual miracle and that the Blacks should not. The ultimate proof of the higher biological intellectuality of the European stock was that they had to their credit the most intellectual of all ancient civilizations. It was inconceivable that Blacks could ever have produced an Aristotle. The black stock could not even produce a language to compare with that evolved by the Greeks. Nor was that the furthest that cultural arrogance could go. In his address to the Congress of Africanists in Accra in December 1962, Nkrumah cited the case of John C. Calhoun, "the most philosophical of all the slave-holders" of the Southern States of America. Calhoun had apparently once said that if he could find a black man who could understand the Greek syntax, he would then consider their race human, and his attitude toward enslaving them would therefore change. Nkrumah agreed with the re-action of a Zulu student at Columbia University who, com-menting on Calhoun's criterion of what is human, said in an oration in 1906:

> What might have been the sensation kindled by
> the Greek syntax in the mind of the famous
> Southerner, I have so far been unable to discover
> but... I could show him among black men of pure
> African blood those who could repeat the Koran

from memory, skilled in Latin, Greek and Hebrew, Arabic and Chaldaic.[4]

It is evident that Calhoun's charge against Blacks was
more severe than the simpler accusation that they were incapable of producing a language to compare with ancient
Greek. Calhoun was asserting that Blacks were not only incapable of inventing such a language; they were also incapable of understanding it when invented by someone else.
Nkrumah was too modest to remind the International Congress of Africanists that when he himself obtained his Master
of Science degree in education from the University of Pennsylvania many years before, he became a full instructor in
philosophy and first year Greek. And Nkrumah was not even
the best African specialist in either of these subjects. He had
countrymen better versed in these subjects than he.[5]

In a book he published two years after the International Congress of Africanists, Nkrumah discussed the influence of the Graeco-Roman mystique on the kind of education
which colonialism bequeathed to Africa. Not only the study
of philosophy but also of history in Africa was to him distorted by that mystique. As he put it:

> The colonized African student, whose roots in his
> own society are systematically starved of suste-
> nance, is introduced to Greek and Roman history,
> the cradle history of modern Europe, and he is
> encouraged to treat this portion of the story of
> man together with the subsequent history of
> Europe as the only worthwhile portion.[6]

It was partly because of such elements of European
cultural pride that movements like that of *Négritude* came
into being. *Négritude* is an idealisation of the traditional culture of the black man. In a profound sense *Négritude* is
therefore the black man's response to the Graeco-Roman

mystique. That mystique had psychological implications for black people that were not shared by other colonised peoples in Asia. As Thomas Hodgkin once pointed out, no Western European seriously questioned the fact that there had been periods in the past when Arab and Indian civilizations, owing little to European stimulus, flowered. But, in the words of Hodgkin, "the case of the peoples of Africa is different."[7] For them it was not a simple case of recovering a dignity that every one concedes they once had. It may indeed be an attempt to recover their own respect for themselves, but it is also an endeavor to exact for the first time an adequate respect from others. As I have said elsewhere, self-respect and respect by others, difficult to separate as they usually are, are in the Africans' case even more so. And in regard to *Négritude*, there prevails a deep conviction that there is dignity in cultural defiance itself.

Jean-Paul Sartre was right when he described *Négritude* as "evangelical."[8] Perhaps there might even be a mystical link between, say, Elijah Masinde, the so-called prophet of *Dini ya Misambwa* in East Africa and Aimé Césaire, the sophisticated poet of *Négritude* in Martinique. At any rate, literary *Négritude* and certain African messianic and separatist movements are different responses to one inter-related cultural phenomenon. We should remind ourselves here that the sources of European civilization were not exclusively Graeco-Roman. It would perhaps be more correct to regard the ultimate fountains of European culture as being Judea as well as Greece. The achievement of imperial Rome was to fuse the two traditions and bequeath to Europe a civilization that was both Graeco-Roman and Judeo-Christian.

But as these two traditions entered the lives of Blacks they often came wrapped in Europe's cultural arrogance. The Graeco-Roman aspects of that arrogance contributed to the birth of *Négritude*; the Judeo-Christian sense of sacred superiority contributed to the birth of Ethiopianism and African syncretic churches at large. B.C. Sundkler, in his contemplation of the black Christ movements of South Africa, is suddenly reminded of a few verses attributed to Xenophanes:

> The Ethiop's Gods have dusky cheeks,
> Thick lips and woolly hair;
> The Grecian Gods are like the Greeks,
> As tall, bright-eyed, and fair.[9]

Sometimes that old intellectual arrogance of Europe that underestimates the black mind has been extended to the religious sphere. Calhoun might have doubted if a Black could ever understand the Greek syntax; others have sometimes doubted if a Black could ever comprehend the Trinity. And whenever the Black has turned away from European Christianity and embraced a separatist version, some of his judges have felt vindicated. In her book, *New Nations*, Lucy Mair refers to the theory held by some people that "the assimilation of Christian doctrine is an intellectual exercise too difficult for some 'primitive minds.'" She points out that those who hold this theory use it to explain Ethiopianism and similar separatist movements. They argue that such 'primitive minds' not only have misunderstood Christian doctrine and reproduced it in a garbled form but, in the effort, have sometimes become mentally deranged and abandoned themselves to the new cults. Professor Mair herself rejects the theory[10] but, for our purposes here, what matters is that such a theory does exist and is obviously akin to Calhoun's prejudices about the Greek syntax. That is what leads us to the conclusion that both the Graeco-Roman and the Judeo-Christian elements of European civilization have sometimes forced the African into a position of cultural defensiveness. Ethiopianism emerged as a form of poetic protest in action and *Négritude* became, in Sartre's word, "evangelical."

One particularly sophisticated type of African response to the Graeco-Roman mystique of the West is the response of Léopold Senghor, a leading proponent of *Négri-*

tude. Senghor acknowledges that Greek civilization was pre-eminently an intellectual civilization. Did this make Greeks and Westerners at large more intellectual as a group of human beings than black people are? For Senghor the answer is yes. He has argued that the genius of Africa is not in the realm of intellectual abstraction; it is in the domain of emotive sensibility. As he once put it in his own inimitable way: "Emotion is black... reason is Greek."[11] Under attack, Senghor reformulated his views to some extent. His interpretation of original Africa has sometimes exposed him to the charge of having deprived the traditional African of the gift of full rationality. Senghor defends himself with his usual ingenuity. But ultimately he still insists on regarding the African as being basically intuitive, rather than analytical. He said:

> Young people have criticised me for reducing Black-African knowledge to pure emotion, for denying that there is an African 'reason'... I should like to explain myself once again... European reasoning is analytical, discursive by utilization; Negro-African reasoning is intuitive by participation.[12]

Elsewhere Senghor emphasizes that "analytic and discursive reason" was part of the Graeco-Roman heritage of Europe at large. "One could even trace the descent of Marxism from Aristotle!" he asserts. Descartes had once asserted that the ultimate proof that I exist is that I think—in his own famous words "I think, therefore I am." But according to Senghor, African epistemology starts from a different basic postulate. For the African Black the world exists by the fact of its reflection upon his emotive self:

> He does not realise that he thinks; he feels that he feels, he feels his *existence,* he feels himself.[13]

In short, Black-African epistemology starts from the premise "I feel, therefore I am." Kwame Nkrumah, in his book, *Consciencism,* also discusses Descartes' postulate. Nkrumah argues that the fact that "Monsieur Descartes" is thinking is no proof that his body exists. It is certainly no proof that the totality of his person is in being. Nkrumah is out to deny that matter owes its existence either to thought or to perception. In a sense he would disagree with both assertions "I think, therefore I am" and "I feel, therefore I am." But to the extent that "feeling" is a more "physical" experience than thought, it is a greater concession to the autonomy of matter. The kind of philosophical idealism that puts our bodies in our minds instead of our minds in our bodies was, to Nkrumah, no more than an indulgence in "the ecstasy of intellectualism."[14]

But Nkrumah would certainly not go to the extent of denying the African the gift of "analytical and discursive reason." As he himself put it at the inauguration of the University of Ghana in November 1961: "We have never had any doubt about the intellectual capacity of the African."[15] Yet the measure of African capacity has sometimes been deemed to be the extent to which the African could grapple with Greek thought. Calhoun might have used the ability to understand the Greek syntax as a criterion of whether the African was human. But Africans themselves sometimes invoke the ability to grapple with Greek concepts as a criterion that the African was indeed an intellectual being. Cheikh Anta Diop of Sénégal, in trying to establish the academic calibre of the ancient African University in Timbuktu, found it pertinent to assert that,

> Aristotle was commented upon regularly, and the trivium and quadrivium were known as one does not go without the other. Almost all the scholars were completely experienced in the Aristotelian Dialectics and the commentaries of formal logic.[16]

Nkrumah talked proudly of Anthony William Amoo, the Ghanaian who, in the eighteenth century, taught philosophy at the University of Wittenberg in Germany and "wrote dissertations in Latin and Greek."[17] The most intellectual of all Nkrumah's own works is *Consciencism*. To some extent, the book is a collaborative effort. Nkrumah himself acknowledges the assistance of his Philosophy Club, of which Professor William Abraham, the Ghanaian philosopher, was presumably a member. In spite of its many and serious imperfections, there is no doubt that the book is a work of the intellect. Diallo Telli, later Secretary-General of the Organisation of African Unity, took part in a ceremony to launch the book. He stated that the book deprived of all validity "the accumulated lies about the so-called congenital inability of the African man to raise himself to the highest levels on the plane of thought."[18] Telli was substantially right in seeing the book in those terms. Yet *Consciencism* is also the least Africa-oriented of all Nkrumah's books. Descartes is by no means the only Western philosopher discussed in it. Much of the book is in the tradition of Greek "analytic and discursive reason." The dilemma of African cultural nationalism is implicit in Diallo Telli's evaluation. In order to establish her intellectual equality with the West, Africa has to master Western versions of intellectual skills. Africa has to establish that she can be as "Greek" as the next person.

But, sometimes, African nationalists wanted to go further than this. They wanted to assert an African role in the growth of Greek culture itself. A crucial link in the chain of this reasoning is another mystique that we must now look at, the mystique of the Nile. And it is this mystique which brings in not only Northern Africa but also Eastern. A Ghanian intellectual, Michael Dei-Anang, once wrote the following poem:

Dark Africa?
Who nursed the doubtful child

Of civilization
On the wand'ring banks
Of life-giving Nile,
And gave to the teeming nations
Of the West
A Grecian gift![19]

Few would today seriously dispute that there was an Egyptian influence on at least the earlier phases of the Hellenic civilization. In the words of Henry Bamford Parkes, "The Euphrates and the Nile Valleys were the original sources of the civilization of Western man."[20] This consideration affects Eastern Africa in two ways. First, because the precise nature of ancient Egypt's links with countries South of her might be important in determining whether Egypt's civilization was, in any meaningful sense, an "African" achievement. The second consideration which makes Eastern Africa relevant is at once simpler and of more permanent repercussions. If the Nile was a source of civilization, East Africa was the source of the Nile. The latter fact was not fully grasped until centuries later, but the mystery of the source of the Nile came to have important historical consequences for this part of the continent.

To the Greeks, much of Europe was as dark a continent as much of Africa. But the question of where the Nile originated had compelling symbolism. It was at once a symbol of Greek ignorance about Eastern Africa and a symbol of Greek curiosity about it. It was a symbol of Greek ignorance because the Ancients did not as yet know for certain that the great river had its birth in these parts. But the mysterious floods of the Nile, as well as the river's mysterious source, were more a part of Greek scientific interest than anything that ever happened in the remoter parts of Western Europe. The Greeks even looked at the birds disappearing into the African horizon and speculated about their destination. If Nkrumah is right, then "Erastosthenes and Aristotle knew that the cranes migrated as far as the lakes where the Nile had its source."[21] Even if it were true that this part of Africa was "as dark a continent" to the Greeks as much of Europe was, there was one difference. The darkness of Eastern Africa was one of scientific fascination. The darkness of parts of Western Europe was, to the Greeks, devoid of intellectual compensation.

But it might not even be true that this part of Africa was as dark to the ancient Greeks as North-Western Europe was at that time. In a meaningful sense, East Africa was a subordinate sector of the classical world. It had this status partly through its connection with the Nile Valley as a whole and partly through its links with the Middle East proper. It is therefore just conceivable that ancient East Africa might have been more a part of the classical world known by the Greeks than some parts of Europe could ever claim to be. Of course, since much more archaeological work has been done in Western Europe than in Africa, the volume of evidence is seriously uneven. But L.S.B. Leakey has hazarded the generalization that, because of isolation, sub-Saharan Africa as a whole was, for a while, "in a cultural state very similar to that of Britain at the time of the coining of the Romans."[22]

Yet if the isolation of Africa south of the Sahara as a unit was comparable to that of Britain, the isolation of Eastern Africa on its own might have been less severe. There is evidence of trade down the Red Sea, as well as from the Persian Gulf, from very early times. As Gervase Mathew has pointed out, the list of imports into East Africa mentioned by the *Periplus* "suggests the existence of a fairly evolved culture." One could go on to add that it also suggests a significant commercial intercourse much older than the *Periplus* itself.[23] Sir Mortimer Wheeler has put East Africa alongside Mediterranean Africa as the two parts of the continent that, on present evidence, have had the longest intercourse with the outside world:

[...] two regions of Africa... have long looked outwards to worlds across the seas. The first of these is the Mediterranean coastline which has always been inclined to share its ideas with Europe. The second is the East African coastline, the coastline of what we know as Somalia, Kenya and Tanganyika, which has long shared its life with Arabia and India and continues to do so today.[24]

Later on, the Middle East exerted a different kind of cultural influence on Eastern Africa, particularly with the coming of Islam through coastal settlements. And even late in the Christian era, there were areas of Europe that were no more closely integrated with the Middle East. In the nature of the relationship between these areas, Roland Oliver might be exaggerating when he says: "Certainly Islam's African fringe can bear comparison with Christendom's Northern European fringe at any time up to the late sixteenth century."[25] But the exaggeration lies in the dateline he chooses. Well before the sixteenth century, Europe had already become more closely integrated as part of Christendom than the East African coast was with the southern sector of the Middle East. But Oliver is at least right in asserting that the integration of Europe was completed well after Islam had come to East Africa.[26]

What we should not overlook is that the Islamisation of the East African coast was only a new manifestation of an older phenomenon, the phenomenon of East Africa's contacts with certain parts of the classical world. Later developments had their genesis in the general cultural inter-relationship within the classical world as a whole. As Marshall C.S. Hodgson has pointed out in a stimulating article on "the inter-relations of societies in history:"

The Mediterranean Basin formed a historical whole, not only under the Roman Empire but before and since... The core of the Middle East was the Fertile Crescent and the Iranian Plateau, to which lands North and South from Central Eurasia to Yemen and East Africa looked for leadership, as did increasingly even Egypt, despite its distinct roots in its own past.[27]

But, as we mentioned, East Africa's links with this world were not merely through its historical intercourse with the Middle East proper. They were also through its primeval relationship with the Nile Valley as a distinct sub-section of the classical world. This relationship though as yet only vaguely understood, is giving rise to challenging hypotheses. Fifty years ago, a towering British scholar and archaeologist, Sir Ernest Wallis Budge, put forward a hypothesis that, by 1954, was getting incorporated into the movement of historical *Négritude*. In his book on Black civilizations, Dr. J.C. DeGraft-Johnson of Ghana cited the testimony of Sir Ernest Budge that ancient Egyptians might have been, in part, Ugandans. DeGraft-Johnson quotes the following passage from Budge:

> There are many things in the manners and customs and religions of the historic Egyptians, that is to say, of the workers on the land, that suggest that the original home of their prehistoric ancestors was a country in the neighbourhood of Uganda and Punt.[28]

Elsewhere, Budge argues that Egyptian tradition of the Dynastic Period held that the aboriginal home of the Egyptians was Punt. But where was Punt? Budge answers in the following terms:

> Though our information about the boundaries of this land is of the vaguest character, it is quite certain that a very large proportion of it was in Central Africa, and it probably was near the country called in our times 'Uganda.'[29]

Our information about the boundaries of Punt is still vague and controversial. And Budge was sometimes rash. But whatever the accuracy of speculations such as his, there is enough evidence to indicate significant primeval contacts down the Nile Valley, and movements of peoples in both directions. "It is to the Nile Valley that we look for the original link between Egypt and all South of it" a historian once asserted.[30] And two other historians traced back to Egypt an ancient ceremony in Western Uganda on the accession of an Omukama of Bunyoro.[31] Perhaps less scientific was the conviction of a Bishop of Uganda earlier in the century, Bishop Alfred Tucker of the Church Missionary Society, that there were aspects of the Kiganda culture which "must" have been of Egyptian origin.[32]

The distribution of the Nilotes along the Nile Valley is another aspect of interest in trying to determine the degree of contact along the Valley. An essay on ancient Egypt in the 1953 edition of the *Encyclopaedia Britannica* claims that there was significant Nilotic element in the ethnic composition of early Egypt. The evidence for such claims is questionable but the speculations partly arise out of the apparent cultural diffusion along the Nile Valley as a whole, and among populations descended from or affected by the Nilotes and Nilo-Hamites. One line of interpretation is to see Egypt as a recipient of certain influences from the South of her. The other is to see Egypt as the ultimate source of certain cultural elements discerned in the lives of people elsewhere in the continent. "That certain ritual practices and beliefs found in Equatorial Africa are of Egyptian origin need not reasonably be doubted," writes G.W.B. Huntingford, and he too turns to the Bunyoro of Uganda to illustrate his thesis.[33] There is much in the history of the Nile Valley that we have yet to discover. And in any case some of the cultural influences were carried up or down the Valley long after the glories of classical times. But the evidence of primeval contacts down the Nile Valley, and of significant movements of populations, is

already persuasive enough. It is these contacts along the
Nile, plus the intercourse through the Indian Ocean and the
Red Sea, which converted at least some ancient East Africans
into more meaningful members of the classical world than,
say, ancient Britons could claim to be.[34] What this whole
question is related to is, of course, the general problem of
how far ancient Egyptian civilization can, in a significant
sense, be regarded as an African civilization. This latter problem is at the heart of African cultural nationalism at large.
And it is to this that we must now address ourselves more
specifically.

In the final analysis there are at least two basic ways
in which a culture might he alien to Africa. One is when the
culture itself comes from outside Africa. The second is when
the people who develop that culture within Africa are themselves of recent alien extraction. In the latter case, the new
civilization would be one that the alien group did not bring
with them from outside; they cultivated it as something new
after arrival in Africa. So the culture in its new peculiarities
is, in that sense, native-born. But partly because the particular group that develops such culture is itself of alien origin,
the culture falls short of having full indigenous status. The
nearest example in modern Africa is perhaps the Afrikaner
ethos of South Africa. In an important sense the political
thought of Afrikaner-nationalists is nearer to being native-
born than the political thought of a black African Marxist or
a Western liberal. For better or for worse, the ideology of
apartheid is an outgrowth of a particular sociological situation in Africa itself. It is a poisonous plant that has grown out
of the soil of Africa. To that extent it is more native to Africa
than Marxism.

Apartheid is a poisonous growth that the rest of Africa
would rather weed out. And the plant falls short of full indigenous status partly because those who are cultivating it with
such care and affection are of recent alien-extraction as a
group. Their alien nature would have become less pro-

nounced if they had allowed themselves to mix more with the natives and to be influenced by them. But their exclusiveness preserves their alien-ness in Africa as well as their alienation from those they live with. The question that needs to be asked is whether Afrikaner culture is really a plant of the African soil. The calculated foreignness of the cultivator arouses the suspicion that although the plant might have grown in Africa, the seed might be as foreign as the cultivator. Apartheid as an ethos might therefore be deemed to be a product of Africa without being elevated to the status of being native to Africa. A similar kind of reasoning has tended to affect the status of the ancient Egyptian civilization. Even if that civilization flourished on African soil, its status as an African civilization would partly depend on whether the Egyptians themselves were African. Were the ancient Egyptians immigrants from Eurasia or were they really native to the African continent?

Cultural nationalism in modern Africa has wanted to emphasize that ancient Egyptians were indeed African. But how can one establish this point? Logically, there is no reason why a people should not be considered to be native of Africa because it is not black. The idea that all the people of each continent ought to be of one color is a dogma that has completely ignored the example of multi-colored Asia. The yellow peoples of Japan and China, the dark Tamils of Ceylon, the brown Gujarati in India, are today all part of the Asian continent. The ancient Egyptians need not therefore have been black in order to qualify as natives of Africa. And yet, if they can be shown to have been black, their links with sub-Saharan Africa would be easier to take for granted. There is evidence that at least a section of ancient Egyptians were Blacks (or Negroid). Basil Davidson, in his romanticism, sometimes over-argues the vision of a glorious African past. But he is probably well within the evidence available when he tells us the following:

An analysis of some 800 skulls from pre-Dynastic

Egypt—from the lower Valley of the Nile, that is, before 3000 B.C.—shows that at least a third of them were Negroes or ancestors of the Negroes whom we know; and this may well support the view, to which a study of language also brings some confirmation, that remote ancestors of the Africans today were an important and perhaps dominant element among populations which fathered the civilization of ancient Egypt.[35]

Whether the black element among ancient Egyptians was a third, or more, or less, the fact that it was there has become part of African cultural nationalism in our own day. As one such nationalist, Cheikh Anta Diop, put it:

It remains... true that the Egyptian experiment was essentially Black, and that all Africans can draw the same moral advantage from it that Westerners draw from Graeco-Latin civilization.[36]

What makes Cheikh Anta Diop's position extreme is not his Africanisation of the Pharaohs. It is not even the simple claim that ancient Egypt influenced the Hellenic civilization, a claim which few scholars would dispute. Diop's extremism is in the magnitude he assigns to that Egyptian influence. At his most reckless, he virtually credits ancient Egypt with all the major achievements of the Greeks. But even when he does not go quite as far, he at least claims that Egypt was to the Greeks what the Western impact has been to Africa in our own times. To use his own words:

From Thales to Pythagoras and Democritus, Plato and Eudoxus, it is almost evident that all those who created the Greek philosophical and scientific school and who pass for universal inventors of mathematics... were disciples educated at the school of the Egyptian priests.[37]

Diop goes on to assert that if Plato, Eudoxus, and Pythagoras had remained in Egypt for thirteen to twenty years, "it was not only to learn recipes." He then draws the telling analogy in the following terms:

> The situation is similar to that of under-developed countries in relation to their ancient metropolises. It does not occur to a national of these countries, whatever his nationalism, to dispute the fact that modern technique has been spread from Europe to the whole world. The rooms of the African students at the *cités universitaires* in Paris, London, etc., are comparable from all points of view to those of Eudoxus and Plato at Heliopolis, and they may well be shown to African tourists in the year 2,000.[38]

But here again a dilemma faces Africa as she seeks to demonstrate that she has a past as glorious as that of other nations and peoples. She needs the testimony of those other nations for that purpose. Even in the attempt to establish that ancient Egyptians were at least partly black, contemporary black nationalists sometimes turn to the Greeks for evidence. Cheikh Anta Diop himself cites from Graeco-Roman sources at large. And the late W.E.B. DuBois, the distinguished American Black, used to cite the testimony of Herodotus that ancient Egyptians were "woolly haired" in the African sense.[39] All this is understandable; since Africans were often trying to combat Western disparaging assertions, it made sense that they should on occasion have to turn to authorities regarded as respectable by Westerners themselves. The appeal to the Greeks, to Aristotle and Herodotus, was inevitably one respectable source of authority.

The question of whether or not ancient Egypt was African was only an acute form of a broader confrontation between African cultural nationalism on the one hand and certain assumptions of orthodox Western scholarship on the other. There was one compound Western assumption in particular which could not but clash with African pride. This compound assumption took one of two main forms. One form was the belief that whatever was worthwhile in ancient and medieval Africa was of alien origin. Professor C.G. Seligman belonged substantially to this school. He regarded the Hamites as "the great civilizing force of black Africa from a relatively early period" and he considered the Hamites to be "Asiatic" in origin, with ties of kinship with what he called "the European representatives of the Mediterranean race."[40] Seligman might have overestimated the amount of Hamite blood in Africa, or the prevalence of alien influence behind old African civilizations. In any case, the conception of Hamites as related to what Seligman called "the Mediterranean race" could be one extra piece of evidence that Eastern Africa was part of the classical world in a sense in which much of ancient Europe was not. In short, Seligman was granting more to Africa than would be granted by some of his contemporaries in Europe. We referred, at the beginning of this article, to the inaugural lecture of a Regius Professor of History at Oxford in December 1841. Professor Thomas Arnold had, as we indicated, talked about a moving center of civilization that had traveled from classical Greece to England. More than 120 years later, another Regius Professor of History at Oxford, Professor Hugh Trevor-Roper, put forward the other side of this particular coin of ethnocentrism. In 1963, Trevor-Roper went on record as saying: "Perhaps in the future there will be some African history to teach. But at present there is none; there is only the history of Europeans in Africa. The rest is darkness... and darkness is not a subject of history."[41]

Both the Seligman and the Trevor-Roper theses were manifestations of a somewhat arrogant historiography, but the Seligman version had compensating factors that were absent from the latter version. In any case, a revolution has already started in Western scholarship on Africa. In this same month of August 1966, Ethiopia expressed Africa's appreciation of the work of Roland Oliver, Professor of African History at the University of London. Professor Oliver was awarded a prize by the Haile Selassie I Trust for what the citation described as "very considerable contribution to the development of African historical studies." Partly on the success of this revolution in Western scholarship depends the transformation of Africa's response to the Graeco-Roman mystique. *Négritude* is, as we indicated, an essential part of that response. For too long, Africans had been too blatantly denied a creative capacity. They had been too often denied moments of civilization in their past. The black man became the most deprived of all colonized peoples and his reactions became peculiarly his own. As Melville J. Herskovits once exclaimed, "but there isn't the Indian equivalent of Négritude."[42] The Indians had, after all, been allowed to keep their *Ashokas* in full regal splendor.

As Africans begin to be given credit for some of their own civilizations, African cultural defensiveness will gradually wane. Not everyone need have the confidence of Léopold Senghor as he asserts that "Black blood circulated in the veins of the Egyptians."[43] But it is time that it was more openly conceded not only that ancient Egypt made a contribution to the Greek miracle, but also that she in turn had been influenced by the Africa which was to the south of her. To grant all this is, in a sense, to universalise the Greek heritage. It is to break the European monopoly of identification with ancient Greece.

And yet this is by no means the only way of breaking Europe's monopoly. In order to cope with the cultural offensive of the Graeco-Roman mystique, African cultural defenders have so far emphasized the Africanness of Egypt's civilisation. But a possible counter-offensive is to demonstrate that ancient Greece was not European. It is not often remembered how recent the concept of "Europe" is. As a matter of fact, it may be easier to prove that ancient Egypt was "African" than to prove that ancient Greece was "European." In the words of Palmer and Colton:

> There was really no Europe in ancient times. In the Roman Empire we may see a Mediterranean world, or even a West and an East in the Latin- and Greek-speaking portions. But the West included parts of Africa as well as of Europe, and Europe as we know it was divided by the Rhine-Danube frontier, South and West of which lay the civilised provinces of the Empire, and North and East the 'barbarians' of whom the civilised world knew almost nothing.[44]

The two historians go on to say that the word "Europe," since it meant little, was scarcely used by the Romans at all.[45] Even as late as the seventeenth century, the notion that the landmass south of the Mediterranean was something distinct from the land mass north of it was something yet to be fully accepted. Melville Herskovits has pointed out how the Royal Geographer of France, writing in 1656, described Africa as "a peninsula so large that it comprises the third part, and this the most Southerly, of our continent."[46] Nevertheless, it was perhaps the Romans who laid the foundation for the incorporation of Greece into Europe as we know it today. A crucial part of the process was the spread of culture. William H. McNeill reminded us that "under the Roman Empire, an increasingly cosmopolitan, though still basically Hellenic, civilisation extended tentacles even to remotest Britain."[47] And so Northwestern and Northern Europe gradually became, in a sense, "Greek" in culture. And yet there was no logical necessity why Greece herself should in turn become "European" in physical context. The fact that the rest of Europe was Hellenised did not in itself make Greece "European"—any more than the fact that Jamaicans who are Anglicised need today to convert England into a West Indian island.

The logic of this point might be incontrovertible, but European map-makers had other ideas. By the eighteenth century they had made fairly sure that the seat of the most intellectual of all civilizations was placed firmly within the arbitrary boundaries that they increasingly called "the continent of Europe." Greek Philosophers might have conquered the minds of Europeans; but European map-makers had their own back, when, in their projections, they quietly captured the territory of Greece on the battlefield of the atlas. In that article on "The Inter-relations of Societies in History," Marshall Hodgson discussed some ethnocentric elements in the world-image of the West. He opened the substance of his analysis with the following assertion:

> We must begin with the map. A concern with maps may seem trivial; but it offers a paradigm of more fundamental cases. For even in maps we have found ways of expressing our feelings.[48]

Hodgson goes on to ask why Europe was classified as one of the continents while India was not. He asserts that it is not because of any geographical features, nor even because of any marked cultural breach of the limits chosen. "The two sides of the Aegean Sea have almost always had practically the same culture, and usually the same language or languages and even the same government." Why then did Europe become classified as a continent? In making it a continent, Hodgson points out, it was given a rank disproportionate to its natural size. Despite all of that, Hodgson asserts: "Europe is still ranked as one of the 'continents' because our cultural ancestors lived there."[49] And yet, for an Anglo-Saxon or a Frenchman to talk confidently of "our ancestors, the Greeks" is no less absurd than a reference by a Senegalese schoolboy to "our ancestors, the Gauls." Imperial ideologues had legitimised their expansion into Asia and Africa partly on their being heirs to the only valid civilization, the Graeco-Roman one. But in fact, the first act of cultural imperialism that Europe committed was that of incorporating Greece into the map of Europe. So successful has Europe been in this that, today, even the Greeks themselves would, if forced to choose, perhaps regard themselves as European first and Mediterranean only second.

The only mitigating factor in this blatant act of cultural impersonation is that Europeans did become the great carriers of the Graeco-Roman heritage in these later periods of world history. In an act of cultural piracy, Europe had stolen classical Greece. But later, in an act of territorial annexation, "Europe stole the world" and, in the colonies that she annexed, she passed on the message of Greece. In Eastern Africa, that old mystique of the Nile was to have a new relevance. The quest for the elusive source of the Nile helped to prepare the way for a new European penetration into the region. In the olden days, Eastern Africa might indeed have been more a part of the classical world than ancient Britain was. By the end of the nineteenth century, the brightest jewel of Britain's African crown was perhaps Egypt itself. The British Foreign Office inherited from history the doctrine of the Unity of the Nile, and converted it into a new imperial postulate. Historians differ as to the practical significance of the doctrine in British policy but the balance of the evidence is probably on the side of those who regard it as an important conditioning factor on British attitudes. Robinson and Gallagher remind us that "the idea that the security of Egypt depended upon the defense of the Upper Nile was as old as the pyramids." They point out its effect on Salisbury who in 1889-1890 decided that if Britain was to hold on to Egypt, she could not afford to let any other European power obtain a hold over any part of the Nile Valley. The two historians contend that, in so doing, Salisbury took what was perhaps the critical decision of the partition of Africa. "Henceforward almost everything in Africa North of the Zambesi River was to hinge upon it."[50] Under Salisbury's successors, the doctrine of the Unity of the Nile Valley helped to seal the fate of Uganda. As Robinson and Gallagher put it with reference to Rosebery's vision: "the Cabinet quarrels over Uganda were really quarrels over Egypt."[51]

And so the snowball of imperial annexation proceeded. Egypt was important for Britain's whole Middle Eastern strategy and so Egypt had to remain occupied. But Egypt depended so much on the Nile, and the Nile passed throughout the Sudan. Thus the loose Egyptian suzerainty over Sudan had to be converted into a strong British sovereignty. But the unity of the Nile Valley was not complete unless its very source was controlled by the same power. So Uganda had to be under British control. And again, the way to the Lakes from the important port of Mombasa was through what came to be known as Kenya, and hence Kenya had to be annexed too. The forceful torrent of British expansionism shared a valley with the Nile River and overflowed into other areas the East African land surface. With that imperialism, Eastern Africa has also sensed a strong cultural impact. She has felt herself in communion with a civilization that is at once new and strangely reminiscent of ancient ties. The gift of Greece has come with a new bearer, acquiring a new luster on the way. Ancient Britons might have been less immediately connected with the Hellenic miracle than were the inhabitants of the Nile Valley but it is the modern Britons who have brought the spirit of Greece back to the banks of the river.

But can we concede to Europe the role of bearer of Greek culture without conceding her the right to Greece itself? The answer is, indeed we can. The point is that Europe's title to the Greek heritage is fundamentally no different from Europe's title to Christianity. In these later phases of world history, Europe has been the most effective bearer of both the Christian message and the Greek heritage. But just as it would be a mistake to let Europe nationalize Christianity, it would be a mistake to let her confiscate the Hellenic inheritance. The Greeks must at last be allowed to emerge as what they really are: the fathers, not of a European civilization, but of a universal modernity. The distinction is a matter of importance to a modern university in Africa where medical graduates might take the Hippocratic oath, where historians trace their origins to Herodotus, and where political scientists study *The Politics* of Aristotle. In his inaugural address, the first Principal of the University College of the Gold Coast, D. M. Balme, complained about the careless use of term "European civilization" as the central preoccupation of a university. He said:

> It may be justifiable that the things which are studied at universities... are themselves the instruments of civilization. If so, it then follows that there is only one *modern* civilization. It happens to have started in Greece... and it spread first through Europe. But it is high time we stopped calling it European.[52]

Traces of ethnocentrism are still very evident in the address of this European classicist. He seems to insist that the Graeco-Roman heritage is the only profitable preoccupation for a modern university. But at least he no longer insists that the heritage is "European." This is a step forward. In the meantime, the classics could increasingly be made to serve the purposes even of African nationalism itself without offending the ultimate postulates of that nationalism. One area of possible service is the area of language. It was Aristotle who once remarked:

> Nature, as we often say, makes nothing in vain, and man is the only animal whom she has endowed with the gift of speech.[53]

Many centuries later, Léopold Senghor proclaimed: "Language is a power in Negro-Africa. Spoken language, the word, is the supreme expression of vital force, of the being in his fulfillment."[54] Yet Aristotle's own ancient language had by now a different kind of power within Africa itself, and was not even primarily a spoken language. On the eve of Ghana's independence, Nkrumah lamented the following situation:

> At present such is the influence of Europe in our affairs that far more students in our University are studying Latin and Greek than are studying the languages of Africa.[55]

What Nkrumah might have overlooked was the potential value of Greek and Latin as allies of African languages in their war against modern European languages. In a recent paper on "Swahili in the Technical Age," Dr. Mohamed Hyder, Lecturer in Zoology at the University College, Nairobi, posed the problem in stark terms. He asked whether it was possible to write a serious scientific paper in Swahili on the subject of "The Effect of Thyroid Stimulating Hormone on the Radioactive Iodine Uptake Beef Thyroid Tissue *in vitro*." His answer was that if a serious attempt was made to develop a "technical limb" to Swahili, this was indeed possible. The title of the paper would, it is true, include terms like *"thairodi, hormoni, ayodini, redioaktivu na invitro."* However, Dr. Hyder goes on to say that,

> There is no good reason why this development of a 'technical limb'...of Swahili through the Swahilisation of such terms should weigh heavily on our consciences. Examination of any technical or scientific journal, English, French, German, Russian or Chinese, shows clearly that such technical terms are really international in usage. Look up the word 'thyroid' or 'radioactive' in any of these

languages and you would find that apart from the token digestive processes exerted on them, they are practically the same the world over.[56]

In a *Présence Africaine* lecture delivered in November 1961, Pierre Alexandre, the French linguist and Africanist, linked this issue more specifically to the scientific utility of the classics. He said:

> It would be wrong to say that African languages are a barrier to the teaching of science and technical subjects. The syntactical structure of those known to me would not provide any major obstacle to the pursuit of logical reasoning. The absence of technical terminology in the vocabulary is all the more easy to remedy since, in fact, the international technical terminology is based on an artificial assembly of Greek and Latin roots. The Parisian who speaks of a 'telegram' rather than 'far-off writing' is expressing himself in Greek, in the same way as a Duala who speaks of 'telefun.'[57]

In no other field is the international neutrality of the classical languages better illustrated than in the sciences. In their war against the deadly encroachment of English and French, the African languages must therefore seek the alliance of Latin and Greek. For some African languages such an alliance might indeed be a matter of life and death.

Sometimes the classics are not only neutral as between modern European languages and modern African. The classical languages are sometimes called upon to be neutral between one African language and another. Margaret Macpherson reminds us how, late in the 1940s, Makerere decided that its motto should no longer be in Luganda and so representative of only a fraction of the academic population of the College. The motto became the Latin one of *Pro Futuro aedificamus* because, as Mrs. Macpherson explains:

It may be protested that Latin represents no section of the community at all, but its use is hallowed by academic and heraldic custom and many
may feel it is better to represent none than only
some.[58]

In this case then, Latin is called upon to help the
cause of Pan-Africanism at Makerere and spare Luganda the
envy of others. But when called upon to build up Swahili and
Luganda to the level of scientific respectability, Greek and
Latin would be serving the cause of linguistic *Négritude* as
well. Perhaps that is the road towards the universalisation of
the Graeco-Roman heritage. There is already evidence that
even the most radical of African nationalists are beginning to
assert a claim to that heritage without being culturally defensive at the same time. In June 1964, *The People*, the militant
newspaper of the ruling party in Uganda, carried an article
entitled "The Formative Years of Dr. Milton Obote." According to the article, Dr. Obote's headmaster at the college in
Mwiri "made it a practice to read the *Republic* of Plato with
the top form every Tuesday." The article then asked: "had
this reading of Plato anything to do with the moulding of
Obote's thoughts?" The question is left tantalizingly in the
air.[59]

When Kwame Nkrumah returned to Achimota as a
famous man twenty years after his student days there, he
gave a talk on "The Political Philosophy of Plato." After the
talk, his old teacher, Lord Hemingford, went to congratulate
him and added humorously that, although he had to admit
that he had taught Nkrumah, he wanted to make it quite
clear that he was in no way responsible for the political ideas
he had just heard.[60] But perhaps one of the most important
speeches of Nkrumah's career was the speech with which he
moved what came to be known as "The Motion of Destiny," a
motion on fundamental constitutional reform prior to independence. It was in that speech that Nkrumah referred to Aristotle as "the master." At that mature stage of African na-

tionalism such an acknowledgement was not a submission but a conquest, not a retreat into subservience but a move to transcend. As Nkrumah said "Aristotle, the master," the whole edifice of Europe's monopoly of the Graeco-Roman heritage began to shake because of only three words casually included in a speech. The speech was indeed on "A Motion of Destiny" but in a sense far deeper than the speaker realized. In simple terms, and with confidence, an African was claiming his share of the Hellenic heritage of man.[61]

NOTES

This chapter is a revised version of an inaugural lecture delivered on August 25, 1966, at Makerere University College, Uganda, which originally appeared in *Présence Africaine*, Volume 61 (1967), N° 149/150, pp. 68-93, and which was also published as a pamphlet by The East African Publishing House (Nairobi, Kenya) in 1967.

1. *Towards Colonial Freedom* (London: Heinneman, 1962 reprint), p.1.

2. See T. Arnold, *Introductory Lecture on Modern History* (New York, 1842), pp. 46-47. Consult also Philip D. Curtin, *The Image of Africa, British Ideas and Action, 1780-1850* (Madison: University of Wisconsin Press, 1964), pp. 375-377. See also Arthur Penrhyn Stanley, *Life and Correspondence of Thomas Arnold* (London: Ward, Lock and Co., 1845), pp. 435-438.

3. F.D. Lugard, *The Dual Mandate in British Tropical Africa* (Edinburgh: William Blackwood and Sons, 1926), p. 618.

4. See Nkrumah's address opening the Congress in *Proceedings of the First International Congress of Africanists* (11th–18th December, 1962), edited by Lalage Bown and Michael Crowder (Longmans, 1964), p. 12.

5. See *Ghana: The Autobiography of Kwame Nkrumah* (Edinburgh: Thomas Nelson, 1960 reprint), p. 27.

6. Nkrumah, *Consciencism* (London: Heinneman Educational Books, 1964), p. 5.

7. Hodgkin, *Nationalism in Colonial Africa* (London: Frederick Muller, 1956), p. 172. See also Ali A. Mazrui, "On the Concept of 'We are all Africans,'" in *The American Political Science Review*, Vol. LVII, no. 1, March 1963, p. 97—reproduced in the first volume of the *Collected Essays of Ali A. Mazrui* entitled *Africanity Redefined* as Chapter 4, pp. 43-64.

8. See Sartre, *Orphée Noir*, Preface to *Anthologie de la Nouvelle Poésie Nègre et Malgache*, ed. L. S. Senghor, 1948.

9. Sundkler, *Bantu Prophets in South Africa* (London: Oxford University Press, 1961 edition), p. 279. Consult also F.B. Welbourn, *East African Rebels: A Study of Some Independent Churches* (London: S.C.M. Press, 1961), and Sylvia L. Thrupp (ed.), *Millennial Dreams in Action* (The Hague: Mouton et Cie, 1962).

10. Lucy Mair, *New Nations* (London: Weidenfeld and Nicholson, 1963), pp. 172-173.

11. L.S. Senghor, *Négritude et Humanisme* (Paris: Seuil, 1964), p. 24.

12. Senghor, *On African Socialism* (London: Pall Mall, 1964), p. 74.

13. Senghor, "The Spirit of Civilization, or the Laws of African Negro Culture," The First International Conference of Negro Writers and Artists, *Présence Africaine*, Special Issue, June-November 1956, pp. 64-71. Elsewhere Senghor describes Descartes as "The European *par excellence*." See his *De La Négritude, Psychologie du Négro-Africain* (in *Diogène*, no. 37, 1962), parts of which are available in English under the title "The African Apprehension of Reality" in *Senghor, Prose and Poetry*, ed. and trans. By John Reed and Clive Wake (London: Oxford University Press, 1965), pp. 29-35.

14. *Consciencism*, op. cit., pp. 16-19.

15. See "Ghana's Cultural History," extracts from Nkrumah's speech at the inauguration, in *Présence Africaine*, Vol. 13, no. 41, Second Quarter 1962.

16. Cited by Erica Simon, *Présence Africaine*, "Négritude and Cultural Problems of Contemporary Africa," Vol. 18, no. 47, Third Quarter 1963, p. 135.

17. Nkrumah, "Ghana's Cultural History," op. cit., p. 9.

18. See *Ghana Today*, vol. 8, no. 4, April 22, 1964.

19. From his poem, "Africa Speaks." Immanuel Wallerstein uses these as opening lines for his book *Africa: The Politics of Independence* (New York: Vintage, 1961).

20. Parkes, *Gods and Men: The Origins of Western Culture* (New York: Alfred A. Knopf, 1959), p. 52.

21. See his Address to the Congress of Africanists, December 12, 1962, op. cit. For a short but comprehensive account of the Nile as a question of scientific speculation, see B.W. Langlands "Concepts of the Nile," *The Uganda Journal*, Speke Centenary Number, vol. 26, no. 1, march 1962, pp. 1-22.

22. See Leakey, *the Progress and Evolution of Man in Africa* (London: Oxford University Press, 1961), p. 16.

23. See Mathew, "The East African Coast Until the Coming of the Portuguese," in Roland Oliver and Gervase Mathew (eds.), *History of East Africa*, vol. 1 (Oxford: Clarendon Press, 1963), pp. 94-95; 97-99. See also the *Periplus of the Erythrean Sea*, ed. by H. Frisk (Goteburg, 1927).

24. See the chapter by Wheeler in *the Dawn of African History*, ed. Roland Oliver (London: Oxford University Press, 1961), p. 2.

25. See Oliver's concluding chapter, *The Dawn of African History*, ibid., p. 97.

26. See also Roland Oliver and J.D. Fage, *A Short History of Africa* (Penguin, 1961), esp. chapter 8.

27. *Comparative Studies in Society and History*, vol. 5, no. 2, January 1963, pp. 232-233.

28. DeGraft-Johnson, *African Glory: The Story of Vanished Black Civilizations* (London: Watts and Company, 1954), p. 8.

29. *A Short History of the Egyptian People* (London: J.M. Dent, 1914), p. 10.

30. A.J. Arkell, "The Valley of the Nile" in *The Dawn of African History*, op. cit., p.12.

31. The ceremony was that of "shooting the nations" by firing arrows to the four points of the compass. Roland Oliver and J.D. Fage link this with the concept of divine kingship: "Egypt's eventual legacy to so much of the rest of Africa." See their book *A Short History of Africa*, op. cit., p. 37. For a different interpretation of the concept of divine kingship in Uganda see Merrick Pos-

nansky, "Kingship, Archeology and Historical Myth," *The Uganda Journal,* vol. 30, no. 1 (1966), pp. 1-12.

32. Alfred R. Tucker, *Eighteen Years in Uganda and East Africa* (London: Edward Arnold, 1908), vol. 1, 86 ff.

33. See Huntingford. "The Peopling of the Interior of East Africa by its Modern Inhabitants," *History of East Africa,* vol. 1, op. cit., pp. 88-89.

34. The situation was, of course, changed when Rome expanded more significantly westward in Europe.

35. Basil Davidson, *Old Africa Rediscovered* (London: Victor Gollancz, 1961), p. 28.

36. For a brief version of his views on this, see Cheikh Anta Diop, "The Cultural Contributions and Prospects of Africa," Proceedings of the First International Conference of Negro Writers and Artists, *Présence Africaine,* Special Issue, June-November 1956, pp. 347-354.

37. Cited by Erica Simon, "Négritude and Cultural Problems of Contemporary Africa," *Présence Africaine,* vol. 18, no. 47, Third Quarter 1963, p. 140.

38. Ibid.

39. See, for example, DuBois, *The World and Africa* (New York: International Publishers, 1965 enlarged edition).

40. See, for example, his *Races of Africa* (London: Oxford University Press, 1957 edition), pp.10-87.

41. For this brief account of Trevor-Roper's views, see *West Africa* (London), no. 2433, 18 January 1964, p. 58. See also Basil Davidson's article on the following page of the same issue.

42. See Wellesley College, *Symposium on Africa* (Wellesley, 1960), p. 37.

43. See his "Négritude and the Concept of Universal Civilization," *Présence Africaine,* vol. 18, no. 46, Second Quarter 1963, p. 12.

44. See R. R. Palmer and Joel Colton, *A History of the Modern World,* Second edition (New York: Alfred A. Knopf, 1962), p. 13.

45. Ibid.

46. See Wellesley College, *Symposium on Africa,* p. 16.

47. McNeill, *The Rise of the West* (Chicago and London: University of Chicago Press, 1963), p. 250.

48 Hodgson, "The Inter-relations of Societies in History," *Comparative Studies in Society and History*, Volume V, no. 2, January 1963, pp. 227-228.

49. Ibid., p. 228.

50.Roland Robinson and John Gallagher with Alice Denny, *Africa and the Victorians* (New York: St. Martin's Press, 1961), p. 283.

51. Ibid., p. 320.

52. D.M. Balme, "Inaugural Address to First Ordinary Convocation, 2nd December, 1950," *University College of the Gold Coast Notices, 1950-51*, no. 5. The emphasis is mine.

53. *Aristotle's Politics*, trans. Benjamin Jowett (Oxford: Clarendon Press, 1953 reprint), pp. 28-29.

54. "The Spirit of Civilization," First International Conference of Negro Writers and Artists," op. cit., p. 58.

55. Nkrumah, *I Speak of Freedom* (London: Mercury Books, 1962 edition), p. 103.

56. "Swahili in the Technical Age," *East Africa Journal*, vol. II, no. 9, February 1966, p. 6.

57. "Linguistic Problems of Contemporary Africa," *Présence Africaine*, vol. 13, no. 41, Second Quarter 1962, p. 21.

58. *They Built for the Future: A Chronicle of Makerere University College* (Cambridge University Press, 1964), p. IX.

59. *The People* (Kampala), June 13, 1964, p. 5.

60. *Ghana, The Autobiography of Kwame Nkrumah* (Edinburgh: Thomas Nelson, 1957), p. 16.

61. Ibid, p. 157.

TWELVE

ROUSSEAU AND INTELLECTUALIZED POPULISM IN AFRICA (1968)

At a state dinner marking Ghana's independence in March 1957, Kwame Nkrumah first invoked the dramatic device of asking the band to play Ghana's new national anthem. He then made his point, saying:

> ... [H]ere today the work of Rousseau, the work of Marcus Garvey, the work of Aggrey, the work of Caseley Hayford, the work of these illustrious men who have gone before us, has come to reality at this present moment.[1]

Of these figures mentioned only Rousseau was not black. Nkrumah was suggesting that a triumph of nationalism on that great day of Gold Coast liberation was a triumph for the revolutionary spirit of Rousseau as well as of the black heroes. Thomas Hodgkin has also claimed that "the spiritual ancestor" of the kind of popular nationalism that inspired movements for independence in some African countries was indeed "Jean-Jacques Rousseau."[2] The relevance of Rousseau in Africa is partly direct, partly derivative, and partly by analogy. When it is direct it is, of course, the impact of Rousseau's own ideas that we are looking at. When it is derivative we might be looking at the impact of, say, an aspect of French revolutionary tradition. When Rousseau's relevance is by analogy we are in fact asserting the meaningfulness of comparative political ideology even where no interplay of ideas between two ideological universes is immediately discernible.

Empirical populism in Africa has taken a variety of forms, ranging from messianic movements and separatist popular churches in South Africa and Zambia to general rural discontent in the Congo. What we are concerned with in this paper is not empirical populism as an outburst of activity, but intellectualized populism as a relationship of ideas. It is the populist elements of African political thought that we are here examining, rather than the behavior of, say, Alice Lenshina or Elijah Masimde as leaders of sub-intellectualized popular religious movements.

Many of the leaders of thought in Africa are also decision-makers in government. Their ideas are sometimes in danger of being underestimated simply because they are not themselves putting them into practice. An African leader may propound populist ideas and yet pursue different policies. There might indeed lie a fundamental insincerity between a man's behavior and the ideas he propounds. Yet insincerity of this kind is a moral rather than an intellectual fault. A man's ideas may have intellectual worth even if his behavior is morally dubious. Rousseau himself was the prime example of intellectual greatness combined with what was at times nothing less than moral depravity. We would like to stress here that African ideologies can have important populist components even if African policies are not always in accord with them. It is on these components, when intellectually refined, that Rousseau has a bearing.

Populism and the Individual

It is not merely with the masses that populism concerns itself. It also makes assumptions about the worth of the individual. This is not to be confused with the kind of glorification of the individual that we normally associate with liberalism. Populism tends to glorify the ordinary individual and is often a romanticization of the ordinary. This is a different frame of reference from that of the liberal ethic. The liberal ethic has not tended to value the ordinariness of an individual; it has more often tended to value his individuality. The concept of "individuality" is more intimately connected with the notion of distinctiveness than with that of ordinariness. That is one reason why that great champion of individualism, John Stuart Mill, was always fearful of the "mediocrity" of ordinary people. It was not the ordinary person that Mill wanted to protect and cultivate; it was the extraordinary one. It was often against the ordinariness of others that Mill sought to protect his intellectually exceptional citizen. In short, the paramount value for Mill was not the concrete individual. It was more the quality of individuality, with all its suggestions of uniqueness. We can, therefore, say that opposition to mediocrity is quite consistent with the liberal ethic but such an opposition cannot easily be reconciled with the values of populism.

If we now turn to Rousseau's thought, a different picture presents itself from what we get in Mill. Many of the assumptions of Rousseau's thought amount to a glorification of the ordinary. There is first his view that every individual ought to participate directly in government. To Rousseau, government by consent is a poor substitute for real self-government. The former principle allows for the possibility of being ruled by others. That is what representative government is all about. But real self-government demands direct participation by each individual in decision-making. Rousseau realizes that if you get the exceptional few and the ordinary multitudes to participate together in ascertaining the General Will, there is a danger that simplemindedness might prevail. When he idealized the ordinary people, he did not necessarily go to the extent of attributing to them an infallible collective wisdom. He found in them purity of intention rather than clarity of judgment. "Of itself the people wills always the good, but of itself it by no means always sees it."[3] Unlike Mill, Rousseau is not repelled by "collective mediocrity." For Rousseau the intellectually gullible can still be morally glorious, for "the general will is always in the right, but the judgment which guides it is not always enlightened."

In the *Discourse on the Origin of Inequality*, Rousseau has a similar theme, but here more individualized. He says: "Above all, let us not conclude, with Hobbes, that because man has no idea of goodness, he must naturally be wicked."[4] Again he insists that ignorance is not ignominy. His defense of the simpleminded sometimes attains lyrical dimensions. But it is easy to move from a romanticization of what is average to an idealization of what is below average. The cult of the ordinary moves a step further back and becomes a cult of the sub-ordinary. It is the latter concept that leads to the pedestal of the "Noble Savage." According to this new frame of reference, ultimate heroism lies not with the lower classes of civilized society—for these have already been partially corrupted. The real heroes are those who are yet untouched by the full rigors of technical and rational complexity.

This concept of the "Noble Savage" was to constitute an intellectual tradition that, for the black man, culminated in *Négritude*. It was Aimé Césaire, the West Indian poet, who eulogized his black brothers by describing them as:

> Those who have invented neither powder nor the compass;
> Those who have tamed neither gas nor electricity;
> Those who have explored neither the seas nor the skies...

Jean-Paul Sartre describes this as "a proud claim of nontechnicalness."[5] It is certainly a revelling in simplicity that echoes aspects of Rousseau's romantic primitivism. In both *Négritude* and Rousseau's primitivism one characteristic particularly stands out: it is a pervasive distrust of rationality and a faith in emotive sensibilities. The great exponent of *Négritude* in Africa itself was Léopold Senghor of Sénégal. He contrasts *Négritude* with Cartesian coldness in the following terms:

> "I think therefore I am," wrote Descartes, the European *par excellence*. The African might say, "I smell, I dance... I am."

Senghor goes on to assert: "It is this gift of emotion which explains Négritude."[6] To some extent this return to the emotions is a quest for authenticity and such a quest amounts to a rebellion against imitation. Rousseau rejected the eighteenth-century theory of aesthetics in which imitation was the real purpose of art. He substituted for it the view that the act of creation was not to copy but to fill the art form with an emotional and passionate content. To create then becomes an act of emotional liberation.

Sartre traces the issue of Black authenticity to the very basis of prejudice against Blacks. Prejudice against Jews can be cultural or religious. And culture and religion are artificial to the extent of being the outgrowth of man-made institutions in historical perspective. But prejudice against "Blackness" is a prejudice against bare nature itself. In Sartre's words:

> A Jew, white among white men, can deny that he is a Jew, can declare himself a man among men. The Black cannot deny that he is a Black nor claim for himself this abstract uncolored humanity. He is Black. Thus he is held to authenticity.[7]

Prejudice against Blacks is, therefore, based on one of

their indissoluble bonds with nature. It is sometimes argued by white liberals that color should not matter as it is "only skin-deep." Black is a characteristic of the African's appearance, and appearance is equated with superficiality. But the African's appearance is not a superficial irrelevance; it is part of his essential authenticity. If there must be prejudice, let it by all means be based on the essential uniqueness of the black individual, his "Blackness."

This romanticization of what is natural is also what leads to a glorification of intuition over reflection, emotion over rationality. Senghor never approaches Rousseau's denunciation of the thinking man as "a depraved animal."[8] But he does share Rousseau's conviction that "the human understanding is greatly indebted to the passions."[9] And it is the African rather than his white conqueror that had the good sense to permit the human passions to yield their maximum wisdom. Thus the central feature of the cultural values of Africans is what Senghor calls "their *emotive attitude* towards the world."[10]

And yet there is a danger in romanticizing simple emotions too much, if one is at the same time eager to demonstrate the essential ordinariness of the African. *Négritude* is apt to drift into an exaggerated portrayal of traditional pre-colonial Africa as a Garden of Eden. Perhaps this is part of a larger African phenomenon. There are occasions when African nationalism itself rebels against the myth of eternal innocence. To be inherently innocent is to cease to be ordinary. Nationalists like Julius Nyerere of Tanzania have been known to protest in terms like these:

> It would be absurd to imply that... pre-colonial Africa was an ideal place in which the "noble savage" of Rousseau lived his idyllic existence. The members of this social unit were no more "noble" than other human beings...[11]

Ezekiel Mphahlele, the South African writer, is more specifically rebellious against the pristine assumptions of *Négritude*. At a conference in Dakar, Mphahlele once exploded into saying:

> I do not accept ... the way in which too much of the poetry inspired by Négritude romanticizes Africa—as a symbol of innocence, purity and artless primitiveness. I feel insulted when some people imply that Africa is not also a violent Continent. I am a violent person, and proud of it because it is often a healthy state of mind.[12]

In Mphahlele, the cult of African ordinariness therefore triumphs over the myth of African innocence. As an inspiration for populist enthusiasm either the myth of innocence or the cult of ordinariness could be effective. Indeed, in Rousseau and in African nationalistic thought the two concepts are often difficult to disentangle. Yet they can be logically contradictory and still not lose their inspirational functionality.

Populism and Society

For analytical purposes, it is possible to argue that the myth of innocence is an exclusive feature of the nationalistic component of African thought, while the cult of ordinariness retains crucial relevance for problems of resource allocation and quest for a classless society after independence. All African political leaders are self-consciously engaged in the activity of nation-building. In broad terms, this activity expresses itself in the search for the appropriate institutional arrangements, the appropriate economic structure, and the appropriate emotional involvement by the masses. The cult of ordinariness now interacts with other aspects reminiscent of Rousseau. It interacts with an ethos of anti-pluralism and a desire for mass participation in national affairs.

The supremacy of the General Will in Rousseau is a denial of the validity of pluralistic interests. The wills of competing interest groups can only encumber the discovery of the composite will. This thesis is one that, in various ways, has been embraced by a number of African leaders. Before independence, the idea of a General Will was translated into a concept of popular sovereignty to be embodied in a united movement against colonial rule. As Thomas Hodgkin pointed out once, a congress-type political party in the colonies was apt to claim that it embodied the national will and represented "all the people." According to Hodgkin, the party's "dominant concept is 'popular sovereignty,' and its spiritual ancestor is Jean-Jacques Rousseau."[13]

After independence the idea of "popular sovereignty" has sometimes been even more insistently argued. Immanuel Wallerstein has argued that the political ideology of Sekou Touré's political party, *Parti Démocratique de Guinée* (PDG), has been a combination of Hobbes, Rousseau, and Lenin. Wallerstein himself tends to think that there is more of Hobbes than of Rousseau in the intellectualized ethos of the PDG. But he does concede there is much in the tone of Guinean ideology that favors a community of sentiment and a reverence for citizenship similar to Rousseau's.[14]

The anti-pluralistic implications of the General Will take the form of an opposition both to "tribalism" and to the formation of competing social classes. Here again the myth of a previous age of innocence is often invoked. Certain social characteristics of the past, notably communalism and cooperation, are mobilized to strengthen a new anti-pluralistic ethos. In using certain aspects of the past as building blocks for the future, African thinkers are perhaps departing radically from one aspect of Rousseau's thought in the *Social Contract*. The new social order created by the contract was supposed to be an autonomous entity, rather than a stage in a process of evolution going back to the age of innocence. What Rousseau's social contract created was a communal entity with no historical antecedents, but having instead an absolute validity of its own from the moment of its creation.

In a sense, the achievement of the African version of anti-pluralism is to bridge the gulf between two otherwise contradictory aspects of Rousseau's thought. The age of primitive innocence is, in some of its aspects, converted by Africans into a model for the new form of popular order. The new order should avoid conditions for class conflict. For its inspiration it should look to the essential "classlessness" of African traditional arrangements. Intellectualized African populism is, in this way, apt to go on denying the previous existence of classes in Africa. But if the existence of classes is ever admitted, then "historically" it is regarded to have no attribution of social distance and no accompanying feeling of social deprivation or social injustice. In the African version of anti-pluralism drawn from the past to glorify community and cooperation, it does so at the expense of ignoring a clear lack of trans-tribal cooperation in the traditional model. Though wedded to the ideal of authenticity, African leaders are now obliged to invoke an artificial identification of interests in the hope of raising enthusiasm and transcending ethnic differences.

Here again the cult of ordinariness comes into play. This cult now becomes a weapon against social pluralism. To glorify ordinariness is to assert a form of egalitarianism. And the latter in turn is a commitment against the growth of privileged groups in conflict with each other and with the underprivileged. In practice, the new political class in most African countries is itself creating a mode of living often marked by a certain amount of affluence, and probably out of gear with the national ideology that the leaders themselves are propagating. The leaders themselves are a living and agonizing example of the problem of reconciling personalism with patriotism, the will of the individual with the General Will. But the cult of ordinariness can sometimes ease the process of reconciliation by encouraging demonstrative identification. And so, President Nyerere digs with the people. The leaders of Tanzania assert their ordinariness by the ritual of using a shovel or pushing a wheelbarrow. Indeed, the presidential shovel becomes one more symbol of a general ethos of anti-pluralism. Rousseau's concept of popular sovereignty becomes wedded to the Marxist concept of proletarian solidarity.

From this position there is an easy transition to the ethic of mass involvement, which also has antecedents in Rousseau: no political system is legitimate unless it rests on the active participation of all its citizens. This in turn involves the suppression of selfish impulses and the emergence of the secular reign of the common good. Out of a personal maladjustment is therefore supposed to spring a moral activism, marked by a rejection of hedonism. And so the Arusha Declaration of the Tanzania African National Union demands hard work and self-reliance from all citizens in a shared involvement in nation-building.[15] To some extent this is a departure from Rousseau. According to the ideology of the PDG in Guinea and of TANU in Tanzania, the route to personal and national regeneration is explicitly through sacrifice and hard work. Yet under Rousseau's scheme there appears to be no incompatibility between moral activism and physical laziness.[16] Nevertheless, Rousseau's notion of individual participation in fulfilling the General Will does have logical connections with those Africans policies that put a premium on mass involvement in nation-building.

Is this the path by which the masses become virtuous? To be virtuous in the eighteenth-century sense did not require the accidental influence of climate or geography. The total involvement of the masses in an appropriate political structure provided both a path to virtue and an escape from a pre-moral society. But in contemporary Africa, mass involvement in "human investment" or in "self-help" schemes is regarded as a return to an older moral order. As Nyerere once put it:

In traditional African society everybody was a worker [...] as opposed to "loiterer" or "idler" [...] it was taken for granted that every member of society—barring only the children and the infirm—contributed his fair share of effort towards the production of its wealth. [...] A society which fails to give its individuals the means to work, or, having given them the means to work, prevents them from getting a fair share of the products of their own sweat and toil, needs putting right. Similarly, an individual who can work—and is provided by society with the means to work—but does not do so, is equally wrong.[17]

Thus an intricate interplay between the cult of ordinariness, the ethos of anti-pluralism, and the ethic of mass involvement has in this case led to the emergence of ideological toil. For a country like Tanzania this is one more step away from the colonial legacy. There had been something rather unfeeling about the "Law and Order" administrative ethos of the colonial period. The whole apparatus of this colonial legacy came to be something of an impediment to the emotional engagement of the people at large. The political neutrality of the civil service—supposedly linked to the notion of a two-party or multiparty system—had all the coldness of bureaucratic rationality. Further, the political neutrality of the civil service was inconsistent both with the ethos of anti-pluralism and with the ethic of mass involvement. In the words of Nyerere again:

Once you begin to think in terms of a single national movement instead of a number of rival factional parties, it becomes absurd to exclude a whole group of the most intelligent and able members of the community from participation in the discussion of policy simply because they happen to be civil servants. In a political movement which is identified with the nation, participation in political affairs must be recognised as the right of every citizen, in no matter what capacity he may have chosen to serve his country.[18]

And to this wisdom Rousseau might perhaps give a nod of approval.

Populism and International Relations

It is not merely domestic policy that is affected by populist notions. Recent events would seem to indicate a growing impact on some ideological postulates of international relations also. It is to this phenomenon that we must now turn. Early in 1965, Léopold Senghor had occasion to say:

> For my part, I think Afro-Asianism has been superseded, for this form of solidarity should be extended to Latin America and to *tiers monde* in general.[19]

A few months later, an unusual conference took place in Havana. Cuba was host to an Asian-African-Latin American conference of solidarity sponsored by the Afro-Asian People's Solidarity Organization. The conference went on from January 5 to 15, 1966. The outcome was the creation of a Tricontinental People's Solidarity Organization, with an executive committee provisionally seated in Havana. The Havana conference was primarily of leftist radicals. The United Nations Conference on Trade and Development in Geneva had preceded it, in the spring of 1964. At Geneva, Africa, Asia, and Latin America had confronted the developed countries of the world and demanded a transformation of the international trade system in the direction of better terms for producers of primary products and more concern for the needs of the underdeveloped world at large.²⁰ The whole concept of the Third World perhaps signifies the emergence of a new form of populism: global populism. Both the Havana conference of radical leftists and the Geneva conference of governmental representatives of all ideological persuasions are symptoms of a new movement just emerging. It is perhaps the bare beginning of global protest of the indigent against the affluence of the developed world.

For African intellectuals, the concept of the Third World is an attempt to transcend their old nationalistic bonds of color and emphasize instead the bonds of shared poverty. Perhaps that is what Senghor meant by "Afro-Asianism has been superseded, for this form of solidarity should be extended to Latin America and to *tiers monde* in general." Global populism as conceived in Africa is particularly drawn towards using Marxian tools of analysis. Nyerere, for example, used them in the following way:

> Karl Marx felt there was an inevitable clash between the rich of one society and the poor of that society. In that, I believe, Karl Marx was right. But today it is the international scene which is going to have a greater impact on the lives of individuals... And when you look at the international scene, you must admit that the world is divided between the "Haves" and the "Have-nots"... And don't forget the rich countries of the world today may be found on both sides of the division between "Capitalist" and "Socialist" countries.²¹

If we accept this analysis, the Soviet Union would itself be a bourgeois country, being a member of the middle and upper classes of the global society. But within this global society, there is no global state that Africa, Asia, and Latin America could capture in their global proletarian revolution against the rich. The Africans and Asians on their own may have captured the votes in the United Nations General Assembly but that is an instrument which is hardly strong enough to "oppress" the rich countries. Indeed, the United Nations would almost certainly collapse tomorrow if American support were withdrawn. The utopia of this international class system cannot therefore be the "withering away" of a global state already existing. At its most ambitious it can only be the creation of a world state or world government. For the time being there is no world state to "wither away" and perhaps a world government is not possible either. What can be conceived is at best an equitable global authority that would "administer things," even if it would never "govern men."

Of this whole line of reasoning, however, Rousseau would be suspicious. The idea of a world government tends to be a brainchild of what Rousseau called "cosmopolitans." And it is these people whom Rousseau accused of trying to "justify their love of their country by their love of the human race and make a boast of loving all the world in order to enjoy the privilege of loving no one."[22] For Rousseau, the *patrie* or fatherland is the widest loyalty that the human heart can authentically be capable of. But now a few African intellectuals were going beyond the bonds of nationality, or even of Blackness. Indeed, the concept of the Third World signifies a shift of emphasis from pan-pigmentationalism, or the affinity of color, to pan-proletarianism, the affinity of being economically underprivileged. Mamadou Dia, the former Prime Minister of Sénégal, called the first section of his book "The Revolt of the Proletarian Nations." He quoted Gabriel Ardant's powerful line that "the geography of hunger is also the geography of death."[23] Sekou Touré describes Africa itself as a "continent of the proletarian peoples."[24] This view of Touré's is different from the view that sees Africa as a "classless continent." A "proletarian Africa" is, after all, a class in itself, one class within a global class system.

African populism then, in its global dimension, owes

much more to Marx than to Rousseau. Yet the distinction might not perhaps be all that rigid. To save the ancient age of innocence Rousseau had wished someone had cried out to his fellow men: "... you are undone if you once forget that the fruits of the earth belong to us all, and the earth itself to nobody."[25] The movement of pan-proletarianism as captured in the concept of "the Third World" is perhaps a new version of that cry which alas was never uttered to save Rousseau's age of innocence. Global populism is a new form of anti-pluralism. "It is one of the most important functions of government to prevent extreme inequality of fortunes," Rousseau had asserted.[26] The mitigation of inequalities is a mitigation of antagonistic pluralism. This is as true internationally as it is true intra-nationally. In the ultimate analysis then, populism at the international level is a dream that seeks to globalize the General Will and turn it from being the will of society to being the will of man.

NOTES

This chapter is a revised version of an article co-written with G. F. Engholm that originally appeared in *The Review of Politics* (Notre Dame, USA), Vol. 30, N⁰ 1, January 1968, pp. 19-32.

1. K. Nkrumah, *I speak of Freedom* (London, 1961), p. 107. Marcus Garvey was, of course, the Jamaican who fired the imagination of American Blacks and started a "Back to Africa" movement in the United States in the beginning of the twentieth century. Aggrey was a Ghanian philosopher, and Casley Hayford, a barrister, was one of the founding fathers of Gold Coast nationalism.

2. T. Hodgkin, *Nationalism in Colonial Africa* (London, 1962 reprint), p. 144.

3. This rendering is from the Everyman's edition of *The Social Contract and Other Essays* with an introduction by G. D. H. Cole (London, 1955 reprint), p. 31.

4. *A Discourse on the Origin of Inequality*, in *The Social Contract and Other Essays*, op. cit., p. 181.

5. Jean-Paul Sartre, *Black Orpheus*, trans. S. A. Allen, (Paris, n.d.), pp. 42-43.

6. *De la Négritude, Psychologie du Négro-Africain* (1962). The above rendering in English is from *L. Senghor, Prose and Poetry*, trans. John Reed and Clive Weke (London: Oxford University Press, 1965), pp. 32, 35.

7. Jean-Paul Sartre, *Black Orpheus*, p. 15.

8. J. J. Rousseau, *A Discourse on the Origin of Inequality*, op. cit., p. 161.

9. Ibid., p. 171.

10. *L. Senghor, Prose and Poetry*, p. 35. The emphasis is original.

11. See *J. Nyerere, Freedom and Unity: A Selection from Writings and Speeches, 1952-1965* (Dar-es-Salaam, 1966), p. 12.

12. "Négritude and Its Enemies: A Reply," *African Literature and the Universities*, ed. Gerald Moore (Ibadan, 1965), p. 23.

13. T. Hodgkin, *Nationalism in Colonial Africa,* op. cit., p. 144.

14. I. Wallerstein, "The Political Ideology of the P. D. G.," *Présence Africaine*, Vol. 12, N° 40, First Quarter 1962, pp. 38-39.

15. *The Arusha Declaration and TANU's Policy on Socialism and Self Reliance* (Dar-es-Salaam: Publicity Sections TANU, 1967).

16. In *A Discourse on the Origin of Inequality* Rousseau satirizes the excessive preoccupation with "work" which civilized society tends to promote. He mentions that in the Northern temperate countries this work mania is aggravated by climate.

17. J. Nyerere, *Ujamaa: The Basis of African Socialism* (1962). Reprinted in the collection of Nyerere's works entitled *Freedom and Unity* (Dar es Salaam: Oxford University Press, 1966), pp. 165-166.

18. "Democracy and the Party System" (1963) in *Freedom and Unity*, op. cit., p. 203.

19. See *Africa Diary*, June 19-25, 1965.

20. See Ali A. Mazrui, "Africa and the Third World," *On Heroes and Uhuru-Worship: Essays on Independent Africa* (London, 1962), pp. 209-210.

21. "The Second Scramble" (1961). For a later version of the same theme, see *Freedom and Unity*, pp. 207-208.

22. J. J. Rousseau, *Contrat Social* (First Version). See C. E. Vaughan, *The Political Writings of J. J. Rousseau* (Cambridge, 1915), Vol. I, p. 453.

23. See M. Dia, *The African Nations and World Solidarity*, trans. Mercer Cook (London, 1962). Ardant is quoted on p. 19. See also Mazrui, "Africa and the Third World," op. cit., p. 211.

24. See S. Touré, "Africa's Destiny," *Africa Speaks*, edited by James Duffy and Robert A. Manners (Princeton, 1961).

25. J. J. Rousseau, *A Discourse on the Origin of Inequality*, p. 192.

26. Ibid., p. 250.

THIRTEEN

EDMUND BURKE AND REFLECTIONS ON THE REVOLUTION IN THE CONGO (1963)

There are at least five ways of treating a political theory. One is to consider it a form of intellectual exercise, pure and simple, an adventure in abstraction to sharpen the mind. Another is to go through it, and through other theories, seeking a personal practical philosophy for oneself. A third is to distill the history out of a political theory, examining what light the theory can throw on the age from which it emerged. A fourth is also to treat the theory as a source of historical data, but not in the sense in which a river may conceivably be a source of some dissolved substance from the silt it carries, but in the sense in which a river may be a source of water. In this latter sense, a political theory is not distilled to yield history; it is itself part of the flow of history—part of what Americans sometimes call "intellectual history." A fifth way may involve tearing the theory out of its historical context altogether, and bringing the logic of all or some of its ideas to bear on a specific situation in perhaps one's own time. The object of such an exercise would be to determine whether the ideas scattered within the theory help in the understanding of the situation, on the one hand, and on the other, whether the situation can lend a new depth to the theory or perhaps expose an old shallowness within it.

For those who are called upon to teach European political theory to students outside Europe, this last approach may often be particularly profitable. The "Europeanism" of the theory is thus played down as the ideas are pulled out of their temporal and geographical context and analysed for what they may have to say about some situation in, say, Asia or Africa at the present time. One non-European situation with which many European ideas on the nature of society could be mated as an experiment in conceptual cross-breeding is, no doubt, the Congo situation. Indeed, the situation has all the signs of great virility, and if the European ideas are fertile, there may well be interesting results. If, for example, the Congo is mated with Hobbes' arguments on the need for a strong government, a vindication may be produced if nothing more. The Congolese nationalists demanded self-government and they got it. But they then found that the logical extreme of self-government meant too much "self" and not enough "government." If one cannot hear the voice of Hobbes saying: "I told you so," one can at least hear the voice of Tom Stacey of the *Sunday Times* suggesting that the withdrawal of Belgian rule deprived the Congolese of "the mental comfort of being dominated."[1] But what would Burke's reaction have been? He admonished the French for choosing to "act as if you had never been moulded into civil society and had everything to start anew."[2] He was reprimanding them for letting their behaviour tell a lie. It was a lie that the French had not been moulded into civil society and the French told that lie not by a verbal declaration, but worse, by attempting to destroy the truth. But could Burke have admonished the Congolese in the same vein? Were they telling a lie when they acted as if they had "never been moulded into civil society and had everything to start anew"?

This is where it is important to remember that so much of Burke's philosophy presupposes a long-established nation. In popular usage today it is normal to speak of the "new nations" of Africa and Asia. To Burke a "new nation" would be virtually a contradiction in terms "because a nation is… an idea of continuity, which extends in time as well as in numbers and in space."[3] It is a moral essence, not a geographical arrangement. Many who would find a "moral essence" unclear would at least agree that a nation is more than "a geographical arrangement." Dankwart A. Rustow, for example, once defined a nation as "a population inhabiting a given territory and willing to subordinate all other purposes to the common aims."[4] It has been suggested that under such a definition very few of those within the United Nations are, in effect, "nations" at all, let alone "united." Their populations had yet to develop a willingness to subordinate particular interests to some over-riding common aims. Among such populations many would include the great majority of the African member-states of that world organization. But what then do we mean by Congolese nationalism or African nationalism? Has the definition of a "nation" become entirely irrelevant to the definition of "nationalism"? Has the term "nationalism," in other words, won its independence from the term "nation"? Perhaps it has and all that nationalism now means is: "kick the foreign ruler out and let us rule ourselves." But the question arises: what is a foreign ruler? If the answer is something like "a ruler who belongs to a people different from the people he rules," then we have now shifted the problem from trying to determine what a "nation" is to attempting to grasp what a "people" is. On this, Burke maintains:

> In a state of rude nature there is no such thing as a people. A number of men in themselves have no collective capacity. The idea of a people is the idea of a corporation. It is wholly artificial; and made, like all other fictions, by common agreement.[5]

For the populations that Burke was concerned with, this common agreement was supposed to be of long standing, each population thereby developing into an organized group, with similar prejudices and similar loyalties, and with a capacity to see themselves collectively as a cohesive, really personal "we." In the case of the Congo, the population had yet to convert itself into "a people" by virtue of what Burke considered to be the crucial transforming element of "common agreement" among its members, or what modern sociologists may call "consensus." It thus made sense for Joseph Ileo, then Prime Minister under the Kasavubu regime, to observe in February 1961:

> The Congo is not a people; it is a collection of large ethnic groups and each of them is a people.[6]

And yet in the same month, though in another context, the same Joseph Ileo was telling representatives of these "peoples" of the Congo: "the Congo is a homogeneous entity."[7] Why did he imagine that this kind of language could in any sense be meaningful to an audience which collectively, on his own addition, did not constitute "a people"?

This is where we come to one dilemma of present-day Africa. Burke's insistence that a "people" is a people by "common agreement" has indeed been met, but in a manner that was certainly not the one he had in mind. In this sense, the Congolese were transformed into a people by a "common agreement" several decades ago, only that agreement was not between Congolese but between European powers out to settle their own rivalries in their scramble for the continent as a whole. If Katanga, for example, had fallen to the British in that scramble, we could today think of Katangese as perhaps Zambians instead of as Congolese. If the Portuguese had realised their dreams, then the Katangese may well have been Angolans today. Indeed, Katanga nearly fell to the French and if it had, our image of them today might have been as perhaps a section of another "people."

Are we then to say that a "common agreement" among Europeans some time ago was really enough to convert any African population into a "people"? Is a native of Brazzaville in former French Congo really a foreigner in Kinshasa? In other words, is the man from across the border a foreigner, even if that border was drawn up by other foreigners, when they scrambled for Africa several generations ago? What if the man from across the border belonged to the same ethnic group of the Bakongo as the man on this side of it? As for the foreign ruler, must he have come from across the seas in order to be really foreign? Must he be distinguishable by the color of his skin? Or is it enough that he comes from another ethnic group even if that group is represented on some map or atlas as part of the share of King Leopold of the Belgians in a "common agreement" among Europeans three generations ago? What all this means is that in the Congo, as in so much of the rest of Africa, Burke's notion that a people is a people by common agreement has posed the question: "agreement between whom?" Africa is landed with the consequences of the common agreement of others.

Of course, all would be well if the consequences of that external agreement could be reversed on the withdrawal of European rule. Unfortunately for the argument, that is not so easy. And it is not easy substantially because among the most ardent converts to European fictitious creations are none other than the African nationalists themselves. At least insofar as he sought to preserve the frontiers of the Congo, Patrice Lumumba, for example, was a complete and devout convert to the European fiction of "one Congo." In a sense, his tragic career was one hectic attempt to put some Congolese substance into this European fiction. If, in pursuit of that end, secessionist Tshombe of Katanga was not cooperative, then Tshombe had to be compelled. In other words, if at this late stage the Congo could only become a people by the agreement of the Congolese themselves, and if such an agreement was not forthcoming voluntarily, then it had to be exacted by force—as federal Nigeria had exacted it from secessionist Biafra. And if there were logical contradictions within the notion of "enforced common agreement," then so much the worse for logic!

And yet the Luba tribesman, for example, may well ask: "who was that King Leopold anyhow—foreigner that he was—to determine for now and for all time which man I, a Luba, shall consider a foreigner like him and which other man I shall accept as 'my fellow countryman' from among 'my own people'? The so-called nationalists call me a tribalist and anti-African, if I refuse to bow to some line drawn up by a conference in Berlin by white foreigners many, many moons ago. They call me a stooge of the whites because I refuse to recognise a map drawn up by the whites or to accept concepts imported by the whites. Actually, the trouble with me is that I am anti-foreign-rule, be it white or black, be it the foreigner Leopold or Lumumba (or Tshombe, for that matter). As a Muluba tribesman I am all for self-government—government of the Baluba, by the Baluba, for the Baluba." This argument by the hypothetical Luba tribesman may sound artificial. Why would it be considered artificial if, at the same time, it is a rebellion against the artificiality of the frontiers drawn up by European colonial powers? "Government by the Baluba": isn't that the most meaningful expression of "government by the people," if we accept Burke's insistence on "common agreement" as a defining characteristic of a "people" and if we specify that it must be agreement from within? If we accept that, we may then proceed to ask whether the trouble with the European agreement from without was not the fact that it was not accompanied by vigorous attempts to create the necessary conditions for ultimate agreement from within. In the Congo, for example, the effect, if not necessarily the intention, of Belgian policy was the development of tribal governments based on district councils, with ethnic loyalties fostered.[8] This was by no means the most effective way of creating consensus for the ultimate conversion of the Congolese into one people by a criterion over and above a settlement in Berlin.

Indeed, Belgian preference when independence finally came was, in fact, for a centralised unitary government—again, by no means the most logical culmination of the policy they had pursued up to independence. As for the parliamentary system by which the Congolese could realise "government by the people," it was something just added at the end of their rule, bearing little relationship to the Congolese ethnic realities that the Belgians themselves had helped to perpetuate. And so, there was Lumumba trying to uphold an unrealistic constitution passed to him by the departing Belgians. And perhaps, there behind him was the voice of Burke lamenting:

> When I hear of the simplicity of contrivance aimed at and boasted of in any new constitutions, I am at no loss to decide that the artificers are grossly ignorant of their trade or totally negligent of their duty.[9]

Yet the trouble with the Belgians may well have been that they were too Burkean. With some intervals, they kept on reverting back to the policy of recognising, if not really respecting, the traditions of individual groups in the Congo, with all the ethnic loyalties inherent in those traditions.

In British "Indirect Rule" policy, this ambivalence was even more clearly manifest. On the one hand, there was a calculated neo-Burkean reluctance to radically suppress the ways and customs of their dependent peoples; and on the other, a calculated policy (at least in recent decades) to "prepare" those peoples for parliamentary government. How that preparation could exclude revision of major areas of such old traditions as, say, the powers of chiefs was something that does not seem to have been worked out. Perhaps there is a case for this policy that Britain pursued. Perhaps there is a case for the Belgian policy, at least to the extent that, consciously or unconsciously, the policy has left the ultimate reconciliation between old folkways on the one hand and new forms of government on the other to the domestic forces in those countries themselves after independence.

Open to African reformers after independence are at least three ways for disentangling the contradictions of colonial policies. Unfortunately for Burke, each of these ways involves some kind of revolution. One way is to revise radically the form of government inherited from colonialism and try to make it more consistent with the realities of the traditions of the country. Another is to stamp out ruthlessly those traditional ways themselves that are inconsistent with the Western concepts and values implied in the new governmental system. A third is to combine the other two. Is Burke at all helpful to us in the attempt to see which of the three is the best way of going about it? His guiding principle was: "it is a presumption in favour of any settled scheme of government against any untried project that a nation has long existed and flourished under it."[10] In a situation like that of the Congo after independence, Burke's choice between "a settled scheme of government" and an "untried project" is not open to him. What is open to him is a tried project (a unitary system) which has not proved "settled" and an untried project (looser, federal structure) which may or may not be more settled.

Shifting the analysis to the time before independence was granted, the nature of the choice becomes more akin to what Burke had in mind. The question then arises as to how sympathetic he would have been to the demands for independence. Perhaps a clue may lie in the following observation of his:

> A brave people will certainly prefer a liberty accompanied with a virtuous poverty to a depraved and wealthy servitude. But before the price of

comfort and opulence is paid one ought to be pretty sure it is real liberty which is purchased, and she is to be purchased at no other price. I shall always, however, consider that liberty as very equivocal which has not wisdom and justice for her companions and does not lead prosperity and plenty in her train.[11]

The Congolese "liberty" which has followed the withdrawal of the Belgians is of a type which Burke would most definitely regard as "equivocal" for it is a liberty which does not seem to have had wisdom and justice for her companions and has certainly not led prosperity and plenty in her train. In modern terminology, Burke would then have concluded that the Congolese were "unfit" to govern themselves. Certainly in his thought the capacity to be "wise" is one criterion of capacity to govern. He says so specifically in the observation that "there is no qualification for government but virtue and wisdom, actual or presumptive."[12] And to ensure that this qualification is met, he would insist that "the road to eminence and power, from obscure condition, ought not to be made too easy"[13]—not easy enough, at any rate, for any postal clerk like Patrice Lumumba to take over.

This snobbish argument may fit a situation where the choice is, in fact, between clerks and long-established princes. But what happens in a situation like that of pre-independence Congo when the choice was between governors from thousands of miles away and governors from within the territorial frontiers? Perhaps here it would be relevant to recall that one of the arguments actually used against Congolese independence was that it could lead to "inter-tribal strife." Such an argument presupposed that a tribe which would submit to white foreigners from far away would not find the humility to submit to a fellow black man from the next ethnic group and that there were latent inter-ethnic passions which could only be restricted by a power from outside. In this respect what Burke said of mankind at large is better substantiated in the context of such rival factions of mankind as "tribes." To Burke, among our needs as human beings is what he calls "a sufficient restraint upon the passions of men." He argues that:

> This can only be done *by a power out of themselves* and not, in the exercise of its function, subject to... those passions which it is its office to subdue.[14]

He emphasizes this notion of "a power out of themselves." In the case of the French at the time of the French Revolution, it was hard to portray the French nobility as a power out of the French nation. In the case of the ethnic diversity of the Congo, the Belgians were more manifestly distinct from those whose passions they were to restrain. It was all very well for the Congolese nationalists to demand "liberty." But to Burke "the restraints on men, as well as their liberties, are to be reckoned among their rights."[15]

How relevant, however, was all this to whether Belgian rule was to continue or not? *The Economist* (London), in an article in December 1960, made the remark that in Rhodesia "fitness or unfitness to govern is ceasing to be relevant." The line of argument involved was that the forces of nationalism in so many parts of Africa, coupled with the Cold War and its ideological competition, had reached a stage when it was no longer true to say of Africa: "to be independent or not to be independent: that is the question." That was simply not the question any longer. One could almost say that *The Economist* would recognize the forces of nationalism in Africa as among those of which Burke might say that "they who persist in opposing this mighty current in human affairs will appear rather to resist the decrees of Providence than the mere designs of men." Given that, it was pointless to argue which was to be given priority: the Congolese right to their liberty or the Congolese right to a restraint on their passions. This, in essence, was *The Economist's* point about fitness or unfitness to govern becoming no longer relevant. And yet it is profitable to glance at the rejoinder to this. A white Kenya reader of *The Economist* protested in a letter that "the lesson of the Congo" was "surely exactly the opposite." And then he clinched this protest with the rhetorical question: "is fitness or unfitness to enunciate no longer relevant on the London stage?"[16] The reader intended no light-hearted witticism about politicians generally. Capacity for self-government to him was to be viewed from the same angle as talent for the stage: if it is lacking in one person then someone else must take the part.

In order to relate this to Burke's thought, it may be profitable first to examine this "must" in "someone else must take the part." Very often the "must" is presented as if it was a species of the logical "must." Thus many arguments in favour of colonial rule seem to take it for granted that all one has to do to prove that colonial rule is justified in a particular territory is to prove that the territory is incapable of governing itself. What is often overlooked is that there is a logical jump from the premise that such a territory cannot govern itself to the conclusion that others must "therefore" govern it. Nothing, of course, in the premise really entails the conclusion. If we assumed that "incapacity for self-government" was a factual and descriptive rather than a normative concept, then the whole argument becomes a simple case of the fallacy of deriving an ethical judgment ("ought to be ruled by others") from a non-ethical premise ("incapable of self-government"). If, however, even the premise itself is, at least indirectly, an ethical standpoint (as for those who would equate capacity for self-government with some particular norm of "legitimate" political institutions) then the conclusion could be logically derived but at the expense of having the premise or premises now divorced from the sanction of logic. These become a moral standpoint and leave the door open for a conflict with other standpoints without a common criterion to resolve the conflict. As Lord Milverton is reported to have put it:

> ... when we talk of the premature grant of self-government, the adjective presupposes a point of view which is not admitted by Africans.[17]

There is room for not admitting it because the choice is not one of "either you are capable of governing yourselves or you must be governed by others." There is at least one more possible alternative-expressed in the nationalist's stand: "we have a right to misgovern ourselves" if need be. The right to self-government is here extended then to the right to self-misgovernment.[18]

It is very difficult to see how Burke could accept this. If the Congolese insisted that even self-misgovernment was free government, Burke could indeed concede them that. He may even say to the Congolese as he said to the Sheriffs of Bristol:

> If any man ask me what a free government is, I answer that, for any practical purpose, it is what the people think so, and that they, and not I, are the natural, lawful and competent judges of the matter.[19]

But even after conceding that the Congolese were a people, and that their "self-misgovernment" was at least free government, it would still be open to Burke to say: "All the same, you should not have free government if it amounts to self-misgovernment." Freedom to Burke was not an ultimate value and was not something for which any price may be paid with justification. Men have other rights apart from the right to be free, and they have no right to sacrifice too many of those rights for the sake of only one of them. But what if the demands for independence were a current let loose by the decrees of Providence? Burke then would not blame the Belgians for giving in to them, though he may still have a grievance against the Congolese "nationalists" for being the instruments of an unhappy providential decree.

Now that the decree has had its way, what solutions could Burke offer as to what kind of constitution the Congolese should have? The constitution which Burke would choose is a constitution in which choice is, in fact, irrelevant: "a constitution made by what is ten thousand times better than choice; it is made by peculiar circumstances, occasions, tempers, dispositions and moral, civil, and social habitudes of the people, which disclose themselves only in a long space of time."[20] The Congo has not had the requisite space of time in which to disclose such a constitution. But, paradoxically, it would still be open to Burke to advise: "never entirely nor at once depart from antiquity."[21] The Congo as one unit may not have an antiquity but the Congolese within their respective ethnic groups have. It is with this antiquity—perhaps these antiquities—that compromises have to be made. And by this argument, the mistake that Lumumba made was in his total opposition to the localised traditional loyalties of individual regions and tribes. What was taken for granted by Lumumba, as perhaps a representative African "nationalist," was that tribalism (or regionalism) militated against the effort to build one nation. A love for one's ethnic group and a love for one's country were, it was implied, forces that were in opposition one against the other. Indeed, it seems to be taken completely for granted by many today that ethnic loyalty and a love for the country are mutually exclusive. To this hypothesis Burke would retort that:

> To be attached to the sub-division; to love the little platoon we belong to in society is the first principle (the germ as it were) of public affections. It is the first link in the series by which we proceed

toward a love to our country and to mankind.[22]

By this argument, ethnic loyalty, far from being destructive of love for the country, is the very basis on which patriotism should be built. In war, for example, by all means ask the soldier to think of his country. But his patriotism is the greater if you ask him also to think of his family. His love for his own family is, in practice, not destroyed to make him more patriotic; it is used to give patriotism more meaning to his innermost emotional responses. And within the army itself, what Burke calls the attachment to the subdivision is cultivated, not to keep sub-division from sub-division and lead the army to disintegration, but to strengthen the ties between sub-divisions and give meaning to the war effort as a whole. If this be the reasoning behind Burke's observation, then it bears a striking similarity to some of President Kasavubu's assumptions, particularly soon after the Congo's independence. In his speech to the General Assembly in November 1960, when he spoke as President of an independent Congo, he noted how, in taking oath as head of the state, he had undertaken to "safeguard the unity of the Congolese people." After the Tananarive Conference in March 1961 it became tempting to conclude that his acceptance of the confederal demands of Tshombe, for example, amounted to a betrayal of his oath on Congolese unity. And yet, in justice to Kasavubu, it must be admitted that he always had reservations about the feasibility of keeping the Congo united on a basis other than federalism. At the time of the Brussels Conference on the Congo's independence he envisaged a possible "clash" in the future between the unionists and the federalists. And he remarked that should that clash come, "we would... have to start all over again trying to unite the country on a federal basis, beginning from the bottom."[23]

He himself had, of course, a vested interest in an autonomous Lower Congo, at least until he became the head of the state as a whole. But whatever the motives behind his contention that federalism was the only way unity could be achieved, events following independence have yet to invalidate it. On the contrary, it is as arguable as ever that the country can only be united by conceding institutional recognition to its de facto disunity; that the Congo can be either a unitary state, as it is, or a united people, as it is not, but not both together. It must, of course, be admitted that it is an open question how much institutional recognition to the Congo's diversity can, in effect, be conceded short of making the idea of a "Congolese people" even less tenable than it is now, nor is it certain in what way any dissent from the die-hard unionists would affect the ensuing situation. There is evidence, however, for at least a suggestion that by this acceptance of the principle of a looser structure Kasavubu may have been fulfilling, rather than betraying, his oath of office on ensuring Congolese unity. In January 1961, he himself said the following in reference to the unitary system bequeathed by the Belgians:

> We have inherited a system of institutions which turned out to be ineffective to the situations to which it was intended to be applied. We must give fresh thought to the 'Loi Fondamentale' and the institutions derived from it, with a view to adapting them to our ideas and the requirements of a country which is so large in the geographical sense and whose peoples are so diverse.[24]

And in agreement Burke might say, as he said in a letter to Sir Hercules Langrishe, and as he put it in the Appeal to the Old Whigs, that "the circumstances and habits of every country... are to decide upon the form of government."[25] It is fair to take this to mean not merely whether the government is republican or monarchical, as the choice was sometimes put in Burke's time, but also, in more modern contexts, whether the government is centralized or devolutionary, unitary or federal. It is not enough to think of a unitary government in the abstract as something good. If it is intended for the Congo, look first at the Congo. What is good for the Congolese consists in their advantages and these are "often in balances between differences of good; in compromises between good and evil and sometimes between evil and evil."[26] Even then if a decentralised system is something to be regretted, so surely is civil strife, and a compromise may be needed between one evil and the other. What is to be remembered is:

> [t]he science of constructing a commonwealth or renovating it... is, like every other experimental science, not to be taught a priori... Nor is it a short experience that can instruct us in that science.[27]

And if it is something new you are constructing, be sure to base it on what there is of the experience of what is old. "For people will not look forward to posterity who never look backward to their ancestors."[28] It is here, in fact, that Burke is at his most African, not the African who has just graduated from a university in far-away Manchester or far-away Princeton, but the African who is still steeped in ancestral ways—the Luba tribesman if you like.

> In a politically organized community a particular right, duty or sentiment exists only as an element in a whole body of common, reciprocal, and mutually balancing rights, duties and sentiments, the body of moral or legal norms. Upon that regularity and order with which this whole body of interwoven norms is maintained depends the stability and continuity of the structure of society.

This quotation could have come from Burke, or from a Burkean at any rate. Actually, it is a description of native political systems in Africa by two eminent British anthropologists.[29] They go on to observe: "An African ruler is not to his people merely a person who can enforce his will on them... His credentials are mystical and are derived from antiquity."[30]

With this Burke would be in sympathy. And in his turn, the African tribesman who reveres what he takes to be the will of his ancestors, who in his old age would expect to have his wisdom revered by those of the younger generation, and who believes that this is all part of a spiritual order of things, would listen with attentiveness and understanding as Burke expounds on:

> [a] partnership not only between those who are living but those who are living, those who are dead and those who are to be born, (a partnership in which) each contract of each particular state is but a clause in a great primeval contract of eternal society, linking the lower with the higher natures, connecting the visible and the invisible world, according to a fixed compact sanctioned by the inviolable oath which holds all physical and moral natures, each in their appointed place.[31]

The tribesman in the Congo, after giving his assent to this wisdom, may then turn to the younger constitution-makers in the country's capital and say:

> If you want me to cooperate in constructing the future you dream of, you must cooperate in respecting the past I know of. I have no intention of looking forward to your posterity if you do not have the humility to look backward to my ancestors.

NOTES

This chapter is a revised version of an article that was originally published, under the same title, in *Comparative Studies in Society and History* (The Hague, Netherlands), Vol. 5, N°2, January 1963, pp. 121-133.

1. "Communists Pin Their Hopes on Tribal Insecurity," *Sunday Times*, February 5, 1961. As it stands Stacey's theory is nearer to Fromm than to Hobbes. With Hobbes the "mental comfort" would be derived from knowing that others are dominated along with you rather than from direct satisfaction with being dominated yourself.

2. *Reflections on the Revolution in France* (1790), *Works*, Vol. IV, World's Classics edition (London, 1907), p. 38.

3. *Reform of Representation in the House of Commons* (1782), *Works*, Vol. VI, Bohn's edition (London, 1861), pp. 146 f. Italics are mine.

4. The definition was put forward as a basis of discussion in a class at Columbia University of which the author was a member.

5. *Appeal from the New to the Old Whigs* (1791), *Works*, Vol. V, World's Classics edition (London, 1907), p.96.

6. Reported in "News of the Week Review," *New York Times,* February 12, 1961, p. E9.

7. Address delivered on February 16, 1961. Annex XV, Report of the United Nations Conciliation Commission for the Congo. UN Document N° A/4711, 20 March, 1961, p. 91.

8. Belgian policy was not consistent on this, but in general it bore out the observations made by Daniel Biebuyck and Mary Douglas that "the administration was based on tribal units, local notables were used as assessors in disputes tried by the district tribunals, and affairs were conducted in the appropriate native commercial language. The Belgians tried to rule through the traditional native chiefs, and where this did not make for efficient government, the latter were given honorific positions, and the administrative framework was built on 'administrative' chiefs, chosen from the most intelligent and co-operative people that could be

found." See *Congo Tribes and Parties* (London: Royal Anthropological Institute, 1961), p. 15.

9. *Reflections on the Revolution in France* (1790), op. cit., p. 67.

10. *Reform of Representation in the House of Commons* (1782), op. cit., pp. 146 f.

11. *Reflections of the Revolution in France* (1790), op. cit., p. 147.

12. Ibid., p. 54.

13. Ibid., p. 55.

14. Ibid., p. 65.

15. Ibid.

16. E. B. Cunning, *The Economist*, London, December 24, 1960, p. 13.

17. Quoted by Harold Cooper in his "Political Preparedness for Self-Government," *The Annals of the American Academy of Political and Social Science,* Vol. 306, July 1956, p. 71.

18. Commenting on a "politically sophisticated" African nationalist, Arch Parsons notes: "On the one hand he may argue that he was 'ready' (for independence) as soon as he felt it was necessary (he is inclined to recall that, two centuries ago, the United States did not waste much time on this point). On the other hand he is likely to say 'Ready or not, here I come'." *New York Times Magazine*, October 2, 1960.

19. *Letter to the Sheriffs of Bristol, Works*, Vol. III, Bohn's edition (London, 1861), p. 183.

20. *Reform of Representation in the House of Commons* (1782), op. cit., pp. 147 f.

21. *Reflections on the Revolution in France* (1790), op. cit., p. 109.

22. Ibid., p. 50.

23. See Colin Legum, *Congo Disaster* (A Penguin Special, 1961), pp. 87-88.

24. Address delivered on January 25, 1961. Quoted in Report of the United Nations Conciliation Commission for the Congo. UN Document N° A/4711, 20 March, 1961, p. 27.

25. *A Letter to Sir H. Langrishe* (3rd January, 1792), *Works*, Vol. V, World's Classics edition (London, 1907). The quotation is from the *Appeal* in the same edition, Vol. IV, p. 44.

26. *Reflections on the Revolution in France* (1790), op. cit., p. 67.

27. Ibid., p. 66.

28. Ibid., p. 36.

29. M. Fortes and E. E. Evans-Pritchard, "Introduction," *African Political Systems* (London, 1955), p. 20. The book was published for the International African Institute by Oxford University Press.

30. Ibid., p. 16.

31. *Reflections on the Revolution in France* (1790), op. cit., p. 107.

FOURTEEN

TOWARDS THE DECOLONIZATION OF RUDYARD KIPLING (1972)

One could look at Rudyard Kipling's poem, "The White Man's Burden," as symbolic of that massive historical phenomenon, Euro-American imperialism. There is no doubt that Kipling was the poet of militant expansionist patriotism, and was, in some sense, a hero of both the British and the American wings of Anglo-Saxon militancy. Kipling's poem first appeared in *The Times* of London, on February 4, 1899. This was on the occasion when the United States emerged triumphant out of the Spanish-American War. In May, 1898, Commodore Dewey defeated a Spanish fleet in Manila Bay and the annexation of the Philippines followed, in the face of some significant opposition in the Congress of the United States. The imperial mission, which had already been under way for quite a while among Europeans, was now manifesting itself more blatantly among Americans. "The White Man's Burden" was in part addressed to white Americans as they stood on the threshold of becoming, like their European parent nations, an imperial power.

> Take up the White Man's Burden—
> Send forth the best ye breed—
> Go bind your sons to exile
> To serve your captive's need;

To wait in heavy harness,
On fluttered folk and wild—
Your new caught sullen peoples.
Half-devil and half-child.

The American Government was certainly entering into this mood of legitimation in terms of civilizing the natives, raising their moral stature, and improving their material standards. President McKinley denied emphatically any colonial mission in the Philippines and salved his conscience by affirming that:

> [...] there was nothing else for us to do but to take them all, and to educate the Filipinos, and uplift and civilize and Christianize them, and by God's grace do the very best we could by them, as our fellowmen for whom Christ also died.[1]

Partly because "The White Man's Burden" was composed on the eve of the American colonization of the Philippines, we might say that Rudyard Kipling was not only the voice of the British Empire but the voice of the "Anglo-Saxon Destiny." In this essay, we shall attempt to place him in that wider context, to touch upon other symbols of this line of imperial thinking, and then to indicate the degree to which Kipling and his language were diffused to other societies as part of the emergence of a world culture.

In sentiment, Rudyard Kipling belonged to the second half of the nineteenth century and the first decade of the twentieth. At this time, the Anglo-Saxons were deemed both a "race" and a linguistic group and there was optimism that the race would dominate the world. This prediction has not been borne out by history, but there was also optimism that the English language would conquer the world. This latter prediction continues on the road towards fulfillment. The militancy of Rudyard Kipling's rhetoric and poetry was animated by the forces of enthusiasm implicit in both those prophecies. In 1868, Sir Charles Wentworth Dilke published his two-volume study, *Greater Britain*, after his travels in the United States, New Zealand, Australia, Ceylon, India, and Egypt. "Everywhere [I] was in English-speaking, or in English-governed land," he detected the resilience of "the essentials of the race" and the power of both the English language and English laws. He was particularly impressed by the potentialities of America as a field for the dissemination of English values:

> Through America, England is speaking to the world ... Alfred's laws and Chaucer's tongue are theirs whether they would or no.

Sir Charles shared the view that Britain could claim the glory of "having planted greater Englands across the seas" and here he was capturing a sentiment made even more immortal by Kipling's lines:

> Winds of the World, give answer! They are whimpering to and fro—
> And what should they know of England who only England know?[2]

In the United States, Josiah Strong, a Congregationalist minister, associated the destiny of the Anglo-Saxon "race" more explicitly with the destiny of the English language, and saw the latter as the carrier of Christian ideas and as the medium of "Anglo-Saxonizing mankind." Strong heartily quoted Jacob Grimm's predictions about the English language:

> ...[t]he English language, saturated with Christian ideas, gathering up into itself the best thoughts of all the ages, is the great agent of Christian civilization throughout the world; at this moment affecting the destinies and moulding the character of

half the human race... It seems chosen, like its people, to rule in future times in still greater degree in all the corners of the earth.[3]

Strong took up this solemn prophecy about the infinite conquering power of the English language. The racial chauvinism detracts from what would otherwise be a prediction still very far from being invalidated. In his own exaggerated way, Strong saw the potentialities of the English language as a factor in world order problems. He tied this issue to Tennyson's vision of a future "Federation of the World." Half a true prophet, this Congregationalist minister in the United States asserted that "the language of Shakespeare would eventually become the language of mankind," and then asked whether Tennyson's noble prophecy about the end of war and the beginning of world federalism would not, also, find its fulfillment:

[I]n Anglo Saxondom's extending its dominion and influence—'Till the war-drum throbs no longer, and the battle-flags are furl'd
In the Parliament of man, the Federation of the world.[4]

The British certainly extended their sway across much of the globe as an imperial power; and the United States rose as the most powerful nation in the history of humankind. But then other forces in the world began to conspire against the political domination or hegemony of both the British and the Americans. With the Americans, it took longer for the hegemony to be fully on the defensive and to start beating a retreat to some limited extent following challenges which ranged from the war in Vietnam to the nationalism of France. In fact, the American decline in world stature is still in its initial stages, but the British decline is more firmly demonstrable. Africa was among the last sectors of the British

Empire to be liberated. With the exception of the continuing legal fiction of British power over rebellious Rhodesia (now Zimbabwe), 1966 marked the virtual end of British colonialism in Africa. But at the same time, newer reports about the expansion of the English language began to emerge. For example, in December of that year, an East African magazine reported that the English language had already become the primary language of science in the world and of aviation, sports, and increasingly of literature and the theatre. As the magazine put it using its delightfully pungent journalistic style:

> When a Russian pilot seeks to land at an airfield
> in Athens, Cairo, or New Delhi, he talks to the
> control tower in English.[5]

The same weekly magazine referred to recent estimates to the effect that 70 per cent of the world's mail was by 1966 written in English and an even bigger percentage of cable and wireless transmissions. Sixty per cent of the world's broadcasts were already in English and more and more countries were introducing English as a compulsory second language in schools.

The world picture as a whole does prove the significance of French and English as the two most important languages of international politics, but it is also clear that English continues to outstrip French even in diplomatic importance. Within the old European Economic Community itself, there was anxiety among champions of French at the moment that Britain was about to become a member of the Community. The British, far less nationalistic about their language than the French, had indicated a readiness to let French continue to hold a special position in the councils of Europe, but English has often spread and conquered in spite of Britain's own lack of interest in promoting that spread. The European Union has fallen under the spell of the English language, whatever reassurances Mr. Heath may have once given to President Pompidou. In May 1971, President Pompidou was asked why he insisted on the importance of the French language. His answer, which became more elaborate as the time of British entry approached, conceded first the idea of equality of languages, but then intimated that French had to remain the first among equals in Europe. President Pompidou wanted to safeguard the special role of French within the bodies of the European Economic Community (later the European Union) and the working parties of experts. Why did he want to do so? "Because the language reflects a certain way of looking at the world."6

In some ways, the conquest of continental Europe by the English language would be an even more dramatic victory for the language than its triumphs in Asia and Africa. After all, within Europe the overpowering rivalry of French and German as adequate languages of science and culture for so many years would normally have been expected to present an intractable obstacle to the new hegemony of a language from outside the continental mainland. English has indeed been replacing German as the second language in places such as the Scandinavian countries, but French has continued to resist the encroachment of English in other places.

President Pompidou's concerns about the linguistic implication for the European Economic Community of the British entry were an illustration of a continuing vigilance by France to protect the interests of its language. Of course, Prime Minister Edward Heath's reassurances to President Pompidou on the linguistic question were by no means an adequate safeguard for French since English has been known to extend its frontiers in spite of the lukewarm support from England. Fears still remain that English may push back French in Europe in one sweeping invasion. Such an event would be even more impressive than the acquisition of English by Indians and Nigerians who were more vulnerable because they were colonized and because their languages had not as yet acquired the kind of scientific and modern technological capability which French and German had already imbibed prior to the English challenge on the continent. And yet English, even at its most victorious, can only be a foreign language in Europe. England and Ireland are destined to be the only European countries that have English as their official language. Everywhere else, English will be playing a secondary role within the European continent.

In Africa, however, the position is different. Dr. Tom Soper, Deputy Director of the Overseas Development Institute in London at the time, once estimated that two-thirds of Black Africa was English-speaking and one third was French-speaking. What Dr. Soper meant was that two-thirds of the population of Black Africa was under a system of government that had adopted English as the official language, or one of the official languages, whereas about one third or less of Africa's population was under systems of government that had adopted French for that purpose. In terms of the number of independent states in sub-Saharan Africa, there are indeed about as many French-speaking governments as there are English-speaking, but in terms of population, the picture is different. Nigeria alone has more than the population of former French Africa put together, and out of the two hundred million or more Commonwealth Africans half are Nigerians. This must be balanced by two factors though. First, French-speaking Africa does not consist merely of former French Africa; it also includes former Belgian Africa: The Congo, Rwanda, and Burundi. The population of this former Belgian part of the continent is over forty million. In addition, there may be more people who actually speak French in French-speaking Africa than there are people who speak English in English-speaking Africa. But this calculation is impressionistic, based partly on observations in major centers of population, and partly on the sophistication in the command of French maintained by the French-speaking elite. It is probable that many African users of French have a more sophisticated command of the language than African users of English may have.

Calculating the population as a whole, it is not really certain that the number of people who speak French in French-speaking Africa is greater than the number of people speak English in English-speaking Africa. But even if it were certain, another difference has to be borne in mind. The schools in English-speaking Africa are producing educated Africans more rapidly than the schools in French-speaking Africa are. There is a greater commitment towards promoting education in Commonwealth Africa and towards disseminating it widely. Former French Africa still inclines towards an elitist conception of education, and the expansion of the primary and secondary sectors of education in even such a rich francophone country as the Ivory Coast does not compare with the expansion of pre-university education in, say, Kenya, Tanzania, and Ghana. These are impressionistic assessments but they do add up to the phenomenon of dual Franco-English cultural and linguistic penetration into the African continent. Of the two languages, however, there is no doubt that English is the more dominant in the affairs of the continent.

What all this means is that Strong's prediction concerning the conquest of the world by the English language is coming into conflict with another prediction made famous by Rudyard Kipling himself. We had indicated before that Kipling belonged to that school of militant Anglo-Saxon patriotism which saw the world falling under the influence of those that spoke "the tongue that Shakespeare spake." Kipling also bequeathed to human thought the witticism captured in the verse:

Oh. East is East, and West is West, and never the twain shall meet,
Till Earth and Sky stand presently at God's great Judgment Seat.[7]

The English language itself is helping to contradict the prediction that "never the twain shall meet." The language of Shakespeare, even more so the language of Kipling, has established points of contact, avenues of meeting, between Americans and Ceylonese, Australians and Nigerians, Jamaicans and New Zealanders. Thanks to Kipling's own language, East may still be East and West may still be West but it is harder than ever to assert that "never the twain shall meet." Kipling himself can be regarded as a symbol of the language in some ways more up-to-date than Shakespeare. Looking at the history of English as a whole, it is true that among the poets it was Shakespeare and Alexander Pope who contributed most to the phraseological heritage of English, but Kipling was the nearest modern equivalent to Shakespeare and Pope as a contributor to popular English. In the words of George Orwell:

> Kipling is the only English writer of our time who has added phrases to the English language. The phrases and neologisms which we take over and use without remembering their origin do not always come from writers we admire.[8]

Orwell refers to phrases coined by Kipling that "one sees quoted in leaderettes in the gutter press or overhears in saloon bars from people who have barely heard his name." Orwell mentions phrases like "East is East, and West is West," "the female of the species is more deadly than the male," "paying the Dane-Geld" and, of course, "the white man's burden." He sees in Kipling's capability to enrich the language a capacity to capture the urgency of things. One did not have to agree with the philosophy put forward by Kipling but a phrase may capture an area of importance, even if there is a divergence of values:

"White man's burden" instantly conjures up a real problem, even if one feels that it ought to be altered to "black man's burden."[9]

Orwell's modification of the concept in the direction of the oppressed black man was already echoed earlier by other users of English. Edmund D. Morel, founder of the newspaper *West African Mail* and of the Congo Reform Association in defence of the rise of the Congolese against the King of the Belgians, wrote a book entitled *The Black Man's Burden*. This was in 1920. Taking a point of view diametrically opposed to that of Kipling, Morel nevertheless echoed the rhetoric of his more jingoistic compatriot:

It is (the peoples of Africa) who carry the "Black Man's Burden." They have not withered away before the white man's occupation... The African has survived, and it is well for the white settlers that he has... [But] in fine, to kill the soul in a people— this is a crime which transcends physical murder.[10]

We are taking Orwell's analysis of Kipling a little further in order to illustrate the importance of linguistic dissemination and the power of words. Orwell asks "[b]ut how true is it that Kipling was a vulgar flag waver, a sort of publicity agent for Cecil Rhodes?" Orwell himself, basically an anti-imperialist, conceded that it was true that Kipling provided rhythmic legitimation of British jingoism ant British imperialism. Kipling also helped to romanticize the values popular with the ruling classes of Britain.

In the stupid early years of this century, the blimps, having at last discovered someone who could be called a poet and who was on their side, set Kipling on a pedestal, and some of his more sententious poems, such as "If", given almost biblical status.[11]

What Orwell did not realize was that the very poem "If" captured the imagination not simply of the blimps and jingo imperialists but of African nationalists far away from Britain. On the eve of an election in Nairobi before a massive crowd waiting to hear his last speech before the great day, Kenya's Tom Mboya stood there and recited to that African audience the whole of Rudyard Kipling's poem "If." The whole concept of leadership unflappable in the face of adversity, unwilling to pass the buck ("Here the buck stops"), unwilling to collapse under the weight of pressures, and characterized by the supreme British virtue of the "stiff upper lip" seemed captured in those lines from a supreme British nationalist:

> If you can keep your head when all about you
> Are losing theirs and blaming it on you,
> If you can meet with Triumph and Disaster
> And treat those two imposters just the same,
> If you can talk with crowds and keep your virtue,
> Or walk with kings—nor lose the common touch,
> If you can fill the unforgiving minute
> With sixty seconds' worth of distance run,
> Yours is the Earth and everything that's in it,
> And—which is more—you'll be a Man, my son.[12]

There in Nairobi was this immortal son of Kenya, Tom Mboya, worn out by the exertions of campaigning, nervous about the election the next day, confronting an eager audience of fellow black people listening to his words of wisdom. Mboya was later to communicate to posterity the following paragraph:

> I read out to the great crowd the whole of Rudyard Kipling's poem "If." When facing the chal-

lenge of nation-building, nobody can claim to have played a manly part if he (or she) has not
"...filled the unforgiving minute
With sixty seconds' worth of distance run."[13]

Across the border in Uganda, Rudyard Kipling had had a similar impact. Mr. J. W. Lwamafa, Minister and Member of Parliament, commemorated President A. Milton Obote's ten years in Parliament with the observation:

> He is essentially a man of crisis—he has a unique flair for solving them, but once solved, he will never wait for applause, he simply moves on to the next problem as if nothing had happened. No one reminds me more than President Obote of Rudyard Kipling's poem *If* (which, by the way, I have got framed and hangs in my office) and more particularly the verse, "If you can keep your head when all about you are losing theirs..."[14]

Kipling, the poet of "The White Man's Burden," had turned out also to be the poet of "The Black Man's Leader." The man who had contributed significantly to the phraseological heritage of the English language was also serving inspirational purposes for African politicians within their own domestic systems. The cultural penetration of the English language was manifesting its comprehensiveness. That was in part a form of colonization of the African mind. But when Rudyard Kipling is being called upon to serve purposes of the Africans themselves, the phenomenon we are witnessing may also amount to a decolonization of Rudyard Kipling. It was Kipling who said in 1923: "Words are, of course, the most powerful drug used by mankind."[15] The drug of words may hypnotize individuals away from rationality. But there are times when drugs are used for medicinal and curative purposes. And there are times when one drug is used to neutralize the hypnotic effects of another. In these latter two cases, the story of the English language and its role in the world may include the remedial functions of mitigating the human inclination towards cultural autarky.

NOTES

This chapter is a revised version of an essay originally published, under the same title, in *Quadrant* (Australia), Vol. XXI, September/October 1972, pp. 12-17.

1. Cited by Michael Edwardes, *Asia in the European Age, 1498-1955* (New York: Frederick A. Praeger, 1962), p. 162.

2. Kipling, "The English Flag." For the quotations from Dilke see Sir Charles Wentworth Dilke, *Greater Britain: A Record of Travel in English Speaking Countries* (London, 1868), Vol. 1, pp. vi-viii.

3. Cited by Josiah Strong, *Our Country* (New York, 1885), pp. 178-179.

4. Strong, ibid. The lines from Tennyson are from his poem "Locksley Hall" (1842), Lines 1-7, 8.

5. See the section on "Education," *Reporter* (Nairobi), Dec. 30, 1966, p. 13.

6. See *The Daily Telegraph* (London), May 27, 1971, p. 4.

7. "The Ballad of East and West." The rest of the stanza goes thus:
"But there is neither East nor West,
Border nor Breed, nor Birth.
When two strong men stand face to face,
though they come from the ends of the earth."

8. Orwell, "Rudyard Kipling," in *Decline of the English Murder and Other Essays* (Penguin Books in association with Seeker and Warburg, 1965 edition), pp. 56-57.

9. Ibid.

10. E. D. Morel, *The Black Man's Burden* (London: 1920), pp. 7-11.

11. Orwell, "Rudyard Kipling," op. cit., pp. 50-51.

12. Kipling, "If" (1903).

13. Tom Mboya, *Freedom and After* (London: Andre Deutsch, 1963), p. 114.

14.*Thoughts of an African Leader*, compiled by the editorial department of the *Uganda Argus* (Kampala: Longmans Uganda Ltd., 1970), p. 68.

15. Speech, Feb. 14, 1923. See *The Times* (London), Feb. 16, 1923.

FIFTEEN

EURAFRICAN LESSONS FROM SHAKESPEARE, SHAKA, PUCCINI, AND SENGHOR (1982)

Shaka, the great Zulu warrior who lived from 1787 to 1828, founded the Zulu kingdom, one of the most powerful states in nineteenth-century Africa. He was Black Africa's nearest approximation to Napoleon: a strong ruler, an empire builder, and a leader larger than life. From the point of view of this paper, Shaka symbolizes the military factor in Africa's experience. If Shaka stands for the culture of combat, Shakespeare signifies the culture of words. For Africa, Shakespeare also exemplified the impact of Western culture, certainly on the new elite of the postcolonial era. His work has fascinated a number of contemporary African leaders. For example, Tanzania's Julius K. Nyerere has translated both *Julius Caesar* and *The Merchant of Venice* into Swahili, and Nigeria's Chief Obafemi Awolowo wrote the following in his autobiography about Shakespeare's effect on him:

> Shakespeare is my favourite. I have read all his plays, and re-read some of them—like *Julius Caesar, Hamlet, The Tempest, Anthony and Cleopatra* and *Henry V*—more than three times. Some of the mighty lines of Shakespeare must have influenced my outlook on life.[1]

Beyond Shakespeare, Western culture in general has impressed Africa's new elite. Kwame Nkrumah of Ghana found inspiration in Tennyson. Milton Obote of Uganda adopted the name "Milton" out of admiration for the author of *Paradise Lost*. Léopold Senghor continues to draw inspiration from a wide range of European thinkers and artists. Kenneth Kaunda of Zambia has been influenced by the imagery of the *King James Bible*. The most important carrier of Western culture into the deepest retreats of African villages, however, has been Western technology and commerce. African values have been modified, tastes distorted, resources exploited, new needs fulfilled, and new frustrations created, partly as a result of the broad intrusion of transnational companies.

Shaka provides the techniques of force and war; Shakespeare, the sensibilities of culture and tradition; and the multinational corporations, the instruments of seduction, distribution, and exchange. Added together, those three kinds of forces yield the fourth force: the compound force of politics and power. This essay focuses especially on culture as a way of looking at Africa's relations with Europe. It shall use a bit of Shaka's tragic love for the woman, Noliwe; a little of Shakespeare's tragedy of *Othello* and Desdemona; and Giacomo Puccini's operatic tragedy *Madama Butterfly*, as one way of looking at how the West has sometimes dealt with the non-Western world. Why have I decided in this essay to use culture and art as a way of examining politics? I employ two fellow scholars to defend me in this regard. One is Paul Kress, the social theorist, who has argued that political science and creative literature are comparable in that they are two symbolic systems.[2] The other is Murray Edelman who has argued as follows:

> We may be able to learn something about expressive political symbols from aesthetic theory, for an art form consists of condensation symbols[3]

Let me also cite the poet T. S. Eliot through his theory of "objective correlative:"

> [a] set of objects, a situation, a chain of events which shall be the formula of... [a] particular emotion; such that, when the external facts, which must terminate in sensory experience, are given, the emotion is immediately evoked.[4]

I would like to turn T. S. Eliot upside down, by arguing that there are occasions when the only way of evoking an objective "chain of events" is by recalling its "sensory experience" in literature. Symbols try to capture and condense the world of implications and associations. Like art and creative literature, political analysis has to resort sometimes to the use of analogy and metaphor.

One promising metaphor in discussing the relationship between Europe and Africa is the metaphor of marriage. The very compound term "Eurafrica" is based on matrimonial premises. Ideally in a world without sexism, each partner might adopt at least part of the name of the other. If, however, the links between Europe and Africa are to be seen as a marriage, one issue to bear in mind is that it was initially a forced marriage. Africa was not a willing partner, though contracts were sometimes written, signed, and sealed. It was a mixed marriage, racially, and one wonders whether it is bound to be a tragic marriage. We shall explore these issues partly in the symbolic context of the marriage between Othello and Desdemona in Shakespeare's play, and the marriage between Pinkerton, a lieutenant in the American navy, and Cio-Cio-San or Madama Butterfly in Puccini's opera. Tragedies are not merely interracial, however. They often occur within the same race, hence the third symbolic case in our book of examples, that of the marriage between Shaka and Noliwe.

Involved in the three tragedies is the theme of betrayal. In *Othello*, the white partner, Desdemona, is betrayed by the non-white: Othello, the Moor, kills the fair woman he married. In *Madama Butterfly*, the nonwhite is betrayed by the white: Pinkerton treats Madama Butterfly as a concubine and then betrays her—and she is driven to self-destruction. In our third case, black betrays black: Shaka, the emperor, betrays Noliwe for reasons of state and high politics. But even in the third uniracial betrayal, there are implications for interracial relations. When black betrays black, how can the white world avoid being affected? Let us look at these three scenarios of betrayal more closely in relation to wider themes of contact between Europe and Africa, between white people and nonwhite people, and between the world of yesterday and the world of tomorrow.

Othello in Shaka's Land

The land of Shaka, South Africa, was one of the earliest areas in Black Africa to be colonized by the white man. It was also the last to be liberated. In 1815, Shaka's father, the ruler of the Zulu chiefdom in the wider federation of Dingiswayo, died. When Emperor Dingiswayo was killed in battle, Shaka seized the Zulu throne in 1816. Much of his confederation disintegrated but Shaka managed to absorb these holdings under his own Zulu rule. More ruthless than Dingiswayo, he proceeded to consolidate his power and to establish wider empires. At about the same time, the whites were establishing their own presence in Southern Africa. There had been white settlers in Southern Africa for nearly two centuries before Shaka but the nineteenth century was witnessing a different scale of white empire building, and for a while, both black rulers and white immigrants vied for greater imperial glory. In 1818, Shaka dealt a particularly severe blow to the rival confederation of Ndwandwe, routing them from Ndwandwe country and scattering both them and their allies into what is now northern Swaziland. It should be

noted that at the same moment in history, Europe was recovering from the Napoleonic wars during which that great
white Shaka, Napoleon Bonaparte, had terrorized his own
continent and taken France to new levels of grandeur.

The meeting points between these forms of imperialism must not be forgotten.On October 24, 1818, the following
announcement was made at the Cape of Good Hope:

ENGLISH THEATRICALS:
Under the sanction of His Excellency, The Gover-
nor...
This Evening the amateur company will perform
the Tragedy of *Othello*
With the musical farce of *The Poor Soldier*.

These were the lighter moments of European colonization of Africa. But for that very reason they were the most
pregnant with meaning. The white man was now in Africa
not merely with his ship anchored in the harbor, not merely
with his guns, and not merely with his technology of production, but also with his culture and his art. The play was given
in Dutch for the first time on May 28, 1836 under the title
"Othello, Of De Jaloersche Zwart" ("Othello or the Jealous
Black").[5] It was quite popular against the background of "il-
licit" interracial intimacy in South Africa. Dutch-speaking
South Africans had been among the most vociferous opponents of marriages and sexual relations between interracial
couples and yet the great majority of the Cape's colored
population of South Africa (peoples of mixed origin) is
Dutch-speaking—hence betraying their Afrikaner paternity.
Some of the performance history of *Othello* in 19th century
South Africa is illustrative. In March 1837, a Dutch-speaking
society, *Voor Vlyt en Kunst* (For Diligence and Art), attempted a production of *Othello*, with Iago played by "a gentleman lately arrived from India." The nearness of tragedy to
comedy is sometimes emphasized in situations of anxiety.

Even in the nineteenth century, South Africa was in such a situation. *Othello* was sometimes produced as a comedy, with white men taking the part of both Othello and Desdemona, and making the most of "Desdemona's little endearments towards her black 'hobby.'" That production, apparently hilarious, was given again a few days later.

On December 30, 1854, Gustavus V. Brook, from the Theatre Royal of Liverpool, arrived at the Cape and announced that he would stage *Othello*. Sometimes alterations were made to spare combined Calvinist and Victorian sensibilities, but on balance *Othello* continued to be to white South Africans "a play better understood here than any other of Shakespeare's works. Its hero (a *colored* man) who has wooed and won a *white* lady, ships, bay soldiers, a castle and a governor, being all—familiar in the colonist's ear."[6] The literary historian Eric Rosenthal has shown that by the end of the nineteenth century, few towns in South Africa had failed at some or another time to witness at least an amateur performance of Shakespeare. And because of the real racial predicament, the most popular play was *Othello*, a play that is not really a tragedy of racial incompatibility but a tragedy of subversion. The evil factor in *Othello* is the force that seeks to separate black from white: the harbinger of hate, Iago. And whatever the producers at Cape Town might have done when they made Iago an Indian in the nineteenth century, William Shakespeare in his wisdom made the evil Iago well and truly white. Iago might therefore be seen as apartheid itself, constantly seeking to cultivate jealousies in human beings otherwise destined to live together.

The spirit of subversion is in Iago and what feeds his hate are two forces familiar in the history of racism: on one side is occupational insecurity and jealousy, and on the other, sexual insecurity and jealousy. In Shakespeare's character, both forces feed Iago's venomous villainy, as he confessed:

[...] Now I do love her too;
Not out of absolute lust, though peradventure
I stand accountant for as great a sin
But partly led to diet my revenge,
For that I do suspect the lusty Moor
Hath leap'd into my seat; the thought whereof
Doth, like a poisonous mineral, gnaw my inwards;
And nothing can or shall content my soul
Till I am even'd with him, wife for wife:
Or failing so, yet that I put the Moor
At least into a jealousy so strong
That judgment cannot cure. 7

Shakespeare's Iago is the philosophy of apartheid incarnate. Both white and black South Africans have deeply loved the land on which Shaka once trod. Yet unless the pernicious Iago of hate in their midst is exorcised in time, one patriot from either side may one day be forced to say when it is too late:

When you shall these unlucky deeds relate,
Speak of me as I am, nothing extenuate.
Nor set down aught in malice: then must you speak
Of one that loved not wisely, but too well.8

On Puccini and Casual Imperialism

If Othello's was a crime of passion, Lieutenant Pinkerton's crime in *Madama Butterfly* was a crime of casualness. In Japan, the American naval officer sought a temporary marriage of convenience then returned home while his Japanese woman waited, nursing their child, preparing for his return. When at last his ship was sighted, Pinkerton was back with an American wife—the "real" wife. He had come to collect his child to be brought up with the "civilized" in the

United States. Pinkerton's betrayal was an incomplete crucifixion, but Madama Butterfly gave it the dignity of finality:
she killed herself. The political symbolism of the opera has a
dimension of its own for it is not without significance that
Pinkerton is a white American and Cio-Cio-San is Japanese.
The relationship was in part one between two cultures, two
different races, two different structures of values and priorities.

The casualness of the American relationship was in
turn symptomatic of a wider American reality. Unlike Western Europe, the United States did not try hard to acquire territory and establish direct political control over lands and societies far from its shores. Americans, on the contrary, often
abhorred territorial annexation, although the United States
did occupy the Philippines and annex Puerto Rico. However,
it was European imperialism that became intimate, establishing governments and institutions in large parts of Africa
and Asia and beyond. European imperialism was far from
casual; it involved day-to-day administration of colonies and
constant accountability in policymaking. American imperialism, on the other hand, was casual and irresponsible. Much
of Latin America was ostensibly independent, but the United
States retained the right to intervene wherever it suited its
interests. At times, it did not even bother to intervene but
simply manipulated local forces through less direct means,
as was the case with Salvador Allende in Chile. The United
States poured in money to help create conditions of instability: strikes were subsidized and rioters were bribed, but no
direct American troops were deployed. By contrast, the killing of eleven people in a prison at Hola in colonial Kenya,
seemingly beaten to death while in governmental custody,
was a matter of intense political controversy in Great Britain.
A colonial power that claims sovereignty over another country accepts legal responsibility when things go wrong. Herein
rests the paradox in American criticism of Europe's imperial
role.

The tragedy of *Madama Butterfly* captures the essence of this casual penetration of other societies by Americans. Pinkerton is a personification of casual imperialism, exploiting another society then returning home with a clear conscience. When Pinkerton came later to collect his baby, he exemplified the profit motive in the perverse form of a human product. In Africa, the nearest thing to an American colony was Liberia.Established in the early nineteenth century as the home of freed slaves, it was to some extent an exercise in humanitarianism. In other respects, however, it was an exercise in escapism: exporting a portion of Black Americans in the hope that others would follow, and attempting to ease the racial situation of the United States by providing encouragement and inducement for voluntary Black repatriation. Once again the casualness of American imperialism revealed itself. American Liberians in turn colonized their indigenous brethren, and when such forms of repression and exploitation occurred, the United States was not held responsible. It could provide money to start a rubber industry, it could encourage American economic penetration, but it did not have to do what the British and French were forced to do in their own colonies: to establish more broadly based opportunities for local populations. It did not feel under pressure to make at least an effort in the direction of purposeful development and social change.

Senghor's Shaka and Masochism

If Othello was a case of black betraying white, and *Madama Butterfly* a case of white betraying nonwhite, the case of Shaka illustrates black betraying black. Othello killed Desdemona and then himself; the play presented a murder followed by a suicide. Madama Butterfly, on discovering Pinkerton's betrayal, killed herself; the opera presented a straight case of suicide. With Shaka, we have a black killing black. On an individual basis, this might be a case of murder;

on a collective basis and for political ends, this might be a case of collective suicide. Both cases present the interplay between sadism and masochism. Noliwe was perhaps Shaka's only woman since her beauty captivated the Zulu's imagination and her modesty flattered his ego. Shaka had all along refused ever to marry, but Noliwe was the nearest thing to a common-law wife that the great Zulu ever had. The diviners of the tribe gave Shaka the agonizing dilemma. He was already a great chief, but were his ambitions greater than his accomplishments? Were there any more worlds to conquer? For Shaka, the answer was emphatically yes. Some of Shaka's feelings must have been similar to Nkrumah's when, in 1934, Nkrumah applied to the dean of Lincoln University in the United States for admission. In his application, he quoted from Tennyson's "In Memoriam":

> So many worlds, so much to do,
> So little done, such things to be.

In his autobiography, Nkrumah said that this verse "was to me then, as it still is today, an inspiration and a spur. It fired within me a determination to equip myself for the service of my country."[9] A century earlier, we might say that Shaka the Zulu's tragedy in relation to Noliwe hinged on "so little done, such things to be." The tribal diviners told Shaka that absolute greatness depended on absolute sacrifice. If he wanted new worlds to conquer, he needed to sacrifice some of the old worlds already conquered. What about the conquest of a woman's heart? Could that be sacrificed for a greater conquest of a new empire? The fate of Noliwe, the woman he loved, was hanging in the balance. Was Shaka going to serve the bigger ends of his society or the private longings of his psyche? Torn by doubt and anguish, pushed on by political ambition, worried by the fear of being regarded as a coward, inspired by broader visions of imperial grandeur, Shaka betrayed Noliwe. Like Othello, Shaka killed her whom he loved most. But unlike Othello, he did not kill her for reasons rooted in his love for her, for personal jealousy, but for reasons of state. One might argue that it did work. Shaka succeed in building a larger empire, carving for himself a place in nineteenth-century history perhaps greater than that acquired by any other black man. He inspired black cultural nationalists for generations to come:

> Shaka stands out as the greatest of them all—both Romulus and Napoleon to the Zulu people—and his legend has captured the imagination of both European and African writers, inspiring novels, biographies, and historical studies in several tongues. As a violent autocrat he is both admired and condemned: admired by those who love conquerors, condemned by those who hate despots. [10]

Léopold Sédar Senghor of Sénégal composed a dramatic poem for several voices, in honor of Shaka but dedicated "To the Bantu Martyrs of South Africa." In the poem, Senghor has a white voice taunting Shaka, partly for the murder of Noliwe, but more broadly for his brutality:

> *White Voice:*
> Ha ha ha ha Shaka. It is very well for you to talk about Noliwe, the beautiful girl you were to marry
> Her heart like butter, her eyes the petals of the waterlily
> Her words soft as a water spring.
> You have killed her to escape from your conscience.
>
> *Shaka:*
> And you talk about conscience to me?
> Yes, I killed her, while she was telling of the blue lands
> I killed her yes! My hand did not tremble

A flash of fine steel in the odorous thicket of the
armpit.

White Voice:
So you admit it Shaka? Will you admit to the millions
of men you killed
Whole regiments of pregnant women and children
still at the breast?
You, provider-in-chief for vultures and hyenas, poet of
the Valley of Death.
We looked to find a warrior. All we found was a
butcher...

Shaka:
The weakness of the heart is holy...
Ah! You think that I never loved her
My Negress fair with Palmoil, slender as a plume
Thighs of a startled otter, of Kilimanjaro snow [...]
Ah! You think I never loved her!
But these long years, this breaking of the wheel of
years,
This carcan strangling every act
This long night without sleep...
I wandered like a mare from the Zambezi running and
rushing at the stars.
Gnawed by a nameless suffering, like leopards in the
trap
I would not have killed her if I loved her less. [11]

Once again there is a fusion between the sadism of
murder and the masochism of suicide. To kill that which you
love most is to some extent, to kill a little of yourself. According to tradition, Shaka was never the same again after the
murder of his own black Desdemona. The worst excesses of
Shaka, the most brutal elements of his conquest and of his
rule are sometimes traced to the times when, given a choice

between retaining his beloved Noliwe and conquering new worlds, he chose to destroy his mistress. This is the third and most ominous scenario of the Africa of Shaka as well as of contemporary Africa. Senghor equated Shaka's love for Noliwe with love for black-skinned people: in Shaka's brutal betrayal of Noliwe is a masochistic betrayal of all Blacks:

> I had to escape from doubt
> Prom the intoxication of the milk of her mouth,
> From the throbbing drum of the night of my blood
> From my bowels fervent lava, from the Uranium
> mines of my heart in the depth of my blackness
> From love of Noliwe
> From the love of my black-skinned People. [12]

We have so far discussed different scenarios of possible betrayal in Africa's relations with Europe. The three scenarios mentioned earlier were either Europe's betrayal of Africa, or Africa's betrayal of Europe, or Africa's betrayal of Africa in such a way that it dooms relations with others abroad. But of course there has all along been at least one other scenario, the fourth one, the scenario of a successful marriage between Africa and Europe. Is there not a chance that new Eurafrican loyalties might be forged and endure? We do not know the answer; what we do know is that there have been signs of successful Eurafrican partnerships—as in the case between France and French-speaking Africa. Such partnerships are, of course, unequal, and the marriages may not endure, nonetheless they do present us with Eurafrican lessons. Léopold Sédar Senghor may offer us an illustration of such a marriage that may have the capacity to endure precisely because one is well aware of the inequality at its basis. Senghor, with his philosophy of *Négritude*, affirmed the validity and dignity of Africa's own indigenous cultural heritage. Yet Senghor is also famous as a supreme product of French culture, a master of the nuances and powers of the French language, a devout admirer of French civilization, and a dedicated friend of the French nation. We have here a paradox: on the one hand, Senghor seeks to rescue African cultures and civilizations from the contemptuous arrogance of Europeanized Africa, but at the same time, he is in love with the country which once possessed his own. In his own words:

> Lord, among the white nations, set France at the right hand of the Father.
> O, I know she too is Europe, that she has stolen my children like a brigand to fatten her cornfields and cotton fields, for the negro is dung.
> She too has brought death and guns into my blue villages, has set my people one against the other, like dogs fighting over a bone...
> Yes, Lord, forgive France who hates her occupiers and yet lays so heavy an occupation upon me...
> For I have a great weakness for France...[13]

We have in Léopold Senghor the perfect illustration of a fusion of philosophical rebellion and political collaboration, the quest for African cultural authenticity combined with the imperial legacy of Africa's cultural dependence.

Conclusion

In this essay, we have not only looked at the intimacy of Europe and Africa in a historical context, but also confronted three scenarios of betrayal: the betrayal of a white partner by a nonwhite, as Desdemona was betrayed by Othello; the betrayal of a nonwhite partner by a white, as Madama Butterfly was betrayed by Pinkerton; and most ominous of all, a black partner betrayed by a fellow black, as Noliwe was betrayed by Shaka. I once wrote an article entitled "The Resurrection of the Warrior Tradition In African Political Cultures: From Shaka the Zulu to Amin the Kakwa."

Some commentators denounced me for elevating Idi Amin to the status of Shaka and yet, on balance, Amin killed far fewer people than Shaka ever did. Admirers of Shaka in the twentieth century all too easily forget that he killed so many people in the nineteenth century. Time plays a part in selecting the scale of casualties attributed to a particular historical butcher. But what matters in the history of both Shaka and Amin is that strange combination of masochism and sadism in Africa's historical experience. It is still true that when all the killing is done and narrated, all the brutality committed and said, Africans kill fellow Africans far more than they kill anybody else. Even in the land of Shaka, the martyrdom of Noliwe still persists, as African blood is shed by African spears.

There is, however, another level to the symbolism of this essay. This applies especially to the dialectic between Shaka and Shakespeare in Africa's experience. Shaka was a warrior while Shakespeare was a writer. Africa's history, especially in the second half of the twentieth century, has been an agonizing competition between the specialists in weaponry, the soldiers, and the experts in words, the westernized intelligentsia. When Idi Amin captured power from Milton Obote, it was in part a triumph of the rustic warrior over the westernized African. Indeed, until Amin captured power, it was not possible for a Ugandan to enter politics without the command of English required for membership in the Ugandan parliament and cabinet. Amin was the Shaka replacing an African Milton, if not an African Shakespeare. In 1979, Idi Amin was overthrown and was succeeded by the former head of Makerere University. When President Yusufu Lule was in turn dismissed, he was succeeded by Godfrey Binaisa, counsel to Her Majesty Queen Elizabeth II of Great Britain. In West Africa, a similar trend was discernible when Ghana restored civilian rule after several years of military government. Members of the westernized intelligentsia once again scrambled for parliamentary seats. Many were academics from universities, abandoning professional positions for parliamentary opportunities. The African inheritors of the legacy of Shakespeare reached for power almost as soon as the African inheritors of the legacy of Shaka returned to the barracks. Indeed, the most central dialectic in Africa's political experience in our present times is likely to be precisely the basic tension between the men of weapons and the men of words, between soldiers and westernized politicians, between Shaka and Shakespeare. In the ultimate analysis, the pendulum of power in postcolonial Africa will continue to swing between the killer of Desdemona and the killer of Noliwe, between the black man infatuated with an aspect of the white world, and the black man obsessed with an aspect of the Black world.

NOTES

This chapter is a revised version of an article entitled "Through the Prism of the Humanities: EurAfrican Lessons from Shakespeare, Shaka, Puccini, and Senghor" that originally appeared in *African Cultural and Intellectual Leaders and the Development of the New African Nations*, edited by Robert W. July and Peter Benson (New York: The Rockefeller Foundation, and Ibadan: Ibadan University Press, 1982), pp. 197-220.

1. See *Awo: The Autobiography of Chief Obafemi Awolowo* (Cambridge: Cambridge University Press, 1960), p. 70.

2. Paul S. Kress, "Self, System and Significance: Reflections of Professor Easton's Political Science," *Ethics* LXXVII, No. 1 (October 1966), p. 3.

3. Murray Edelman, *The Symbolic Uses of Politics* (Urbana: University of Illinois Press, 1964), p. 11. See also Ernest Cassirer, *The Philosophy of Symbolic Forms*, 3 vols, (New Haven: Yale University Press, 1953-1957).

4. T. S. Eliot, "Hamlet and His Problems," *The Sacred Wood* (London: Methuen, 1920), p. 100.

5. Cited by Eric Rosenthal, "Early Shakespeare Productions in South Africa," *English Studies in Africa*, 7, no. 2 (Sept. 1964):

210. I am greatly indebted to Rosenthal's research for these insights into early productions of *Othello* in Shaka's land.

6. Cited by Eric Rosenthal, ibid., pp. 212-13.

7. *Othello*, act 2, sc. 1, lines 300-311. Cited by Eric Rosenthal, op. cit., pp. 212-13.

8. Ibid., act 5, sc. 2, lines 341-344.

9. Nkrumah, Preface to *Ghana: The Autobiography of Kwame Nkrumah* (New York:Thomas Nelson, 1957), p. viii.

10. Eugene Victor Walter, *Terror and Resistance: A Study of Political Violence with Case Studies of Some Primitive African Communities* (London and New York: Oxford University Press, 1959 and 1972), pp. 109-10.

11. Senghor, "Shaka," in *Senghor: Prose and Poetry*, ed. and trans. by John Reed and Clive Wake (London: Oxford University Press, 1965), pp. 143-45.

12. Senghor, "Shaka," in ibid., p. 145.

13. Senghor, "Prayer for Peace," in ibid., pp. 135-136.

CONCLUSION

AFRICA AND OTHER CIVILIZATIONS
CONQUEST AND COUNTER-CONQUEST
(1995)

Introduction

As we enter the new millennium let us examine Africa's cultural balance sheet. One of the most intriguing aspects of the historical sociology of Africa in the preceding century has been its remarkable cultural receptivity. For example, Christianity has spread faster in a single century in Africa than it did in several centuries in Asia. European languages have acquired political legitimacy in Africa more completely than they have ever done in formerly colonized Asian countries like India, Indonesia, and Vietnam. Africa's readiness to welcome new cultures is both its strength and its weakness. There is an African preparedness to learn from others but there is also the looming danger of Africa's dependency and intellectual imitation. What has so often been overlooked is the third dimension of this equation. Africa's cultural receptivity can over time make others dependent on Africa because there is a cyclical dynamic at play. Those who have culturally conquered Africa have, over time, become culturally dependent upon Africa. The biter has sometimes been bitten; the conqueror has sometimes been counter-conquered. This essay is about this boomerang effect in acculturation and assimilation and about how Africa has sometimes counter-penetrated the citadels of its own conquerors.

This process of Africa's counter-penetration has been sometimes facilitated by Africa's political fragmentation in the egalitarian age. The majority of the members of the Non-aligned Movement are from Africa. Almost half the members of the Organization of the Islamic Conference are members also of the Organization of African Unity. Although African countries are only a third of the 54 members of the Commonwealth, they have been by far the most influential regional group in shaping its agenda and its decisions since the 1960s. In the United Nations, countries from Africa were also almost a third of the total global membership until the Soviet-Union and Yugoslavia collapsed and Czechoslovakia split. Africa's fragmentation in an egalitarian age had for a while helped Africa's voting power in the General Assembly but Africa's percentage of the total membership has declined in the 1990s. Even in this relatively egalitarian age in human history, real power continues to be decisive, when there is enough at stake to invoke it.

Similarly, Africa's cultural receptivity, although often excessive and a cause of Africa's intellectual dependency, has sometimes become the basis of Africa's counter-influence on those who have conquered her. This essay about Africa's counter-penetration is supposed to be illustrative rather than exhaustive. We shall start by examining Africa's relationship with the Arab civilization before analyzing the French connection as an illustration of Africa's potential in counter-influencing the Western World. We will then examine Africa's interaction with India, with special reference to the legacies of Mahatma Gandhi and Jawaharlal Nehru. We shall conclude with Africa's conquest of Africa, closing with the full circle of auto-colonization. The Arab factor in Africa's experience is illustrative of the politics of identity. With the French connection we enter the politics of language. The Afro-Indian interaction conveys the politics of liberation. Finally, we speculate on the future politics of self-conquest.

Africa Conquers the Arabs

In the seventh century, the Arabs captured various parts of Africa in the name of Islam. Three factors speeded up the Arabization of North Africa and the Lower Nile Valley. One factor was indeed Africa's cultural receptivity and its remarkable degree of assimilability. The second factor that facilitated Arabization was the Arab lineage system and how it defined the offspring of mixed marriages. The third factor behind Arabization was the spread of the Arabic language and its role in defining what constitutes an Arab. At first glance the story is a clear case of how the Arabs took over large chunks of Africa. But on closer scrutiny the Afro-Arab saga is a story of both conquest and counter-conquest. It is comparable to the British role in colonizing North America. Much later, what was imperial Britain was being protected and led by her former colonies, the United States of America. But there is one important difference in the case of reciprocal conquest between the Arabs and the Africans. The actual creation of new Arabs is still continuing. Let us examine this remarkable process of "Arab-formation" in Africa across the centuries more closely.

The Arab conquest of North Africa in the seventh and eighth centuries initiated two processes: Arabization (through language) and Islamization (through religion). The spread of Arabic as a native language created new Semites (the Arabs of North Africa). The diffusion of Islam created new monotheists, but not necessarily new Semites. As an example, the Copts of Egypt were linguistically Arabized but they have not been, of course, Islamized. On the other hand, the Wolof and Hausa were preponderantly Islamized, but they were not Arabized. The process by which the majority of North Africans became Arabized was partly biological and cultural. The biological process involved intermarriage and was considerably facilitated by the upward lineage system of the Arabs. Basically, if the father of a child is an Arab the child is automatically considered Arab, regardless of the ethnic or racial origins of the mother. This lineage system could be described as ascending miscegenation since the offspring ascends to the more privileged parent. This is in sharp contrast to the lineage system of, say, the United States where the child of a white father and a black mother descends to the less privileged race of that society. Indeed, in a system of descending miscegenation like that of the United States, it does not matter whether it is the father or the mother who is black. An offspring of such racial mixture descends to black under-privilege. The American system does not therefore co-opt "impurities" upwards across the racial barrier to high status; it pushes "impurities" downwards into the pool of disadvantage.

It is precisely because the Arabs have the opposite lineage system (ascending miscegenation) that North Africa was so rapidly transformed into part of the Arab world (and not merely the Muslim world). The Arab lineage system permitted considerable racial cooptation. "Impurities" were admitted to higher echelons as new full members, provided the father was an Arab. And so the colors in the Arab world range from the whites of Syria and Iraq to the browns of Yemen, from blonde-haired Lebanese to the black Arabs of Sudan. Within Africa, the valley of the White Nile is a particularly fascinating story of evolving Arabization. The Egyptians were of course not Arabs when the Muslim conquest occurred in the seventh century. The process of Islamization, in the sense of actual change of religion, took place fairly rapidly after the Arab conquerors had consolidated their hold on the country. On the other hand, the Arabization of Egypt turned out to be significantly slower than its Islamization. The Egyptians changed their religious garment from Christianity to Islam more quickly than they changed their linguistic garment from ancient Egyptian and ancient Greek to Arabic. And even when Arabic became the mother tongue of the majority of Egyptians, it took centuries before Egyptians began to call themselves Arabs. But this is all relative. When one considers the pace of Arabization in the first millennium of Islam, it was still significantly faster than average in the history of human acculturation. The number of people in the Middle East who called themselves "Arabs" expanded dramatically in a relatively short period. This was partly because of the exuberance of the new religion, partly because of the rising prestige of the Arabic language, and partly due to the rewards of belonging to a conquering civilization. Religious, political, and psychological factors transformed Arabism into an expansionist culture that absorbed the conquered into the body politic of the conquerors. In the beginning there was an "island" or a peninsula called "Arabia." But in time there were far more Arabs outside Arabia than within. At the end of it all there was an "Arab world."

Along the valley of the White Nile, Northern Sudan was also gradually Islamized, and more recently it has been increasingly Arabized. Again a people who were not originally Arabs have come to see themselves more and more as Arabs. The question that arises is whether there is a manifest destiny of the White Nile pushing it towards further Arabization. It began with the Egyptians and their gradual acquisition of an Arab identity. The Northern Sudanese have been in the process of similar Arabization. Are the Southern Sudanese the next target of the conquering wave of Arabization within the next hundred to two hundred years? Will the twin forces of biological mixture (intermarriage between Northerners and Southerners) and cultural assimilation transform the Dinkas and Nuers of today into the black Arabs of tomorrow? It is not inconceivable, provided the country as a whole holds together. As intermarriage increases, Northern Sudanese will become more black in color. As acculturation increases in the South, Southerners will become more Arab. Biological Africanization of the North and cultural Arabization of the South will reinforce each other and help to forge a more integrated Sudan, provided peace is restored to the country. Without peace the country will break up sooner or later.

Southern Sudanese are the only sub-Saharan Africans who are being Arabized faster than they are being Islamized. They are acquiring the Arabic language faster than they are acquiring Islam. This is in sharp contrast to the experience of such sub-Saharan peoples as the Wolof, the Yoruba, the Hausa, or even the Somali—among all of whom the religion of Islam has been more triumphant than the language of the Arabs. This rapid Arabization of the Southern Sudanese linguistically has two possible outcomes in the future: the Southern Sudanese could became Sudan's equivalent of the Copts of Egypt, a Christian minority whose mother tongue would then be Arabic; or, the Arabization of the Southern Sudanese could be followed by their religious Islamization, in time making Southern and Northern Sudanese truly intermingled and eventually indistinguishable. Meanwhile, the Swahili language has been creeping northwards towards Juba from East Africa as surely as Arabic has been creeping southwards from the Mediterranean. The Swahilization of Tanzania, Kenya, Uganda, and eastern Zaire (now Congo) has been gathering momentum. With Arabic coming up the Nile towards Juba, and Kiswahili coming down the same valley, Southern Sudanese will find themselves caught between the forces of Arabization and the forces of Swahilization. Historically, these two cultures (Arab and Swahili) can so easily reinforce each other. It is because of this pattern of trends that the manifest destiny of the Valley of the White Nile appears to be a slow but definite assimilation into the Arab fold over the next century or two. Ironically, the Arabization of Southern Sudan may continue even if the South breaks away and forms a separate country.

Nevertheless, racial ambivalence will maintain a linkage with Africanity. Indeed, the Southern Sudanese are bound to be the most *Négritudist* of all Sudanese, even if they do become Arabized and do not secede. There is a precedent of black nationalism even among Northern Sudanese. It is not often realized how much *Négritude* sentiment there is among important sectors of Northern Sudanese opinion. Muhammad al-Mahdi al-Majdhub has been described as "probably the first Sudanese poet to tap the possibility of writing poetry in the Arabic language with a consciousness of a profound belonging to a 'Negro' tradition."[1] The poet al-Mahdi has indeed affirmed:

> In the Negroes I am firmly rooted though the Arabs may boastfully claim my origin... My tradition is: beads, feathers, and a palm-tree which I embrace, and the forest is singing around us.[2]

Muhammad Miftah al-Fayturi is another Arab *Négritudist*. Information about his ancestry is somewhat contradictory. His father was probably Libyan and his mother Egyptian but of Southern Sudanese ancestry. In his words:

> Do not be a coward
> Do not be a coward
> say it in the face
> of the human race:
> My father is of a Negro father,
> My mother is a Negro woman,
> and I am black.[3]

In some notes about al-Fayturi's early poetic experiences there is the anguished cry: "I have unriddled the mystery, the mystery of my tragedy: I am short, black and ugly." Then there are the Arab *Négritudists* who sometimes revel in the fact that they are racially mixed. They can also be defiant and angrily defensive about their mixture. Salah A. Ibrahim, in his piece on "The Anger of the Al-Hababy Sandstorm," declared:

Liar is he who proclaims:
"I am the unmixed..." Yes, a liar![4]

In the Sudan of the future, there may be even less room for such "lies" than there is at present. After all, Arabization is, almost by definition, a process of creating mixture and its relentless force along the White Nile is heading southwards towards Juba and beyond. How has the boomerang effect worked in relation to the Arabization of Africa? In what sense has there been an Africanization of the Arab world? In what way has the whole process been cyclical?

It is worth reminding ourselves that the majority of the Arab people are in Africa. Over 60% of the population of the Arab world is now west of the Red Sea on African soil. The largest Arab country in population is Egypt. The headquarters of the Arab League is in Africa. The largest city in the Arab world is located on its African side: the population of Cairo is more than the population of Saudi Arabia as a whole. Cairo also has become the cultural capital of the Arab world. The greatest singers and musicians of the Arab world, including the incredible Umm Kalthum, affectionately known as "the Star at Sunrise," used to mesmerize the Middle East from the studios of the Voice of the Arabs Broadcasting System in Cairo. The most famous Arab musical composer of the twentieth century, Al-Ustadh Muhammad Abdul Wahab, has also come from the African side of the Arab world. Finally, Egypt is by far the most important filmmaking country in both Africa and the Arab world. Egyptian shows feature prominently on cinema screens and television programmes on both sides of the Red Sea. There are other skills of the Arab people that also disproportionately emanate from the African side. Dr. Boutros Boutros-Ghali, as Egypt's Minister of State for Foreign Affairs, estimated that Egypt's technical assistance to other Arab countries is sometimes as high as two million Egyptians scattered in the region.[5] All this is quite apart from the importance of Egypt in the Arab military equation in the Arab world. It is clear that the Egyptian armies played a primordial role in most of the Arab-Israeli wars. In the year 639 A.D., the Arabs crossed into Africa and conquered Egypt. By the second half of the twentieth century, Egypt had become the most important pillar of the military defense of the Arab world. History has once again played its cyclical boomerang game in the interaction between Africa and her conquerors. The ancestral home of the Arabs in Asia is now heavily dependent culturally and militarily on the African side of the Arab nation.

Eurafrica: The French Connection

France invented the concept of "Eurafrica," asserting an organic relationship between Europe and Africa. It is indisputable that the majority of French-speaking states are in Africa. Over twenty members of the Organization of African Unity are French-speaking, in the sense of having adopted French as an official language. Without Africa, the French language would be almost a provincial language. If the Congo (Zaire) succeeds in stabilizing itself, and in assuming effective control over its resources, it may become France's rival in influence and power in French-speaking Africa as a whole. When we look at the global scene, the French language is shrinking in usage in the northern hemisphere while it is still spreading and gaining in influence in the southern hemisphere, especially in Africa. The most important challenge to the French language in the northern hemisphere has been caused by the vast expansion of American influence in the twentieth century. The language has of course been English. While the spread of the English language in Africa has been mainly due to the impact of imperial Britain, the spread of the English language in Europe, and its expanding role in international affairs, has been largely due to the new American hegemony. The triumph of the English language globally has ranged from increasing usage in diplomacy to its pre-eminent role as the eminent role as the supreme language of aviation and air-control. A related reason for the shrinkage of French in the northern hemisphere concerns the computer revolution and the Internet. The amount of information circulating in English is so much greater than what is transmitted in French that English is gaining the ascendancy even further. The old adage that "nothing succeeds like success" has now been computerized. The global influence of American computer firms like IBM and Microsoft have reinforced this Anglo-computer revolution. The third factor behind the decline of French in the northern hemisphere was Britain's entry into the European Economic Community (later European Union). This made English more decisively one of the official languages of the community. The new language became increasingly influential in the affairs of the European Union, both written and oral.

Having described some of the main factors that resulted in the decline of the French language in the northern hemisphere, we need to explore next a few some factors that contributed to its expansion in the South. What must be emphasized in the first instance is that the southern expansion is mainly in Africa. Factors that have favoured expansion in Africa included the type of states that French and Belgian imperialism created during the colonial period. These were often multi-ethnic countries that needed a *lingua franca*. Colonial policy had chosen the French language as the *lingua franca* and the entire educational system and domestic political process consolidated that linguistic choice. A related factor was the assimilationist policy of France as an imperial power, which created an elite mesmerized by French culture and civilization. With some subsidies and technical assistance, the French language is also featuring more and more in classrooms in Anglophone Africa. The global French fraternity of *Francophonie* has currently a secretariat in Paris partly headed by an African, Boutros Boutros-Ghali. Membership of the *Francophonie* club now enlists countries that have not adopted French as a national language but that can be persuaded to teach more French in their schools. The difference which Africa's independence has made partly consists in greater readiness on the part of Anglophone governments to accept France's offers of teachers of the French language. Many an African university in the Commonwealth has been the beneficiary of technical assistance and cultural subsidies from the local French Embassy or directly from France. France's policy in Africa is consolidated partly through an aggressive cultural diplomacy: considerable amounts of money are spent on French-style syllabi and curricula in African schools, and on the provision of French teachers, advisors, and reading materials. A residual French economic and administrative presence in most former French colonies has deepened Africa's orientation towards Paris. In addition, every French President since Charles de Gaulle has attempted to cultivate special personal relations with at least some of the African leaders.

Here again is a case of reciprocal conquest. There is little doubt that the French language and culture have conquered large parts of Africa. Many decisions about the future of Africa are being made by people deeply imbued by French values and perspectives. Moreover, French is expanding its constituency in Africa, at least outside Algeria. It is true that the post-colonial policy of re-Arabization in Algeria was designed to increase the role of Arabic in schools and public affairs at the expense of the pre-eminent colonial role of the French language. The rise of Islamic militancy in Algeria may pose new problems to aspects of French culture. It is also true that the late Mobutu Sese Seko's policy of promoting regional languages in Zaire (Lingala, Kikongo, Tchiluba, and Kiswahili) was successful partly at the expense of French in Zairean (now Congolese) curricula. Since 1994, French has also suffered a setback in Rwanda, led by Anglophone Tutsi originally educated in Uganda. But such setbacks for French in Africa are the exception rather than the rule. On the whole, French is still on the ascendancy in Africa though the pace of expansion has drastically declined. However, when all is said and done, France's aspiration to remain a global power requires a cultural constituency as well as an economic one. The 1990s witnessed a change in France's economic priorities in favour of the new pan-European opportunities and against the older investments in Africa. But it seems certain that a more open Europe after the end of the Cold War will favour the English language at the expense of the French language, even within France itself. As custodian of the fortunes of French civilization, France could not afford to abandon the cultural constituency of Africa entirely in favour of the more open Europe. The collapse of the Soviet empire has been a further gain for the English language, and France may need Africa more culturally, but less economically. Its cultural constituency in Europe has been declining; its cultural constituency in Africa is becoming more valuable than ever. A remarkable interdependence has emerged, still imperfect and uneven but real enough to make Africa indispensable for the recognition of France as a truly global power and the acceptance of the French language as a credible world language. "Eurafrica" as a concept gets its maximum meaningfulness in the destiny of the French language.

Afrindia: Between Gandhi and Nehru

Quite early in his life, Mahatma Mohandas Gandhi saw non-violent resistance as a method that would be well suited for the African as well as the Indian. In 1924, Gandhi said that if the black people "caught the spirit of the Indian movement their progress must be rapid."[6] To understand his claim, one should perhaps link it up with something that was later said by his disciple, Jawaharlal Nehru. Nehru said: "Reading through history I think the agony of the African continent... has not been equaled anywhere."[7] To the extent then that the black man had more to be angry about than other men, he would need greater self-discipline than others to be "passive" in his resistance. But by the same token, to the extent that the black man in the last three centuries had suffered more than any other, passive but purposeful self-sacrifice for the cause should come easier to him. And to the extent that the black man had more to forgive the rest of the world for, that forgiveness when it came should be more weighty. Perhaps in response to adding up these considerations, Gandhi came to the conclusion by 1936 that it was "maybe through the Negroes that the unadulterated message of non-violence will be delivered to the world."8

And so it was that in America the torch passed onto Martin Luther King, Jr. In South Africa, where Gandhi first experimented with his methods, it passed to Albert Luthuli and later to Desmond Tutu. In Northern Rhodesia (Zambia after independence), Kenneth Kaunda became a vigorous Gandhian, saying "I reject absolutely violence in any of its forms as a solution to our problems."9 In the Gold Coast (Ghana before independence), Nkrumah had translated *Satyagraha* (soul force) into a programme of "Positive Action," a programme which he himself defined as "non-cooperation based on the principle of absolute non-violence, as used by Gandhi in India."10 In 1949, the *Morning Telegraph* of Accra went as far as to call Nkrumah the "Gandhi of Ghana."11 African conceptions of dignity now seemed very different from what was implied by that old ceremonial affirmation of young Kikuyu initiates, which Kenyatta once said consisted of the glorification of the spear as "the symbol of our courageous and fighting spirit." But these new conceptions of dignity could now also be differentiated from the submissive virtues of early missionary teachings. Yet one question remained to be answered: could passive resistance survive the attainment of independence? Would Gandhism retain political relevance once its immediate objective of liberation from colonialism was achieved? It is perhaps not entirely accidental that the two most important Indian contributions to African political thought were the doctrines of non-violence and nonalignment. In a sense, they were almost twin-doctrines. Gandhi contributed passive resistance to one school of African thought; Nehru contributed nonalignment to almost all African countries. We should note how Uganda's Milton Obote put it in his tribute to Nehru on his death in 1964: "Nehru will be remembered as a founder of nonalignment... The new nations of the world owe him a debt of gratitude in this respect."[12]

However, Gandhi and Nehru both taught Africa and learnt from it. But how related are the two doctrines in their assumptions? For India itself, Gandhi's non-violence was a method of seeking freedom, while Nehru's nonalignment came to be a method of seeking peace. And yet nonalignment was, in some ways, a translation into foreign policy of some of the moral assumptions that underlay passive resistance in the domestic struggle for India's independence. As independent India's first Prime Minister, Nehru's armed ejection of Portuguese colonialism from Goa in 1961 had a different impact on Africa. India's then Foreign Minister, Krishna Menon, described colonialism to the UN as "permanent aggression." Particularly "permanent" was the colonialism of those who regarded their colonies as part of the Metropole, as Portugal had pretended to do. In such a situation when colonialism threatened to be durable, even "permanent," the military solution was a necessary option. Nehru's use of armed force against the Portuguese set a grand precedent for an Africa still shackled by Portuguese imperialism in Angola, Mozambique, and Guinea-Bissau. What has seldom been adequately examined is the reverse flow of influence from Africa into both Gandhi's vision of *Satyagraha* and Nehru's concept of nonalignment. Experience in the southern part of Africa must be counted as part of the genesis of Gandhi's political philosophy. Similarly, the 1956 Suez war in the northern part of Africa was probably a major influence on Nehru's vision of nonalignment. Gandhi first confronted the problem of politicized evil in the context of racism in South Africa. He lived in South Africa from 1893 to 1914 and racial humiliation in that part of the continent helped to radicalize him— and therefore helped to prepare him for his more decisive historical role in British India from 1919 onwards. Gandhi's political philosophy developed from both the world of ideas and the world of experience. Moreover, in the realm of ideas he relied heavily on both Western liberalism and Indian thought. But what helped to radicalize Gandhi's own interpretation of those ideas was the power of experience. And within that crucible of experience we have to include Gandhi's exposure to sustained segregation in South Africa, a deeper form of racism than even the racist horrors of British India at that time. If Gandhi's *Satyagraha* was a response to the moral confrontation between good and evil, Nehru's nonalignment was a response to the militarized confrontation between Capitalism and Socialism. If Gandhi's political philosophy was originally a response to racial intolerance, Nehru's nonalignment was originally a response to ideological intolerance. The regime in South Africa became the symbol of racial bigotry for Gandhi. The Cold War between East and West became the essence of ideological bigotry for Nehru. South Africa as an inspiration for Gandhi is well documented. North Africa as an inspiration for Nehru's nonalignment has been less explored.

Two wars in North Africa in the 1950s were particularly important in Afro-Asian interaction. The Algerian war from 1954 to 1962 took African resistance beyond the passive level into the militarized active domain. The second great war in North Africa in the 1950s was the Suez conflict of 1956. If the Algerian war marked a possible end to *Satyagraha* as a strategy for African liberation movements, the Suez war marked a possible birth of nonalignment as a policy of post-colonial era. The United States, Britain, and the World Bank economically punished Gamal Abdel Nasser of Egypt for purchasing arms from the Communist bloc. Washington, London, and the Bank reneged on their commitment to help Egypt build the Aswan Dam. Nasser's nationalization of the Suez Canal was thus an assertion of self-reliance: revenues from the Canal were supposed to help Egypt construct the Great Dam. Egypt's sovereign right to purchase arms from either East or West was not for sale. In retrospect, Nasser's nationalization of the Suez Canal was a kind of unilateral declaration of nonalignment. This was before the Nonaligned Movement itself was as yet formally constituted. Before the actual outbreak of the Suez hostilities, the diplomatic division at the level of the big powers was indeed East/West. Socialist governments were also neatly in support of Nasser, while the capitalist world was alarmed by his nationalization of the Canal. However, when Britain, France, and Israel actually invaded Egypt, the Western world was divided. The United States was strongly opposed to the military action taken by its own closest allies, although Washington was also very hostile to Nasser. The Soviet Union helped Egypt by providing pilots and engineers to operate the canal after the nationalization until Nasser could train his own engineers. And in the wake of the West's reneging on the commitment to build the Aswan High Dam, the Soviet Union stepped into the breach and became its builder.

Jawaharlal Nehru helped to mobilize Third World opinion on the side of Gamal Abdel Nasser during the whole crisis. Although there was not as yet a Nonaligned Movement in world politics, the Suez conflict was part of the labour pains of its birth—and Jawaharlal Nehru was the leading midwife in attendance. It is these factors that have made the Suez crisis part of the genesis of Nehru's diplomatic thought and vision, just as racism in South Africa was an integral part of the genesis of Mahatma Gandhi's principle of *Satyagraha*. Suez was the most dramatic test of a Third World country: never before had a Third World country been the subject of aggression by two members of NATO—and yet with the leader of NATO, the United States, protesting against its allies. Nehru was both a teacher over Suez and a learner from its experience. Forty years later, in the mid-1990s, South Africa had its first multiracial election and Nelson Mandela became President. When the new Republic of South Africa joined the Nonaligned Movement, the heritage of Gandhi and the legacy of Nehru were at last fused on the very continent on which they were once separately born. Morally, "Afrindia" was about to be vindicated. Five black men influenced by Gandhi have won the Nobel Prize for Peace: Ralph Bunche (1950); Albert Luthuli (1960); Martin Luther King, Jr. (1964); Desmond Tutu (1984); and Nelson Mandela (1993). Two were Black Americans and three Black South Africans. By a strange twist of fate Mahatma Gandhi himself never won the Nobel Prize but his black disciples did.

Towards an African Conquest of Itself

Africa's capacity to turn weakness into a form of influence has found a new arena of fulfillment. Fragmentation and excessive cultural receptivity are weaknesses. And weakness is not an adequate currency in the market place of power. But quite often the power of the weak is, in human terms, less dangerous than the weakness of the powerful. And yet, when all is said and done, the ultimate conquest is Africa's conquest of itself. The ultimate colonization is self-colonization under the banner of *Pax Africana*. It is to this ultimate full circle that we must now turn. As thousands are falling victims to strife and instability across the continent, can Africa create conditions through which some kind of recolonization becomes possible? In the 1990s, a thousand people a day were dying in the Angolan civil war, from time to time. Somalia was (and still is) torn between chaos and clanocracy (rule on the basis of clans). Burundi has a long history of brutal ethnocracy (rule by a particular ethnic group). Rwanda collapsed into genocide and civil war in 1994. Liberia and Sierra Leone had a tumultuous and bloody decade in the 1990s. Is recolonization feasible? Indeed, could colonization itself be part of yet another cyclical rather than a unilinear experience? Could colonialism have different incarnations, a kind of transmigration of the imperial soul? The imperial soul had previously resided in separate European powers: Britain, France, Portugal, Belgium, etc. Has the imperial soul transmigrated to the United States? Or is the soul trying to decide whether to settle in the bosom of the United Nations? Is this a period of cosmic imperial indecision between the United States and the United Nations as voices of "the world community"?

The next phase of colonialism can be collective rather than through individual powers. It may indeed be the transmigration of the soul of the United Nations Trusteeship Council to some new UN decision-making machinery. Will Africa play a role both as guardian and as ward? Although colonialism may be resurfacing, it is likely to look rather different this time around. A future trusteeship system will be more genuinely international and less western than it was under the old guise. Administering powers for the trusteeship territories could come from Africa and Asia, as well as from the rest of the membership of the UN. For example, might Uganda be officially invited by the UN to administer a fragile Rwanda? Might Nigeria be officially invited to administer Sierra Leone for a while on behalf of the United Nations or on behalf of a reconstituted Organization of African Unity? However, regional hegemonic power can lose influence as well as gain it. Just as there is sub-colonization of one African country by another, there can be sub-decolonization as the weaker country reasserts itself. This is part of what has happened between Egypt and Sudan in the 1990s. Sudan under the Bashir Islamic regime started asserting greater independence of Egypt than anytime since the *Mahdiyya* movement under Seyyid Muhammad el Mahdi in the nineteenth century. Relations between Somalia and Egypt in the era after Siad Barre may also be a case of sub-decolonization—the reassertion of the weaker country (Somalia) against the influence of its more powerful brother (Egypt). If sub-colonization of one African country by another is possible, and sub-decolonization has also been demonstrated, what about sub-recolonization? Will Egypt reestablish its big brother's relationship with Sudan and Somalia? Will there be another full circle?

In West Africa, the situation is especially complex. Nigeria is a giant of over 100 million people. Its real rival in the region was never Ghana under Kwame Nkrumah, or Libya under Muammar Qaddafi, or distant South Africa. The real rival to post-colonial Nigeria has all along been France. By all measurements of size, resources, and population, Nigeria should rapidly have become in West Africa what India is in South Asia or South Africa has been in Southern Africa: a hegemonic power. Nigeria was marginalized not only by civil war, in 1967-70, but also by its own chronic incompetence and by the massive French presence in West Africa—mainly in its own former colonies but also in Nigeria itself. In the 21st century, France will be withdrawing from West Africa as she gets increasingly involved in the affairs of Eastern and Western Europe. France's West African sphere of influence will in time be filled by Nigeria, a more natural hegemonic power in West Africa. It will be under those circumstances that eventually Nigeria's own boundaries could expand to incorporate the Republic of Niger (the Hausa link), the Republic of Benin (the Yoruba link), and conceivably Cameroon (part of which anyway nearly became Nigerian in a referendum in 1959). The case of post-apartheid South Africa also raises questions about a regional hegemonic power. On the positive and optimistic side, this will make it possible to achieve regional integration in Southern Africa. Regional unification is easier where one country is more equal than others and can provide the leadership necessary for the task. On the negative side, post-apartheid South Africa could be a kind of sub-imperial power and questions of sub-colonization, sub-decolonization, and sub-recolonization may become part of the future historical agenda of Southern Africa. Yet another full circle!

If I have presented some frightening possibilities, it is because some African countries may need to be temporarily controlled by others. The umbrella of *Pax Africana* is needed, an African peace enforced by Africans themselves. Africa may have to conquer itself in order to stop the recurring carnage and the loss of innocent lives across the continent. If we were to take the case of the Angolan Civil War, a war that was very costly in terms of African lives, South Africa could have intervened has it been already black-ruled; benevolent sub-colonization could have been attempted for the greater good. It would have been comparable to India's intervention in East Pakistan, in 1971, when the Pakistani army was on the rampage against its own Bengali citizens. India intervened and created Bangladesh, but it had a vested interest in dividing Pakistan. Post-apartheid South Africa could intervene in a civil war in Angola for humanitarian and Pan-African reasons, and could still preserve the territorial integrity of its smaller neighbours. South Africa's intervention in Lesotho, in 1998, was bungled and inept, but the basic principle of *Pax Africana* behind it was sound! New possibilities are on the horizon. We may yet learn to distinguish between benevolent intervention and malignant invasion in the years ahead. Africa could conquer itself without colonizing itself.

Conclusion

We have sought to demonstrate in this essay the paradox of counter-penetration and the cyclical boomerang effect in Africa's interaction with other civilizations. Africa's cultural responsiveness to its Arab conquerors has now tilted the demographic balance and changed the Arab cultural equation. The majority of the Arabs are now in Africa and the

African side of the Arab world has become the most innovative in art and science. Africa's responsiveness to the French language and culture has already made Africa the second most important home of French civilization after France itself. The majority of "French-speaking" countries are already in Africa and the Congo (Zaire) stands a chance of one day becoming a rival to France in leading this French-speaking part of the world. Africa's response to Gandhi's ideas, reinforced by Christian pacifism, has already given Africa more Nobel Prizes for peace than India. Gandhi himself had once predicted that the torch of *Satyagraha* would one day be borne by the Black world. Africa's response to Nehru's ideas of nonalignment has resulted in a majority of the nonaligned countries being from Africa. Africa was in fact the first continent to become almost completely nonaligned. If nonalignment once penetrated Africa, Africa has now truly penetrated the Nonaligned Movement.

In the future, Africa's cultural receptivity has to be more systematically moderated by cultural selectivity. Counter-penetrating one's conquerors may be one worthy trend. But at least as important for Africa is a reduced danger of being excessively penetrated by others. Perhaps one day the sequence of cultural penetration will be reversed. Instead of Africans being Arabized so completely that the majority of the Arabs are in Africa, some other Asians will be Africanized so completely that they are indistinguishable from native Africans. Instead of the Congo (Zaire) being the largest French-speaking nation after France, some other European nation will become the second heartland of Yoruba civilization after West Africa. Meanwhile, Africa has to conquer itself, if it is to avoid further colonization by others. Africa needs to establish a *Pax Africana*, an African peace promoted and maintained by Africans themselves. One day, each African person will look in the mirror and behold the fusion of the guardian and the ward rolled into one.

NOTES

This chapter is a revised version of an article that appeared, under the same title, in *Africa in World Politics*, edited by John W. Harbeson and Donald Rothchild (Boulder, CO: Westview Press, 1995), pp. 69-94.

1. See Muhammad Abdul-Hai, *Conflict and Identity: The Cultural Poetics of Contemporary Sudanese Poetry*, African Seminar Series No. 26 (Khartoum: Institute of African and Asian Studies, University of Khartoum, 1976), pp. 26-27.

2. *Nar al Majadhib* (Khartoum: Dar al-Jil and Sharikat al-Maktabah al-Ahliyah, 1969), pp. 195, 287. See also p. 24.

3. Cited by Abdul-Hai, *Conflict and Identity*, pp.40-41.

4. *Ghadhbat al Hababy* (Beirut: Dar al Thaqafah, 1968) and Abdul-Hai, *Conflict and Identity*, p.52.

5. Dr. Boutros Boutros-Ghali interviewed by the author in Cairo, 1985.

6. *Young Indian*, August 21, 1924 (Madras: S. Ganesan, 1927), pp.839-40. Consult also Pyarelal, "Gandhi and the African Question," *Africa Quarterly*, II, 2 (July-September 1962). See as well the selection from Gandhi entitled "Mahatma Gandhi on Freedom in Africa," *African Quarterly*, II, 2 (July-September 1962). For a more extensive discussion by Gandhi on non-violence consult Gandhi, *Non-Violence in Peace and War* [2nd ed.] (Ahmedabad: Navajivan Publishing House, 1944).

7. Jawaharlal Nehru, "Portuguese Colonialism: An Anachronism," *Africa Quarterly*, I, 3 (October-December, 1961), p. 9. See also Nehru "Emergent Africa," *Africa Quarterly*, I, 1 (April-June 1961), pp. 7-9.

8. *Harijan*, October 14, 1939.

9. See Colin M. Morris and Kenneth D. Kaunda, *Black Government? A Discussion between Colin Morris and Kenneth Kaunda* (Lusaka: United Society for Christian Literature, 1960).

10. Kwame Nkrumah, *Ghana: The Autobiography of Kwame Nkrumah* (New York: International Publishers, 1957), p. 112.

11. *Morning Telegraph*, June 27, 1949.

12. See *Uganda Argus*, May 29, 1964 and Ali A. Mazrui, *Africa's International Relations: The Diplomacy of Dependency and Change* (London: Heinemann Educational Books and Boulder: Westview Press, 1977), pp. 117-121.

INDEX

A

Africa
  Anglophone, 91, 104, 250,
  257, 459, 460
  Francophone Africa, 105,
  142, 257
  Global Africa, 157
  North Africa, 10, 113, 117,
  205, 225, 226, 227, 228,
  230, 234, 260, 269, 335,
  451, 452, 463, 464
  postcolonial, 79, 97, 101,
  102, 103, 106, 108, 121,
  124, 126, 128, 129, 131,
  138, 162, 174, 234, 236,
  237, 239, 240, 241, 243,
  245, 246, 247, 270, 273,
  459, 464, 467
  South Africa, 21, 100, 112,
  140, 153, 160, 227, 230,
  235, 251, 269, 270, 297,
  300, 318, 329, 331, 350,
  359, 374, 380, 385, 434,
  435, 436, 437, 441, 447,
  461, 463, 465, 467, 468
  Sub-Saharan, 225, 227,
  228, 248, 253, 258, 261,
  262, 355, 360, 423, 454
  Traditional Africa, 68, 125,
  249, 351, 389
  West Africa, 113, 115, 117,
  157, 165, 227, 228, 229,
  230, 233, 240, 242,
  245, 246, 248, 254, 283,
  306, 313, 318, 325, 376,
  426, 446, 467, 470
African agriculture, 325
African Institutions, 61
African Religions, 100, 115,
  143, 235, 241
African Socialism, 144, 374,
  394
African traditions, 84, 97,
  235, 252
Africana, 143, 154, 469
Africanity, 112, 241, 374, 454
Amin, Idi, 104, 107, 130, 141,
  142, 237, 246, 269, 445
Anglo-Saxon, 3, 25, 26, 27,
  28, 29, 30, 31, 33, 34, 35,
  36, 37, 38, 40, 41, 42, 43,
  44, 45, 46, 47, 48, 49, 51,
  52, 53, 178, 181, 182, 190,
  267, 283, 366, 417, 418,
  419, 424
Angola, 125, 126, 128, 133,
  153, 155, 158, 296, 463,
  468

Apartheid, 108, 223, 226, 230, 269, 300, 329, 331, 342, 359, 436, 437, 468
Arabian Peninsula, 228, 248
Arabization, 9, 226, 227, 230, 451, 452, 453, 454, 456, 459
Arabs, 2, 3, 8, 11, 40, 51, 66, 90, 151, 184, 225, 226, 227, 228, 230, 268, 269, 311, 333, 451, 452, 453, 454, 455, 456, 469, 470
Ashanti, 98, 108, 139
Association of South East Asian Nations (ASEAN), 134, 338
Atatürk, 92, 203, 204, 209, 211, 212, 216, 217, 219, 220, 221, 222, 257, 275
Atatürk Revolution, 204, 217, 220
Azikiwe, Nnamdi, 71, 129, 242

B

Baganda, 100
Bantu, 82, 131, 374, 441
Belgian Congo, 129, 208, 318
Belgium, 205, 208, 256, 466
Berbers, 10, 228
Berlin Conference, 150, 165, 289
Biafra, 209, 243, 402
Bismarck, Otto von, 282, 284, 289, 290, 292, 295, 297, 298, 300
Black Africa, 22, 24, 69, 70, 100, 152, 164, 174, 236, 237, 268, 363, 423, 431, 434
Boutros-Ghali, Boutros 457, 459, 470
Brazil, 110, 264, 266, 337
Brazzaville, 401
Burundi, 74, 108, 113, 155, 247, 290, 313, 423, 466
Bush, George, 284, 297, 331, 333, 334, 336

C

Cameroon, 246, 313, 468
Capitalism, 4, 16, 18, 20, 25, 30, 31, 32, 33, 34, 35, 44, 47, 49, 50, 51, 52, 118, 122, 138, 165, 325, 326, 463
Capitalist, 1, 17, 30, 33, 34, 35, 47, 49, 50, 62, 63, 98, 123, 124, 128, 134, 153, 213, 261, 263, 264, 274, 304, 320, 321, 325, 326, 464
Césaire, Aimé, 111, 349, 382
China, 27, 85, 87, 105, 127, 134, 141, 212, 218, 219, 263, 264, 272, 273, 276, 283, 292, 316, 360
Christianity, 2, 6, 7, 8, 37, 39, 46, 50, 143, 153, 171, 173, 235, 237, 238, 239, 240, 241, 245, 251, 350, 368, 449, 452
Christians, 6, 8, 10, 40, 147, 172, 187, 231, 237, 238, 239, 240, 241, 250
Yoruba Christianity, 241
Churchill, Winston, 25, 252
City-state, 50, 229, 248

Civilization, 3, 5, 41, 52, 71, 78, 85, 86, 87, 88, 111, 149, 150, 152, 153, 156, 164, 169, 170, 171, 174, 178, 179, 194, 197, 219, 230, 239, 248, 258, 274, 327, 345, 346, 349, 350, 351, 354, 359, 360, 361, 363, 364, 367, 368, 369, 374, 376, 377, 419, 444, 450, 453, 459, 460, 469, 470

Civilizations, 79, 84, 87, 92, 149, 150, 151, 153, 154, 161, 178, 218, 272, 288, 347, 349, 357, 363, 364, 366, 444, 469

Clash of civilizations, 147, 148, 149, 151, 161

Cold War, 139, 142, 143, 148, 149, 151, 152, 153, 161, 162, 163, 166, 262, 263, 264, 266, 272, 329, 332, 333, 334, 339, 340, 341, 406, 460, 463

Colonialism, 92, 144, 156, 471

Colonization, 6, 24, 44, 118, 151, 152, 158, 159, 162, 165, 245, 256, 264, 274, 282, 284, 297, 331, 418, 428, 435, 450, 466, 467, 470

Colonial Powers, 134, 213, 311, 314, 402, 475

Columbus, Christopher, 22, 281, 282, 283

Communication, 3, 5, 10, 11, 15, 20, 21, 22, 23, 25, 29, 51, 59, 70, 74, 78, 152, 177

Communication revolution, 20, 23, 24

Computer, 258, 458

Congo, 113, 125, 140, 147, 154, 155, 156, 199, 208, 235, 247, 301, 313, 319, 380, 397, 398, 400, 401, 402, 403, 404, 405, 406, 407, 409, 410, 411, 412, 413, 414, 415, 416, 423, 426, 454, 457, 469, 470

Consciencism, 238, 352, 353, 374

Cuba, 26, 128, 266, 296, 390

Culture, 2, 3, 4, 5, 8, 12, 14, 18, 21, 25, 32, 36, 38, 41, 43, 44, 45, 47, 49, 50, 55, 58, 59, 60, 61, 65, 66, 67, 68, 69, 70, 71, 72, 73, 74, 76, 78, 80, 81, 83, 84, 85, 87, 88, 89, 91, 95, 98, 99, 100, 101, 102, 104, 110, 112, 114, 118, 120, 122, 125, 127, 132, 137, 138, 148, 149, 150, 151, 152, 154, 155, 156, 170, 171, 176, 178, 180, 183, 189, 190, 204, 206, 207, 209, 218, 219, 221, 222, 237, 240, 241, 249, 250, 252, 253, 256, 257, 258, 261, 270, 271, 274, 288, 292, 303, 319, 325, 339, 341, 347, 335, 339, 341, 347, 348, 349, 353, 355, 358, 359, 360, 365, 366, 368, 383, 418, 422, 431, 432, 435, 438, 443, 444, 445, 449, 453, 454, 458, 459, 469, 473, 476

Cultural paradigm, 58, 66, 67

Spread of, 4

D

Davidson, Basil, 227, 228, 254, 360, 376
Declaration of Independence, 29, 189
Decolonization, 29, 79, 91, 163, 265, 312, 314, 319, 428, 467, 468
Democracy, 144, 198, 327, 394
    Democratic, 28, 31, 34, 113, 120, 129, 132, 134, 136, 137, 147, 153, 155, 156, 177, 179, 296, 335, 337
    Democratization, 28, 134, 136, 137, 216
Dependency, 33, 37, 57, 60, 62, 65, 67, 68, 69, 70, 72, 74, 75, 78, 85, 92, 271, 275, 313, 317, 449, 450
Development, 21, 33, 35, 57, 63, 67, 78, 84, 113, 135, 136, 162, 170, 171, 177, 178, 179, 180, 181, 182, 194, 195, 197, 198, 199, 208, 258, 259, 261, 265, 271, 273, 281, 298, 313, 318, 320, 321, 337, 364, 370, 402, 439
Diaspora, 6, 90, 109, 110, 116, 157, 159, 172, 311
Diversity, 20, 81, 87, 131, 218, 235, 244, 305, 306, 406, 411
Domestication, 79, 88, 91, 218
DuBois, W.E.B., 109, 116, 148, 151, 197, 362, 376

E

Economic, 1, 4, 17, 23, 28, 30, 32, 33, 40, 43, 45, 50, 51, 60, 63, 78, 79, 84, 85, 90, 95, 110, 112, 119, 120, 122, 124, 125, 126, 128, 129, 134, 135, 136, 137, 138, 149, 150, 154, 157, 159, 160, 161, 162, 163, 165, 166, 189, 190, 196, 198, 203, 204, 206, 211, 212, 214, 215, 220, 223, 241, 242, 243, 244, 245, 255, 257, 258, 259, 262, 263, 266, 267, 270, 271, 272, 289, 297, 325, 330, 333, 334, 336, 337, 338, 339, 341, 385, 439, 459, 460
Education, 58, 59, 64, 65, 67, 69, 70, 71, 72, 74, 75, 76, 78, 79, 91, 177, 126, 156, 207, 208, 209, 239, 242, 291, 348, 424
Egypt, 9, 14, 87, 105, 108, 111, 113, 124, 130, 141, 143, 153, 225, 228, 234, 235, 260, 269, 275, 330, 334, 354, 357, 358, 361, 362, 364, 367, 368, 376, 419, 451, 452, 454, 456, 464, 467
    Enlightenment, 15, 19
Ethiopia, 28, 45, 108, 125, 128, 132, 225, 235, 237, 244, 255, 270, 364
Eurafrica, 433, 457, 460
Europe, 5, 8, 9, 11, 14, 16, 17, 20, 21, 23, 33, 34, 44, 50, 58, 61, 63, 64, 84, 89, 90,

100, 110, 111, 113, 128, 135, 139, 142, 143, 151, 152, 153, 158, 160, 162, 163, 165, 166, 173, 194, 198, 205, 206, 214, 217, 219, 264, 281, 282, 283, 284, 287, 289, 291, 329, 332, 335, 339, 346, 348, 349, 350, 351, 354, 355, 356, 362, 363, 364, 365, 366, 367, 368, 369, 370, 373, 376, 398, 421, 422, 432, 433, 434, 435, 438, 443, 444, 445, 457, 460, 467

F

France, 10, 18, 23, 27, 30, 31, 36, 38, 39, 62, 143, 205, 256, 264, 276, 290, 292, 313, 315, 335, 365, 414, 415, 416, 420, 422, 435, 443, 444, 457, 458, 460, 464, 466, 467, 469, 470
French Revolution, 18, 29, 31, 186, 288, 406

G

Gandhi, Mahatma, 3, 23, 41, 269, 273, 323, 450, 460, 461, 462, 465, 469, 470
Garvey, Marcus, 116, 379, 393
Gender, 48, 49, 251, 321, 323, 324, 325, 326, 327
Genocide, 147, 149, 151, 155, 269, 283, 303, 310, 466
Ghana, 23, 24, 58, 59, 71, 98, 130, 133, 135, 136, 145,

182, 183, 238, 242, 258, 259, 260, 271, 275, 352, 357, 370, 374, 375, 377, 379, 424, 432, 446, 447, 461, 467, 471
Global apartheid, 151, 161, 163, 165, 342
Gold, 1, 2, 3, 4, 12, 14, 16, 17, 20, 27, 32, 33, 49, 50, 51, 89, 173, 231, 290
Graeco-Roman, 8, 14, 171, 173, 347, 348, 349, 350, 351, 362, 364, 367, 369, 372, 373
Greece, 7, 11, 14, 113, 189, 345, 346, 349, 363, 364, 365, 366, 367, 368, 369
Ancient, 197, 345
Greek, 7, 85, 112, 345, 347, 348, 350, 351, 352, 353, 354, 361, 364, 365, 366, 368, 370, 371, 372, 452

H

Hausa, 69, 118, 154, 156, 233, 236, 241, 242, 252, 451, 454, 468
Hausaland, 233
Hegemony, 18, 25, 27, 44, 47, 123, 150, 189, 245, 264, 295, 313, 314, 319, 331, 420, 422, 458
Hitler, Adolf, 290, 298, 301, 303, 310, 315
Hutu, 74, 75, 147, 155

I

Iberian Peninsula, 10

Ibo, 74, 235, 241, 242
Ideology, 20, 21, 75, 85, 95,
    99, 114, 118, 122, 123, 125,
    126, 129, 134, 137, 138, 141,
    143, 147, 148, 158, 169,
    194, 207, 222, 273, 296,
    335, 359, 380, 386, 387,
    388, 478
Imperalism, 23, 28, 33, 40,
    45, 59, 62, 111, 123, 126,
    148, 149, 152, 157, 161, 163,
    173, 196, 233, 245, 246,
    264, 272, 273, 274, 289,
    313, 314, 318, 332, 346,
    347, 367, 368, 417, 426,
    435, 437, 438, 439, 458,
    462
India, 5, 9, 11, 23, 24, 40, 41,
    62, 74, 212, 218, 219, 232,
    242, 256, 260, 262, 263,
    272, 273, 281, 282, 283,
    284, 285, 286, 287, 288,
    289, 292, 300, 318, 356,
    360, 366, 419, 436, 449,
    450, 461, 462, 467, 468,
    469
    Indian, 9, 23, 26, 84, 152,
    266, 268, 270, 272, 273,
    282, 285, 286, 288, 349,
    359, 364, 366, 382, 436,
    450, 461, 462, 463, 470
Indirect Rule, 71, 97, 99, 140,
    403
Industrial Revolution, 19, 22,
    33
International Labour
    Organization (ILO), 29,
    319

International Monetary Fund
    (IMF), 34, 136, 160, 164,
    169, 338
International Order, 318,
    320, 327
Iraq, 9, 164, 238, 330, 331,
    333, 334, 452
Islam, 2, 8, 9, 10, 11, 13, 14,
    40, 44, 45, 46, 50, 66, 87,
    90, 113, 115, 141, 143, 205,
    218, 225, 226, 227, 228,
    229, 230, 231, 232, 233,
    234, 235, 237, 238, 239,
    240, 241, 243, 244, 245,
    246, 247, 248, 249, 250,
    251, 252, 253, 254, 267,
    268, 275, 329, 330, 331,
    334, 341, 356, 451, 452,
    454
    Islamic, 2, 10, 11, 13, 40,
    42, 45, 50, 84, 90, 115,
    134, 204, 219, 225, 226,
    229, 231, 234, 235, 237,
    240, 241, 243, 244, 245,
    247, 248, 249, 251, 252,
    253, 254, 268, 330, 459,
    467
    Islamization, 9, 226, 227,
    230, 244, 248, 270, 451,
    452, 454
Israel, 39, 40, 162, 172, 310,
    330, 332, 333, 464
Ivory Coast, 71, 424

J

Japan, 34, 65, 69, 162, 203,
    204, 205, 206, 209, 211,
    212, 213, 214, 216, 218,
    219, 220, 221, 222, 257,

264, 274, 315, 339, 360, 437

Jewish, 7, 39, 40, 43, 114, 170, 172, 173, 187, 194, 299, 310, 311.

Jesus (Christ), 7, 8, 13, 46, 170, 173, 194, 239, 240

Jews, 2, 3, 6, 7, 14, 39, 40, 51, 108, 164, 170, 172, 173, 184, 187, 194, 299, 303, 311, 383.

Jihad, 233

Jihads, 2, 4, 246

Judaism, 6, 13, 39, 172, 173, 196, 235, 310

K

Kenya, 71, 72, 73, 98, 101, 103, 113, 117, 120, 124, 133, 139, 144, 229, 230, 231, 247, 248, 258, 260, 269, 301, 310, 356, 368, 373, 407, 424, 427, 438, 454

Kenyatta, Jomo, 62, 71, 72, 98, 102, 103, 109, 125, 139, 461

Kipling, Rudyard, 42, 196, 206, 417, 418, 419, 424, 425, 426, 427, 428, 429, 430

Kuwait, 40, 164, 331

L

Labor, 32, 46, 60, 83, 95, 206, 306

Labour, 158, 171, 196, 251, 261, 284, 465

Language, 9, 21, 25, 36, 38, 43, 57, 59, 69, 71, 72, 73, 81, 82, 84, 87, 113, 114, 116, 117, 132, 138, 141, 191, 214, 215, 216, 226, 227, 251, 257, 270, 292, 347, 348, 361, 366, 369, 370, 400, 414, 418, 419, 420, 421, 422, 423, 425, 428, 450, 451, 454, 457, 458, 459

African languages, 69, 70, 80, 81, 82, 88, 127, 215, 231, 251, 370, 371

Arabic language, 226, 227, 251, 451, 453, 454, 455

English language, 25, 38, 40, 43, 70, 73, 238, 252, 418, 419, 420, 421, 422, 424, 425, 428, 458, 460

French language, 217, 422, 444, 457, 458, 459, 469

Kiswahili language, 59, 69, 70, 73, 82, 113, 127, 231, 252, 454, 460

Swahili language, 73, 110, 113, 229, 230, 231, 252, 370, 372, 377, 431, 454

Lebanese, 162, 339, 452

Lesotho, 468

Liberalism, 12, 18, 30, 31, 34, 41, 75, 96, 177, 187, 381, 463

Liberal, 6, 14, 30, 34, 35, 65, 68, 75, 98, 118, 120, 134, 136, 158, 170, 177, 178, 188, 273, 274, 305, 307, 308, 359, 381

Liberia, 42, 113, 158, 263, 439, 466

Libya, 113, 232, 234, 245, 247, 296, 331, 334, 467

Locke, John, 15, 31, 184, 186

Lugard, Lord, 71, 288, 346

Lumumba, Patrice, 143, 160, 401, 402, 403, 405, 409

M

Malawi, 103, 107, 113, 124, 133, 231

Mali, 136, 229, 230, 246, 248

Marginalization, 150, 283, 299, 338

Marx, 32, 33, 35, 44, 46, 68, 69, 86, 126, 127, 163, 174, 188, 189, 191, 192, 194, 195, 196, 200, 243, 391, 393

Marxism, 33, 44, 45, 46, 86, 87, 95, 125, 169, 188, 190, 192, 238, 272, 309, 335, 351, 359

Mbiti, John, 100, 140

Mecca, 40, 90, 225, 232, 248, 249, 253

Medina, 40, 143, 225, 248, 253

Meiji Restoration, 65, 92, 203, 204, 205, 210, 211, 212, 213, 217, 219, 220, 221, 257, 275

Mill, John Stuart, 177, 381

Missionaries, 171, 207, 232, 239, 241, 251

Missionary Work, 231, 232, 233, 240

Modernity, 88, 143

Modernization, 34, 41, 42, 65, 79, 174, 177, 180, 194, 195, 197, 198, 203, 204, 205, 206, 208, 209, 210, 211, 212, 214, 215, 216, 217, 218, 219, 220, 221, 222, 257, 258, 261, 271, 275

Mombasa, 229, 248, 368

Monotheism, 14, 50, 249

Mozambique, 113, 123, 125, 128, 153, 231, 463

Mugabe, Robert, 124, 155

Muhammad (Prophet), 9, 50, 115, 225, 228, 232, 233, 244, 249, 252, 253455, 456, 467, 470

Muslims, 9, 10, 11, 40, 85, 91, 147, 162, 229, 230, 231, 232, 234, 237, 238, 239, 240, 241, 244, 245, 246, 247, 249, 250, 252, 330, 331, 332, 334, 339, 341

N

Nairobi, 65, 73, 92, 140, 197, 269, 370, 373, 427, 429

Namibia, 153, 296, 313, 318

Nasser, Gamal Abdel, 105, 125, 141, 464, 465

National consciousness, 138, 324

Négritude, 86, 111, 306, 309, 350, 351, 357, 364, 372, 382, 33, 384, 385, 443, 455

New World Order, 165, 330, 331, 334, 335, 339, 341

Niger, 230, 246

Nigeria, 23, 71, 72, 85, 90, 101, 118, 119, 121, 129, 130, 133, 140, 147, 164, 165, 182, 209, 220, 232, 233,

235, 237, 238, 239, 240,
241, 242, 243, 246, 250,
254, 259, 263, 402, 423,
431, 467
Nile River, 368
Nkrumah, Kwame, 23, 71,
109, 123, 135, 144, 145,
238, 242, 259, 345, 352,
372, 374, 377, 379, 432,
447, 467, 471
Nobel Prize, 299, 465, 469
Nonaligned Movement
(NAM), 263, 265, 266,
270, 272, 450, 464, 465,
469
North Atlantic Treaty
Organization (NATO), 153,
263, 265, 464
Nyerere, Julius, 2, 65, 71,
105, 106, 125, 126, 141,
144, 237, 247, 252, 384,
388, 389, 391, 394, 431

O

Obote, Milton, 126, 131, 141,
237, 372, 428, 432, 445,
462
Oil, 90, 124, 209, 217, 232,
240, 245, 260, 331
Oman, 40, 230
Oral tradition, 68, 83, 97, 101
Organization of African Unity
(OAU), 90, 117
Organization of Petroleum
Exporting Countries
(OPEC), 90, 247
Organization of the Islamic
Conference (OIC), 450

P

Palestinians, 162, 311, 333,
339
Pan-African, 87, 109, 110,
111, 112, 113, 116, 143, 154,
220, 233, 372, 468
Pan-Africanism, 87, 109, 110,
112, 113, 116, 143, 154, 233,
372
Pan-Arabism, 233
Paradox, 207, 217, 256, 304,
312, 439, 444, 469
Pax Africana, 113, 154, 157,
163, 466, 468, 470
Pax Americana, 157, 263,
314, 316, 317, 333, 341
Pax Britannica, 26
Pluralism, 85, 87, 132, 306,
307, 385, 387, 389, 393
Poetry, 252, 385, 418, 455
Political systems, 48, 72, 78,
147, 179, 183, 198, 199,
210, 323, 413, 416
Portugal, 38, 113, 134, 205,
256, 283, 462, 466
Post-colonial, 79, 97, 101,
102, 103, 106, 108, 121,
124, 126, 128, 129, 131,
138, 162, 174, 234, 236,
237, 238, 239, 240, 241,
243, 245, 246, 247, 270,
273, 459, 464, 467
Production, 4, 5, 11, 20, 25,
30, 32, 60, 74, 78, 98, 121,
152, 258, 259, 261, 316,
325, 326, 389, 435
Protestant, 15, 16, 17, 18, 19,
36, 50, 66, 122, 237, 257,
271

Protestant ethic, 16, 122, 257, 271

Protestantism, 17, 20, 37, 38

R

Race, 2, 3, 5, 16, 20, 36, 42, 95, 98, 108, 114, 116, 117, 138, 148, 149, 150, 153, 154, 157, 161, 163, 165, 176, 181, 188, 196, 197, 210, 265, 267, 273, 282, 284, 294, 300, 322, 329, 335, 339, 340, 341, 342, 346, 347, 363, 392, 418, 419, 420, 433, 452, 455

Racism, 21, 153, 163, 175, 335

Re-Africanization, 116

Reagan, Ronald, 26, 284, 297, 300, 301, 334

Red Sea, 225, 355, 359, 456

Reformation, 6, 15, 16, 18, 19, 20, 36, 50, 233

Regional integration, 112, 329, 335, 468

Religion, 17, 66, 84, 140, 143, 165, 201, 222, 226, 330, 341

Renaissance, 14, 19, 112, 187, 203

Reparations (for slavery) 149, 157, 158, 159, 160, 161, 164, 232

Republic of South Africa, 112, 135, 220, 260, 266, 318, 465

Rhodesia, 118, 258, 406, 421, 461

Romantic gloriana, 111, 112

Romantic primitivism, 111, 383

Rousseau, J.J., 15, 379, 380, 381, 382, 383, 384, 385, 386, 387, 388, 390, 392, 393, 394, 395

Rwanda, 75, 108, 113, 147, 154, 155, 156, 164, 166, 247, 290, 313, 423, 460, 466, 467

S

Sadat, Anwar, 234

Saudi Arabia, 40, 90, 232, 456

Semites, 2, 3, 5, 8, 12, 14, 25, 48, 51, 53, 184, 451

Sénégal, 71, 86, 111, 157, 230, 236, 237, 244, 246, 248, 352, 383, 392, 441

Senghor, Léopold Sédar, 71, 86, 93, 100, 105, 111, 125, 126, 144, 236, 350, 351, 364, 370, 374, 383, 384, 390, 391, 394, 432, 439, 441, 443, 444, 446, 447

Slave trade, 149, 151, 152, 157, 158, 162, 196, 246, 266, 268, 270, 283, 289, 298

slaves, 22, 29, 41, 61, 76, 89, 152, 153, 189, 227, 230, 231, 256, 267, 283, 299, 336, 439

Smith, Adam, 32, 118, 134, 156, 171, 174

Socialism, 123, 125, 144, 394, 463

Somalia 113, 129, 132, 158, 238, 244, 245, 246, 254, 301, 356, 456, 466, 467

Songhay, 228, 229

South Africa, 21, 100, 112, 140, 153, 160, 227, 230, 235, 251, 269, 270, 297, 300, 318, 329, 331, 350, 359, 374, 380, 385, 434, 435, 436, 437, 441, 447, 461, 463, 465, 467, 468

Southern African Development Community (SADC), 112

Soviet Union, 127, 135, 148, 152, 183, 214, 264, 292, 303, 330, 332, 335, 338, 339, 391, 464

Spain, 10, 38, 113, 183, 283

Spread of Islam, 228, 229, 230, 231, 232, 234, 239, 245, 247

State, 5, 12, 14, 15, 16, 18, 25, 29, 34, 36, 37, 39, 40, 41, 45, 46, 47, 48, 49, 51, 52, 72, 75, 79, 95, 104, 105, 106, 112, 119, 121, 125, 129, 130, 131, 134, 135, 138, 178, 184, 185, 188, 189, 191, 192, 199, 204, 216, 217, 221, 227, 229, 237, 247, 261, 263, 266, 273, 290, 297, 300, 301, 303, 304, 305, 306, 307, 308, 309, 310, 311, 320, 321, 322, 323, 324, 325, 326, 335, 336, 355, 379, 385, 391, 399, 410, 411, 413, 434, 441

State system, 16, 29, 47, 303, 305, 308, 311, 321, 326

Sub-colonization, 467, 468

Sub-recolonization, 467, 468

Sudan, 70, 115, 129, 130, 143, 226, 227, 228, 233, 234, 237, 244, 245, 246, 268, 306, 368, 452, 454, 456, 467

Northern Sudan, 226, 268, 453, 454, 455

Southern Sudan, 226, 227, 268, 453, 454, 455

Swaziland, 108, 435

T

Tanzania, 2, 65, 71, 105, 106, 113, 115, 126, 128, 142, 144, 183, 229, 230, 231, 237, 252, 313, 339, 384, 388, 389, 424, 431, 454

Technology, 3, 4, 5, 11, 14, 20, 25, 49, 64, 65, 67, 85, 111, 171, 203, 207, 209, 211, 325, 432, 435

Third World, 20, 23, 29, 45, 90, 126, 128, 169, 196, 220, 254, 264, 271, 276, 300, 304, 305, 306, 307, 312, 316, 317, 318, 319, 321, 333, 334, 338, 340, 391, 392, 393, 395, 465

Togo, 133, 313

Transnational corporations, 325

Tribe, 96, 114, 140, 141, 159, 160, 210, 211, 286, 406, 440

Tribes, 96, 132, 159, 161, 220, 241, 268, 406, 409, 415
Retribalization, 329
Triple Heritage, 239
Trusteeship, 313, 318, 466
Tunisia, 103, 113, 124, 141
Turkey, 203, 204, 205, 206, 209, 211, 212, 213, 214, 216, 218, 219, 220, 221, 258, 275, 333
Tutsi, 74, 147, 154, 156, 460

U

Uganda, 58, 64, 76, 80, 104, 113, 118, 130, 131, 139, 141, 154, 155, 156, 183, 229, 231, 237, 246, 269, 310, 357, 358, 368, 372, 373, 375, 376, 428, 430, 432, 454, 460, 462, 467, 471
United Kingdom, 10, 25, 26, 28, 319
England, 17, 26, 30, 32, 33, 34, 36, 37, 39, 60, 90, 92, 109, 116, 176, 186, 207, 269, 285, 287, 346, 363, 366, 419, 422
Great Britain, 51, 61, 62, 285, 315, 439, 446
United Nations, 28, 29, 40, 41, 154, 157, 160, 265, 268, 273, 275, 276, 277, 296, 312, 314, 315, 316, 317, 318, 319, 321, 331, 338, 340, 390, 392, 399, 414, 416, 450, 466
General Assembly, 392

Secretary-General, 296, 353
Security Council, 28, 157, 160, 164, 296, 312, 315, 316
UNESCO, 29, 109, 296, 319
United States, 17, 21, 26, 27, 28, 30, 33, 34, 35, 38, 39, 40, 42, 43, 44, 51, 82, 90, 93, 110, 116, 133, 139, 152, 153, 157, 159, 160, 162, 163, 198, 214, 264, 282, 284, 292, 294, 295, 296, 297, 298, 300, 304, 314, 315, 316, 317, 319, 331, 332, 334, 336, 337, 393, 415, 417, 419, 420, 438, 439, 440, 451, 452, 464, 465, 466

W

Weber, Max, 17, 50, 257, 306
West, 3, 18, 19, 44, 46, 58, 61, 64, 65, 67, 68, 71, 74, 79, 86, 87, 89, 90, 93, 109, 113, 115, 117, 126, 127, 128, 148, 149, 151, 153, 157, 158, 159, 160, 162, 165, 170, 177, 178, 182, 195, 198, 218, 227, 228, 229, 230, 233, 240, 242, 245, 246, 248, 252, 254, 257, 259, 263, 264, 266, 267, 271, 272, 282, 283, 297, 299, 306, 313, 314, 315, 318, 325, 329, 330, 331, 334, 337, 339, 341, 347, 350, 353, 354, 365, 366, 376,

377, 382, 424, 425, 426, 429, 432, 446, 463, 464, 467, 470

Western, 3, 4, 5, 11, 16, 20, 21, 26, 33, 41, 42, 44, 45, 57, 58, 59, 61, 63, 64, 65, 68, 69, 70, 71, 72, 74, 75, 76, 77, 78, 79, 80, 81, 82, 83, 84, 85, 87, 88, 89, 90, 91, 92, 96, 97, 104, 109, 110, 116, 120, 124, 126, 127, 128, 147, 150, 152, 156, 157, 158, 161, 163, 169, 170, 171, 174, 177, 178, 179, 180, 183, 184, 189, 194, 196, 198, 200, 203, 204, 205, 206, 207, 209, 210, 212, 213, 214, 215, 216, 218, 219, 220, 221, 222, 228, 230, 238, 239, 240, 242, 245, 246, 255, 256, 257, 258, 259, 261, 262, 263, 264, 268, 269, 271, 272, 273, 283, 284, 285, 287, 289, 290, 291, 293, 295, 297, 299, 313, 314, 317, 319, 321, 329, 330, 331, 332, 334, 335, 336, 337, 338, 339, 340, 349, 353, 354, 355, 358, 359, 361, 362, 363, 364, 375, 404, 431, 432, 438, 450, 463, 464, 466, 467

Westernism, 85, 90, 180, 206, 209

Westernization, 42, 68, 69, 71, 76, 126, 127, 156, 241, 251, 257, 258, 259, 445

White Man's Burden, 43, 173, 417, 418, 428

Women, 2, 48, 49, 51, 52, 75, 89, 158, 251, 321, 322, 323, 324, 325, 326, 442

World Bank, 33, 136, 144, 160, 164, 169, 261, 262, 276, 338, 464

World Trade Organization (WTO), 265

World War I, 23, 27, 33, 34, 39, 43, 62, 65, 152, 162, 164, 205, 212, 213, 255, 258, 281, 292, 293, 303, 312, 315

First World War, 152, 221

World War II, 23, 27, 33, 34, 43, 62, 65, 152, 162, 164, 213, 255, 258, 281, 292, 293, 303, 312, 315

Second World War, 116, 152, 296, 314

Y

Yemen, 230, 270, 357, 452

Yugoslavia, 96, 265, 335, 338, 450

Z

Zaire, 113, 129, 154, 156, 231, 235, 247, 301, 313, 319, 454, 457, 460, 469, 470

Zambia, 23, 380, 432, 461

Zanzibar, 26, 106, 108, 229, 231, 247, 270

Zimbabwe, 111, 118, 124, 126, 153, 155, 156, 258, 274, 421

Zionism, 39, 40, 42, 115, 245, 318